First published in England in 1956
by Faber and Faber Limited
3 Queen Square London WC1
First published in this edition 1967
Reprinted 1969 and 1972
Printed in Great Britain by
Latimer Trend & Co Ltd Whitstable
All rights reserved

Copyright, 1954 by the Regents of the University of California

ISBN 0 571 08154 1

CONDITION OF SALE

ART

AND VISUAL

PERCEPTION

a psychology of the creative eye

BY RUDOLF ARNHEIM

FABER AND FABER
3 QUEEN SQUARE
LONDON

ART AND
VISUAL PERCEPTION

INTRODUCTION

Art may seem to be in danger of being drowned by talk. Rarely are we presented with a new specimen of what we are willing to accept as genuine art. Yet we are overwhelmed by a flood of books, articles, dissertations, speeches, lectures, guides—ready to tell us what is art and what is not, what was done by whom and when and why and because of whom and what. We are haunted by the vision of a small, delicate body dissected by crowds of eager lay surgeons and lay analysts. And we feel tempted to assume that art is unsure in our time because we think and talk too much about it.

Probably such a diagnosis is superficial. True enough, the state of affairs seems unsatisfactory to almost everyone, but if we look for its cause with some care we find that we are heirs to a cultural situation particularly unsuited to produce art and likely to encourage the wrong kind of thinking about it. Our experiences and ideas tend to be common but not deep, or deep but not common. We are neglecting the gift of comprehending things by what our senses tell us about them. Concept is split from percept, and thought moves among abstractions. Our eyes are being reduced to instruments by which to measure and identify—hence a dearth of ideas that can be expressed in images and an incapacity to discover meaning in what we see. Naturally we feel lost in the presence of objects that make sense only to undiluted vision, and we look for help to the more familiar medium of words.

The mere exposure to masterworks will not do. Too many persons visit museums and collect picture books without gaining access to art. The inborn capacity to understand through the eyes has been put to sleep and must be reawakened. This can best be done by handling the pencil, the brush, the chisel. But here again bad habits and misconceptions will block the path unless there are protection and help. Inevitably such assistance must come through words, since eyes say little to eyes. At this point we are stopped by powerful prejudices.

One of these prejudices asserts that visual things cannot be expressed in words. There is a core of truth in the warning. The particular quality of the experience created by a Rembrandt painting is reducible only in part to descriptive and explanatory concepts. This limitation, however, is not peculiar to our dealing with art. It holds true for any object of experience. No description or explanation—whether a secretary's verbal portrait of her employer or a physician's account of a patient's glandular system—can do more than use a few general categories in a particular configuration. The scientist builds conceptual models, which, if he is fortunate, will furnish the essentials of what he wants to understand about a given phenomenon. But he knows that there is no such thing as the full representation of the individual and that there is no need for the duplication of what already exists.

Similarly, the artist uses his categories of shape and color to capture something universally significant in the particular. He too is neither intent on seizing the unique as such nor able to do so. And if we try to understand or explain works of art, all we need do in preparation is to formulate some guiding principles. To achieve this for art should be no more difficult than to achieve it for such other complex things as the physical or mental make-up of living creatures. Art is the product of organisms and therefore probably neither more nor less complex than these organisms themselves.

If we see and feel certain qualities in a work of art yet cannot describe or explain them, the reason for our failure is not that we use words but that our eyes and thoughts do not succeed in discovering generalities able to do the job. Language is no avenue for sensory contact with reality—it serves merely to name what we have seen or heard or thought. It is not a foreign medium, unsuitable for visible things. It fails us when and because visual analysis breaks down. But fortunately visual analysis can go far and can also call forth the potential capacity to "see," by which we reach the unanalyzable.

Another prejudice maintains that verbal analysis will paralyze intuitive creation and comprehension. Again there is a core of truth. The history of the past and the experience of the present provide many examples of how destructive the formulas and recipes can be. But are we to conclude that in the field of the arts one power of the mind must be put out of action so that another may function? Is it not true that disturbances occur precisely when any one mental faculty operates at the expense of the other? The delicate balance of all our powers—which alone permits us to live fully and to work well—is upset, not only when the intellect interferes with intuition, but also when feeling dislodges reasoning. An orgy of self-expression is no more productive than blind obedience to rules. Reckless analysis of the self will do harm, but so will the artificial primitivism of the man who refuses to know how and why he works. Modern man can, and therefore must, live with unprecedented self-awareness. Perhaps the task of living has become more difficult—but there is no way around it.

It is the purpose of this book to discuss some of the virtues of vision and thereby to help refresh and direct them. As long as I can remember I have concerned myself with art, studied its nature and history, tried my eyes and hands at it, and sought the company of artists, art theorists, art educators. This interest has been enhanced by my psychological studies. All seeing is in the realm of the psychologist, and nobody has ever discussed the processes of creating or experiencing art without talking psychology. (By psychology I mean, of course, the science of the mind in all its manifestations, not merely the limited preoccupation with what nowadays goes under the heading of "emotion.") Some art theorists have used the work of psychologists to advantage. Others do not realize or are not willing to admit what they are doing; but inevitably they too use psychology, either homemade or left over from theories of the past and mostly below the standards of our present knowledge. For this reason I am trying to apply approaches and findings of modern psychology to the study of art.

The experiments I am citing and the principles of my psychological thinking derive largely from gestalt theory. This preference seems justifiable. Even psychologists who have certain quarrels with gestalt theory are willing to admit that the foundation of our present knowledge of visual perception has been laid in the laboratories of that school. But this is not all. From its beginnings and throughout its development during the last half century, gestalt psychology has shown a kinship to art. The writings of Max Wertheimer, Wolfgang Köhler, Kurt Koffka are pervaded by it. Here and there in these writings the arts are explicitly mentioned, but what counts more is that the spirit underlying the reasoning of these men makes the artist feel at home. In fact, something like an artistic look at reality was needed to remind scientists that most phenomena of nature are not described adequately if they are analyzed piece by piece. The realization that a whole cannot be attained by adding up isolated parts was not new to the artist. For many centuries scientists had been able to say valuable things about reality without going beyond the relatively simple level of reasoning that excludes the complexities of organization and interaction. But at no time could a work of art have been made or understood by a mind unable to conceive the integrated structure of a whole.

In the essay that gave gestalt theory its name, von Ehrenfels pointed out that if each of twelve observers listened to one of the twelve tones of a melody the sum of their experiences would not correspond to what would be perceived if someone listened to the whole melody. Much of the later experimentation was designed to show that the appearance of any element depends on its place and function in the pattern as a whole. A thoughtful person cannot read these studies without admiring the active striving for unity and order manifest in the simple act of looking at a simple pattern of lines. Far from being a mechanical recording of sensory elements, vision turned out to be a truly creative grasp of reality—imaginative, inventive, shrewd, and beautiful. It became apparent that the qualities that give dignity to the activities of the thinker and the artist distinguish all performances of the mind. Psychologists also began to see that this fact was no coincidence. The same principles operate in the various mental capacities because the mind always functions as a whole. All perceiving is also thinking, all reasoning is also intuition, all observation is also invention.

The relevance of these views to the theory and practice of the arts is evident. No longer can we consider the artistic process as self-contained, mysteriously inspired from above, unrelated and unrelatable to what people do otherwise. Instead, the exalted kind of seeing that leads to the creation of great art appears as an outgrowth of the humbler and more common activity of the eyes in everyday life. Just as the prosaic search for information is "artistic" because it involves giving and finding shape and meaning, so the artist's conceiving is an instrument of life, a refined way of understanding who and where we are.

As long as the raw material of experience was considered an amorphous agglomeration of stimuli, the observer seemed free to handle it according to his arbitrary pleasure. Seeing was an entirely subjective imposition of shape and meaning upon reality. In fact, no student of the arts would deny that individuals or cultures form the world after their own image. The gestalt studies, however, made it clear that more often than not the situations we face have their own characteristics, which demand to be perceived "correctly." The process of looking at the world turned out to be an interplay between properties supplied by the object and the nature of the observing subject. This objective element in experience justifies attempts to distinguish between adequate and inadequate conceptions of reality. Further, all adequate conceptions could be expected to contain a common core of truth, which would make the art of all times and places potentially relevant to all men—

a badly needed antidote to the nightmare of unbounded subjectivism and relativism.

Finally, there was a wholesome lesson in the discovery that vision is not a mechanical recording of elements but the grasping of significant structural patterns. If this was true for the simple act of perceiving an object, it was all the more likely to hold also for the artistic approach to reality. Obviously the artist was no more a mechanical recording device than his organ of sight. The artistic representation of an object could no longer be thought of as a tedious transcription of its accidental appearance, detail by detail. In other words, here was scientific support for the growing conviction that images of reality could be valid even though far removed from "realistic" semblance.

It was encouraging for me to discover that similar conclusions had been reached independently in the field of art education. In particular, Henry Schaefer-Simmern, inspired by the theories of Gustaf Britsch, had given a great deal of practical thought to the artistic process. He had confirmed the assertion that the mind, in its struggle for an orderly conception of reality, proceeds in a lawful and logical development from the perceptually simplest patterns to increasing complexity. There was evidence, then, that the perceptual principles revealed in the gestalt experiments were also manifest genetically. Chapter IV of the present book offers a psychologist's comments on the basic aspects of the theory, which will be documented more fully in a forthcoming book by Mr. Schaefer-Simmern. In *The Unfolding of Artistic Activity,* Schaefer-Simmern has already convincingly illustrated his belief that the capacity to deal with life artistically is not the privilege of a few gifted experts but belongs to the equipment of every sane person whom nature has favored with a pair of eyes. To the psychologist this means that the study of art is an indispensable part of the study of man.

At the risk of giving my fellow scientists good reasons for displeasure I am applying the principles in which I believe with a somewhat reckless one-sidedness, partly because the cautious installation of dialectic fire escapes, side entrances, emergency closets, and waiting rooms would have made the structure impractically large and orientation difficult, partly because in certain cases it is useful to state a point of view with crude simplicity and leave the refinements to the ensuing play of thrust and counterthrust. I must also apologize to the art historians for using their material less competently than might have been desirable. At the present time it probably would be beyond the power of any one person to give a fully satisfactory survey of the relations between the theory of the visual arts and the pertinent work in psychology. If we try to match two things which, although belonging together, have not been made for each other, many adjustments are necessary and many gaps

have to be closed provisionally. I had to speculate where I could not prove
and to use my own eyes where I could not rely on those of others. I have
taken pains to indicate problems that are waiting for systematic research.
But after all is said and done, I feel like exclaiming with Herman Melville:
"This whole book is but a draught—nay, but the draught of a draught.
Oh, Time, Strength, Cash, and Patience!"

The book deals with what can be seen by everybody. It deals with what
can be read only to the extent to which it has helped me and my students
to see better. But there is also the hangover from the reading of many things
that do not serve the good purpose. One of the reasons for writing this book
is that I believe many people to be tired of the dazzling obscurity of arty
talk, the juggling with catchwords and dehydrated aesthetic concepts, the
pseudo-scientific windowdressing, the impertinent hunting for clinical
symptoms, the elaborate measurement of trifles, and the charming epigrams.
Art is the most concrete thing in the world, and there is no justification for
confusing the minds of people who want to know more about it.

Even concrete things are often intricate. I have tried to discuss them as
simply as I could. This does not mean that I have clung to measurably short
words and sentences, because when the form is simpler than the content
the message does not reach its destination. Nor is any writer entitled to help
reduce our language to the starvation level of the lowest common denominator. To be simple means to say things straight, constantly illustrating
them with examples. To some readers the approach may seem inappropriately sober and pedestrian. They might be answered by what Goethe once
wrote to a friend, Christian Gottlob Heyne, professor of rhetoric in
Göttingen:

"As you can see, I am starting very much from down at the earth, and it
may seem to some that I treated the most spiritual matter in too terrestrial
a fashion; but I may be permitted to observe that the gods of the Greeks
were not enthroned in the seventh or tenth heaven but on Olympus, taking
a giant-sized stride not from sun to sun but, at most, from mountain to
mountain."

A first attempt to write this book dates back to the years 1941–1943, when
I received a grant from the John Simon Guggenheim Memorial Foundation
for the purpose. In the course of the work I had to convince myself that the
tools available in the psychology of perception at that time were not sufficient
to deal with some of the more important visual problems in the arts. Therefore, instead of writing the book I undertook a number of particular studies,
mainly in the areas of space, expression, and movement, designed to fill some
of the gaps. The material was tested and increased by my courses in the psychology of art at Sarah Lawrence College and the New School in New York.

When, in the summer of 1951, a fellowship of the Rockefeller Foundation made it possible for me to take a year's leave of absence, I felt ready to give a reasonably coherent account of the field. Whatever the worth of this book, I am greatly indebted to the officers of the Humanities Division for enabling me to satisfy the need of putting my findings on paper. It should be understood that the foundation assumed no control over the project and has no responsibility for the result.

I wish also to express my gratitude to three friends, Henry Schaefer-Simmern, the art educator, Meyer Schapiro, the art historian, and Hans Wallach, the psychologist, for reading some of the chapters of the manuscript and helping me with valuable suggestions and corrections. The alert comments of my students throughout the years have acted as a constant stream of water, polishing the pebbles that make up this book. Acknowledgments to the individuals and institutions that permitted me to reproduce works of art owned by them are contained in the notes at the end of the volume. I wish explicitly to thank the children, most of them unknown to me, whose drawings I have been able to use. In particular, I am happy that the book preserves some of the drawings of Allmuth Laporte, whose young life of beauty and talent was destroyed by illness at the age of thirteen years.

The second printing has enabled me to add a concluding statement to page 443 and to make some twenty corrections nearly all suggested by one most alert reader, Mrs. Alice Bradley Sheldon of Washington, D.C. In the present paperback edition, some forty further corrections have been made.

R.A.

Sarah Lawrence College, Bronxville, New York

CONTENTS

I   BALANCE

The Hidden Structure of a Square

Cut a disk out of dark cardboard and put it on a white square in the position indicated by Figure 1.

The location of the disk could be determined and described by means of measurement. A yardstick would tell in inches the distances from the edges of the square. Thus it could be inferred that the disk lies off center.

Figure 1

But this result would come as no surprise. We do not have to measure—we can see that the disk lies off center. How is this "seeing" done? Which faculty of the mind provides such information? It is not the intellect, because the result is not obtained by means of abstract concepts. It is not emotion, for although the sight of the eccentric disk may produce discomfort in some persons and a pleasurable stir in others, this can happen only after they have spotted its location. Emotion is a consequence, rather than an instrument, of discovery.

We constantly make statements that describe things in relation to their environment. "My right hand is larger than the left." "This flagpole is not straight." "That piano is out of tune." "This cocoa is sweeter than the brand we had before." An object is seen immediately as having a certain size, that is, as lying somewhere on the scale between a grain of salt and a mountain. On the scale of brightness values, our white square lies high, our black disk low. Similarly, every object is seen as having a location. The book you are reading appears at a certain spot, which is defined by the room about you and the objects in it—among them notably you yourself. The square appears somewhere on the book page, and the disk is off center in the square. No object is perceived as unique or isolated. Seeing something means assigning it a place in the whole: a location in space, a score on the yardstick of size or brightness or distance.

In other words, every act of seeing is a visual judgment. Judgments are sometimes thought to be a monopoly of the intellect. But visual judgments are not contributions of the intellect, added after the seeing is done. They are immediate and indispensable ingredients of the act of seeing itself. Seeing that the disk lies off center is an intrinsic part of seeing it at all.

The observations of the eye are not only geographical. In looking at the disk we may find that it does not merely occupy a certain place but exhibits restlessness. This restlessness may be experienced as a tendency of the disk to get away from where it is placed or, more specifically, as a pull in a particular direction—for example, toward the center. Although bound to its place and incapable of actual motion, the disk may nevertheless show an inner tension in its relation to the surrounding square. Again, this tension is not a supplementary contribution of intellect or fancy. It is as much part and parcel of the percept itself as size, location, or blackness. Since the tension has a magnitude and a direction, it may be described as a psychological "force."

If the disk is seen as striving toward the center of the square, it is being attracted by something not actually contained in the picture. The center point is not revealed to the eye by any marking in Figure 1; it is as invisible as the North Pole or the Equator, and yet it is more than an idea. It is clearly a part of the perceived pattern, an invisible focus of power, established at a considerable distance by the outline of the square. We may say it is "induced" (as one electric current can be induced by another).

There are, then, more things in the field of vision than those that strike the retinas of the eyes. Examples of "induced structure" are not infrequent. For example, in a picture done in central perspective the vanishing point may be established by the convergent lines even though no actual object can be seen at their meeting point. In a melody there may be "heard" by mere induction the regular beat, from which a syncopated tone deviates, as our disk deviates from the center. Again it must be emphasized that such an induction is not an intellectual operation. It is not an interpolation based on previously acquired knowledge but an integral element of what is immediately perceived.

A visual figure such as the square is empty and not empty at the same time. The center is part of a complex hidden structure, which can be explored by means of the disk, somewhat as iron filings will reveal the lines of force in a magnetic field. If the disk is put in various places within the square, it may be found that at some points it looks solidly at rest; at others it exhibits a pull in some definite direction, or its situation may be unclear and wavering.

The disk is most stably settled when its center coincides with the center of the square. In Figure 2 it may be seen as drawn toward the contour to the right. With changing distance this effect will weaken or even turn into its opposite. For example, we can find a distance at which the disk looks "too close," possessed by the urge to withdraw from the boundary. Then the empty interval between the boundary and the disk will appear compressed, as though more "breathing" space was needed.

Figure 2

Investigation reveals that the disk is influenced also by the diagonals of the square as well as by the cross formed by the central vertical and horizontal axes (Figure 3). The center is established by the crossing of these four main structural lines. Other points on the lines are less powerful than the center, but the effect of attraction can be established for them also.

Wherever the disk is located, it will be affected by the forces of all the hidden structural factors. The relative strength and distance of these factors will determine their effect in the total configuration of forces. In the center all the forces balance each other, and therefore the central position makes for rest. Another comparatively restful position can be found, for example, by moving the disk along a diagonal. The point of balance seems to lie somewhat nearer to the corner of the square than to the center, which may mean that the center is stronger than the corner and that this preponderance has to be compensated by greater distance, as though they were two magnets of unequal power. In general, any location that coincides with one of the features of the "structural map" (Figure 3) will introduce an element of stability, which of course may be counteracted by other factors.

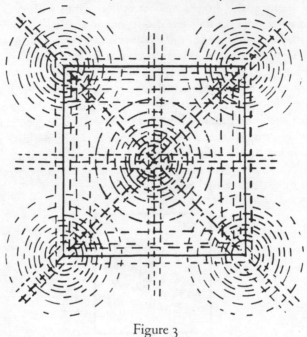

Figure 3

If influence from a particular direction predominates, a pull in that direction will result. When the disk is put exactly in the middle between center and corner, most observers see it striving toward the center.

An unpleasant effect is produced by locations at which pulls are so equivocal and ambiguous that the eye cannot decide whether the disk is pressing in any particular direction. Such wavering makes the visual statement unclear and interferes with the observer's perceptual judgment. In ambiguous situations the visual pattern ceases to determine what is seen, and subjective factors in the observer become more effective, such as his focus of attention or preference for a particular direction.

When conditions are such that the eye cannot keep checking on the actual location of the disk, the forces that are discussed here may, perhaps, produce genuine displacement instead of mere directed tension. If Figure 1 is seen for only a split second, will the disk be seen closer to the center than on

leisurely inspection? According to Wertheimer, an angle somewhat larger
or smaller than ninety degrees will be seen as a right angle when exposed
briefly. A related phenomenon may be observed when the hand of a clock
leaves a position of prominence, such as the twelve-o'clock mark. Interrupt-
ing its smooth rotation, the hand seems to cling to the position for a
moment and then to liberate itself from it with a leap. All these phenomena
are examples of the tendency to reach and maintain structurally simple
configurations—a subject for later discussion.

Are the pulls in the disk active or passive? That is, does it move "under
its own steam" or is it merely yielding to attractions exerted by the square?
The difference is crucial for the expression conveyed by the pattern. Only
exact experimentation will tell whether particular conditions make consistently for activity or passivity. Another question can be answered with more
confidence. It always seems to be the disk that is being influenced by the
square and not the square by the disk. This brings to mind experiments by
Duncker in which luminous line patterns were put in slow motion relative
to each other in a dark room. Regardless of what happened physically, the
enclosed figure was seen as moving, whereas the enclosing one remained
almost or completely still. The effect was found to be particularly strong
when the observer explicitly fixated the disk rather than the square. Similarly in our figures, the surrounding square furnishes a stable basis, in reference to which visual action takes place. When seen in broad daylight the
square is not isolated, as Duncker's figures were in the dark room, but
anchored to the environment. The square acquires additional stability from
the page on which it is printed. It constitutes an enclosure, within which
there is greater freedom from surrounding space. The frame of a painting
creates such an enclosure. It is a fence that to some extent protects the play
of forces in the picture from the fettering influence of the environment.

The roving disk has revealed that a visual pattern consists of more than
the elements recorded by the retinas of the eyes. To the retinas, brightness
differences of black and white have created a pattern, which can be fully
described in terms of size, shape, distance, and direction. Investigation revealed, in addition to this visible pattern, a hidden structural map, the main
features of which were indicated in Figure 3. This map represents a frame
of reference, which helps to determine the balance value of any pictorial
element just as the musical scale helps to determine the pitch value of each
tone in a composition.

In still another and even more important way we had to go beyond the
"stimulus pattern" recorded by the retinas. It became evident that the figure,
plus its hidden structure, is not just a lattice of lines. As indicated in Figure 3,
the visual pattern is really a field of forces. In this dynamic landscape, lines

are actually ridges, from which the level of energy slopes off in both directions. These ridges are centers of attractive and repulsive forces, whose influence covers the entire area of their surroundings. What was called the internal
structure of the square—and, incidentally, there is an external structure as
well, outside the figure—is created secondarily by the meeting of the forces
that emanate from the visible figure, namely, the edges of the square.

No place is free from this influence. It is true that "restful" spots were
found in the square, but their repose does not indicate the absence of active
forces. "Dead center" is not dead; no pull in any one direction is felt, because
at the middle point pulls from all directions balance each other. To the
sensitive eye, the balance of the middle point is alive with tension. Think
of a rope that is motionless while two men of equal strength are pulling it in
opposite directions. It is still, but it is loaded with energy.

Throughout this book it must be kept in mind that every visual pattern
is dynamic. Just as a living organism cannot be described by its anatomy,
so the essence of a visual experience cannot be expressed by inches of size
and distance, degrees of angle, or wave lengths of hue. These static measurements define only the "stimulus," that is, the message sent to the eye by the
physical world. But the life of a percept—its expression and meaning—
derives entirely from the activity of the kind of forces that have been
described. Any line drawn on a sheet of paper, or the simplest form modeled
from a piece of clay, is like a rock thrown into a pond. It upsets repose, it
mobilizes space. Seeing is the perception of action.

What Is Meant by Perceptual Forces?

The reader may have noticed with apprehension the use of the term
"forces." Are these forces merely figures of speech, or are they real? And if
they are real, where do they exist?

They are assumed to be real in both realms of existence—that is, as
psychological and as physical forces. Psychologically, the pulls in the disk
exist in the experience of any person who looks at it. Since these pulls have
a point of attack, a direction, and an intensity, they meet the conditions
established by physicists for physical forces. For this reason, psychologists
have adopted the same term.

In what sense can it be said that these forces exist, not only in experience,
but also in the physical world? Surely they are not contained in the objects
at which we are looking, such as the white paper on which the square is
drawn or the dark cardboard disk. Molecular and gravitational forces are
active in these objects, holding their microparticles together and preventing
them from flying away. But there are no known physical forces that would
tend to push an eccentrically placed paper disk in the direction of the center

of a paper square. Nor will lines drawn in ink exert any magnetic power on the surrounding paper surface. Where, then, are these forces?

Remember how the observer obtains knowledge of the square and the disk. Light rays, emanating from the sun or some other source, hit the object and are partly absorbed and partly reflected by it. Some of the reflected rays reach the lens of the eye and are projected on its sensitive background, the retina. Do the forces in question arise among the stimulations that light produces in the millions of small receptor organs situated in the retina? The possibility cannot be entirely excluded. But the receptor organs of the retina are essentially self-contained. In particular, the "cones," which are largely responsible for pattern vision, have little anatomical connection with each other, many of them having private pathways to the optic nerve.

In the brain center of vision itself, which is located in the back of the head, conditions seem to exist, however, that would allow for this very kind of process. According to gestalt psychologists, the cerebral area contains a field of electrochemical forces. These interact freely; unconstrained by the kind of compartmental division that is found among the retinal receptors. Stimulation at one point of the field is likely to spread to adjoining areas. As an example of a phenomenon that seems to presuppose such interaction, Wertheimer's experiments on illusory movement may be cited. If two light spots appear successively in a dark room for a split second, the observer often does not report two separate and independent experiences. Instead of seeing one light and then, at some distance, another, the observer sees only one light, which moves from one position to another. This illusory movement is so compelling that it cannot be distinguished from the actual displacement of one light dot. Wertheimer concluded that this effect was the result of "a kind of physiological short-circuit" in the brain center of vision, by which energy shifted from the place of the first stimulation to that of the second. In other words, he suggested that local brain stimulations acted upon each other dynamically. Subsequent research confirmed the validity of this hypothesis and provided more information about the exact nature and behavior of cortical forces. Although all these findings were indirect, in that they inferred knowledge of physiological happenings from psychological observations, more recent investigations by Köhler have opened the way for the direct study of the brain processes themselves.

The forces that are experienced when looking at visual objects can be considered the psychological counterpart or equivalent of physiological forces active in the brain center of vision. Although these processes occur physiologically in the brain, they are experienced psychologically as though they were properties of the perceived objects themselves. In fact, by mere inspection they can be no more distinguished from the effects of physical processes taking place in the objects than a dream or hallucination can be distinguished from the perception of "actual" events. Only by comparing various experiences can man arrive at telling the difference between events that are merely produced by the activity of the nervous system and others that occur in the external objects themselves.

There is no point, however, in calling these forces "illusions." They are no more illusory than colors, which are attributed to the objects themselves although they are actually nothing but the reactions of the nervous system to light of particular wave lengths. Psychologically, our visual forces are as real as anything else we perceive or feel or think. The term "illusion" is useful only when a difference arising between the physical and the psychological world makes us commit a mistake in dealing with physical things— for example, walking into a mirror or giving a slant to a wall which is supposed to be vertical. No such danger exists for the artist, because in the arts what looks right is right. The artist does not use his eyes for the purpose of handling paints. He handles paints for the purpose of creating a visible image, since the image. and not the paint, is the work of art. If a wall looks vertical in the picture, it is vertical; and if walkable space is seen in a mirror, there is no reason why images of men should not walk right into it, as has happened in some movies. Thus, the forces that pull our disk would be "illusory" only to a man who decided to use their energy for running an engine. Perceptually and artistically they are quite real.

Two Disks in a Square

In order to get a bit closer to the complexity of the work of art, a second disk is now introduced into the square. What is the result? First of all, some of the effects of the relationship between disk and square also appear with regard to the two disks. When they lie close together, they attract each other and may look almost like one indivisible thing. Also a distance between them can be found at which they repel each other because they are too close together. The distances at which these effects occur will depend on the size of the disks and the square as well as on the locations of the disks in the square.

The locations of the disks may balance each other. Either of the two locations in Figure 4a may look unbalanced by itself. Together they make for a symmetrically located pair that is at rest. However, the same pair may look intolerably unbalanced when moved to another place (Figure 4b). The earlier analysis of the structural map helps to explain why this is true. The two disks form a pair because of their closeness, their similarity of size and shape, and also because they are the only "content" of the square. As members of a pair they tend to be symmetrical—that is, equal value and function in the whole are attributed to them. This perceptual judgment, however, is in conflict with another that derives from the location of the pair. The lower disk lies in the prominent and stable position of the center. The upper is at a less stable location. Thus location creates a distinction between the two that is in conflict with their symmetrical pairness. This conflict is insoluble. The spectator finds himself shifting between two in-

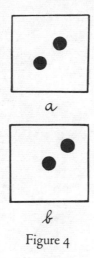

a

b

Figure 4

compatible conceptions. The example shows that a visual pattern cannot be considered without regard to the structure of its spatial surroundings, and also that ambiguity can result from a contradiction between form pattern and location pattern.

Psychological and Physical Balance

In discussing the perceptual effect of location, we become inevitably concerned with the factor of balance or equilibrium. Especially in a work of art all elements must be distributed in such a way that a state of balance results. What is balance, and why is it indispensable?

To the physicist, balance is the state of a body in which the forces that act upon it compensate each other. In the simplest example this is achieved by two forces of equal strength that pull in opposite directions. The definition is applicable to visual balance. Exactly like a physical body, every finite visual pattern has a fulcrum or center of gravity. And just as the fulcrum of even the most irregularly shaped flat object can be determined by locating the point at which it will balance on the tip of a finger, so the center of a pattern can be determined by trial and error. According to Denman W.

Figure 5

Ross, the simplest way of doing this is by moving a frame around the pattern until the two balance; then the center of the frame coincides with the
center of the pattern. Except for the most regular shapes, no method of
rational calculation is available that could replace the eye's intuitive sense of
balance. From our previous speculation it would follow that the eye experi-

ences balance when the physiological forces in the cortical field are distributed in such a way that they compensate each other.

The center of gravity of a painting roughly coincides with the center of the frame. (Slight deviations from the geometric center occur mainly for two reasons: The difference of "weight" between the top and the bottom of a visual object tends to push the perceptual center upward; the interaction between the pictorial pattern and the structural map of the plane may cause the displacement of the center of the framed space.)

In a frameless work of art—for example, a piece of sculpture—the figure determines its own fulcrum, except for the influence of such environmental factors as a niche in which the statue may be placed or the base on which it rests.

When the two pans of a scale are in balance, they will be seen swinging up and down until they settle in a position of rest. No further action of physical force can be observed by the eye. Our observations of the disk in the square have demonstrated that this does not hold true for perceptual balance. In a work of art, the forces that have been balanced remain visible. This is the reason why motionless media, such as painting and sculpture, can represent life, which is action.

There are other differences between physical and perceptual equilibrium. The photograph of a dancer may look unbalanced although her body was in a comfortable position at the time the photograph was made. A model may find it impossible to hold a pose that shows perfect poise on canvas. Sculpture may need an internal armature to hold it upright, although it may be well balanced visually. A duck sleeps peacefully standing on one oblique leg. The reason for these discrepancies is that the visual balance values of such factors as size, color, and direction often do not correspond to equal physical factors. A clown's costume—red on the left side and blue on the right—may be asymmetrical to the eye as a color scheme, although the two halves of the costume—and indeed of the clown—are equal in physical weight. Also, in a painting, a physically unrelated object—such as a curtain in the background—may counterbalance the asymmetrical position of a human figure.

An amusing example is found in a fifteenth-century painting that represents St. Michael weighing souls (Figure 5). By the mere strength of prayer, one frail little nude figure outweighs four big devils plus two millstones. The difficulty is that prayer carries only spiritual weight and provides no visual pull. As a remedy, the painter has used the large dark patch on the angel's dress just below the scale that holds the saintly soul. By visual attraction, which is nonexistent in the physical object, the patch creates the weight that adapts the appearance of the scene to its meaning.

Why Balance?

Why is pictorial balance indispensable? It must be remembered that visually, just as physically, balance is the state of distribution in which everything has come to a standstill. In a balanced composition all such factors as shape, direction, and location are mutually determined by each other in such a way that no change seems possible, and the whole assumes the character of "necessity" in all its parts. An unbalanced composition looks accidental, transitory, and therefore invalid. Its elements show a tendency to change place or shape in order to bring about a state better fitted to the total structure. Under such conditions the artistic statement becomes incomprehensible. The pattern is ambiguous and allows no decision as to which of the possible configurations is meant. We get the impression that the process of creation has been suddenly and accidentally frozen somewhere in its course. Since change is needed, the stillness of the work becomes a handicap. Timelessness gives way to the frustrating sensation of arrested time.

This phenomenon is related to my earlier assertion that every act of perception is a perceptual judgment. A blimp floating in an empty universe would be neither large nor small, neither high nor low, neither fast nor slow, and it would be neither at rest nor moving in any direction. Any visual quality must be defined by its environment in space or time. A balanced pattern does just this.

Naturally, the artist always wants to express some kind of inequality. For example, in one of El Greco's paintings of the Annunciation the angel is much larger than the Virgin. But this symbolic disproportion is compelling only because it is fixated by counterbalancing factors. Otherwise the unequal size of the two figures would lack finality and, therefore, meaning. It is only seemingly paradoxical to assert that disequilibrium can be expressed only by equilibrium, just as discord can be shown only by harmony, or separateness by unity.

The following examples are adapted from a test designed by Maitland Graves to try the artistic sensitivity of students. Compare *a* and *b* in Figure 6. The left figure is well balanced. There is plenty of life in this combination of squares and rectangles of various sizes, proportions, and directions, but they all hold each other in such a way that every element stays in its place, everything is necessary, nothing can be changed. Compare the clearly established internal vertical of *a* with its pathetically wavering opposite number in *b*. In *b,* proportions are based on small differences, which leave the eye uncertain whether it deals with equality or inequality, square or rectangle. We cannot tell what the pattern is trying to say.

Somewhat more complex, but no less irritating in its ambiguity is Figure 7*a*. Relations are neither clearly rectangular nor clearly oblique. The four lines are not sufficiently different in length to assure the eye that they are

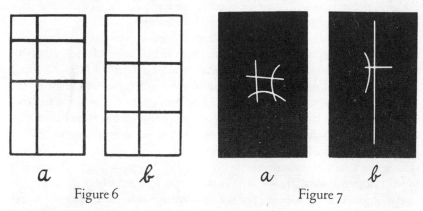

| *a* | *b* | *a* | *b* |
| Figure 6 | | Figure 7 | |

unequal. The pattern, which drifts in space without anchor, approaches, on the one hand, the symmetry of a crosslike figure of vertical-horizontal orientation and, on the other, the shape of a kind of kite with a diagonal symmetry axis. Both interpretations, however, are equally inconclusive. They have none of the reassuring clarity of Figure 7*b*.

Figure 8

Disequilibrium does not always render the whole configuration fluid. In Figure 8 the symmetry of the Latin cross is so firmly established that the unfitting curve may look like an injury. Here, then, a balanced pattern is present to such an extent that it is capable of segregating the rest as an intrusive element. Under such conditions disequilibrium makes for local interference with the unity of the whole.

Weight

At this point it may be useful more systematically to describe the two factors that determine balance: weight and direction.

Weight depends on location. A pictorial element lying in or close to the center of the composition or on the central vertical axis pulls less compositional weight than one lying off the main tracks indicated in the structural map (Figure 3). For example, the centrally located figure of Christ or the Virgin may be quite large or weighted by color or some other factor without overthrowing the balance of the composition. Van Pelt has pointed out that in a symmetrical arrangement of three arches the central one should be larger. It would look too weak if it had merely the size of the other two. (Compositional weight must not be confused with "importance." A centrally located object assumes more importance than a lateral one.)

An object in the upper part of the composition is heavier than one in the lower; and location at the right side makes for more weight than location on the left. Also, the lever principle of physics has been applied to pictorial composition. According to this principle, the weight of a pictorial element increases proportionally to its distance from the center of balance. Although this is probably true, it must be kept in mind that pictorial weighing does not occur in empty space, as physical weighing does, and that usually the other powerful factors of location will strongly interfere with the lever effect.

There seems to be a lever effect in the depth dimension—that is, the farther away from the observer objects are located in pictorial space, the more weight they carry. Puffer has observed that "vistas," which lead the glance to distant space, have great counterbalancing power. This may be a special case of a more general distance effect. The factor is hard to evaluate, because a distant object appears relatively large for reasons of perspective. By appearing larger, it may pull more weight than a picture area of its size would do otherwise. In Manet's *Déjeuner sur l'herbe,* the figure of a girl picking flowers at a distance has considerable weight in relation to a group of three large figures in the foreground. How much of this derives from the fact that being far away she looks perspectively larger than the space she occupies?

Weight depends also on size. Other factors being equal, the larger object will be the heavier. As to color, red is heavier than blue, and bright colors are heavier than dark ones. A black area must be larger than a white one in order to counterbalance it. This is due in part to the irradiation effect, which makes a bright surface look relatively larger.

"Intrinsic interest" has been found by Puffer to be a factor of compositional weight. An area of a painting may hold the attention of the observer either because of the subject matter—for example, the spot around the Christ child in an Adoration—or by its formal complexity, intricacy, or other peculiarity. (Compare the multicolored bouquet of flowers in Manet's *Olympia*.) The very tininess of an object may cause a fascination capable of compensating the light weight that would otherwise go with small size. Also, recent experiments have suggested that perception may be influenced by the observer's wishes and fears. It would be interesting to find out whether pictorial balance is changed by the introduction of a highly desirable object or a frightening one.

Isolation makes for weight. The sun or moon in an empty sky will be heavier than an object of similar appearance surrounded by other things. On the stage, isolation is known as a means of emphasis. Star actors often insist on not being approached too closely by others during important scenes.

Shape and direction seem to influence weight. Regular shape, as it is found in simple geometric forms, is probably heavier than irregular shape. Also compactness—that is, the degree to which mass is concentrated around its center—seems to produce weight. Figure 9, taken from the Graves test, shows a relatively small circle counterweighing a larger rectangle and triangle. Vertically directed forms seem to be heavier than oblique ones. Most of these "rules" need to be verified by exact experiment.

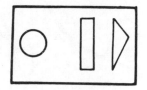

Figure 9

What about the influence of knowledge? In a picture, no knowledge on the part of the observer will make a bundle of cotton look lighter than a lump of lead of similar appearance. The problem has come up in architecture. According to Mock and Richards, "We know from repeated experiences how strong wood or stone is for we frequently handled them in other contexts, and when we look at a piece of wood or masonry construction we are immediately satisfied that it is able to do the job it has to do. But reinforced concrete construction is different; so is a building of steel and glass. We cannot see the steel bars inside the concrete and reassure ourselves that it can safely span several times the distance of the stone lintel it so much resembles, nor can we see the steel columns behind a cantilevered store window, so that

Figure 10

Figure 11

a building may appear to stand unsafely on a base of glass. It should be realized, however, that the expectation that we shall be able to understand at a glance why a building stands up is a survival of the handicraft age that had disappeared even in the days of William Morris."

This kind of reasoning is common nowadays, but seems open to doubt. Two things must be distinguished. On the one hand there is the technical understanding of the craftsman, who deals with such factors as methods of construction and strength of material. Most of these data cannot be obtained by looking at the finished building, and there is no artistic reason why they should. Quite another matter is the visual comprehensibility of the building. The beholder must be able to understand such things as the distribution of *visual* weight and the relations between load and carrier. Technical information or misinformation is likely to influence visual evaluation very little. What perhaps does count is certain stylistic conventions—for example, as to the width of the span. Such conventions oppose change everywhere in the arts. Some of the resistance to the visual statics of modern architecture may be owing to this conservatism. But the main point is that the purely visual discrepancy between a large mass and a thin supporting pole is in no way touched by the assurance of the architect that the thing will not collapse physically. Wherever the architect abandons the appearance of the solid cube or wall, which are remnants of the older construction method, and reveals the skeleton of slender girders, style catches up with technology and the eye ceases to have trouble.

Direction

Direction, as well as weight, determines balance. Like weight, direction is influenced by location. The weight of any compositional element, whether it is a part of the hidden structural map or a visible object, will attract things in the neighborhood and thus impose direction upon them. I have already shown the centripetal pull in the disk caused by the center of the square. In Figure 10 the horse is seen to be drawn backward through the attraction of the figure of the rider, whereas in Figure 11 it is pulled forward by the other horse. In Toulouse-Lautrec's drawing, from which this sketch was made, the two factors balance each other. Weight by attraction was demonstrated also in Figure 5.

Elongated forms whose spatial position deviates from the vertical or horizontal only by a small angle show a pull toward that structurally strong direction. A similar striving toward the diagonal may also exist.

The shape of pictorial objects creates axes, and these axes create directed forces. This is true not only for such well-defined objects as a human figure, which in an upright position may show a vertically directed force, but also for any detail—as, for example, the line of the mouth—or any grouping of objects—say, a row of men forming a large rectangle. Compositional triangles forge groups of figures into upward-moving pyramids—for example, in the El Greco *Pietà* (Figure 12).

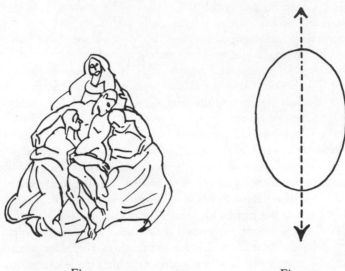

Figure 12   Figure 13

The axes produced by shape allow for movement in two opposite directions. An ellipse (Figure 13) is directed upward as well as downward. Preference for one of the two directions is caused by various factors. A shape may be seen as directed to the right rather than to the left because of the general tendency to read visual patterns from left to right. If one point of the shape is "anchored," for example, by coinciding with the fulcrum, the force will be seen as issuing from there. If one side of the shape is anchored to the frame and the other ends in free space—as, for example, the triangle of Figure 12—the force will move toward the free end. Similarly, the shape of an arm will move toward the hand and that of the branch of a tree toward its tip.

Subject matter also creates directed forces. It will define a human figure as walking forward or falling backward. In Rembrandt's *Portrait of a Young Girl* at the Chicago Art Institute the eyes of the girl are turned to the left, thus providing the almost symmetrical shape of the front-face figure with a strong lateral force. Spatial directions created by the glance of actors are known as "visual lines" on the stage.

In any particular work of art many of the above factors act with and against each other to create the balance of the whole. Weight through color may be counteracted by weight through location. The direction of shape may be balanced by movement toward a center of attraction. The complexity of these relations contributes greatly to the liveliness of a work of art.

When actual motion is used, as in the dance, the theater, or the movies, direction is indicated by the movement. Balance may be obtained between events that occur at the same time—as when two dancers walk symmetrically toward each other—or in succession. Film cutters often have a scene of movement toward the right followed, or preceded, by one of movement toward the left. The elementary need for such balancing compensation was shown clearly by experiments in which observers, after fixating a line bent at the middle into an obtuse angle, saw an objectively straight line as a line bent in the opposite direction. Also when observers inspected a straight line that was moderately tilted from the vertical or the horizontal, the objective vertical or horizontal later appeared bent in the opposite direction.

Speech creates visual weight at the place from which it issues. For example, in a duet between a dancer who speaks poetry and another who is silent the asymmetry may be compensated by more active movement of the silent dancer.

Patterns of Balance

Balance is often centered in one or more nodal elements or focuses that carry the main weight. For example, a pair of human figures may furnish the twin centers of the work. Each figure in turn will be organized within itself around secondary balance centers, which may be located in the face, the lap, the hands, depending on the composition. The same will be true for the rest of the picture. In this way a chief theme is created, which represents the top of a hierarchic order. From the two figures and their over-all balance in the whole work the eye descends toward lower levels of organization reaching smaller and smaller units. What may be called the steepness of the hierarchic order differs with the style of the work. Some are dominated by a powerful theme surrounded by a subservient "background." On the other hand—for example, in certain works by Klee, Matisse, Braque, the cubists, or the impressionists—the balance of the whole may be maintained by a large number of minor centers, all of similar strength. In its extreme consequence, this latter method leads to an even distribution of substance, better suited to interpret the over-all character of a mood or mode of existence than to describe life as depending upon the effects of central powers or events. In paintings of this kind the influence of the structural map is weak. The result is a homogeneity that may well be termed "atonal," in that the relation to the underlying structural "key" is given up and replaced by a network of connections between the elements of the composition itself.

Top and Bottom

It has often been remarked that the lower part of a visual pattern demands more weight. A distinction must be made here between adding just enough weight to the bottom part to make the whole look balanced and giving the bottom overweight so that it looks heavier than the top. Langfeld says: "If one is asked to bisect a perpendicular line without measuring it, one almost invariably places the mark too high. If a line is actually bisected, it is with difficulty that one can convince oneself that the upper half is not longer than the lower half." When this occurs, an increase of the lower length will act simply as a compensation. It will make both halves look equal. But Horatio Greenough speaks of a different matter: "That buildings, in rising from the earth, be broad and simple at their bases, that they grow lighter not only in fact but in expression as they ascend, is a principle established. The laws of gravitation are at the root of this axiom. The spire obeys it. The obelisk is its simplest expression." Here the pattern is made to look heavier at the bottom.

Gravitation is probably at the root of this asymmetry in the vertical dimension, but how its effect on vision comes about is not known. Man's experience in handling physical objects teaches him that bottom heaviness assures stability. It is possible that this knowledge affects the observer when visual balance is evaluated. It is equally possible that, independent of experience, a physiological feature of the brain makes for this asymmetry; or there may be a combination of both factors. The strictly spherical building at the New York World's Fair in 1939 aroused the unpleasant impression of wanting to rise from the ground but being tied to it. Whereas a securely balanced building points freely upward, the contradiction between the symmetrical sphere and asymmetrical space made for frustrated locomotion in this particular structure. The use of a completely symmetrical form in an asymmetrical context is a delicate undertaking. As an example of how the task can be solved, the position of the rose window in the façade of Notre Dame in Paris (Figure 14) may be studied. Relatively small enough to avoid any danger of drifting, it "personifies" the balance of vertical and horizontal elements obtained around it. The window finds its place of rest somewhat above the center of the square-shaped surface that represents the main mass of the façade.

The compensation, which keeps the lower part of a pattern from looking too light or too small, is needed everywhere, except for the structurally strongest shapes, which resist the distortion of angles. For example, a picture frame can be strictly rectangular because any rectangle maintains its regular shape; but in a less regular shape, allowance must be made for compensation.

Figure 14

It cannot be maintained, however, that general artistic practice makes patterns look heavier at the bottom—that is, lowers the center of gravity. True, in the landscape that man, the land animal, sees around himself the lower part of the visual field is crowded with buildings, fields, trees, and events whereas the sky is relatively empty. A corresponding effect is sought in the arts wherever the realistic representation of solid material bodies is intended. By lowering the center of gravity the painter or sculptor adapts his work to the asymmetry of physical space. This practice, however, is not universal. It goes with certain styles only. For instance, modern art— because of its trend toward abstraction—has little use for this uneven distribution of masses. Suspended in space and reposing in itself, the picture demonstrates its emancipation from material reality by shirking earthly weight. This tendency can be found even in certain works of modern sculpture and architecture.

The experience of flying through the air and the upsetting of visual conventions in photographs taken from the air have contributed to this development. The motion-picture camera refuses to keep its line of sight parallel with the ground, thus presenting views in which the gravitational axis is freely displaced and the lower part of the picture not necessarily more crowded than the upper. The modern dance has run into an interesting inner conflict by stressing the weight of the human body—which the classical ballet had tried to deny—and at the same time following the general trend in moving from realistic pantomime to abstraction.

Some modern abstractionists have maintained that their works can be turned around freely because they balance in all spatial orientations. Since this rules out compensation for the asymmetry of space, the claim sounds suspicious. In a recent experiment twenty observers were asked to judge which way some abstract paintings were "right side up." They were correct significantly often, non-art students doing as well as art students.

Right and Left

A knotty problem is posed by the asymmetry of right and left. I shall discuss it here only as far as it concerns the psychology of visual balance. The art historian Wölfflin called attention to the fact that pictures change appearance and lose meaning when turned into their mirror images. He realized that this happens because pictures are "read" from the left to the right, and naturally the sequence changes when the picture is inverted. Wölfflin noted that the direction of the diagonal that runs from bottom left to top right is seen as ascending, the other as descending. Any pictorial object looks heavier at the right side of the picture. For example, when the figure of Sixtus in Raphael's *Sistine Madonna* is moved to the right by inversion of the painting, he becomes so heavy that the whole composition seems to topple (Figure 15). Gaffron carried the investigation further, notably in a

Figure 15

book in which she attempted to show by detailed analysis that Rembrandt's etchings reveal their true meaning only when the observer looks at them the way the artist drew them on the plate and not in the inverted prints, to which we are accustomed. According to Gaffron, the observer experiences a picture as if he was facing its left side. He is subjectively identified with the left, and whatever appears in that part of the picture assumes greatest importance. This agrees with Dean's observations on the so-called stage areas of the theater. He says that as the curtain rises at the beginning of an act, the audience can be seen to look to its left first. The left side of the stage is considered the strong one. In a group of two or three actors, the one to the left dominates the scene.

It will be evident that when the observer experiences facing the left side, a second and asymmetrically located center is created in the picture at that side. Just like the center of the frame, this subjective center carries importance and can be expected to influence the composition accordingly. A contrapuntal relationship between the two competing centers will result.

Like the area around the center of the frame, the area of the subjective center to the left is able to carry more weight, which seems to be the reason why the heavy figure of Sixtus (Figure 15) at the left does not upset the balance. As soon as it is moved to the right, it profits from the "lever effect" in relation to both centers. It therefore becomes heavy—it looks conspicuous. There is, then, a curious difference between being important and "central," at the left, and being heavy and conspicuous, at the right. In Grünewald's crucifixion of the Isenheim altar the group of Mary and the Evangelist to the left assumes greatest importance next to Christ, who holds the center, whereas John the Baptist to the right is the conspicuous herald, who calls attention to the scene at which he is pointing. If an actor comes on the stage from the right, he is noticed immediately, but the focus of the action lies at the left if it does not occupy the center. In the traditional English pantomime, the Fairy Queen, with whom the audience is supposed to identify, always appears from the left whereas the Demon King enters on the prompt side, that is, on the audience's right.

At the end of his observations on the right-left phenomenon Wölfflin reminds his readers that he has described but not explained it, and he adds: "Apparently it has deep roots, roots that reach down to the nethermost foundations of our sensuous nature." At present the most common explanation runs along empiricist lines. The reading of pictures from left to right is a habit taken over from the reading of books. The neuropsychiatrist Stanley Cobb, speaking of handedness, says: "Many fanciful ideas have been put forward, from the theory that the left hemisphere has a better blood supply than the right to the heliocentric theory that the right hand dominates because man originated north of the equator and, looking at the sun, was impressed with the fact that great things move towards the right! Thus right became the symbol of rectitude and dexterity and things on the left were sinister. It is an interesting observation that about 70 per cent of human foetuses lie in the uterus in the 'left occiput posterior' position, i.e., facing to the right. No one has ever found out whether or not these become the right handed majority of babies. Probably the dominance of right hand-edness is due to chance in heredity."

Gaffron relates the phenomenon to the dominance of the left brain cortex, which contains the higher brain centers for speech, writing, and reading in a right-handed person. If this dominance applies equally to the left visual center, it means that "there exists a difference in our awareness of visual data in favor of those which are perceived within the right visual field." Vision to the right would be more articulate, hence the conspicuousness of objects appearing in that area. The attention for what goes on at the left would make up for that asymmetry, and the eye would move spontaneously from the place of first attention to the area of most articulate vision. This is the state of the hypothesis at the present time.

Balance and the Human Mind

Thus far I have described balance as a means of eliminating ambiguity and disunity, that is, as an indispensable device for making an artistic statement comprehensible. This is not the usual way of dealing with the subject. The more common assertion is that the artist strives for balance because it is desirable for its own sake. Why is it desirable? "Because it is pleasing and satisfying." This is the hedonistic theory, which defines human motivation as the striving for pleasure and the avoidance of unpleasant feelings. It should be evident by now that this venerable theory is correct but useless. It explains everything and nothing. What we need to know is why a par-ticular activity or situation is pleasing.

It has been asserted that the artist strives for balance because the mainte-nance of bodily equilibrium is one of man's most elementary needs. When looking at an unbalanced pattern, the observer is said to experience a feeling of unbalance in his own body by some kind of spontaneous analogy. Hence the need for balanced composition.

This assertion is based on theory rather than on observation. There is no concrete evidence to show that such muscular reactions to visual experiences are frequent, strong, or decisive. The tendency to explain visual (or auditory) reactions by kinesthetic ones is not limited to the psychology of balance. It will be discussed critically later. I have already offered an alternative theory to the effect that the visual reaction of an observer may be considered the psychological counterpart of the striving for balance assumed to exist in the physiological forces of the cortical brain field.

Neither theory, however, can be sufficient. Both refer to specific tendencies of the body, and therefore cannot do justice to the deep spiritual function fulfilled by art. We must expect the need for balance to correspond to a universal human experience of much greater range. The phenomenon of balance must be seen in a wider context.

The psychology of motivation has recently profited from a way of thinking that has led workers in different fields of knowledge to similar conclusions. In physics the principle of entropy, also known as the second law of thermodynamics, asserts that in any isolated system each state represents an irreversible decrease of active energy. The universe tends toward a state of equilibrium, in which all existing asymmetries of distribution will be eliminated. Thus all physical activity can be defined as a striving for balance. In psychology the gestalt theorists have come to the conclusion that every psychological field tends toward the simplest, most balanced, most regular organization available. Freud has interpreted his "pleasure principle" as the belief that the course of psychical events is stimulated by an unpleasant tension and takes a direction that will lead to a reduction of tension. Finally, the physicist L. L. Whyte has been so impressed by the universality of the idea that he has formulated a "unitary principle," underlying all natural activity, according to which "asymmetry decreases in isolable systems."

In line with this trend of thinking, psychologists have defined motivation as "the disequilibrium of the organism which leads to action for the restoration of stability." The establishment of this principle unquestionably represents a decisive step forward. At the same time its one-sided application leads to an intolerably static conception of motivation. The organism appears as something like a stagnant pool, stimulated to activity only when a pebble disturbs the balanced peace of its surface, limiting its activity to the reëstablishment of that peace. Freud came closest to accepting this view in its radical consequences. He described man's basic instincts as an expression of the conservative nature of living matter, as an inherent tendency to go back to a former state. He spoke of the basic importance of the "death instinct," a striving for return to inorganic existence. According to Freud's economy principle, man constantly tries to expend as little energy as possible. Man is lazy by nature.

In opposition to this view, it can be pointed out that a human being, not handicapped by physical or mental ailment, finds his fulfillment not in inactivity but in doing, moving, changing, growing, going ahead, producing, creating, exploring. There is no justification for the strange notion that life consists of attempts to put an end to itself as rapidly as possible. In fact the chief characteristic of the organism may well be that it represents an anomaly of nature because it wages an uphill fight against the universal law of entropy by constantly drawing new energy from its environment.

Such a view does not deny the importance of balance. Balance remains the final goal of any wish to be fulfilled, any task to be accomplished, any problem to be solved. But the racing is not done only for the winning's sake.

In human life, balance can be achieved only partly and temporarily. Even so, as a person is engaged in striving and activity, he constantly tries to organize the competing forces that make up his life situation in such a way that the best possible equilibrium results. Needs and duties, which often pull in opposite directions, have to be reconciled, and within the group of people of which he is a part there will be a constant maneuver of re-arrangement to keep the friction of divergent interests at a minimum.

Balance Conveys Meaning

The above discussion concerns art in two ways. First of all, compositional balance reflects a tendency that is probably the mainspring of all activity in the universe. Art accomplishes what can never be realized by the overlapping strivings that make up human life. But at the same time the work of art is far from being merely an image of balance. If we define art—and this is my second point—as the striving for, and achievement of, balance, harmony, order, unity, we arrive at the same perverting one-sidedness as the psychologists did when they formulated the static conception of human motivation. Just as the emphasis of living is on directed activity and not on empty repose, so the emphasis of the work of art is not on balance, harmony, unity, but on a pattern of directed forces that are being balanced, ordered, unified.

A work of art is a statement about the nature of reality. From an infinite number of possible configurations of forces, it picks and presents one. In any such configuration the whole determines place, character, and magnitude of each force, and in turn a unified structure results from the together-ness of all the forces of which it consists. This means that each pattern of existence is presented in its valid form. The work of art is the necessary and final solution of the problem of how to organize a reality pattern of given characteristics.

If, instead, the layman is told that art deals with the presentation of balance or harmony, he ought to conclude, with surprise, that apparently the celebrated craft of the artist is concerned with nothing better than the modest satisfaction experienced by a housemaid who arranges knickknacks on the mantelpiece in a symmetrical order. And when a lecturer endeavors to explain the *raison d'être* of a painting by showing in detail how the colors, masses, and directions balance each other, the layman should be expected to assume that, for reasons of their own, artists have expanded the game of the housemaid into a tricky trade.

Much of what is being said about art these days leaves the bystander in the position of a person to whom the functioning of an unknown machine is explained without any intimation of the use of the machine. Only when he is told that the work of art has a content—and that all the organizing of color and shape occurs exclusively for the purpose of conveying that content—only then will he understand why those balanced forms might regard him.

The notion that art is concerned with perfecting formal relationships, such as balance, misleads and alienates the public. It has equally devastating effects upon the practice of art. An artist who approaches his work with the sole intention of achieving balance and harmony without considering what he is trying to balance will get lost in the arbitrary playing with form that has wasted so much talent during the past few decades. Regardless of whether the work is representational or abstract, only the content can determine which pattern is to be chosen and subjected to the business of pictorial organization or composition. Therefore the function of balance can be shown only by pointing out the meaning it helps to make visible. According to Leonardo, in a good work of painting "the distribution or arrangement of the figures is devised in agreement with the conditions you desire the action to represent." Focusing upon the content need not be conscious or be formulated intellectually. It is a question of the attitude, which may be entirely beyond the awareness of the artist himself.

Madame Cézanne in a Yellow Chair

After so much theory, here is a concrete example of the approach I advocate. I have deliberately chosen a painting that at first glance looks simple—beautiful but perhaps artless—the kind of work on which many a museumgoer does not spend much time. My analysis will have to be detailed to bring out some of the richness of this masterpiece.

Cézanne's portrait of his wife in a yellow chair (Figure 16) was painted in 1888–1890. What strikes the observer first is the combination of external tranquillity and strong potential activity. The reposing figure is charged with energy, which presses in the direction of the woman's glance. The figure is stable and rooted, but at the same time it is as light as though suspended in space. It rises, yet it rests in itself. This subtle blend of serenity and vigor, of firmness and disembodied freedom, may be described as the particular configuration of forces that represents the theme of the work. How is the effect achieved?

The picture has an upright format, the proportion being approximately 5:4. This stretches the whole in the direction of the vertical and reinforces the upright character of the figure, the chair, the head. The chair is somewhat slimmer than the frame, and the figure slimmer than the chair. Thus there is a scale of increasing slimness, which leads forward from the back-

Figure 16

ground over the chair to the foreground figure. At the same time the shoulders and arms form an oval around the middle point of the picture, a centric core of stability that counteracts the pattern of rectangles and is repeated in small scale by the head.

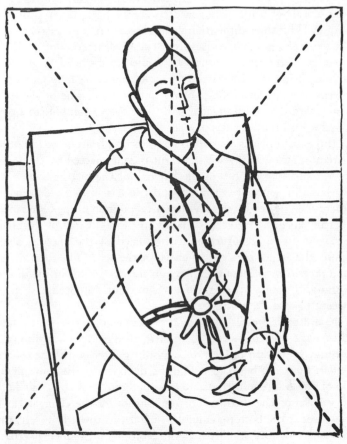

Figure 17

A dark band divides the background into two rectangles (Figure 17). Both are more elongated than the whole frame, the lower rectangle being 3:2 and the upper, 2:1. This means that these rectangles are stressing the horizontal more vigorously than the frame stresses the vertical. Although the rectangles furnish a counterpoint to the vertical, they also enhance the upward movement of the whole by the fact that vertically the lower rectangle is taller

than the upper. According to Denman Ross, the eye moves in the direction
of diminishing intervals—that is, upward in this picture.

A scale of increasing slimness, which leads from the background toward
the observer was noted above. This crescendo effect is enhanced by a number
of other features. The three main elements of the picture overlap each other
spatially: a scale of three planes leads from the background over the chair
to the figure. This three-dimensional scale is supported by a two-dimensional
one—a series of steps—that rises from the small fraction of the dark band
at the extreme left over the corner of the chair to the head. Similarly, a scale
of increasing brightness leads from the dark band to the light face and hands,
which represent the two focuses of the composition. The bright red of the
coat also makes the figure advance. All these factors combine to a powerful,
stepwise forward movement.

The three main planes overlap in the direction from far left to near right.
This lateral movement toward the right is counteracted by the location of
the chair, which lies mainly in the left half of the picture and thus establishes a retarding submovement toward the left. But the dominant right
movement is enhanced by the asymmetrical position of the figure in relation
to the chair, since the figure lies mainly in the right half of the chair. The
trend toward the right is further strengthened by the unequal division of
the figure, the larger part of which is on the left. (The nose divides the
face in a proportion of about 5:2.) Again the eye moves in the direction of
diminishing intervals—that is, from left to right. The wedge-shaped collar
also sweeps toward the right.

Figure and chair are tilted at about the same angle relative to the frame.
It will be remembered that in themselves all directions are ambiguous; so
this tilt may be toward top left, or bottom right, or both. The composition
as a whole, however, helps to define the direction of the movement. Both
the top of the figure and the center of the bottom of the chair lie on the
central vertical of the picture. This establishes for the chair an anchoring
point or pivot at the bottom, around which it tilts toward the left; the head
of the woman, doubly stabilized by its position on the medial vertical and
in the center of the upper background rectangle, is the basis around which
the body of the figure tilts forward toward the right. Thus the two focuses
of the composition are set against each other. The head—where we localize
the mind—reposes firmly; the hands—the instruments of labor—are thrust
slightly forward in potential activity. But an ingenious counterpoint com-
plicates the situation. The head, although at rest, contains activity in the
watchful eyes and the dynamic asymmetry of the quarter profile. The hands,
although moved forward, lie folded in restful symmetry.

The forward tilt of the figure is counterbalanced by the fact that, like the chair, it is solidly founded at the bottom of the picture whereas the top ends in free space. But the free rising of the head is checked not only by central location but also by its nearness to the upper border of the frame. It rises so much that it is caught by a new harbor. Just as the musical scale rises from the base of the key tone only to return to a new base at the distance of the octave, so the figure rises in the frame from the bottom base only to find new repose at the top base at the upper edge of the frame. Like the so-called "leading" tone of the scale, the head in its high location is not only as far away as possible from the bottom base of departure but at the same time captured by the new top base, which it approaches. (There is, then, a similarity between the structure of the musical scale and the framed composition. They both show a combination of two structural principles: the gradual increase of intensity by the rising from bottom to top; and the symmetry of bottom and top, by which the act of ascension from the base finally transforms itself into an upward fall toward a new base, so that withdrawal from a state of rest turns out to be the mirror image of the return to a state of rest.)

If this analysis is correct, it will not only exhibit the wealth of dynamic relationships that a work of art contains but also demonstrate that these relationships establish the particular balance of rest and activity that was earlier described as the theme or content of the picture. Only by realizing how these relationships interpret the content can we understand and appreciate their artistic excellence.

Two general remarks should be added. It will be seen that the subject matter of the picture is an integral part of the conception. Only because shapes are recognized as head, body, hands, chair, do they play their particular compositional role. The fact that the head harbors the mind is at least as important as its shape, color, or location. As an abstract pattern, the formal elements of the picture would have to be quite different to convey a similar meaning. And the observer's knowledge of what a seated, middle-aged woman signifies contributes strongly to the deeper meaning of the work.

Then too, it will have been noticed that the composition rests on a kind of counterpoint—that is, on many counterbalancing elements. But these antagonistic forces are not contradictory or conflicting. They do not create ambiguity. Ambiguity confuses the artistic statement because it leaves the observer on the edge between two or more assertions that do not add up to a whole. As a rule, pictorial counterpoint is hierarchic—that is, it sets a dominant force against a subservient one. Each relationship is unbalanced in itself; together they all balance each other in the structure of the whole work.

II   SHAPE

I see an object. I see the world around me. What do these statements imply?
For the purposes of everyday life, seeing is essentially a means of practical
orientation. In that sense, seeing is determining through one's eyes that a
certain thing is present at a certain place. This is identification at its bare
minimum. A husband entering the bedroom at night may perceive a dark
patch on the white pillow and thus "see" that his wife is in the familiar
place. Under better lighting conditions he will see more, but, in principle,
orientation requires only a minimum of cues. After a brain injury a man had
lost the capacity of seeing shape to the extent that he could not even recognize a circle by merely looking at it. He was, however, able to hold a job and
get along in daily life. He could distinguish a human being, which is narrow
and long, from a car, which is much wider. This kind of rudimentary information was all he needed to hold his own in the streets. Many people are
using their unimpaired sense of sight to no better advantage during much
of the day.

Vision as Active Exploration

Obviously, seeing can mean more than that. What does it involve? The
optical process, as described by the physicists, is well known. Light is emitted
or reflected by objects of the environment. The eye lenses project images
of these objects upon the retinas, which transmit the message to the brain.
But what about the corresponding psychological experience? There has been
a tendency among scientists to describe the experience of vision in analogy
to the physical process. As far as seeing is concerned, the mind was assumed
to perform much like a photographic camera. But if, instead of assuming
things, scientists observe the facts with an unprejudiced mind, they discover

that vision is anything but a mechanical recording device. First of all, vision is not mere passive reception. The world of images does not simply imprint itself upon a faithfully sensitive organ. Rather, in looking at an object, we reach out for it. With an invisible finger we move through the space around us, go out to the distant places where things are found, touch them, catch them, scan their surfaces, trace their borders, explore their texture. It is an eminently active occupation.

Impressed by this experience, early thinkers described the physical process of vision correspondingly. For example, Plato, in his *Timaeus,* asserts that the gentle fire that warms the human body flows out through the eyes in a smooth and dense stream of light. Thus a tangible bridge is established between the observer and the observed thing, and over this bridge the impulses of light that emanate from the object travel to the eyes and thereby to the soul. Primitive optics has had its day, but the experience it illustrates remains alive and still becomes explicit in poetical description—for example, in these words by T. S. Eliot: "And the unseen eyebeam crossed, for the roses had the look of flowers that are looked at."

Vision, then, differs from what the photographic camera does by being active exploration rather than passive recording. Vision is highly selective, not only in the sense of concentrating on what attracts attention, but also in its way of dealing with any one object. The camera will register all detail with equal faithfulness, but vision will not. Physically, vision is limited only by the resolving power of the retinas; if we intently examine some object, we find the eyes equipped to see every minute detail. But commonly, seeing is not scrutinizing. What do we see when we see?

Grasping the Essentials

Seeing means grasping a few outstanding features of the object—the blueness of the sky, the curve of the swan's neck, the rectangularity of the book, the sheen of metal, the straightness of the cigarette. A few simple lines and dots are readily accepted as "a face," not only by civilized Westerners, who may be suspected of having agreed among each other on such "sign language," but also by babies, savages, and animals. Köhler aroused terror in his chimpanzees by showing them "most primitive stuffed toys" with black buttons for eyes. A clever caricaturist can create the speaking likeness of a person through a few well-chosen lines. We identify an acquaintance at long distance by nothing more than the most elementary proportions or motions. A crudely printed photograph may reduce a face to dots of varying grays and still allow spontaneous recognition.

Thus a few selected marks are able to conjure up the recollection of complex things. In fact, not only are they sufficient for identification, but they even convey the lively impression of being the complete, "real" thing. The power of salient perceptual features to stand for the whole exerts itself most impressively in certain primitive inborn reactions of animals. Lorenz has reported on experiments that show, for example, that a male robin will start to fight when shown a square inch of the russet breast feathers of its species. Dummies that reproduce one or more basic features of size, shape, color, or motion are reacted to by birds or fish as though the actual animal were present. Lorenz points out that geometric regularity of form and movement, pure notes, and unmixed spectral colors are the typical qualities of such perceptual "releasers."

Naturally, these experiments prove only that the isolated features elicit the same behavior as the sight of the complete animal and not that the two stimuli actually look alike. In fact, Lorenz has also noted, for example, that a fish will distinguish between its own mate and a hostile intruder of the same species, although both display the identical fighting colors. Certainly, human beings are readily aware of even slight changes in objects they know well. The tiny modifications of muscle tension or skin color that make a face look tired, a small change of the line drawn by an eyebrow pencil, or the effect of a few more pounds of body weight will be noticed, even though the observer may be unable to tell precisely what causes the change of the over-all impression.

In short, a few outstanding features determine the identity of a perceived object and create an integrated pattern, which is also influenced by a number of secondary qualities. It takes special training to see pictures that contain a great deal of realistic detail but do not clearly bring out the salient perceptual features. Jung tells the story of African natives who were unable to recognize the magazine pictures he showed them until one of them, tracing the outlines with his fingers, exclaimed, "These are white men!"

Perceptual Concepts

There is good evidence that in organic development perception starts with the grasping of striking structural features. For example, when two-year-old children and chimpanzees had learned that of two boxes presented them the one with a triangle of particular size and shape always contained some attractive food, they were able without difficulty to apply their training also to triangles of very different appearance. The triangle was made smaller or larger or turned upside down. A black triangle on white ground was replaced by a white triangle on black ground, or an outlined triangle by a solid one. These changes seemed to create little difficulty of recognition. Similar results were obtained with rats. Lashley has asserted that simple transpositions of this type "are universal from the insects to primates."

The perceptual process revealed by this kind of behavior is still referred to as "generalization" by psychologists. The term is left over from a theoretical approach, which has been refuted by the very experiments to which it is applied. It was assumed that perception started with the recording of individual cases, whose common properties could be realized only by creatures capable of forming concepts intellectually. Thus the similarity of triangles different in size, orientation, and color was thought to be discoverable only by observers whose brain was mature enough to have drawn the general concept of triangularity from the variety of individual observations. Consequently, the fact that young children and animals, untrained in logical abstraction, performed such tasks without difficulty came as a puzzling surprise.

The experimental findings demanded a complete turnabout in the theory of perception. It seemed no longer possible to think of vision as proceeding from the particulars to the general. On the contrary, it became evident that over-all structural features are the primary data of perception, so that triangularity is not a late product of intellectual abstraction but a direct and more elementary experience than the recording of individual detail. The young child sees "doggishness" before he is able to distinguish one dog from another. I shall soon show that this psychological discovery is of decisive importance for the understanding of artistic form.

The new theory poses a peculiar problem. The over-all structural features of which the percept is thought to consist are obviously not furnished explicitly by any particular stimulus pattern. If, for example, a human head— or a number of heads—is seen as round, that roundness is not a part of the stimulus. Every head has its particular complex outline, which approaches roundness; but if that roundness is not just distilled out intellectually but actually seen, how does it get into the percept? My answer is that the stimulus configuration seems to enter the perceptual process only in the sense that it evokes in the brain a specific pattern of general sensory categories, which "stands for" the stimulation in a way similar to that in which, in a scientific description, a network of general concepts is offered as an equivalent of a phenomenon of reality. Just as the very nature of scientific concepts excludes the possibility of their ever seizing the phenomenon "itself," percepts cannot contain the stimulus material "itself," either totally or partly. The nearest a scientist can get to an apple is by giving the measurements of its weight, size, shape, location, taste. The nearest a percept can get to the stimulus "apple" is by representing it through a specific pattern of such general sensory qualities as roundness, heaviness, fruity taste, greenness.

When we see a human face, is there, even as a first stage, a passive recording of all or some of the specific contours, sizes, shades of color? Does not seeing a face mean producing a pattern of such general qualities as the slimness of the whole, the straightness of the eyebrows, the forward sweep of the nose, the blueness of the eyes? There is a fitting of perceptual characteristics to the structure suggested by the stimulus material rather than a reception of the raw material itself. Are not these whole patterns or categories of shape, size, proportion, color all we get and use when we see, recognize, remember? Are not these categories the indispensable prerequisites that permit us to understand perceptually?

As long as we look at simple, regular shape—say, a square—the phenomenon does not become apparent. The squareness seems literally given in the stimulus. But if we leave the world of well-defined, man-made shapes and look around in a landscape, what do we see? A mass of trees and brushwood is a rather chaotic sight. Some of the tree trunks and branches may show definite directions, to which the eyes can cling, and the whole of a tree or bush may often present a fairly comprehensible sphere or cone shape. Also there may be an over-all texture of leafiness and greenness, but there is much in the landscape that the eyes are simply unable to grasp. And only to the extent to which the confused panorama can be seen as a configuration of clear-cut directions, sizes, geometric shapes, colors, can it be said that it is actually perceived.

The brain processes that make this articulation possible are unknown. We may assume that in response to perceptual qualities, more or less clearly indicated in the raw material of the stimulus, corresponding patterns of simple structure arise in the cortical field of vision. But for the time being, this is pure theory, inferred from what is observed in experience.

If the foregoing presentation is correct, we are compelled to say that perceiving consists in the formation of "perceptual concepts." To the usual way of thinking this is uncomfortable terminology, because the senses are supposed to be limited to the concrete whereas concepts deal with the abstract. The process of vision as it was described above, however, seems to meet the conditions of concept formation. Vision deals with the raw material of experience by creating a corresponding pattern of general forms, which are applicable not only to the individual case at hand but to an infinite number of other cases as well.

In no way should the use of the word "concept" suggest that perceiving is an intellectual operation. The processes that have been described must be thought of as occurring within the visual apparatus. But the term should indicate that there is a striking similarity between the elementary activities of the senses and the higher ones of thinking or reasoning. So great is this similarity that psychologists have often been tricked into attributing the achievements of the senses to secret aid supposed to have been rendered them by the intellect. They have spoken of unconscious conclusions or computations because they took it for granted that perception itself could do nothing better than mechanically register the impingements of the outer world. It seems now that the same mechanisms operate on both the perceptual and the intellectual level, so that inevitably terms like concept, judgment, logic, abstraction, conclusion, computation have to be applied to the work of the senses.

Recent psychological thinking, then, encourages us to call vision a creative activity of the human mind. Perceiving achieves, at the sensory level, what in the realm of reasoning is known as understanding. Every man's eyesight also anticipates in a modest way the admired capacity of the artist to produce patterns that validly interpret experience by means of organized form. Eyesight is insight.

What Is Shape?

Shape is one of the essential characteristics of objects grasped by the eyes. It refers to the spatial aspects of things, excepting location and orientation. That is, shape does not tell us where an object is and whether it lies upside down or right side up. It concerns, first of all, the boundaries of masses. Three-dimensional bodies are bound by two-dimensional surfaces. Surfaces are bound by one-dimensional borders—for example, by lines. The outer boundaries of objects can be explored by the senses without impediment. But the shape of a room, a cave, or a mouth is given by the inner boundaries of solid objects; and in cups, hats, or gloves, outside and inside make up shape together or vie with each other for the title.

In addition, the look of an object is never determined only by the image that strikes the eyes. The hidden back of a ball, which logically completes the round shape partly visible in front, is actually part of the percept. We do not see a partial sphere but a complete sphere. And so intimately is knowledge wedded to observation that while we look at a person's face the unseen hair on the back of the head is part of the picture we receive. Similarly, the internal shape of things is often present in visual conception. The observer may see a watch as something that contains a clockwork. He may see a person's clothes as the wrappers of the body, or he may see the body as containing cavities, organs, muscles, and blood vessels. Various conceptions of what makes up the visible shape of things are reflected in the arts. The Western style of painting, created by the Renaissance, restricted shape to what can be seen from a fixed point of observation. The Egyptians, the American Indians, and the cubists ignore this restriction. Children draw the baby in the mother's belly, bushmen include inner organs and intestines in the picture of a kangaroo, and the sculptor Henry Moore fashions a human head as a hollow helmet whose visible inside is just as important as the outside. More of this later.

Figure 18

Finally, it follows from what was said above that the shape of an object is not necessarily identical with the actual boundary of the physical body. When a person who has been asked what a winding staircase looks like describes with his finger a rising spiral, he is not giving the outline but the characteristic main axis, actually nonexistent in the object. Figure 18 depicts a face, even though the outer boundary is absent. The true shape of an object, then, is constituted by its essential spatial features.

The Influence of the Past

Shape is determined by more than what strikes the eye at the time of observation. The experience of the present moment is never isolated. It is the most recent among an infinite number of sensory experiences that have occurred throughout the person's past life. Thus the new image gets into contact with the memory traces of shapes that have been perceived in the past. These traces of shapes interfere with each other on the basis of their similarity, and the new image cannot escape this influence. Images of clear-cut shape are often strong enough to resist any observable influence of the

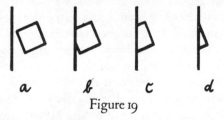

Figure 19

memory traces they meet. Sometimes they may contain ambiguous features, which can change under appropriate influence. Figure 19*d* looks clearly enough like a combination of a vertical line and a triangle. When the same

pattern is presented as the last of the series, however, we are likely to see
the corner of a square that is about to disappear behind a wall. Similarly,
Figure 20 changes its shape abruptly when we are told that it represents a

Figure 20

giraffe passing behind a window. Here the verbal description stirs up a
visual memory trace that resembles the drawing sufficiently to establish
contact with it. Under the pressure of this contact, the spatially ambiguous
drawing assumes an appearance that makes the resemblance even stronger.

In an experiment familiar to all students of psychology, the perception
and reproduction of ambiguous shapes was shown to be subject to influence
by verbal instruction. For example, Figure 21*a* was reproduced as *b* when

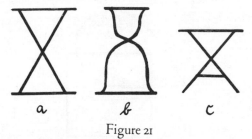

Figure 21

the subject had been told that an hourglass would appear briefly on the
screen, whereas *c* resulted when the subject expected a table. Such experiments have been mistakenly used to prove that what we see is determined
simply by what we have known before. Actually they merely illustrate the
fact that the most recent image is an indivisible part of the huge stock of
images stored in our memory. This tie with the past may or may not have a
tangible effect, depending on whether traces are mobilized that are strong
enough to take advantage of the structural weaknesses (ambiguities) in the
perceived figure. It is a matter of the relative strength of the stimulus structure as compared with the structural strength of the pertinent traces.

Other experiments have shown that if a given figure is impressed upon the memory of observers by being presented to them hundreds of times, it may nevertheless remain invisible when it appears in a new context. For example, after Figure 22*a* has been learned thoroughly, *b* still appears spon-

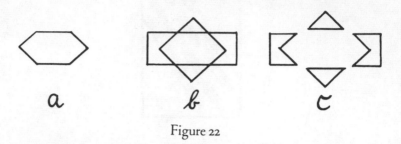

Figure 22

taneously as a rectangle and a square and not as the familiar hexagon surrounded by the shapes *c*. The observer is also unlikely to see the well-known number 4 in Figure 23 spontaneously. Such examples of camouflage demonstrate that when the inherent structure of the stimulus pattern vigorously contradicts that of a previously learned figure, even an overdose of past experience will be unable to exert its effect.

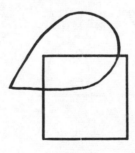

Figure 23

The influence of memory is particularly great when a strong personal need makes the observer want to see objects of given perceptual properties. Gombrich says: "The greater the biological relevance an object has to us the more will we be attuned to its recognition—and the more tolerant will therefore be our standards of formal correspondence." A man waiting at a street corner for his girl friend will see her in almost every approaching female, and this tyranny of the memory trace will get stronger as the minutes pass on the clock. A psychoanalyst will discover genitals and wombs in every work of art. The stress exerted by needs on perception is used by psychologists in the Rorschach test. The structural ambiguity of the ink blots employed in this test admits a large variety of interpretations, so that the individual observer has a chance of spontaneously choosing one that is characteristic for his state of mind.

Seeing Shape

How can the spatial features, which represent shape, be described? The most accurate way would seem to be to determine the spatial locations of all the points that make up these features. This may be exemplified by a procedure highly recommended to the sculptors by the Renaissance architect Leon Battista Alberti in his treatise *Della Statua,* from which Figure 24 is taken. By means of ruler, protractor, and plumb line, any point of the statue can be described in terms of angles and distances. A sufficient number of such measurements can be used to make a duplicate of the statue. Or, says Alberti, half the figure can be made on the island of Paros and the other in the Carrara Mountains, and still the parts will fit together. It is characteristic of this method that it allows reproduction of an individual object but that the result comes as a surprise. In no way can the nature of the statue's shape be gleaned from the measurements, which must be applied before the result is known.

The procedure is very similar to what happens in analytic geometry when, in order to determine the shape of a figure, the points of which the figure consists are defined spatially by their distances from a vertical (y) and a horizontal (x) Cartesian coördinate. Here too a sufficient number of measurements will permit construction of the figure. Whenever possible, however, the geometrician will go beyond the mere accumulation of unrelated data. He will try to find a formula that indicates the location of any and every point of the figure—that is, he looks for an over-all law of construction. For example, the equation for a circle with the radius *r* is:

$$(x-a)^2 + (y-b)^2 = r^2$$

if the center of the circle lies at the distance *a* from the y-axis and at the distance *b* from the x-axis. Even a formula of this kind, however, does little more than summarize the locations of an infinite number of points, which happen to add up to a circle. It does not tell us much about the nature of the resulting figure.

What is the situation in perception? In order to see shape, the eyes could register and then add up the spatial locations of many of the points constituting that shape. Closest to this method is the practice used by persons with brain injuries who have lost the capacity of seeing form. By means of

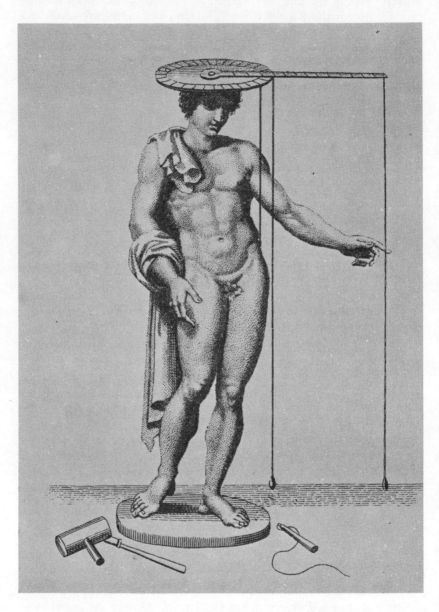

Figure 24

head or finger movements they trace the outlines of a given figure and then conclude from the results that the whole must be, say, a triangle. But they are unable to see the triangle. They behave like the tourist who, by reconstructing his meandering path through the maze of an unknown town, concludes that he has walked in a circle.

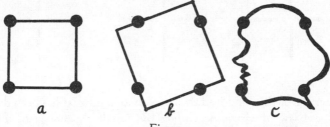

Figure 25

The normal eye does nothing of the sort. Usually it grasps shape immediately—that is, it seizes on the over-all law of construction. What shape does the eye see? The answer is obvious with very simple, regular figures,

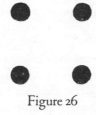

Figure 26

which dictate their shape to the eye in unambiguous terms. A square will be seen as a square. But how about Figure 26? It is worth considering why

Figure 27

most persons see spontaneously a square (Figure 25*a*) rather than something like the other figures suggested in *b* or *c*.

If four more dots are added to Figure 26, the square disappears from the now octagonal or even circular pattern (Figure 27). White circles or——for some observers—squares appear in the centers of the crosses shown in Figure 28, even though there is no trace of a circular or square-shaped contour. Why circles and squares rather than any other shape?

Figure 28

Phenomena of this kind find their explanation in what has been described as the basic law of visual perception by gestalt psychologists. This law asserts that any stimulus pattern tends to be seen in such a way that the resulting structure is as simple as the given conditions permit.

Simplicity

What is meant by simplicity? First of all, simplicity may be defined by the effect certain phenomena have upon the observer, and its meaning may be limited to such subjective reactions. For example, Spinoza made a statement about order that may be applied to simplicity also. According to him, we firmly believe that there is order in the things themselves even though we know nothing about these things or their nature. "For, when things are arranged in such a way that when they are represented to us by the senses we can easily imagine and, in consequence, easily remember them, we call them well ordered and, in the opposite case, call them badly ordered or confused." In a similar vein, simplicity may be defined by the degree of tension that a phenomenon creates in the experience of the observer and in the correlated processes occurring in his brain. Such definitions are incomplete for more than one reason. In the first place, an observer's reaction may be inadequate. Owing to his own state of mind, he may consider a phenomenon highly complicated or confused because he cannot grasp its simplicity; or, conversely, he may experience a situation as simple because he is blind to its intricacies.

For our purposes it is necessary to define simplicity not only by its effects on individuals but by the precise structural conditions that make a pattern simple. This must be done not only for the experienced pattern but also for the stimulus that elicits the experience. In fact the nature of simplicity can be understood only if it is considered also as a property of physical patterns in themselves, regardless of whether someone looks at them or not. In practice, the term "simplicity" is used in two ways. It may be said that a folk song is simpler than a symphony, or that a child's drawing is simpler than a painting by Tiepolo. This implies using the term almost in a quantitative sense by referring to patterns that contain only a few elements and allow for correspondingly few relations. Here the antonym of simplicity is complexity.

In the field of the arts the word frequently refers to something different and more important. Typical drawings of children as well as truly primitive art objects achieve simplicity of the whole by simple means. This does not hold in any mature style of art. Even works that look "simple" turn out to be quite complex. If we examine the surfaces of a good Egyptian statue, the shapes that make up a Greek temple, or the form relationships in a good piece of African sculpture, we find that they are anything but elementary. The same holds true for the bisons of the prehistoric caves, the Byzantine saints, or Henri Rousseau's paintings. The reason why we may hesitate to describe the average child's drawing or an Egyptian pyramid or certain "functional" buildings as "works of art" is precisely that a minimum of complexity, or richness, seems to be indispensable. Recently, the architect Peter Blake wrote: "In another year or so there will be only one type of industrial product in the U.S.—a shiny, smoothly finished lozenge. The small lozenges will be vitamin capsules; the bigger ones will be television sets or typewriters; and the big ones will be automobiles, planes or trains." Blake was not implying that in his opinion we were moving toward a peak of artistic culture.

When a work of art is praised for "having simplicity," it is understood to organize a wealth of meaning and form in an over-all structure that clearly defines the place and function of every detail in the whole. It seems paradoxical for Kurt Badt to say that Rubens is one of the simplest of all artists. He explains: "It is true that in order to grasp his simplicity one must be able to understand an order which dominates an enormous world of active forces." Badt defines artistic simplicity as "the wisest ordering of the means based on insight into the essentials, to which everything else must be subservient." As examples of artistic simplicity he mentions, for example, Titian's method of creating a painting from a tissue of short brush strokes. "The double system of surfaces and outlines is abandoned. A new degree of simplicity is reached. The entire picture is accomplished by one procedure only. Until then, line was determined by the objects; it was used only for boundaries or shadows or, perhaps, highlights. Now the line also represents brightness, space, and air, thus fulfilling a demand for greater simplicity, which requires that the lasting stability of form be identified with the ever changing process of life." Similarly, Rembrandt, at a certain point of his development, for simplicity's sake, abandoned the use of the color blue, because it did not fit his chords of golden brown, red, ocher, and olive green. Badt also cites the graphic technique of Dürer and his contemporaries, who represented shadow and volume by the same curved strokes they used for outlining their figures, thus again achieving simplicity through a unification of means.

In a mature work of art all things seem to resemble each other. Sky, sea, ground, trees, and human figures begin to look as though they were made of one and the same substance, which falsifies the nature of nothing but re-creates everything by subjecting it to the unifying power of the great artist. Every great artist gives birth to a new universe, in which the familiar things look the way they have never before looked to anyone. This new appearance, rather than being distortion or betrayal, reinterprets the ancient truth in a grippingly fresh, enlightening way. The unity of the artist's conception leads to a simplicity that, far from being incompatible with complexity, shows its virtue only when it masters the abundance of existence rather than escapes to the poverty of abstinence.

The law of parsimony—or the principle of economy—in scientific method demands that when several hypotheses fit the facts, the simplest should be chosen. According to Cohen and Nagel, "one hypothesis is said to be simpler than another if the number of independent types of elements in the first is smaller than in the second." Such a hypothesis must permit the scientist to cover all aspects of the phenomenon under investigation with a minimum of assumptions and, if possible, should explain not only a particular variety of things or happenings but the whole range of the phenomena that fall into this category.

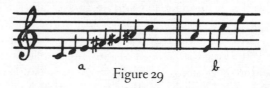

a   Figure 29   b

The principle of parsimony is valid esthetically in that the artist must not go beyond what is needed for his purpose. He follows the example of nature, which, in the words of Isaac Newton, "does nothing in vain, and more is in vain when less will serve; for Nature is pleased with simplicity, and affects not the pomp of superfluous causes." It will have become apparent by now, however, that simplicity cannot be defined by the number of elements a pattern contains. It is true that the number of elements has an influence on the simplicity of the whole, but the examples given in Figures 29 and 30 show that the pattern with the larger number of elements may still have the simpler structure. The seven elements of the full-tone scale are combined in a pattern that grows consistently and by equal steps. Figure 29b has only four elements but is less simple because it consists of a downward fourth, an

upward fifth, and an upward third. Two different directions and three different intervals are used. The structure of the pattern is more complex in
spite of the smaller number of elements. Similarly, the regular square, with
its four edges and four angles, is simpler than the irregular triangle (Figure
30). In the square all four edges are equal in length and lie at the same distance from the center. Only two directions are used, the vertical and the
horizontal, and all angles of the same size. The whole pattern is highly
symmetrical (around four axes). The triangle has fewer elements, but they
vary in size and location and there is no symmetry.

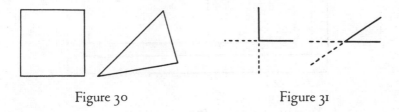

| Figure 30 | Figure 31 |

A straight line is simple because it uses one unchangeable direction.
Parallel lines are simpler than lines meeting at an angle because their relationship is defined by one constant distance. A right angle is simpler than
other angles because it produces a subdivision of space based on the repetition of one and the same angle (Figure 31). Figures 32*a* and *b* are identical
except that the relative location of parts in *b* provides for a common center
and in this way makes the pattern simpler.

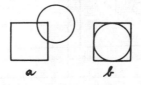

Figure 32

Elements that are simply shaped in themselves can be arranged in a
highly complex whole. By this method some modern abstractionists, such as
Josef Albers, Piet Mondrian, or Ben Nicholson, have given sufficient richness to compositions built of geometric elements. Figure 33 shows the compositional scheme of a relief by Ben Nicholson. Its elements are as simple
as can be found anywhere in a work of art. The composition consists of one
regular and complete circle plus a number of rectangular figures, which lie

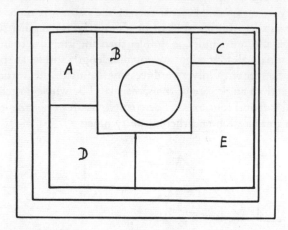

Figure 33

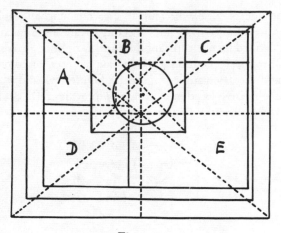

Figure 34

parallel to each other and to the frame. Yet, even without the differences of depth, which in the original relief play the various planes against each other, the total effect is not elementary. On the whole the various form units do not interfere with each other, but rectangle B overlaps D and E (Figure 34). Also, a complicating inconsistency is produced by the fact that B is attached, with its top edge, to the frame of the outer large rectangles, which surround it at large distance otherwise. The three outer rectangles are roughly but not exactly of the same proportion, and their centers lie close together but do not coincide. The close approximation of proportion and location produces considerable tension in that it compels the observer to call on his sensitivity for subtle distinctions. This holds true for the entire composition. Two of the inner units, A and C, are clearly rectangular; D—when completed—makes for a square (since it is slightly broader than high, which compensates for the familiar overestimation of the vertical); B and the completed E look rectangular, but they are only so slightly upright that their proportions flirt with squareness; again this approximation creates tension by requiring subtle distinction. The center of the whole pattern does not coincide with any point of the composition, nor does the central horizontal touch any corner. The central vertical comes close enough to the center of B to create an element of simplicity in the relationship between that rectangle and the total area of the work. The same is true for the circle, and yet both B and the circle deviate enough from the central vertical to look clearly asymmetrical in relation to each other. The circle lies neither in the center of B nor in the center of the whole pattern; and the overlapping corners of B have no simple relationship to the structures of the rectangles D and E, into which they intrude.

Why does the whole pattern hold together nevertheless? Some of the simplifying factors have already been mentioned. In addition the prolongation of the bottom edge of C would touch the circle; and if A were enlarged to a square, the corner of that square would touch the circle also. These coincidences help to keep the circle in place. And, of course, there is the over-all balance of proportions, distances, and directions, which creates the indispensable simplicity of the work as a whole. Even so, it will be seen from this illustration that very simple elements may combine into a complex pattern.

I am now ready to define simplicity by the number of structural features that make up a pattern. In an absolute sense, a thing is simple when it consists of a small number of structural features. In a relative sense, a thing has simplicity when it organizes complex material with the smallest possible number of structural features.

By "features" I do not mean elements. They are structural properties that, as far as shape is concerned, can be described in terms of distance and angle. If I increase the number of the radii drawn in a circle from ten to twenty, the number of elements has increased but the number of structural features is unchanged. For whatever the number of the radii, one distance and one angle are sufficient to describe the build of the whole. Structural features must be determined for the total pattern. Fewer features in a limited area will often make for more features in the whole, which is another way of saying that what makes a part simpler may make the whole less simple. In Figure 35 a straight line is the simplest connection between points *a* and *b*

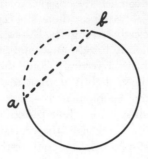

Figure 35

only as long as we overlook the fact that a curve will make for a simpler total pattern.

The Conditions of Simplicity

I have suggested that the tendency to simplest structure in the brain field makes the percept as simple as possible. But the simplicity of the resulting experience depends also upon (a) the simplicity of the stimulus, which gives rise to the percept; (b) the simplicity of the meaning to be conveyed by the percept; (c) the relationship between meaning and percept; and (d) the mental "set" of the individual observer.

The stimulus is the geometric pattern projected upon the retinas of the eyes. It is not a psychical experience but a physical thing. As such it has certain objective properties, which can be described independently of the properties of the experiences it creates. For example, if someone looks straight at Figure 26, the stimulus pattern projected upon the background of his eyes consists of four equal round dots. Four of the distances between the dots are equal. In four cases, three dots form a right-angular constellation. Psychologically, these geometric properties press for straight-line connections between the units and for the establishment of right angles. On the other hand, the simplest possible connection of the four units would be a circle. If the simplicity of the percept were the only factor to be considered, we would expect the observer to see a circle. But the perceptual result is determined by the structure of the stimulus in its interaction with the striving for greatest simplicity in the brain field. That is, the perceived pattern will be the one that combines the conditions of the retinal stimulus and the dynamic tendencies of the brain field in the simplest possible structure. In Figure 26 the overriding of the potential rectangularity of the stimulus by the tendency to circularity in the brain would produce more tension (less simplicity) than the brain's "willingness" to settle for the less simple (but still quite simple) square, which fits the stimulus better. In Figure 27 the rectangular relations between the units of the stimulus are less compelling, and circular form is more closely approximated by the locations of the eight dots. Under these conditions a victory of circularity provides the simplest solution. So much for the influence of the stimulus pattern on the percept.

It is in the nature of all artistic form that it carries meaning. Form always points to something beyond itself. A lump of clay or a group of lines may represent a human figure. An abstract painting may be called *Victory Boogie-Woogie*. This meaning or content can be relatively simple (*Reclining Nude*) or quite complex (*Rebellion Tamed by Wise Government*). The character of the meaning and its relation to the visible form intended to express it help to determine the degree of simplicity of the whole work. If a percept that is quite simple in itself is employed to express something complex, the result is not simple. If a deaf mute who wants to tell a story utters a groan the structure of the sound is simple enough, but the total result involves as much tension between the audible form and what it is meant to convey as the squeezing of a human body into a cylindrical corset. A number of short words in short sentences do not necessarily make for a simple statement—popular prejudice to the contrary. The discrepancy between complex meaning and simple form may produce something quite complicated. Of course a very simple meaning clad in correspondingly simple shape will result in great simplicity. (Artistically, it may produce boredom.)

Suppose a painter should represent Cain and Abel by two figures that looked exactly alike and faced each other symmetrically in the identical attitude. Here the meaning would involve the differences between good and evil, murderer and victim, acceptance and rejection, whereas the picture would convey similarity of the two men. The effect of the pictorial statement would not be simple.

These examples show that simplicity requires a correspondence of structure between meaning and tangible pattern. Such structural correspondence has been named "isomorphism" by gestalt psychologists.

Finally, the "set" or attitude of the individual observer must be considered. In a psychological experiment the figure of a square can be made gradually to appear on a screen by means of increasing intensity of light in the projector. If the observer expects to see a square, he is likely to recognize the figure earlier than if he has been misled to believe that he was going to see a circle. The second task is harder because the relationship between what is perceived and what is anticipated has a less simple structure. To a concertgoer familiar with music in the diatonic mode, a composition by Alban Berg may sound much more complicated than it is in its own terms because this listener relates it to the wrong structural model. In addition, factors more deeply imbedded in the human personality may create a complication. El Greco's slim, swinging figures may present difficulties for a beholder to whom ascetic ecstasy is foreign or repulsive. Curves were incompatible with Piet Mondrian's character; apparently his personality demanded the strict stability of straight verticals and horizontals.

Physical Simplicity

The striving for balance (see chapter I) can be described as a striving for simplicity. By eliminating ambiguity and disunity, balance increases the simplicity of a composition. Balance was described as existing not only in psychical situations but also in physical ones. Does this hold true for simplicity in general? Is simplicity an objective property of material things or does it refer only to a subjective experience and judgment of the observer?

It will be seen that the definition of simplicity given earlier can be directly applied to physical structure. The fact that the body of a starfish has fewer structural features than the body of man is independent of any observer's reaction. A daisy is objectively simpler than an orchid. The tomb of Theodoric in Ravenna is a simpler arrangement of stones than the cathedral in Milan, regardless of whether under given cultural conditions people take more easily to the one or to the other.

In physical simplicity, there is a decisive difference between things of nature and works of art. In works of art, simplicity refers only to the outer surface. The simplicity of a clay figure is not a product of the internal structure of the clay but something imposed upon it by man. In the visual arts, except for the effect of such inherent qualities of the medium as the weight of stone, the grain of wood, or the viscosity of paint, form is applied to a material by external influence. In fact the artist tends to avoid highly organized materials such as crystals or plants. The art of arranging flowers is hybrid because it subjects organic shape to human order. And we are inclined to think of the dance and the theater as secondary arts because they rely on the given form and functioning of the human body. Kracauer has pointed out that in photography highly defined compositional form falsifies the medium, which is the joint product of the organizing mind and physical reality.

Artistic shape is made, whereas organic shape is grown. "Although we ourselves are made or fashioned by means of insensible growth, we cannot create anything in that way," according to Paul Valéry. The shape of a seashell or a leaf is the external manifestation of the inner forces that produced the object. A tree makes the story of its development visible to the eyes. The waves of the ocean, the spherical boundaries of planets, the contours of the human body, all reflect the forces that made them and possess them. If the Pythagorean harmony of the spheres existed, it would be an example of art as a direct manifestation of natural processes. But marble, wood, and paint are the amorphous substrata of humanly conceived form.

The striking simplicity of some natural forms is the result of the correspondingly simple distribution of the forces that created the object. These forms visibly manifest the tendency toward simplicity in nature. If this is a general tendency, why is regular, symmetrical shape relatively rare? The answer is that the tendency to simplicity can exert itself undisturbed only in "isolable systems" (to use L. L. Whyte's expression)—that is, in configurations that for all practical purposes may be considered locked off, so that no influence of the environment can take place. Organisms are open systems, which constantly draw and give off energy. This energy is spent on activities that may be described as the functions of the organism. The processes of growth are such a function. The stem or trunk of a plant grows upward. Within the limits of this directed activity, however, the simplest possible form results. Thus the stem or trunk may grow along a relatively straight line, and its section may be circular. The human body is approximately symmetrical in relation to a median vertical plane; and in the details of its build, approximations of spherical, cylindrical, parabolical, or plane shape are found everywhere.

Other interferences with the tendency to simplicity abound in nature. Heat motion stirs up molecules to the kind of amorphous mash we find, for example, in gases or liquids. More specifically, things interfere with each other everywhere. The potential symmetry of a tree is disturbed by the neighborhood of other trees as well as by the directed action of wind, water, and light. We read about the Italian poet Giacomo Leopardi: "While the boy was learnedly mastering obscure folios, his bones were degenerating, his spine was being curved beyond redemption, his eyesight ruined."

Objects or bodies may be considered as processes that we observe at some more or less constant stage. In that stage they show the traces of the tendency to simplicity as well as the traces of those directed activities that make them grow and fulfill their functions or that interfere with their inherent strivings. For this reason man enjoys contemplating, in regular, symmetrical shape, the image of accomplished perfection and peace. But such simplicity, to be valuable, must have been achieved through a victory over the interfering forces of nature. When we pick up an object on the beach because of its regular shape, why do we throw it away, disappointed and contemptuous, when it turns out to be a factory-made comb or can? We do so because the simplicity of the factory product is cheaply achieved. It is not wrested from the forces of nature but forced upon matter from the outside.

Simplification Demonstrated

According to the basic law of visual perception, any stimulus pattern tends to be seen in such a way that the resulting structure is as simple as the given conditions permit. This tendency will be less apparent when a strong stimulus controls the pattern to be perceived. Under such conditions the receptor mechanism is limited to grouping or completing the given material in a way that makes for the simplest result. But the weaker the stimulus, the more radically can the perceptual trend assert itself. Leonardo da Vinci observes that when the figure of a man is seen from afar, "he will seem a very small round dark body. He will appear round because distance diminishes the various parts so much as to leave nothing visible except the greater mass." Why does the reduction make the beholder see a round shape? The answer is that distance weakens the stimulus to such an extent that the perceptual mechanism is left free to impose upon it the simplest possible shape—namely, the circle. Such weakening of the stimulus occurs also under other conditions, as for example, when the perceived pattern is dimly illuminated or exposed for only a split second. Distance in time will have a similar effect as distance in space; when the actual stimulus has disappeared, the remaining memory trace weakens. Experimenters have investigated the effects of these various conditions.

The changes of stimuli that occur in such experiments are manifold. At first the results look confusing and even contradictory, for reasons that are not hard to discover. In the first place, percepts and memory traces are not directly accessible to the experimenter. They must be communicated to him by the observer in some indirect way, either by verbal description, or by drawing, or by comparison with a number of patterns, among which the observer is asked to choose the one most resembling the figure he saw. None of these methods is very satisfactory, because there is no telling how much of the result is due to the primary experience itself and how much to the medium of communication. Fortunately, this distinction is not essential for our purpose.

In considering drawings made by the observers, however, it is necessary to take into account their technical ability as well as their personal standards regarding the required degree of exactness. A person may consider a rather irregular scrawl a sufficiently exact image of an intended form, and it is therefore impossible to take the details of such drawings literally. Unless allowance is made for some leeway between the actual drawing and the intended image, the interpretation of results will lead to confusion.

Secondly, the perceiving and remembering of a pattern are not an isolated process. They are open to the influence of the innumerable memory traces that are potentially active in the observer's mind. Under these conditions we cannot expect the underlying tendencies clearly to manifest themselves in all examples. It is best, therefore, to base the interpretation on those examples that illustrate some clear-cut effect. I shall not deal separately here with results obtained with different techniques and by different investigators, but try to summarize the total outcome.

The traditional theory asserted that, with the passing of time, memory traces slowly fade out. They dissolve, become less distinct, and drop their individual characteristics, thus looking more and more like everything and nothing. This would be a process of gradual simplification through loss of articulate structure. Later investigators raised the question whether this process did not involve more tangible changes from one structural form to another, which could be concretely described.

Figure 36

Such types of changes have in fact been identified. As a simple demonstration, Figure 36 is exposed for a split second to a group of persons. They are asked beforehand to keep paper and pencil ready and to draw without much reflection but as accurately as possible what they have seen. The examples of Figure 37 will schematically illustrate the kind of result that is typically obtained.

The samples give an idea of the impressive variety of reactions, which is partly due to individual differences, and partly to such factors as differences of exposure time and distance of the observer. All represent simplifications of the stimulus pattern. I admire the ingenuity of the solutions, the imaginative power of vision, which reveals itself even though these drawings are done quickly, spontaneously, and with no other pretense than faithfully to record what has been seen. Even though some of the aspects of the figures may be graphic interpretations of the percept rather than properties of the percept itself, such an experiment gives sufficient evidence that the act of vision involves the solution of a problem—namely, the creation of an organized whole.

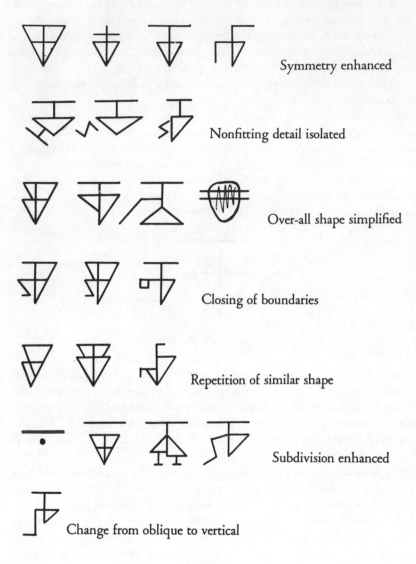

Symmetry enhanced

Nonfitting detail isolated

Over-all shape simplified

Closing of boundaries

Repetition of similar shape

Subdivision enhanced

Change from oblique to vertical

Figure 37

Leveling and Sharpening

Although it is obvious that the drawings reveal a tendency toward the reduction of the number of structural features, it would be incorrect to say that the only tendency discernible in such experiments is the one toward simplest structure. A particularly interesting result has been achieved with patterns that contain ambiguities of the kind illustrated in Figure 38. Both *a* and *d* deviate slightly from symmetrical patterns. When such figures are presented

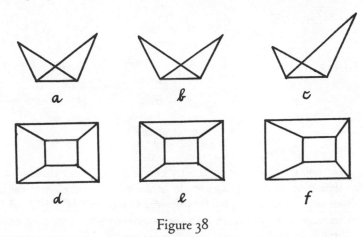

Figure 38

under conditions that keep the stimulus control weak enough to leave the observer with a margin of freedom, two types of reactions follow. Some persons perfect the symmetry of the model (*b, e*) whereas others exaggerate the asymmetry (*c, f*). Now *b* and *e* obviously achieve simplification; but so do *c* and *f*, by changing a figure in which two structural patterns compete for dominance into another that shows clear dominance of one of them. Elimination of ambiguity makes for simplification. It will be noted, however, that solutions *c* and *f*, although simpler than *a* and *d*, are less simple than *b* and *e*. Solutions *c* and *f* enhance factors of complexity inherent in *a* and *d*. Wulf called this tendency "sharpening"; he called the opposite tendency of eliminating complexity "leveling."

Leveling is characterized by such factors as unification, enhancement of symmetry, repetition, dropping of nonfitting detail, elimination of obliqueness. On the contrary, sharpening makes for subdivision, enhancement of differences, stressing of obliqueness. Sharpening involves simplification when it helps to eliminate ambiguity—but not in other examples, where it occurs although no ambiguity is involved. In the latter there is a tendency against simplification. This important exception from the general rule will be discussed later.

Factors of leveling and sharpening frequently occur together in the same drawing. In Figure 39 simplification of the stimulus *a* is achieved in *b* through straightening the vertical contours (leveling) and increasing the difference between the two spikes beyond ambiguity (sharpening). And *d* simplifies *c* by splitting one figure in two (sharpening) and thus achieving two more regular shapes—the circle and the open square (leveling).

      a   b   c   d

Figure 39

To this point I have discussed only changes that occur through the inherent dynamics of specific figures. In other examples the effect cannot be explained only by the interplay between the observer and the isolated figure. When sequences of figures are used for experiments, the resulting drawings often show a mutual influence of different figures in the sense that resemblances between them appear. Also the stimulus patterns are sometimes related to the shape of objects the observer knows from previous experience. In Figure 40 the model (Figure 39*a*) has been adapted to the shape of a twig.

Figure 40

Such a process may lead to simplification or complication of the original shape. It is important, however, that, by adapting new perceptual experiences to existing memory traces, the observer always simplifies his total memory structure. Adaptation to past experiences is therefore no exception from the general rule of simplicity.

A Physiological Theory

Whence this tendency to simplicity? The question puts the psychologist in a peculiar dilemma. If he limits himself to what goes on in the mind, he can go no further than describe and illustrate the phenomenon. He suspects that to find its cause he must explore the happenings in the corresponding brain field But the physiology of brain processes is not sufficiently advanced to permit this. The psychologist can therefore offer a hypothesis only by analogy to what takes place under somewhat similar circumstances in the world of general physics.

The physicist tells us that in any given "field" the forces of which it consists will distribute themselves in such a way that the simplest, most regular, most symmetrical organization results. The more independent the field and the less constrained the play of the internal forces, the simpler the resulting distribution will be. I have pointed out that such simple distribution of forces often manifests itself in regular, symmetrical shape. If the visual cortex of the cerebrum is now assumed to be such a field of forces, the tendency to simplest distribution can be expected to be active in it. A stimulus pattern projected upon the brain field will upset this equilibrium, which the field forces will then try to reëstablish. How successful they will be depends on the strength of the stimulus. Just as a bit of water or oil will more readily assume simple shape than a more cohesive piece of wood, so the visual stimulus will resist simplification of its shape when it is strong—that is, when the eye receives clear-cut impulses from the observed object. When, however, the stimulus is weak, the tendency to simplification will assert itself most effectively. The result is illustrated by the experiments already described.

Even though a strong stimulus will not allow actual modification of its shape, tangible effects of our principle can be observed also under normal conditions of vision. The tendency to simplification will manifest itself in the way in which subdivision of patterns occurs. We know already that when a number of discrete units are given in the visual field, all or some of them may be seen as connected in such a way that the simplest possible organization results. The eight dots of Figure 41 will be seen as a circle or octagon (*a*) and not as two squares (*b*) or the combination of three units shown in *c;* the nine dots of *d* will split up into two main units—the circle plus the outsider.

Subdivision of the whole is thus lawfully controlled by the familiar principle. How about compact figures? Figure 42 is an unbroken, unified disk to everybody; Figure 43 is a star, characterized by a subdivision into spikes;

but in Figure 44 the continuity of the surrounding outline explodes. Immediately or—for some observers—after a period of uncomfortable pushing
and pulling, during which the figure tries to "find its shape," the whole
pattern splits into triangle and rectangle. This subdivision is so compelling
that an observer is surprised to find that no actual dividing lines run through
the black body.

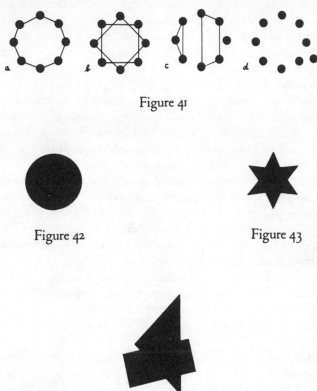

Figure 41

Figure 42

Figure 43

Figure 44

How about line figures? A glance back to Figure 22 shows that again
subdivision occurs according to simplest structure. It will be observed, however, that subdivision does not prevent the pattern from being perceived as
a whole. Figure 22b is a fairly well integrated, starlike whole, which is seen as
being made up of two main parts. These parts again are made up of four
lines each—that is, there are two levels of subdivision. The relative strength
of whole and parts varies from figure to figure. If we compare the patterns

of Figure 45 from left to right, we find that they look less and less like a whole and more and more like a combination of parts. But both whole and parts are seen in all the patterns.

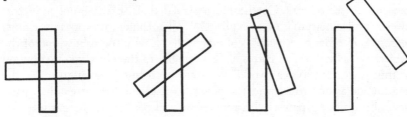

Figure 45

The rule that governs the process is evident. The effect depends on the degree of simplicity of the whole as compared with the degree of simplicity of the parts. Greater simplicity of the whole makes for greater unity. The simpler the parts, the more clearly they tend to stand out as independent entities.

What holds true for isolated figures must be applied to the entire visual field. In complete darkness or when we watch a cloudless sky, there is an unbroken unity. Most of the time, however, the visual world is made up of more or less distinct units. The extent to which a given area of the field is seen as a self-contained unit depends on the simplicity of its connection with the surrounding field. An area may be identified clearly as a unit be-

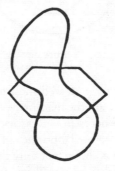

Figure 46

cause it has a simple shape in itself or because no structural features of the environment fuse it into a larger whole. On the contrary, an area may be hard to isolate because its own shape is quite irregular or because, partly or as a whole, it fits snugly into a larger context. (Thus, Figure 22*a* disappears in the context *b*, whereas it retains much of its identity in Figure 46.)

Why the Eyes Tell the Truth

Subdivision is of the greatest biological value because on it depends the capacity to see objects. Goethe has observed that "Erscheinung und entzweien sind synonym"; more explicitly, "What comes into appearance must segregate in order to appear." We may well ask why the subdivision of the subjective field of vision corresponds normally to the objective distribution of things in the physical world. Why are we fortunate enough to see the automobile as one thing and the person in it as another rather than paradoxically unifying part of the automobile and part of the person into one misleading monster? Sometimes our eyes fool us. Wertheimer has cited the example of a bridge that forms a compelling whole with its own mirror image in the water (Figure 47). Constellations are seen in the sky that have no counterpart in the actual locations of the stars in physical space. In military camouflage the unity of objects is broken up into parts that often fuse with the environment—a technique used also by nature for the protection of animals. Modern artists have experimented with reorganizing objects in ways that contradict everyday experience. Gertrude Stein reports that when, during the First World War, Picasso saw the camouflage paint of guns he exclaimed in surprise: "We are the ones who made this—it's cubism!"

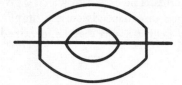

Figure 47

Why, then, do our eyes serve us well most of the time? It is more than a lucky coincidence. First of all, the man-made part of the world is fitted to human needs. Only secret doors in old castles blend with the walls. The letter boxes in London are painted a bright red so that they will stand out from their surroundings. In addition, not only the human mind but also the physical world follows the law of simplicity, which means that the outer appearance of natural things will be as simple as conditions permit; and simple shape enhances segregation. Separate physical processes tend to produce correspondingly separate visual units. The redness and roundness of apples in distinction from the different colors and shapes of leaves and branches are not created for the convenience of pickers but are the outer manifestation of the fact that the biological processes that make apples are separate and different from those that make leaves or branches. Finally, simple shape—notably symmetry—contributes to bringing about physical equilibrium. It keeps walls and trees and bottles from falling and is therefore favored in construction work by nature as well as by man. In the last analysis, then, the useful correspondence between the way we see things and the way they are is the result of the fact that vision, as a reflection of physical processes in the brain, is subject to the same basic law of organization as the things of nature.

Subdivision in the Arts

In the visual arts subdivision is an essential means of composition. It takes place at different levels, which in every work of art are organized in a hierarchy. A primary segregation establishes the main features of the work. The larger parts are again subdivided into smaller ones, and it is the task of the artist to adapt the degree and kind of the segregations and connections to the meaning he is trying to convey. In Manet's painting *The Guitarist* (Figure 48) the primary subdivision distinguishes the entire foreground scene from the neutral backdrop. Within the frontal scene the musician, the bench, and the small still life with the jug make for a secondary division. The separation of man and bench is partly compensated by a countergrouping, which unites the bench and the similarly colored trousers and sets them off against the dark top part of the man. This halving of the man by means of brightness and color stresses the importance of the guitar, which is placed between the upper and the lower section of the body. But the endangered unity of the figure is reinforced by such devices as the all-around distribution of the white areas, which knit together the shoes, the sleeves, the kerchief, and the shirt, of which a tiny but important bit appears below the left elbow. Each of the major parts is subdivided in turn, and on each level one or several local concentrations of more densely organized form appear in relatively empty surroundings. Thus the strongly articulated figure stands against the empty ground, and similarly the face and the shirt, the hands and the finger board, the shoes and the still life, are islands of heightened activity on a secondary level of the hierarchy. The various focuses tend to be seen together as a kind of constellation; they represent the significant high spots, which carry much of the meaning. The specific principles of organization will be examined below.

Subdivision, as I have said, presupposes some simplicity of shape in the units to be separated. Occasionally compositions are crystallized around units that are so self-contained that there is only a one-way relationship between them and their surroundings—that is, they determine the rest of the work but are little influenced by it. (Compare the reference to the rose window in

Figure 48

the façade of Notre Dame de Paris, p. 20.) On the whole, however, the simplicity of any part must be modified or weakened sufficiently to make the part dependent on, and therefore integrated with, its context. This seems to be true even for organic shape. The geneticist Waddington says that although whole skeletons have a "quality of completeness," which resists additions or omissions, the single bones have only "a certain degree of completeness." Their shape carries some implications about the other parts to which they are attached, and when isolated they are "like a tune which breaks off in the middle."

What Is a Part?

What, exactly, do we mean by a "part"? In a purely quantitative sense, any section of a whole can be called a part. This definition is the only possible one when we are dealing with something homogeneous. Any section of the blue sky is as good as any other. But homogeneous structures are rare. Most are subdivided—that is, they contain breaks and seams and joints, which suggest parts defined by the structure itself. Even in a sausage or a straight line of limited length, not all sections are of the same nature. A cut in the middle will produce a subdivision that fits the shape of the whole. Thus there is a difference between sections and parts. A statue may be arbitrarily divided into any number of sections for shipping purposes, but its parts are not arbitrary. They cannot be imposed upon the statue from without, but are determined by its very structure.

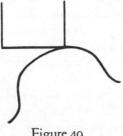

Figure 49

When a line shows sufficiently strong breaks or turns, the sections segregated by the corners or turning points will be its parts—as for example, the sides of an angle or of a parabola. A part, then, is a section of a whole that under the given conditions shows some measure of separation from its environment. The nature and range of the environment determine whether and to what extent a certain section appears as a part. Wertheimer has used Figure 49 to demonstrate that in restricted local terms the horizontal base of the box slides as an undivided whole into the right wing of the curve;

whereas, in terms of the total structure, the same line is broken up into two sections, which belong to different parts. Is the swastika a part of Figure 50*b*? Obviously not, because the local connections and segregations that form the swastika are overruled by others in the context of the square. It is necessary to distinguish between "genuine parts"—that is, sections that represent a segregated subwhole within the total context—and "not genuine parts"—that is, sections that are segregated only in relation to a limited local context and not to the whole.

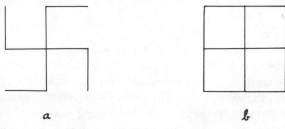

a   *b*

Figure 50

When we speak of a whole and "its" parts, we always mean the genuine parts. The statement "The whole is more than the sum of its parts" refers to this relationship. It is a statement that has been rejected because it sounds as though the whole did consist of the sum of its parts plus a mysterious additional quality. The objection is justified, but, on the other hand, the statement "The whole is different from the sum of its parts" is also unsatisfactory because it may imply that the character of the parts simply disappears in the whole. This is not true. A certain amount of self-containedness is in the very nature of a genuine part. The more self-contained a part, the more likely it is to contribute some of its own character to the whole. The degree to which parts are integrated varies widely, and without this variety any organized whole—particularly a work of art—would be a dull thing indeed. To think of a "gestalt" as a soup made of overcooked ingredients, in which everything dissolves in everything, is just as wrong as to think of harmony exclusively as the kind of perfect blend found in the color schemes for baby bedrooms or the "mood music" for restaurants.

Rules of Grouping

Once it is quite clear that relationships between parts depend on the structure of the whole, we may safely and profitably isolate and describe some specific relationships between parts. To demonstrate such relationships in a "pure" state we can use either relatively chaotic patterns, in which structure is at a minimum except for the features under investigation, or patterns that are chosen in such a way that the whole does not interfere with the part relationship in question. Observations made under such conditions can then be applied to works of art.

The rules of grouping, first formulated by Wertheimer, refer to factors that cause some parts to be seen as belonging more closely together than others. These rules can be treated as applications of one basic principle—the "principle of similarity." This principle asserts that the degree to which parts of a pattern resemble each other in some perceptual quality will help determine the degree to which they are seen as belonging together.

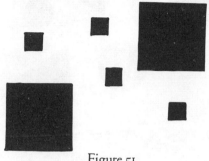

Figure 51

Figure 51 shows a group of six units that are equal in shape and orientation and rather irregularly distributed in space. It will be observed that the difference of size has a grouping effect, the large squares going together as against the smaller ones. This is an example of grouping by "similarity of size." In the same way "similarity of shape" is shown in Figure 52 to group circles versus triangles. In Figure 53 "similarity of brightness or color" separates the black circles from the white ones. "Similarity of location" (called by Wertheimer the "rule of proximity or nearness") produces visual clusters in Figure 54, and the lines of Figure 55 organize according to "similarity by spatial orientation."

Elements linked by similarity also tend to lie in the same plane. Painters like Matisse often moderate the depth effect of their compositions by applying the same color—for example, a strong yellow—to one object placed in the foreground and another farther back, thus safeguarding the unity of the picture in the frontal plane.

Additional factors come into play when objects in motion are considered. If the members of a dance group move in the directions indicated by the arrows in Figure 56, they will be seen as grouped according to "similarity of direction." Again, if some of the dancers move slowly while others move rapidly, "similarity of speed" will produce grouping (Figure 57). Similarity of speed facilitates depth perception when a landscape is observed from a

Figure 52

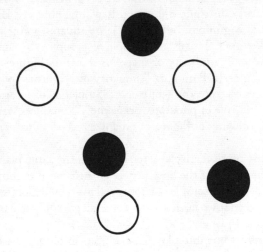

Figure 53

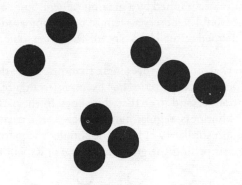

Figure 54

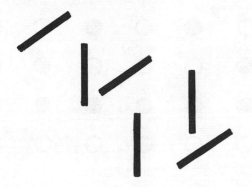

Figure 55

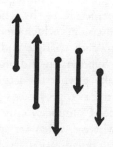

Figure 56

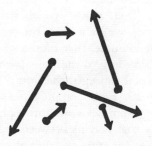

Figure 57

vehicle in motion or photographed by a moving camera. Since objects that lie at identical distance from the observer seem to be moving at identical speed, distances become defined visually by speed, the faster objects being the closer ones.

It will be noticed that similarity does more than just make things "belong together." Similar units form patterns. For example, in Figure 53 the black circles add up to a triangle, and so do the white ones. In the patterns used for the testing of color blindness, regular figures, such as the triangle in Figure 58, are created through similarity of hue. The simpler the pattern formed in this way, the more compelling the grouping of the units will be.

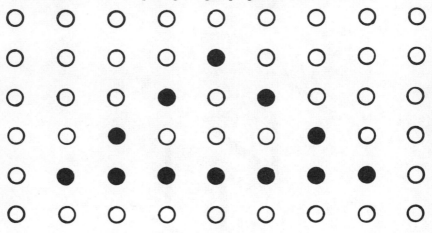

Figure 58

At this point, the effect of grouping cannot be further explained by adding up the similarities of units. The approach "from below" cannot account for the perception of over-all patterns formed by the units. This requires an approach "from above," which starts from the structure of the whole. In other words, we are back at the concept of "subdivision," which would explain, for example, that Figure 58 splits up into dark triangle and background according to the principle of simplicity. Subdivision and grouping are reciprocal concepts, the former doing from above what the latter does from below. The important difference between the two procedures is that in starting from below we can apply the principle of simplicity only to the similarity that obtains between unit and unit whereas, when we apply it from above, the same principle accounts for over-all organization. By adding up the parts we learn something but do not get further than the blind men in the Indian parable who ran into an elephant and set out together to explore the shape of the unknown thing by touching it with their hands at different parts of its body. We can imagine the blind men pooling their information, discovering similarities and differences of shape, size, and texture, but ending with a sum of relationships rather than with the visual concept of an elephant.

One step beyond the mere similarity of units is made in the grouping principle of "consistent shape," which deals with the intrinsic similarity of a visual object. Figure 59 shows that when there is a choice between several possible continuations there will be a spontaneous preference for the one that carries on the intrinsic structure most consistently. Figure 59*a* will be seen more easily as a combination of the two parts indicated in *b* than of the two indicated in *c,* because *b* provides the simpler structure.

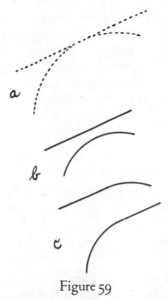

Figure 59

The more consistent the shape of a unit, the more readily it will detach itself from its environment. Figure 60 shows that the straight line is more quickly identified than the irregular ones. If in a milling crowd of actors or dancers one person pursues a consistent path, the eye of the observer will more easily keep track of that one person.

The principle finds interesting applications in what is known as harmonic progression in music. Here the problem consists in maintaining the "horizontal" unity of the melodic lines against the "vertical" harmonic coherence of the chords. This is achieved by keeping the melodic lines as simple and consistent as the musical task permits. For the progression from one chord to the next this means, for example, the use of what we called grouping by similarity of location. Walter Piston writes: "If two triads have one or more notes in common, these are repeated in the same voice, the remaining voice or voices moving to the nearest available condition" (Figure 61).

Figure 60   Figure 61

By considering the structure of the whole we can expand some of the above rules. Similarity of location applies not only when units lie close together but also when they occupy similar—for example, symmetrical—positions in the whole (Figure 62). Similarity of direction and orientation also can be expanded beyond mere parallelism—for example, when dancers move along symmetrical paths (Figure 63).

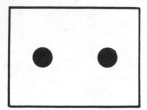

Figure 62   Figure 63

The limiting case of similarity of location is contiguity. When there are no intervals between units, a compact visual object results. It may seem artificial to think of a line or area as an agglomeration of units, and there may seem to be no need for explaining why a.red cherry on a green ground is seen as what it is. It must be remembered, however, that the images formed by the lenses of the eyes are picked up point by point by millions of small retinal receptor organs that are largely isolated from each other. This means that the brain is the receiving end for a mosaic of punctiform stimulations, consisting, in our example, of a few million "red" stimulations and other millions of "greens." The principles by which all these pieces are grouped into visual objects need to be formulated. These principles turn out to be applications of the principle of simplicity, and among them are the rules of similarity. A visual object will be the more unified the more strictly similar its elements are in such factors as color, brightness, speed and direction of movement. A painting is a less unified object than a plain-colored wall, and a cloud of smoke is less unified than a balloon.

Examples from Art

In the visual arts, similarity of location will make for the grouping of objects that appear close together. Obviously a crowd of people will be seen as a unit detached from other figures that are placed at some distance. Compelling groupings may also be achieved between objects that are remote from each other. This can be done by means of the other similarities. In Picasso's *Seated Woman* (Plate 1) the similarity of the geometric shapes used throughout the picture emphasizes unity of the whole and understates the distinction between the woman and the screenlike background. The distinction, however, is made clear by other means. Essentially a left slant is used for the figure, a right slant for the ground—that is, similarity of orientation serves to subdivide the picture into its two main subjects. As to shape, it will be seen that the circular units are limited to the figure of the woman and distributed in such a way that they emphasize its pyramidal shape. The one curved form outside the woman's body is the elbow rest of the green chair, which plays the role of an intermediary area between the angular room and the organic body. Color supports the subdivision produced by orientation and shape but at the same time adds variety to the composition by counteracting these structural tendencies to some extent. With the exception of the dark brown shades, which are found outside as well as inside the figure, each color belongs either to the figure or to the background. The vertical chain of the yellows gives unity and distinction to the woman. The steplike head-shoulder-body progression at the left is unified by the light brown, and the orange holds the right side together and connects it with the egg-shaped patch at the bottom. The continuity of the background, which is interrupted by the figure, is reëstablished by similarity of color. Thus the green "mends" the split-up chair, and on the right side a darkish brown connects two parts of the background that are separated by the woman's protruding arm. The relational network created by the interplay of similarities and corresponding dissimilarities in this picture could be analyzed at considerable length.

The rules of grouping serve not only the purely formal organization of compositions but also support their symbolic meaning. A particularly good example can be found in the Grünewald crucifixion of the Isenheim altar. The figures of John the Baptist and John the Evangelist, placed at opposite sides of the panel, are both clad in bright red; white is reserved for the coat of the Virgin, the lamb, the Bible, the loincloth of Christ, and the inscription on the top of the cross. In this way the various symbolic carriers of spiritual values—virginity, sacrifice, revelation, chastity, and kingship—which are distributed over the entire panel, are not only united compositionally but are also interpreted to the eye as having a common meaning. In contrast, the symbol of the flesh is suggested in the pink dress of Mary Magdalene, the sinner, who in this way is associated with the naked limbs of the men. Gombrich has pointed out that there is also in this picture an unrealistic but symbolically significant scale of sizes, which leads from the gigantic figure of Christ down to the undersized Mary Magdalene.

The knitting together of separate units by means of similarity of color, shape, size, or orientation is of particular importance in "diffuse compositions," which are in need of unification because they consist of more or less isolated elements, distributed rhythmically but irregularly over the entire picture area. Examples can be found in Persian miniatures, in Brueghel's paintings, or in the work of some recent artists—for example, in *La Grande Jatte* by Seurat. In this latter picture, the isolation of the city dweller is strikingly shown by a large number of people sitting and walking under the trees, which they share without any social communion. At the same time their similarity as human beings who are satisfying the same needs is expressed through application of the various rules of perceptual grouping.

The rules of similarity that have been discussed thus far can create unity among irregularly distributed items. The factor of "consistent shape" always applies to a global form pattern. Instead of connecting isolated monads by visual ties, it is used to convey unity of interaction. The close spiritual connection of the figures in a Pieta group may be expressed visually by a geometrically simple form that fences them in (see Figure 12). The well-known compositional triangle of the Renaissance is achieved through the visual fusion of various units that together create a consistent shape. An extreme example is found in a piece of sculpture by Brancusi (Figure 64), in which two embracing lovers are united by a symmetrical, rectangular outline to such an extent that they have become one object.

The unifying power of consistent form is used symbolically in Cézanne's *Uncle Dominic* (Figure 65). There is something compelling about the gesture of the crossed arms, which seem chained in their position as though they could never come apart. This effect is achieved partly by fastening the border of the sleeve to the central vertical established by the symmetry of the face and the cross. Thus the powerful connection between a man's mind and the symbol of the faith to which his thought is dedicated ties down the physical activity of his body and creates the stillness of collected energy.

The factor of consistent shape can create connections across fairly large intervals as long as the given units indicate strongly enough a common

pattern. In Figure 66 the observer tends to see a circle and one large cross
rather than four independent small crosses. The curved pieces unite, as do
the straight ones, by bridging over empty intervals.

Figure 64

In a given composition the various factors of similarity may either support
or counteract each other. The circular or oval areas in the Picasso (Plate 1)
resemble each other in shape but differ in color and size—that is, they are
connected and segregated at the same time. In this way a visual counterpoint is obtained, which builds the unity of the whole out of a rich network
of attractions and repulsions. In fact unity of a whole that contains any
subdivision at all can be achieved only if the segregations are counteracted
by connections. If, for example, all perceptual factors in a portrait coöperated
in unifying the figure and separating it from the ground, the picture would
fall apart.

A specific dissimilarity is brought out most clearly when other factors
are kept constant. In van Gogh's painting of his bedroom there are two
chairs of approximately identical color, shape, and position (Figure 67). In
this way the difference in size, which creates depth, is made much more
compelling than it would be if the two objects differed also in shape and
color, because it is by similarity that the eye is induced to relate and compare
them and thus to discover their difference.

Similarity and dissimilarity are always relative. The question "How much
do these two things resemble each other?" is meaningless as long as nothing
is said about the context. A triangle and a square often look quite different

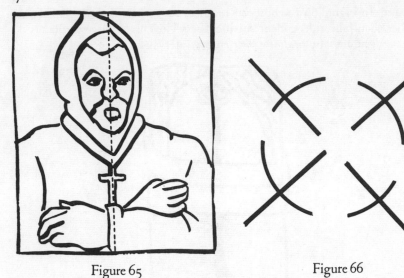

Figure 65   Figure 66

from each other, but when a triangular piece and a circular piece from a child's block-building set are seen lying on an otherwise tidy lawn they are very similar indeed. Two nuns walking in the public street look strikingly alike, but when they are seen by themselves individual differences may come to the fore. Photographers know that similarity of location is relative. In a picture of "midshot" size two people will look much farther apart than they did in reality, because in relation to the narrower picture space the distance between them increases.

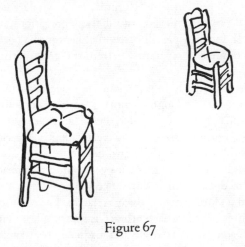

Figure 67

In a work of art, relationships based on any particular perceptual factor are hardly ever limited to the simple dichotomy of groups made up of identical members, for example, five large figures as against five small ones. The similarity generally applies to an extensive scale of values—for example, to all degrees of size, from the largest to the smallest (Figure 68). Even the degree of similarity may change (Figure 69). When such gradated values

Figure 68   Figure 69

are distributed irregularly throughout a composition, the eye will connect them in the order of their position in the scale and thus scan their hierarchic sequence along a path that is compositionally relevant. In Seurat's *Grande Jatte* the eye may start with the largest figures and move to smaller and smaller ones on a zigzag trail that leads gradually from the foreground to the background.

Figure 70

In this last example similarity is shown to guide the eye. Movements of the glance are important compositionally. They often contribute significantly to the artistic effect. El Greco's *Expulsion from the Temple* (Figure 70) is painted in drab yellowish and brownish shades. A bright red is reserved for the clothes of Christ and those of one of the money-changers, who bends down in the left corner of the picture. As the beholder's attention is caught by the central figure of Christ, similarity of color makes his glance sweep to the left and downward to the second red spot. This movement exactly duplicates the stroke of Christ's whip, the path of which is emphasized further by the raised arms of the two interposed figures. Thus the eye actually performs the action that represents the main subject of the picture.

Another example is found in Pieter Brueghel's *Parable of the Blind Men.* The blind men lead each other into the ditch. Consistent shape connects the six figures into a row of bodies, which slopes downward and finally falls rapidly. In this painting are successive stages of one and the same process:

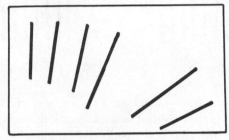

Figure 71

unconcerned walking, hesitation, alarm, stumbling, falling. The similarity of the figures is not one of strict repetition but of gradual change (Figure 71), and the eye of the observer is made to follow the course of the action. The principle of the motion picture is applied here to a sequence of simultaneous phases in space. It will be shown later that the illusory film motion is based on the application of the rules of similarity to the time dimension.

The Structural Skeleton

It may have become apparent that the shape of a visual object does not consist only of its outline. An example will make this point more explicit. A man in the street is asked to take the route indicated in Figure 72a: "Walk two blocks, turn left, walk two more blocks, turn right, walk one block. . . ." When he is through, he will find himself at the point from which he started. This will probably surprise him. Although he has traced the entire contour, his experience is unlikely to have contained the essentials of what we see when we look at a cross-shaped design (Figure 72b), because the distinguishing quality of such a design is that it consists of the two bars that cross each other or of four bars that issue symmetrically from a common center.

Delacroix has said that the first thing to grasp of any object in order to make a drawing of it is the contrast of its principal lines. "One must be well struck by this before one sets the pencil on the paper." Much of the

PLATE 1

time these principal lines do not refer to any contours actually given in the object. They form what I shall call the "structural skeleton" of a visual object. For example, different triangles have different structural skeletons. The five

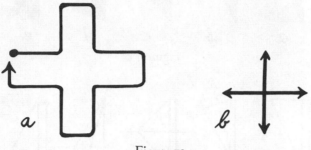

Figure 72

patterns of Figure 73 are obtained by vertically moving one corner point and leaving the other two constant. Wertheimer has noted that as the moving point continuously slides downward the changes occurring in the triangle are not continuous at all. Rather, there is series of transformations culminating in the five shapes shown in Figure 73. Although caused by changes of the contour, the structural differences of the triangles cannot be described in terms of the contour.

Triangle *a* (Figure 74) is characterized by a main vertical and a secondary horizontal axis, which meet at right angles. In *b* the main axis is slanted to the right and divides the whole into two symmetrical halves. The edge to the left, although objectively still a vertical, now looks hardly vertical at all. It has become an oblique deviation from the main axis of the pattern. In *c* the obliqueness of the whole has disappeared, but now the shorter, horizontal axis has become dominant because it is the center of a new symmetrical division. Triangle *d* reverts to obliqueness and so on.

It will be seen that the spontaneous organization of the triangles follows the law of simplicity. It is hard to visualize less simple structures—for example, *c* as an irregular oblique triangle or *d* as a deviation from the right-angled type *e* (Figure 75). Symmetry is used wherever it is available (*b, c, d*); in *a* and *e* right angularity provides the simplest available pattern.

The "identity" of each triangle—its character or nature—depends on its structural skeleton, which consists primarily of the framework of axes and secondarily of characteristic correspondences of parts created by the axes. In the isosceles triangles of Figure 73 the two equal edges correspond to each other; they become the "legs," whereas the third is seen as the base. In the other two triangles the right angle makes for a correspondence between the two sides that oppose the hypotenuse.

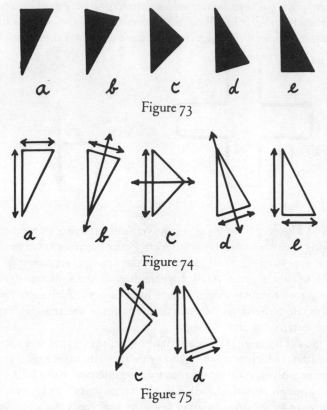

Figure 73

Figure 74

Figure 75

The fact that the structural skeleton establishes the identity of a pattern is of great consequence because it indicates the conditions that must be observed if a given pattern is to resemble or to represent another. When a number of forms within the same work of art are meant to be similar to each other, considerable differences between them will be no obstacle as long as their structural skeletons are reasonably alike. The image of a human figure may be stripped to a very few elements; it may greatly deviate in its detail from the familiar appearance of a person—it will still be recognized without difficulty as long as the structural skeleton of the image corresponds to that of the visual concept that the observer has of a human being. The relationship between visual images and the content they are meant to convey will be discussed further in the next chapter.

Among the various fashions that influence discussions of art these days, one particularly disturbs the artist—that the understanding of a work of art is an entirely subjective affair. We are told that what a person sees depends entirely on who he is, what he is interested in, what he has experienced in the past, and how he chooses to direct his attention. If this were true, the artist would have to believe that what he sees in his painting or sculpture is there only because it is he who is looking at it and that another observer will see nothing of the sort. Balzac's *Unknown Masterpiece,* the portrait of a beautiful woman to its creator and nothing but a chaos of meaningless brush strokes to his friends, would then be the fitting symbol of art. Now it is true that no two persons see the same thing in a work of art. But this does not mean that the picture or statue is only an empty *tabula rasa,* on which every beholder casts the reflections of his mind. In the preceding pages I have discussed visual phenomena that are essentially independent of individual differences. Simplicity was defined in objective terms, as was subdivision and grouping. Given an unimpaired nervous system in the observer, objective conditions in the stimulus will bring about predictable reactions. Admittedly these phenomena are quite elementary. In the arts, however, the elementary form patterns carry the core of meaning. If these patterns have an objective structure of their own, they are likely to offer a solid basis on which the artist can rely.

III   FORM

The words "shape" and "form" are often used as though they meant the same thing. Even in this book I am sometimes taking advantage of this opportunity to vary our language. Actually there is a useful difference of meaning between the two terms. The preceding chapter dealt with shape— that is, with the spatial aspects of appearance. But no visual pattern is only itself. It always represents something beyond its own individual existence— which is like saying that all shape is the form of some content.

Content, of course, is not identical with subject matter, because in the arts subject matter itself serves only as form for some content. But the representation of objects by visual patterns is one of the form problems encountered by most artists. Representation involves a comparison between the model object and its image. Since the image is hardly ever a mechanically exact copy, some questions arise. What conditions must be observed to make an image recognizable? What kinds of visual concept do artists use to represent objects? What accounts for the variety of these concepts?

Change of Orientation

What happens to the identity of a two-dimensional pattern when it is turned within the plane? Will it look different if its geometric shape remains exactly what it is and only its spatial orientation changes?

When a pattern that possesses a relatively clear-cut skeleton of axes is tilted sideways, the resulting figure will not generally show a new structure of its own. In Figure 76 we see the triangle and the rectangle unchanged except for their orientation. They do not appear as new things but simply as the old ones in new positions. This was strikingly illustrated in the experiments by Gellermann in which young children and chimpanzees were confronted with variations of the triangle to which they had learned to react. When the triangle was turned by sixty degrees, the children as well as the animals turned their heads by the same angle to reëstablish the "normal" orientation of the figure.

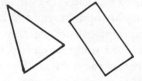

Figure 76

The orientation of an object is not an absolute but a relative phenomenon. In empty space an object would be neither upside down nor right side up, because there would be no other objects to whose orientation it could be compared. We are unaware of the fact that the projective image on the retina is inverted in relation to the physical world, not because the image is "turned around in the brain" or because "the child learns to turn it around"—as can still be read in some textbooks—but because the visual image of the world is in itself neither right side up nor upside down. There is nothing else in either space or time with which to compare it, and therefore one orientation is as good as another. Only within this image are distinctions created between top and bottom, so that we are able to say: "This monkey is hanging upside down" (in relation to the world around him).

Orientation, then, exists only relative to a framework. In fact vision is influenced not only by one but by three such frameworks, by the position of the object in relation to: (1) the structural skeleton of the surrounding visual world; (2) the brain field on which the image is projected; and (3) the structural framework of the observer's body as perceived kinesthetically by muscular sensations and the organ of equilibrium in the inner ear. In the visual world the dominant axes establish a framework of orientation. For example, in a room the orientation of walls, floor, and ceiling determines the position of the vertical and horizontal. When the maid has finished dusting, pictures may be seen hanging obliquely in relation to the framework of the room. If I stand upright, the askew pictures are projected obliquely also on the visual field of the brain. But if I cock my head sideways, I may see a picture as upright in relation to myself even though it still looks tilted in relation to the room. As long as the vertical axis of a picture coincides with the inherent vertical of my field of vision (as determined by the corresponding brain field), the picture will look upright, regardless of whether it is hanging on the wall, lying on the table, or held in any unusual position. My kinesthetic sensations give me the position of my body in relation to the pull of gravity. In daily life these kinesthetic sensations are usually in harmony with those derived from the visual framework of the environment. When I look up at a tall building, the inclination of the visual world and the kines- thetic sensation of my tilted head add up to making me experience myself as tilted in relation to a roughly upright world. When the same view appears on a movie screen, my upright posture together with the upright picture frame make the photographed world look tilted.

If we want to know whether the visual or the postural factor of orientation is the stronger, we must make them act against each other by means of special experimental conditions. Witkin performed the following experi- ment. The observer sat in a completely dark room watching a square frame made of luminous lines and tilted by some angle. Within the frame there was a luminous rod pivoted around its center so that its orientation could be varied. Under these conditions, then, the visual world, reduced to a lu- minous frame, was tipped in relation to the body framework of the observer as perceived by the kinesthetic sense of equilibrium. Thus, when he was asked "to make the rod vertical," he could not satisfy both frames of reference at the same time. Most observers adapted the rod, to varying degrees, to the axis of the square, thus going along with the visual field in spite of differing postural evidence. Some observers were guided by their postural sense to place the rod more or less closely to the physical vertical—that is, they overrode the visual framework. There was a marked difference between the sexes: women went along more often with the visual field in the outer world; men relied on the bodily experiences of the inner world.

In a work of art the orientation of any unit is determined essentially by the main axes of the work, as indicated, for example, by the verticals and horizontals of the picture frame. Within the composition, however, there are often obliquely oriented subwholes that act as local frames of reference in their own right. If a face is turned sideways, the nose will be seen as upright in relation to the face but as tilted relative to the entire picture. Figure 77, taken from an investigation on space perception, shows that the inner figure tends to look like a tilted square under the influence of the rectangular frame although without the frame it is seen more readily as an upright diamond. In Figure 78, which comes from the ornamentation of a tablecloth in a still life by Picasso, the diamonds have a tendency to look parallel to each other although in terms of the picture frame they differ in orientation. Children often draw the chimney perpendicular to the inclined edge of the roof even though this adherence to the more specific framework puts the chimney into an oblique position. As a rule, then, the spatial orien- tation of units in a work of art is determined by a number of different influences. The artist must see to it not only that the desired effect prevails but also that the strength of these influences is clearly proportioned in such a way as to make them overrule each other hierarchically or to compensate each other rather than produce a confusing cross fire. Compare the disturbingly indeterminate orientation of the central line in Figure 79.

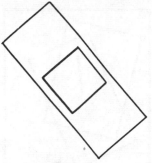

Figure 77

Oblique position produces a strongly dynamic effect. Photographers sometimes tilt their pictures relative to the frame in order to add an element of heightened life or excitement. The cubists and expressionists gave violent action to their landscapes by rendering the vertical dimension of buildings, mountains, or trees as piles of oblique units.

Figure 78

A tilt produces an actual change of shape when no one axis of the pattern is strong enough to prevent its replacement by another. A straight line does not change shape in any position. But when the square is turned by forty-five degrees, it becomes a new object—a diamond—because its diagonals can function as symmetry axes. The reason for this is that the law of simplicity does not operate only within the pattern but governs also the relationship of the pattern to the above-mentioned frames of spatial reference. When several structural skeletons are available, the one that has the simplest relationship to the framework will come to the fore. In the example of the square, the edges run parallel to the axes of the framework and thus determine the shape of the figure. In the diamond, the corners coincide with the framework.

The difference in shape between the square and the diamond has tangible effects. The square, with its explicit verticals and horizontals, is stable, restful, and simple. The diamond balances on an angle rather than on a stable base and, because of the obliqueness of its sides, is more dynamic and perceptually less simple. In oblique position the angles of ninety degrees tend

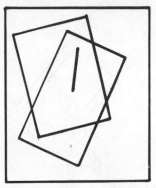

Figure 79

to lose the character of right angularity. Their sides appear to deviate obliquely from a central axis. This difference in simplicity is borne out by the fact that children find it easier to draw a square than a diamond. Results of the Stanford-Binet intelligence test show that the average five-year-old is able to copy a square whereas only the average seven-year-old can successfully copy the diamond.

Things Upside Down

When a pattern in which one axis prevails to such an extent that no other can compete is turned around, the pattern assumes a different shape even though geometrically nothing has been changed. A turn of 180 degrees is not seen as a deviation from the upright position; rather does it result in a new pattern with a stable skeleton of its own. In surrealist motion pictures human faces are sometimes shown upside down. The effect is frightening; even though we know better, visual evidence insists that we are seeing a new kind of face, a monstrous variation, which carries the mouth on top of the eyes, closes its eyelids upward, and wears its hair on the bottom. The new face is sanctioned by a symmetry of its own: it looks self-contained and right side up. Less dramatic examples can be found everywhere—as in the isosceles triangle (Figure 80). Even though both versions share the general property of triangularity, their shapes differ. Version *a* rises from a stable basis to a sharp peak; in version *b* a broad top balances heavily and precariously on a pointed foot.

Why does change of orientation produce this change of shape? The brain field seems to contain a predominance of one orientation, which corresponds to what we call the vertical; within that orientation there must be a predominance of one direction, which makes for the distinction between up and down. In vision the vertical is distinguished as the base to which everything else is related, so that, for example, the symmetry of a pattern is fully acknowledged only when its axis is oriented vertically. A violin is most clearly symmetrical when it is seen upright. In addition, there is a shape difference between a violin held upright and one held upside down. Concerning the physiological basis of this phenomenon, Köhler says: "It seems necessary to assume that the tissue of the visual center is permanently pervaded by a gradient which has a fixed direction, and which contributes to the nature of particular processes in this center just as concretely as does the distribution of retinal stimuli in each case."

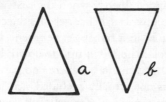

Figure 80

We must not overlook the fact that the vertical orientation is distinguished in physical space also because it coincides with the pull of gravity, and that the gravitational force makes also for an asymmetry of direction within that orientation. Going upward means going against the pull, and going downward means yielding to it. It could be argued, therefore, that the phenomenon is not due to inherent properties of the visual mechanism but to our observations of the physical world. There is some evidence that objects we are accustomed to seeing in varying spatial positions (umbrella, bone, key, trumpet) are more readily recognized at any orientation than others that are commonly seen in one position only (sitting cat, rabbit, toy cannon, sunbonnet). It has also been found, however, that the sensitivity to orientation in daily life is not acquired as quickly as we would expect it to be if it were based exclusively on learning.

Young children pay little attention to these differences in orientation. There is no reason to assume that they do not see these differences, but they do not mind looking, for example, at a picture upside down. Orientation apparently begins to play a role in the sixth year of life. Experiments have suggested that even eleven-year-old children are less impaired in their reading speed than are adults when the text is turned by ninety degrees. Young children's drawings contain no indication of a unified space concept except that units are often distributed with a surprising sense of rhythm and balance. Isolated figures float around in all orientations, and in extreme examples even the various parts of the body are strewn around irregularly. The children will spontaneously draw upside-down figures or turn the paper freely without minding the changing orientation. A unified spatial framework develops only gradually.

The facts in this area are difficult to interpret. It is possible that we are dealing here with an effect of "maturation"—that is, with a developmen: of the nervous system due to physiological growth rather than to learning. However, indifference to orientation has also been observed in adult "primitives." Koffka notes that the Bantu Negroes perceived and understood pictures of things familiar to them with equal ease whether they were right side up or upside down. In the same way, the few of them who knew how to read did so with unchanged fluency when the text was turned around.

Under certain conditions actual changes of subjective orientation can be produced. When Stratton, in a famous experiment, had for a week worn a pair of glasses that turned the world upside down, he began to see things as right side up. In other situations, where comparison with a differently oriented environment is not actually excluded—as it was with Stratton—but limited by concentration on a relatively self-contained object, righting also seems to occur. The example of a printer who saw wallpaper designs right side up while they were running upside down through the machine is cited by Lewin in an investigation in which he discovered that inverted letters or words are righted up when they are shown for split seconds a sufficient number of times.

Projections

A mere change of spatial orientation might not have been expected to interfere with the identity of a visual object, because no actual change of geometric shape is involved. Instead it was found that under certain conditions a new orientation will bring to the fore a new structural skeleton that gives the object a different character. Turning now to deviations that do involve a modification of geometric shape will demonstrate that such a "nonrigid" change may or may not interfere with the identity of the pattern, depending on what it does to the structural skeleton.

Cut a fairly large rectangle of cardboard and observe its shadow cast by a candle or other small light source. Innumerable projections of the rectangle can be obtained, some of them looking roughly like the examples of Figure 81. In spite of their similar origins, these patterns differ in that *a* looks spontaneously like a deviation from a rectangle whereas the other two betray no such kinship. In *a* essential characteristics of the structural skeleton of a rectangle are maintained—the approximate parallelism and equal length of the two pairs of corresponding sides; the other two have clearly different skeletons of their own.

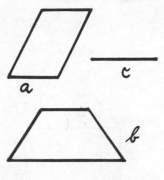

Figure 81

Perception of a cardboard rectangle is based on retinal projections, which are shaped roughly like the shadows on the wall. Depending on the relative positions of object and observer, the retinas will receive a "good" projection or one that is more or less uncharacteristic—that is, one with a clear-cut, different structure of its own. The fact remains that the visual concept of a given rectangle can be represented, more or less convincingly, by a number of patterns, not all of which have rectangular shape. Certain nonrectangular figures are actually seen as rectangles turned or tilted in space.

As long as we deal with a flat object, such as the cardboard rectangle, there exists one projection that does such complete justice to the visual concept we have of the object that the two can be considered identical. That is the orthogonal projection, which is obtained when the plane of the object is hit by the line of sight at a right angle. Under this condition the object and its retinal projection have roughly the same shape.

The situation is much more complicated with truly three-dimensional things, because their shapes cannot be reproduced by any two-dimensional projection. The projection on the retina is created by light rays that travel from the object to the eye along straight lines. Consequently this projection renders only those points of the object whose straight-line connection with the eyes is unobstructed. Figure 82 shows how the selection and relative position of these points change in the example of a cube (*b, c, d*), depending on the angle at which the observer (*a*) sees it. The corresponding projections are indicated approximately in *b', c', d'*.

As the projection changes, the observer should be expected to see an

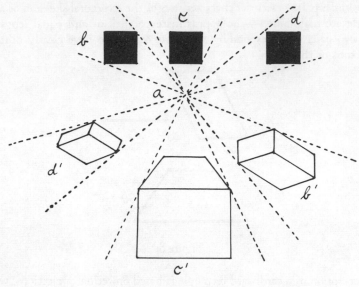

Figure 82

object of changing shape. The cube should undergo constant amoebic transformations into quadrilaterals and hexagons of the most varied proportions.
This, however, would be a desperate situation, because the immutable physical object would be inappropriately represented by a constantly changing
image, which at certain moments would structurally resemble the object and
at others not. The sickening experience produced by a distorting mirror would
be the normal visual reaction to all objects of the environment all the time.
Fortunately, but surprisingly enough, this does not happen. Under the
normal conditions of everyday life the constantly changing shape of the
retinal projection produces the experience of a three-dimensional cube of
unchanging shape. This phenomenon, about which more will be said in
Chapter V, is known to psychologists as the "constancy of shape."

Visual Concept of Solids

The visual concept of the object that we derive from perceptual experiences
has three important properties. It conceives of the object as being three-
dimensional, of constant shape, and not limited to any particular projective
aspect. An illustration can be found in Francis Galton's investigations of
visual imagery. He asserts that "a few persons can, by what they often
describe as a kind of touch-sight, visualize at the same moment all round
the image of a solid body. Many can do so nearly, but not altogether round

that of a terrestrial globe. An eminent mineralogist assures me that he is able to imagine simultaneously all the sides of a crystal with which he is familiar." Now imagery and visual conception are not the same thing. A capacity of actually visualizing an object that is not present is not necessary for conceiving of its visual structure. Even so, Galton's examples serve to show what is meant by a three-dimensional concept, which is not bound to any one aspect. If a person has an all-around concept of a crystal or a globe, no one point of observation predominates. This is true because a person's visual concept of an object is generally based on the totality of observations from any number of angles. Yet it is a visual concept and not a verbal definition derived by intellectual abstraction from perceptual experiences. Intellectual knowledge sometimes helps form a visual concept, but only to the extent to which it can be translated into visual attributes.

Strictly speaking, the visual concept of anything that has volume can be represented only in a three-dimensional medium, such as sculpture or architecture. If we wish to make pictures on a plane surface, all we can hope to do is to produce a translation—that is, to present some structural essentials of the visual concept by two-dimensional means. The pictures achieved in this way may look flat like a child's drawing or have depth like a Renaissance painting, but in both the problem remains that the all-aroundness of the visual conception cannot be reproduced directly in a plane.

Which Aspect Is Best?

One such method of translation consists in picking out one or several aspects (projections) of the object and in making them stand for the conceived whole. The problem arises: which aspects should be chosen?

For some objects all aspects are equal or equally good—for example, for a sphere or an irregularly shaped piece of rock. Usually, however, there are definite distinctions. In a cube the orthogonal projection of any one of the six surfaces is distinguished. In fact oblique aspects of the surfaces are seen as mere deviations from those for which the retinal projection is square-shaped. This distinction is based on the law of simplicity, because the distinguished projections are the ones that produce patterns of the simplest shape.

Are these simplest and perceptually preferred aspects best suited to accomplish the desired translation of the visual concept into a plane picture? Some of them are. Our visual concepts of many objects are characterized by structural symmetries, which are brought out most directly by certain aspects of the object. Thus a straight front view of a human figure displays this striking feature. But consider Figure 83. It is surely the simplest possible representation of a Mexican wearing a large sombrero. Yet such a view will be used only as a joke, which results precisely from the contradiction between the correctness and the inadequacy of the representation. The picture is certainly faithful—it can be obtained photographically from a third-floor hotel window—but it is inadequate for most purposes because it does not distinguish a Mexican from a millstone or a doughnut. The structural skeleton of Figure 83 is too little related to the structure of the visual concept to be conveyed; instead it creates other, misleading associations.

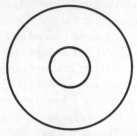

Figure 83

It is true that most works of art try to do more than render the basic structure of things with the utmost clarity. It is also true, however, that no representation of an object will ever be valid visually and artistically unless the eyes can directly understand it as a deviation from the basic visual conception of the object. The eyes cannot do so with the picture of the Mexican, which can be understood only by intellectual knowledge.

The elementary task of depicting on a surface the main properties of an object's shape is a difficult one. Should the portrait of a given person show the front face or the profile? G. K. Chesterton speaks of "one of those women whom one always thinks of in profile, as of the clean-cut edge of some weapon." Police records require both views, as do anthropometric studies, because important characteristics often show up in one view and not in the other. A further complication is introduced by the fact that some parts of an object may show best from one angle whereas others do so from another. The typical shape of a bull is conveyed by a side view, which, however, hides the characteristic lyre pattern of the horns. The spread of the wings of a flying duck does not show in profile. The angle that must be chosen to identify the goblet and stem of a wineglass destroys the circularity of the mouth and the foot. The problem repeats itself in the combination of objects: how can a pond, whose undistorted outline is revealed only through a bird's-eye view, and trees, which display their typical shape in profile, be shown in the same picture?

Take an apparently simple object—a chair (Figure 84). The top view (*a*) does justice to the shape of the seat. The front view (*b*) shows the shape of the chair's back and its symmetrical relations to the front legs. The side view (*c*) hides almost everything, but gives the important rectangular arrangement of back, seat, and legs more clearly than any other view. Finally, the bottom view (*d*) is the only one to reveal the symmetrical arrangement of the four legs attached to the corners of the square seat. All this information is indispensable, and makes part of the normal visual conception of the object. How can it be conveyed in one and the same picture? No more eloquent demonstration of the difficulties involved in this task can be given than by the drawings of Figure 85, which are derived from findings by Kerschen-

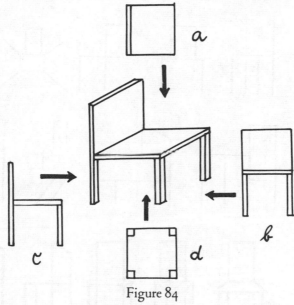

Figure 84

steiner. These drawings schematically present types of solutions worked out by school children who had been asked to reproduce from memory "a three-dimensional picture of a chair drawn in correct perspective."

The Egyptian Method

One solution of the problem is best exemplified by the wall paintings and reliefs of the Egyptians or by the drawings of children. It consists in choosing for each part of an object or combination of objects the aspect that best suits the pictorial purpose. The pictures obtained by this procedure were formerly condemned or, at best, tolerated as the inferior creations of people who did not know how to do better. When somewhat similar methods were adopted by adult artists of our own time and culture, some appreciation of their artistic validity began hesitantly to develop. An adequate psychological interpretation is, however, still far from common.

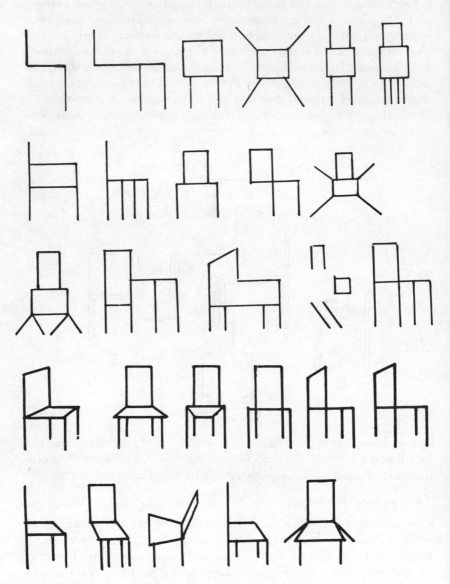

Figure 85

The Egyptians—as well as the Babylonians, early Greeks, Etruscans, who used a similar style of representation—were commonly thought to have avoided foreshortening because it was too difficult. This argument has been disposed of by Schaefer, who has shown that the side view of the human shoulder occurs in a few examples as early as the sixth dynasty but continues to remain an exception throughout the history of Egyptian art. He cites two examples of reliefs that show workmen chiseling or towing a stone statue; the shoulders of the living men are given in the conventional front view, but the statue shows the perspectively "correct" side view (Figure 86). Thus, in order to express lifeless rigidity the Egyptians had recourse to a procedure that, in the opinion of the average nineteenth-century art teacher, created the much more lifelike effect. In addition, Schaefer points out that, for the purpose of carving a sphinx, elevations were drawn on the sides of the rectangular block as early as 1500 B.C. and probably earlier. Naturally, perspective drawing was required for these elevations.

Figure 86

Therefore it is evident that the Egyptians used the method of orthogonal projection, not because they had no choice, but because they preferred it. This method permitted them to preserve the characteristic symmetry of chest and shoulders and the front view of the eye in the profile face.

In evaluating this procedure we must remember that pictorial representation is based on the visual concept of the total three-dimensional object. The method of copying an object or arrangement of objects from one fixed point of observation—roughly the procedure of the photographic camera—is not truer to that conception than the one used by the Egyptians. Drawing or painting directly from the model is quite rare in the history of art. Even in the epoch of Western art that began with the Italian Renaissance, work from the model is much of the time limited to preparatory sketches and does not necessarily make for the use of photographic projection. The figures in Egyptian art may look "unnatural" to a modern observer, not because the Egyptians fail to present the human body the way it "really is," but because the observer judges their work by the standards of a different procedure.

Once the observer has freed himself from this distorting prejudice, it becomes rather difficult to perceive the Egyptian figures as "wrong."

The question may arise: Why bother with primitive attempts to cope with a problem that has been solved satisfactorily by the rules of perspective? Does not Figure 84 contain a drawing of a chair that convincingly yields all the required visual properties? In answer to this question, I shall try to reconstruct the objections an Egyptian might have voiced to a picture done in perspective. Figures 87 and 88 schematically present two versions of the same subject—a square-shaped pond surrounded by trees. One of them (Figure 87) is done in central perspective, the other (Figure 88) according to a method used in Egypt as well as in other cultures and in the drawings of children all over the world.

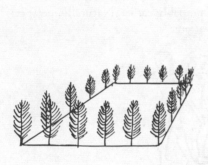

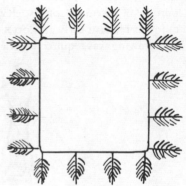

Figure 87

Figure 88

The Egyptian might criticize the perspective drawing as follows: "This picture is all wrong and very confusing! The shape of the pond is distorted. It is an irregular quadrilateral rather than a square. In reality the trees surround the pond symmetrically and meet the ground at a right angle. Also, they are all of equal size. In the picture some of the trees are in the water, some outside. Some meet the ground perpendicularly, others quite obliquely; and some of them are much taller than others." If the Westerner retorted that the Egyptian's own pond was acceptable only as an airplane view and that all the trees were lying flat on the ground, the Egyptian would find this impossible to see and hard to understand.

The apparently modest request that a picture reproduce the structural skeleton of a visual conception seems to lead to disturbing consequences. The Egyptian fulfills this demand to the letter by matching squareness with squareness, symmetry with symmetry, lying outside with lying outside.

Now it is true that the perspectively distorted drawing of the square also looks like a square, not only to the grown-up Westerner, but also to his child or to the Egyptian if he can make himself look at the perspective drawing as though it were not a picture but the real thing. Schaefer reports the experience of an artist who was sketching the house of a German peasant while the owner was watching him. As he was drawing the oblique lines of perspective, the peasant protested: "Why do you make my roof so crooked—my house is quite straight!" But when he later saw the picture finished, he admitted with surprise: "Painting is a strange business! Now it is my house, just the way it is!"

The puzzle of perspective representation is that it makes things look right by doing them wrong. There is an important difference between the two procedures here being discussed. The Egyptian or the child accounts for the squareness he sees in reality with an actual square in his picture. In this way he greatly strengthens the perceptual impact of the shape. It might be said that he actually makes it be what it suggests it is. Even though "constancy of shape" makes the real pond appear approximately square-shaped, there is a weakening indirectness about this experience; the distorted stimulus pattern, which gives rise to the experience, plays its part in the percept although the beholder may not be aware of it and be unable to realize or copy it. This is all the more true for pictures—even the most "lifelike" ones—because the depth effect is reduced and therefore constancy of shape is quite incomplete.

The power of all visual representation derives from the properties directly inherent in the medium and only secondarily from what these properties suggest in an indirect way. Thus the artistically truest and most effective solution is to represent squareness by a square. There is no question that in relinquishing this directness perspective art has suffered a serious loss. It has done so in favor of new expressive capacities that were more important to the men who developed perspective art than the ones they had to give up.

Foreshortening

In both the Egyptian and the perspective procedures a particular aspect or projection of an object is intended to represent the whole. To do so it must fulfill two conditions. First, it must indicate that in itself it is not the complete thing but only a part of something larger; second, the structure of the whole it suggests must be the correct one. When we look at a cube from straight in front, there is nothing in the perceived square to show that it is part of a cubic body. Therefore such a projection is not suitable to represent the three-dimensional structure of the cube.

According to a rule in perception—again an application of the principle of simplicity—the shape of the perceived aspect (projection) is taken spontaneously to embody the law of the whole volume. If we are shown a flat square, we see it as one aspect of a flat thing. The same is true for a disk, which we see as part of a disk-shaped body. If the circular thing is rounded, however—for example, by means of shading—we see it as part of a sphere. This may very well be misleading—the rounded object may be the bottom of a television tube—but perception automatically completes the whole body according to the simplest shape compatible with the perceived projection.

This perceptual tendency often produces satisfactory results. A sphere is in fact what its aspect promises it to be. To some extent this is true also for the human body. The whole volume roughly bears out the suggestion made by the front view. No basic surprises show up when the body is turned. Nothing essential is hidden. Within obvious limits, the shape of the projection embodies the law of the whole.

Figure 89

This is not true in the drawing of the Mexican (Figure 83), where the law of completion suggests a disk-shaped body. Nor is it true in a straight front view of a horse, like the one in Figure 89 taken from a Greek vase. Knowledge may tell us that this is a horse, but contrary perceptual evidence overrules—and should always overrule in the arts—such knowledge and tells us that this is a penguin-shaped creature, a monstrous horse-man. Untypical front views of this kind are artistically suspect.

The term "foreshortening" can be used in three different ways: (1) It may mean that the projection of the object is not orthogonal—that is, its visible part does not appear in its full extension but projectively contracted. In this sense, the front view of the human body would not be called foreshortened. (2) Even though the visible part of the object is given in its full extension, a picture could be called foreshortened when it does not provide a characteristic view of the whole. In this sense, the bird's-eye-view Mexican and the Greek horse would be foreshortened, but not in a truly perceptual and pictorial sense. It is only our knowledge of what the model object looks like that makes us consider these orthogonal views as deviations from a differently shaped object. The eye does not see it. (3) Geometrically, every projection involves foreshortening, because all parts of the body that do not run parallel to the projection plane are changed in their proportions or disappear partly or completely. Delacroix notes in his journals that there is always foreshortening, even in an upright figure with its arms hanging downward. "The arts of foreshortening and of perspective are one and the same thing. Some schools of painting have avoided [foreshortenings], truly believing that they did not use any because they were using no violent ones. In a profile head, the eye, the forehead, etc. are foreshortened; and so the rest."

Projective contraction always involves oblique position in space. What Max Wertheimer used to call the *Dingfront,* or "façade," of the object is seen as turned, and the given projection appears as a deviation from that "façade." Obliqueness gives visual evidence that the object has volume—that is, that different parts of it lie at different distances from the observer. At the same time it retains direct perception of the structural pattern from which the projection deviates. The foreshortening of a face, brought about by a turn to an oblique position, is not perceived as a pattern in its own right but as a mere variation of the frontal symmetry. No trace of that symmetry is left in a straight profile view, which is why the profile is not generally thought of as a foreshortening. The profile has a structure of its own.

It seems best, then, to call a pattern foreshortened when it is perceived as a deviation from a structurally simpler pattern, from which it is derived by a change of orientation in the depth dimension. Not all projective contractions are successful in making clear from what structural pattern they are deviating. A number of perceptual problems are involved here, of which I shall mention only a few. If, for example, the projective pattern has a rather simple shape, this simplicity will tend to interfere with its function because the simpler the shape of an object the more it resists being perceived three-dimensionally—it tends to look flat. It is difficult to see a circle as a foreshortened ellipse or a square as a foreshortened rectangle. In Figure 90 the top view of a sitting man is foreshortened into a square-shaped projection.

Owing to its squareness, the figure displays great stability in the plane and opposes its being decomposed into a less simple three-dimensional object. The conditions for subdivision in plane figures apply also to the third dimension.

Figure 90

Contractions along symmetry axes must be handled with caution. The effect of a face seen from above or from below (Figure 91) is much more violent than a view from the side. This is true, not only because shape and relative location of parts deviate more thoroughly from the basic visual conception, but also because the symmetrical view looks so "frozen," so much more stable in itself. The asymmetrical side view clearly indicates the "normal" front view from which it deviates, whereas the front view has a dangerous tendency to look like a squashed creature in its own right. The same holds true for symmetrical bird's-eye and worm's-eye views of whole figures. It is worth note that these "abnormal" views are rare in the arts and that in the most famous of them—Mantegna's picture of the dead Christ—the fossilizing effect of the symmetry is mitigated by the sideward leaning of head and feet.

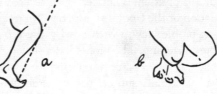

Figure 92

Another problem comes up frequently in the foreshortening of inward-bent forms, when the continuity of the body (Figure 92a) is replaced in the projection by discontinuous, overlapping units (b). The dropping out of the hidden parts, together with the change from continuity to discontinuity, produces a strong interference with the underlying visual concept. Other examples are found in fists that reach out of the picture toward the observer and often look quite detached from their arms, or in the back views of horses

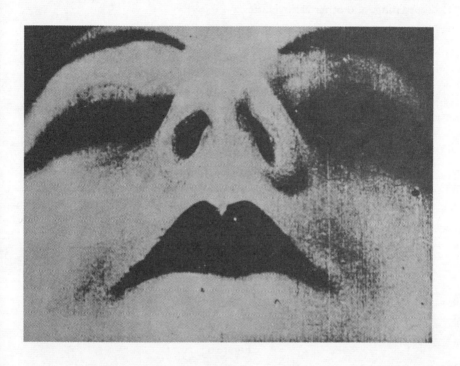

Figure 91

with their buttocks cutting across their necks. In such examples visual comprehensibility approaches its limits. Ernst Barlach, the German sculptor, says: "I do not represent what I, on my part, see or how I see it from here or there but what it *is,* the real and truthful, which I have to extract from what I see in front of me. I prefer this kind of representation to drawing because it eliminates all artificiality. I would say, sculpture is a healthy art, a free art, not afflicted by such necessary evils as perspective, expansion, foreshortening, and other artificialities."

Overlapping

Overlapping—or superposition—is one of the devices that create a deviation from the underlying visual conception. Overlapping occurs when one unit partly hides another that lies behind it, either within one object or in arrangements of objects. Here the requirements for adequate perception are that the units that, by effect of the projection, touch each other in the same plane must be seen as: (a) separate from each other and (b) belonging to different planes. The examples in Figure 93 show that the more consistent the shape of each unit is in itself and the more sharply the individual shapes are set off against each other, the more clearly overlapping is perceived. I shall discuss the more particular problems of "figure and ground" in Chapter V.

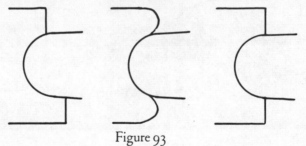

Figure 93

When the overlapping units together form a particularly simple shape, they tend to be seen as one and the same thing. Thus in Figure 94 the shoulder and arm of the woman may be taken to belong to the man—a misinterpretation strengthened by the fact that the resulting simple symmetry also fits the basic visual concept of a human body.

Since, in every example of overlapping, one unit is partly covered by the other, the curtailed unit must not only be made to look incomplete but it must also ask for the right kind of completion. When limbs are cut in the joints (shoulders, elbows, knees), visual amputation rather than overlapping is the result, because the visible part looks complete in itself. Also, when the direction of the cut is in a simple relationship to the structure of the visible unit (for example, a human face cut parallel or perpendicularly to the medial axis), the fragment is more likely to show an unwelcome completeness. Oblique cuts tend to avoid the effect. These rules apply not only to the interior of the picture but also to the way the frame overlaps it. (Compare the rules of thumb for the trimming of photographs, the selection of details for enlargement, the use of the range finder.)

Figure 94

When an arm goes out of sight by overlapping at the point of the wrist, there is visually no hidden hand but a stump. The law of consistent shape continues the interrupted limb logically according to the structure indicated in the visible part. This creates a problem whenever a change of shape or direction occurs in the hidden portion. If a man puts his arm around the shoulder of a woman, a front view of the group will show the arm disappearing behind the back with nothing but the fingers reappearing on the shoulders. It is almost impossible visually to establish the continuity, not only because of the mere size of the interruption, but also because the change of the direction at the elbow and the change of shape from upper arm to fingers are not indicated to the eye.

Finally, there is the rearrangement of organic parts through projective overlapping—hands sprouting from behind the head, ears attached to the chin, knees adjoining the chest. Even the most daring modern artists have rarely matched the paradoxical reshuffling of the human limbs that has been presented as an accurate imitation of nature. Often the organic unity of the body can be reconstructed only by knowledge. How much of this is considered admissible depends on the style of the period. Examination of the work of the great masters reveals how much care they take to keep the underlying visual concept recognizable in the projection. This is true even for the baroque style, which brought the love of foreshortening to a peak— for example, in the work of El Greco or Rubens. Although minor artists are led astray by the challenge of virtuosity and the accidental projections observed in the living model, much of the Egyptian need for visual comprehensibility is left in a Michelangelo.

What Good Does Overlapping Do?

Once we realize the intricate technical problems introduced by projective representation and the threat to visual clarity and impact that the procedure involves, we may well ask why anyone at any time should have been willing to get into such trouble. For centuries we of the West have taken for granted the assumption that only the projective method enabled the artist to represent reality as it actually is. By now we are beginning to see that this method approaches "reality" no more closely than, for example, the Egyptian method does. We suspect that it is quite possible to describe Western "realism" as the most radical deviation from reality in the entire history of art. It is a style that can be called more "realistic" only when that ambiguous term is defined according to Western ideas. A more convincing argument in favor of this method is needed.

If as the point of departure we use the simplest kind of visual representation as it is found, for example, in the drawings of young children or prehistoric cave dwellers or in the Chinese ideogram for "man" (Figure 95), we may say that the projective method involves a twofold deviation from this "key tone."

Figure 95

First, the simple structural skeleton is bent and twisted into those innumerable modifications that result when the body is shown in activity—walking, working, gesticulating, sitting, climbing, falling. This transformation is inevitable wherever the artist wishes to present more than the mere permanent existence of the object. Second, the body is subjected to the deformation that results from the projection upon a surface. It is this transformation that requires a more detailed justification. I shall attempt to give it by first answering the question: What good does overlapping do the artist?

If you compare Figure 96a with another representation in which the two ducks would walk in single file without overlapping (Figure 96b), you will realize that the parallelism of the two animals, which conveys to the eye their belonging together, is brought out more compellingly when it occurs within one and the same visual unit. Similarly, in Figure 97 the contrast between the vertical body and the oblique arm imposes itself more forcefully when the two directions coincide in space within one unit (*a*) rather than being unfolded in the looser lateral succession of *b*. In music the effect of harmony or disharmony is similarly made more compelling when several tones are combined in one chord rather than being played in succession. Overlapping, then, intensifies the formal relationship by concentrating it within a more unified pattern.

Figure 96

The intimate union achieved by overlapping is of a peculiar nature. It impairs the completeness of at least one—and mostly all—of the parties concerned. The result is not simply a "relationship"—that is, the exchange of energy between independent, serenely intact beings. It is togetherness as interference through mutual modification. By renouncing the clarity of juxtaposition, the artist accomplishes a more subtle and more dramatic interpretation of communion. He shows the tension between the conflicting tendencies involved in social intercourse and the need for safeguarding the integrity of the individual.

Figure 97

Strictly speaking, the interference caused by overlapping is not mutual. One unit always lies on top, unimpaired, and violates the wholeness of the other. In Figure 98 the effect is rather one-sided. King Sethos is in front and complete whereas Isis, who gives his majesty the support of her godship, endures all the inconveniences that befall a seat. Thus, overlapping establishes a hierarchy by creating a distinction between dominating and submissive units. A scale of importance leads, through any number of intervening steps, from foreground to background.

The relationship is one-sided, however, only in any specific example of overlapping. In a complex whole the dominance-submission relationship at one place may be counteracted by its reversal at another, so that each partner is shown as active and passive at the same time. A comparison of Figure 98 with the compositional scheme of a Rubens painting (Figure 99) will illustrate this point without need of further analysis.

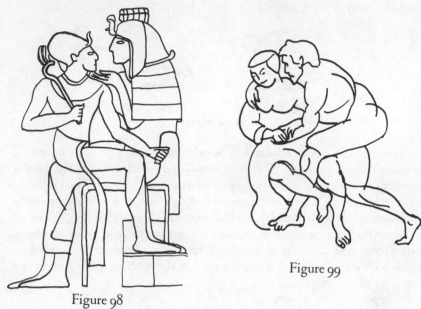

Figure 99

Figure 98

The relationship between inside and outside is most clearly expressed without the use of overlapping. Children draw hair as growing outward from the contour of the head and people as dwelling inside the rectangle of the house. This method has no way of rendering the particular expressive quality of hiding and being hidden, which is conveyed when the difference between inside and outside is given by overlapping. Overlapping shows how dress covers or exposes the body. When the film camera pictures a prisoner behind bars, it makes all the difference for the meaning of the scene whether the shot is taken from the inside or the outside of the cell, even though the objective spatial situation is unchanged. If the scene is shot from inside the cell, we see the margin of freedom that remains to the man against the background of the prison; if the scene is shot from outside, we see the bars shut him off visually by striking across his body. Alschuler and Hattwick have found some evidence that young children who in their "abstract" easel paintings overlaid one patch of color on another, as distinguished from other children who preferred separate placement of color, tended to be "repressed" and (when cold colors were overlaid on warm ones) "of a passive nature."

This finding may suggest that even young children are sensitive to the hiding effect of overlapping and may seek it when it suits their personal attitude. It is well to remember, however, that their response may not be based mainly on the visual result obtained on paper but rather on the motor activity of first doing something and covering it up afterward.

Since overlapping has the property of eliminating parts of objects and preserving their integrity at the same time, it offers a welcome means of selection to any artist who is unwilling to interfere with the physical completeness of things. When a modern artist leaves out arms or eyes he actually deprives the visual pattern of these parts, whereas overlapping moves them out of sight but suggests at the same time that they are present at their proper places. The picture frame selects a section of the infinite continuum of the world but does not interfere with the visual conception of this infinity, provided the frame seems to hide rather than to cut off the rest. Within the picture, figures and objects cover each other in such a way that what is needed is shown and the unnecessary remains hidden.

In addition to permitting selection, overlapping serves to rearrange elements in strikingly new patterns that reveal hidden characteristics of the object by freshly discovered relationships. Thus Wölfflin writes of Michelangelo's *Slaves* of the Sistine ceiling: "The variation from the normal in the structure of these bodies is insignificant by comparison with the way Michelangelo disposes the limbs, for which he discovers new and effective formal relationships; here, he brings one arm and both legs together as a series of parallels; there, he brings the downward-reaching arm across the thigh so that it forms almost a right-angle; there again, he encloses the figure from head to heels in an almost unbroken sweep of line; and these are not mathematical variations which he sets himself as an exercise, for even the most unusual action is made convincing in its effect."

Overlapping offers a convenient solution to the problem of how to represent symmetry in relation to a party within the picture. Suppose a painter wants to depict the Judgment of Paris. The three goddesses are to be presented as having equal chances of being chosen, which means in visual terms that they should be placed symmetrically in relation to their judge. It is simple enough to show this symmetry to the person who looks at the picture (Figure 100*a*), because his glance meets the plane perpendicularly. This, however, is not possible with the same means when the beholder (Paris) is located in the picture plane itself (*b*). The three women do not face him symmetrically; one is closest, the second farther, the third has the poorest chance. This arrangement contradicts the visual concept of the theme. The painter may enlist the second dimension of the plane (*c*). This restores the symmetry but piles the goddesses awkwardly one on the other in totem-pole fashion. To

display the pattern on the ground plane the picture space must be expanded
into the third dimension by oblique arrangement, which often (though not
necessarily) involves overlapping (*d*). The tilt may also be applied vertically (*e*).

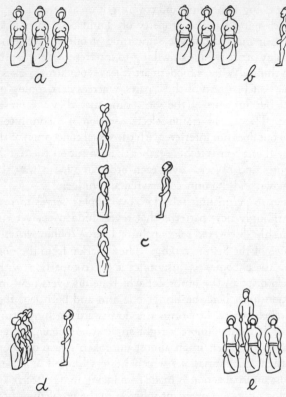

Figure 100

The charioteer with his horses is another illustration of the same problem.
The visual concept of the Horatii and the Curatii would ask for two groups
of three set against each other symmetrically. The task is even more difficult
when the group to be related symmetrically to another party in the picture
is not linear but, for example, circular. Figure 101 shows the compositional
scheme of a twelfth-century calendar picture. St. Ursula, surrounded by
her maidens, is attacked by an archer. The group is symmetrical to the beholder but not to the archer.

The same dilemma arises for the presentation of individual objects. Medieval painters were plagued by the problem of how to make the evangelist

write in his book. The visual concept asks for the book to face the writer symmetrically—which cannot be achieved without overlapping or foreshortening. In the last analysis we are back at the problem of the Egyptian, who presents the shape of each part most strikingly but—we must insist now—falsifies the angular relationships by placing everything in the same plane.

Figure 101

And since I have pointed out that the visual concept of an object is based on a three-dimensional skeleton of axes, I am in no position to maintain that the rendering of angles is less important than that of shape. The only method that unambiguously represents spatial orientation in the three dimensions is the so-called "isometric" perspective. Even though this method permits accurate reconstruction of three-dimensional bodies, it has the visual drawback of distorting angles and shapes. The problem of reproducing volume in a plane remains basically insoluble. It is up to the artist to choose the system for whose advantages he is willing to accept its shortcomings.

Interplay of Plane and Depth

The third dimension creates an enrichment somewhat comparable to what happened in music when harmonic chords were added to the melodic line. There are striking parallels in the development of the two arts. In music additional "voices" are introduced first, and only gradually does the mere simultaneity of the independent melodic lines grow into a genuine new dimension of "vertical" structure. Once this is achieved, each tone belongs to two contexts by holding a position in the melodic sequence as well as in the chord formed by the notes that sound at the same time. The integration of the two structural dimensions produces the complexity of modern polyphonic music. Rather similarly, pictorial scenes are first subdivided into separate horizontal rows or strips, which fuse gradually into one integrated, three-dimensional whole. Here too each element belongs to two different contexts when the integration has been achieved. It has a location in the

Figure 102

frontal plane and at the same time in the three-dimensional space represented in the picture. Correspondingly, each pictorial unit has two shapes: that of the three-dimensional object, and that of its flat projection. The picture as a whole consists of two entirely different compositions: one of them being the arrangement on the "stage" that extends into depth, and the other the arrangement within the frontal plane. The synthesis of both constitutes the meaning of the whole. An example will clarify this matter.

The three-dimensional arrangement of the group of *Silk Beaters* (Figure 102) has four women standing around the table in a rectangular group, which is an oblique variation of the shape of the table itself (Figure 103). Three of the figures face each other symmetrically (II, III, IV); the fourth, getting herself ready to work, stands turned away. Thus the fourfold group is subdivided into a triangle and an outsider, woman IV being the connecting link between the two who are working already and the one who is not. The connections between the two dark robes and the two light robes correspond to the diagonals of the rectangular group. The two dark figures establish the lateral limits of the group. The light ones do the same for the depth dimension, II dominating in the foreground and III being removed to the greatest distance.

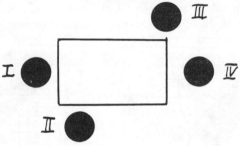

Figure 103

The arrangement in the projective pattern of the picture plane is quite different. The women are not located around the table. Two of them flank it, and the other two are in an overlapping relationship to it. The group now subdivides more clearly into two pairs, each knitted together by overlapping and separated from the other by empty space. The triangular symmetry of II, III, IV has disappeared; the fourth figure is no longer separate. Instead there is something like a sequence of four lunar phases that leads in a decrescendo from the dominating full face of I over the obliqueness of III to the profile of II and finally the almost hidden face of IV. This establishes a linear zigzag connection that is nonexistent in the three-dimensional composition. There are now two outer figures (dark) and two inner figures (light)—an approximate lateral symmetry around a central axis formed by the two sticks. The four heads are the corners of a flat parallelogram in which I and III dominate the other two by their higher position but are overlapped by them if the whole figures are considered.

A wealth of form and meaning springs from the interaction of the two compositional structures, which partly support and partly oppose each other contrapuntally. It would be worth while to study the relative functions of the two patterns more precisely. Obviously, the three-dimensional grouping always describes the factual or "geographic" situation (for example, Christ surrounded by his disciples), and its expressive or symbolic function may well be weaker than that of the visually more direct projective pattern. Since the relative strength of the two depends on the strength of the depth effect in the particular picture, however, an investigation of their functions may lead to different results for different styles.

Dynamics of Obliqueness

Obliqueness always entails a crescendo or decrescendo because it is seen as a gradually increasing deviation from, or approximation of, the stable positions of the vertical and horizontal. In perspective obliqueness the phenomenon operates in two different ways. First, an obliquely placed object shows an inner tension in the direction of moving toward, or away from, the frontal

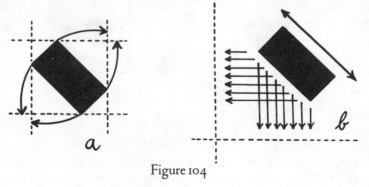

Figure 104

plane or an orthogonal plane (perpendicular to the frontal plane) (Figure 104*a*). An obliquely oriented object is charged with potential energy as distinguished from the stillness of any location parallel to the frontal plane. Compare the table with the walls in Leonardo's *Last Supper*. In an architect's plan they would run parallel to each other (Figure 105). In the perspectively drawn picture the table and the back wall reflect the majestic stability of Christ whereas the side walls are swung outward like pivoted wings in a gesture of revelation that fits the meaning of the scene.

The same painting exemplifies the other dynamic effect, schematically represented in Figure 104*b*. The table is at equal distance from the beholder throughout its length, as is the back wall. As the eye, starting from the center of the picture, moves along one of the side walls, however, the distance decreases rapidly and there is a sensation of powerful approaching and growing that is greatly enhanced by the concomitant increase in size. The process can also be perceived as a gradual withdrawal from the orthogonal plane. In the *Last Supper* this makes pyramid-shaped space dramatically expand or contract.

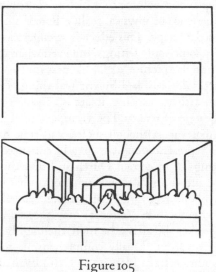

Figure 105

These phenomena can occur only because "constancy" is not complete, thus leaving the room some of its projective obliqueness instead of showing its objective rectangularity. Incomplete constancy is also the cause of a further dynamic effect that occurs in foreshortening. An outstretched figure with its feet facing the observer would be seen in its correct length if constancy entirely compensated foreshortening. Instead the projective decrease in size is partly noticed and the figure looks shrunk. Owing to the ambiguity of pictorial dynamic effects, which was discussed earlier, this contraction may be perceived in different ways. The body may be seen as being, or having been, compressed—as though squashed by a plate of glass; and here the effect may be focused either on the compression itself or on the expansive spring action that arises as a response to the compression. Then too the body may be seen as swelling or unfolding from small to large size. Depending on how the dynamic effect is perceived, the corresponding expressive meaning will vary, so that a foreshortening may convey the crushing power of death, the resistance to destruction, or the life process of growth. This polarity in the symbolism of foreshortening has been described by Rathe. It would be interesting to find out whether the difference of interpretation depends mainly on the subject matter of the picture or the subjective attitude of the observer or whether it is determined by properties of the pictorial pattern.

Realism

The addition of depth and volume to a picture contributes greatly toward duplicating the experience of physical reality. Round shape looks more like the real thing than flat shape. This effect is strongest in actual illusions as they are achieved by some stage settings; but even when the beholder knows that he is looking at a flat picture, its lifelikeness is often sufficient to make him assume the attitude provoked by the real thing. This use of pictures cannot be called an artistic response, if art is considered an interpretation rather than a duplication of reality. The vicarious use of images is, however, widespread and important. Although such an attitude toward art does not require illusionistic representation, it is greatly enhanced by it. In some of Caravaggio's paintings or in certain Dutch still lifes the material presence of particular people and things is so overwhelming that it becomes difficult to see them as symbolic realizations of a more general content. A great master (Giorgione, Rembrandt, Vermeer) may succeed in combining both purposes; but the weaker the artist, the more thoroughly will the illusion of material presence crowd out visually comprehensible meaning. (Compare the *trompe l'oeil* tradition from Harnett to Dali.) Even after many decades of spade work by modern artists, one of the things the "man in the street" finds hardest to accept is that a picture may present a perfect likeness of people or a landscape and yet be entirely incomprehensible visually and therefore devoid of artistic content. This difficulty has been created by the "scientific" approach to copying a model with mechanical exactness as well as by candid photography and the movies. The attitude of contemplation has been extended to images that can be grasped visually only in rough approximation because they use the raw material of reality. In this way the eye has been reduced to registering the presence of the subject matter—a type of reaction suitable only to a civilization in which ideas have been separated from their concrete manifestations, so that the material object is valued only for its own sake as the target of man's social, economic, and instinctual strivings. According to H. Kühn, illusionism in the arts is found in civilizations based on exploitation and consumption. Only in such a climate did it become possible seriously to describe art as springing from the desire for reputation, power, fame, wealth, and the love of women, as Freud did in his lectures on psychoanalysis.

The New Freedom of Modern Art

"Realistic" art has produced the most radical deviation from basic visual conception by faithfully recording the specific appearance and activity of things and objects and by using projection as a means of translating the three-dimensional world into plane images. Realism is, however, not the only method by which artists have rendered the identification of images a strenuous task. "Modern" art, in some of its aspects, is much better known for having done the same thing. In fact "modern" art and "realism" are popularly thought to be opposite extremes; the former is said to be far removed from reality, and the latter to approach it most closely. For my present purpose I must stress the fact that the freedom of the "modern" artist was made possible by his predecessor the "realist," who had stretched the tie between representation and the underlying visual concept of objects to the utmost.

Protected by the "correctness" of their foreshortenings, artists had twisted the axes of objects, destroyed the symmetrical correspondence of parts, changed the proportions, and rearranged the relative location of things. In a realistic painting, a human figure could reach above the trees into the sky, the feet could adjoin the face, and the outline of the body could assume almost any shape. Modern artists took over much of this sovereignty but renounced its traditional justification. They abandoned the realist's double frame of reference, by which violence to the pattern in the plane was permitted because it was the result of correct projection of objects in three-dimensional space. It is true, however, that since they could no longer rely on the organic correctness of their representation in space, even the most radical modern artists have rarely matched the boldness of the deformations that were common when projective realism was at its peak.

Realists had initiated the destruction of organic integrity. They made objects incomplete or separated their parts through intervening foreign objects. Modern artists did the same without the excuse of overlapping. Obliqueness had been introduced to represent depth. Modern artists distorted the orientation of axes without that justification. The destruction of local color had been carried to its extreme by the impressionists, who had used reflections to apply the green of a meadow to the body of a cow or the blue of the sky to the stones of a cathedral. In consequence, modern artists became free not only to make a red object blue but also to replace the unity of one local color with any combination of different colors. In the past, artists had learned to reorganize organic subdivisions with paradoxical results. They fused several human figures into one triangle or detached an arm from the mass of the body and united it with the arm of another figure to a new, continuous whole. This enabled the modern artist, for example, to split up a face and fuse part of it with the background. By illuminating objects from a specific direction, artists had come to cast shadow lines across them, subdividing them in ways that had little organic justification. Carrying this device further, Braque made one female figure consist of two—a black profile woman and a light front-face woman (see Figure 233b).

What Looks Lifelike?

Today we are faced with the curious situation that "modern" art is considered offensively far removed from reality whereas projective illusionism is said to match it closely, even though the above analysis shows that it would be difficult to say which one of the two procedures deviates more boldly from basic visual concepts. Why this different evaluation? What makes us easily recognize familiar objects in pictures that would have puzzled and confused people of most other civilizations? And why did pictures and statues look lifelike to them and do not look so to us?

On what basis is the lifelikeness of images judged? It might be thought that this is done simply by comparing the images with what is seen in "real life," but remarkably enough this is not true. As far as we can judge from written documents that have come down to us from the past, works of art have always been thought of as faithful replicas of the real things. The greatest praise bestowed on them consisted in accounts of their lifelikeness, which was said to be such as to fool man and beast. The theory was often refined to include the artist's selection of what was most beautiful or significant, but even the idealized image was considered as nothing but a faithful copy of what should or could exist.

The Greek and Chinese stories about the illusion of reality created by certain masterworks refer to styles of art that are anything but illusionistic in the modern sense of the word. To cite a more recent example from Western art, we read in Boccaccio's *Decamerone* that the painter Giotto "was a genius of such excellence that there was no thing of nature ... that he did not depict with the pencil or the pen or the brush in a manner so similar to the object that it seemed to be the thing itself rather than merely resembling it; so much so that many times the visual sense of men was misled by the things he made, believing to be true what was only painted." The highly stylized pictures of Giotto could have hardly deceived his contemporaries if lifelikeness was judged by direct comparison with reality rather than with the manner of picture making to which they were accustomed. Compared with the best among his immediate predecessors, Giotto's rendering of expressive gestures, depth, volume, and scenery could indeed be called realistic, and it was this difference that produced the astonishing effect. Even in the recent past, examples have shown that progress in pictorial lifelikeness will create the illusion of life itself. The first motion pictures, which were shown about 1890, were technically crude, but spectators screamed with fear when the train rushed headlong toward them. The phenomenon is being repeated in the so-called "three-dimensional" films.

Actual illusions are, of course, rare; but they are the extreme and most tangible manifestation of the fact that as a rule in a given cultural context the familiar style of pictorial representation is not perceived at all   the image looks simply like a faithful reproduction of the object itself. In our civilization this is true for "realistic" works; they look "just like nature" to many persons who are unaware of their highly complicated and specific style. However, this "artistic reality level" may shift quite rapidly. Today we can hardly imagine that only a few decades ago the Cézannes and Renoirs looked offensively unreal.

Probably only a further shift of the artistic reality level is needed to make the Picassos, the Braques, or the Klees look exactly like the things they represent. Anybody who is concerned with modern art will find it increasingly difficult to remain aware of the deviations from realistic rendition that strike the newcomer so forcefully. Even though our daily life is being permeated with all the devices of modern art by designers who use them for wallpapers, store windows, book covers, posters, and wrappers, the man in the street has hardly gone beyond the reality level of 1850 in painting and sculpture. I must emphasize that I am not referring here to matters of taste but to the much more elementary experience of perception. When confronted with a still life by van Gogh, a modern critic actually sees a different object than his colleague saw in 1890.

As far as the artists themselves are concerned, there seems to be little doubt that they see in their works nothing but the exact equivalent of the object. Their utterances make it quite clear that they think of "style" simply as a means for obtaining this result. "Originality" is the unsought and unnoticed product of a gifted artist's successful attempt to be honest and truthful. The deliberate search for a personal style inevitably interferes with the validity of the work, because it introduces an element of arbitrariness into a process that can be governed only by necessity.

The sculptor Jacques Lipchitz tells of admiring one of Juan Gris' pictures while it was still on the easel. It was the kind of cubistic work in which the layman discovers little but an agglomeration of building material. Lipchitz exclaimed: "This is beautiful! Do not touch it any more! It is complete." At which Gris, flying into a rage, shouted in reply: "Complete? Don't you see that I have not finished the moustache yet?" To him the picture evidently contained the image of a man so clearly that he expected everyone to see it immediately in all its detail.

It would be difficult to explain these facts by a psychology of perception according to which two patterns could be expected to look identical or similar only if one was a rather exact and complete replica of the other as to countable elements and measurable values of size, shape, direction, color. All the paradoxical equations between object and image I have cited are possible only because perception relies on salient structural features, which carry expression, rather than on exactness and completeness. Earlier I spoke of the robin that started to fight when presented with a square inch of russet breast feathers (see p. 34). This is an extreme example, but is it different in principle from our accepting small outline figures on a flat board as speaking likenesses of large physical objects? We say of a Michelangelo drawing, "This is a man!" rather than, "This represents a man!" This usage is more than a convenient abbreviation of speech. It reflects the fact that the lines on the board are actually perceived as a human figure. Once it is realized that the considerable differences between object and picture are no obstacle to perceptual identification, there is no reason to assume that such identification must stop short of the cubists.

(Discussions of "identity" and "identification" have become difficult since Western logic has accustomed us to a kind of all-or-none thinking, according to which an image either creates a complete illusion or assumes a mere "meaning" based on convention. Actually, all images are experienced as literally "being"—to some extent—the thing they represent. Instead of foolishly assuming that the child who uses a stick for a doll is the victim of an illusion, we ought to realize that there is nothing unusual in an object being a piece of wood and a baby at the same time. When American Indians blamed a famine on the white explorer because he had put so many of their bisons in his sketchbook that none were left to eat, they identified object and image on the basis of perceptual similarities. They neither tried to butcher and eat the bisons in the book nor did they take the pictures for mere magic "symbols." The bisons were real and unreal at the same time. Partial identification of the image with the real object is the rule rather than the exception, not only in children and primitives, but in man's reactions to all effigies whether they be in dreams, churches, movie theaters, photographic albums, or art museums.)

Styles of representation seem to be subject to the psychological rule that constant features of a situation tend to drop out of consciousness. An odor, which may be strong when we enter a room, disappears after a while. Millions of Americans spend their winters in overheated rooms without being aware of their own suffering. Noises, pictures on the wall, the habits of our companions, all disappear. A principle of economy seems to limit awareness to changes, which might require reaction. For this reason pictorial representations that come from the observer's own cultural environment appear to him as "styleless"—that is, as done in the only natural and correct way. Thus the modernist is accused of not showing things "as they are." It should be added that adaptations to something new occurs most easily and completely when the features in question fit the character and needs of the observer. Modern art disturbs particularly where its style is not only new but conveys violence and tension; but even violence may remain unnoticed when it fits the state of mind of the person or group. Meyer Schapiro has noted that van Gogh speaks of a painting of his bedroom in Arles as an expression of "absolute repose [although] it is anything but that, with its rapid convergences and dizzying angularities, its intense contrasted colors and the scattered spots in diagonal groups." This observation may be generalized by saying that the creator is least aware of the style of his work, because it is a direct reflection of his own personality.

Probably it can be maintained that every successful work of art, no matter how stylized and remote from mechanical correctness it may be, conveys the full natural flavor of the object it represents. A portrait of a school girl by Picasso is done in wildly overlapping geometrical shapes of strong color. At first glance much of the subject matter is invisible. Yet the picture masterfully renders the elementary liveliness of the young creature, the girlish repose, the shyness of the face, the straightly combed hair, the burdensome tyranny of the big textbook.

Why does the painter insist on artful camouflage, which hides what could have been given more clearly by a realistic portrait of the school child? The answer must be that to Picasso—and not only to him—the method he used made the school child more alive to the eyes than any other method. To achieve this effect the detail of the model's material appearance was less important than the qualities of expression conveyed through Picasso's shapes and colors.

Picasso attempts to get a solid grasp of his subject by presenting it through simple, geometric shapes and pure colors clearly set off against each other. The almost frantic need of much modern art for simple, tangible form can be understood historically. I have shown how the mechanical copying of the model had rendered the pictorial pattern incomprehensible to the eye. In such products art was committing suicide. When Cézanne was told that the public considered a certain painting by Rosa Bonheur "very strong," he commented: "Oui, c'est horriblement ressemblant!" At the same time the impressionists had undertaken to reduce the cognitive capacities of human vision to a minimum. All they wanted the painter to do was faithfully to record the smallest perceivable units of color as they appeared in each particular spot at a particular moment. This procedure, in itself as valid as any other approach to reality, threatened the artist with losing both the object and pictorial form. The visual field was in danger of becoming a continuum of equivalent units, all equally like and unlike each other. The whole picture was one thing and an infinity of things at the same time. If the method was carried to its extreme, there could be no more "grouping" and therefore no shape and no object. At this fatal stage of the development certain artists seized upon the pictorial atom—the color dot—which had no shape and also the simplest shape; from this last tangible remnant they rebuilt anew the alphabet of shape and color, free from the object, and subservient only to visual comprehensibility.

At the same time, however, there was also a need for recuperating the world of things that had slipped away. In 1902, at the age of twenty-three, Paul Klee wrote in his diary: "To have to begin by what is smallest is as precarious as it is necessary. I will be like a newborn child, knowing nothing about Europe, nothing at all. To be ignorant of poets, wholly without verve, almost primordial. Then I will do something very modest, think of something very, very small, totally formal. My pencil will be able to put it down, without any technique. All that is needed is an auspicious moment; the concise is easily represented. And soon it is done. It was a tiny, but real act, and from the repetition of acts that are small, but my own, eventually a work will come, on which I can build. The nude body is an entirely suitable object. In the academies I have caught it little by little from all sides. But now I will no longer project a shadow of it but rather proceed in such a way that everything essential, even though hidden by optical perspective, appears on the plane. And soon a small, incontestable possession is discovered, a style is created."

From the twofold need of the modern painter for object and form, something as simple and concrete as the drawings of children could have emerged—and occasionally it almost did. The shape of things was carried back to the elementary scheme. Realistic trimmings and inflections were dropped in favor of a thrifty geometry. Straight front and side views replaced the foreshortenings. Yet much of this art was anything but simple; rather than reflecting a naïve view of a stable world, it was a refuge from the bewildering complexity that the artist found around and within himself.

Some artists obtained simplicity by withdrawing to the monastery of abstraction. In the work of others the underlying concept of the object seemed simple enough, and the pictorial pattern they employed was not too intricate either; but rather than supporting each other, the structures of object and form paradoxically contradicted each other. Figure 106 gives the main lines of Paul Klee's *Brother and Sister*. The organic separation of the two heads is denied by a rectangle, which fuses them at the same time it

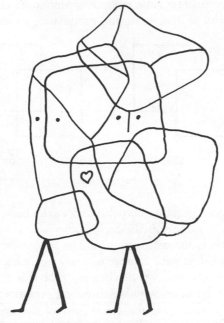

Figure 106

halves the face of the brother. The right pair of legs carries a body that fits either head equally well. It is the picture of a world in which the natural state of things is set off by an equally convincing affirmation of the opposite.

Transparency

The liberties of projective realism had remained within the limits of what was sanctioned by the rules of projection. Modifications of proportion or size had to remain slight unless used for caricature or fantasy. Specifically, there were two principles that could not be violated. One related to over-lapping, the other to projective aspects.

Overlapping, as I have shown earlier, had introduced a new spatial dimension and thus made it possible for more than one object to be located in the same plane of the picture. This coincidence in the projective plane was com-pensated, however, by strict separation in depth. One object had to lie clearly in front of the other (Figure 107a). This meant technically that over-lapping had to remain one-sided except when transparency was to be represented. Modern art dispensed with this limitation—it practiced mutual overlapping (Figure 107*b*). One and the same area was made paradoxically to belong to more than one object, thus destroying the cherished value of well-defined property. The same twilight of ambiguity also blotted out the traditional hierarchy of dominance and submission; no longer was one unit

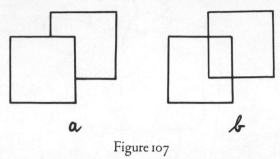

a   *b*

Figure 107

whole and in front, the other curtailed and in the back. Both were whole and curtailed, in front and in the back at the same time, and no decision in favor of either solution was suggested. The price to be paid for the intercourse of one individual with another was no longer clear. There was insistence on completeness, and yet no denying that this integrity was being invaded; and the question who was invading whom remained unsolved. Interpenetration undermined also the solidity of the object; as Figure 107 shows, overlapping involves the paradox that incompleteness maintains solidity (*a*) whereas completeness destroys it (*b*). Thus the pictorial object acquired the transparency of an apparition, which could be suspected of being a product of the mind rather than a thing of matter. The suspicion that reality was only a figment grew at times into the bold affirmation of the subjective origin of all images. Just as the transparency of the solids revealed them to be nothing but painted shapes, so the deliberate exposure of the brush stroke, the movement of the pen, the texture of bare paint, canvas, or paper, all amounted to the proud declaration that the so-called reality was the work of eye, hand, and thought. Here, as in other areas of modern civilization, the subjective or psychological approach was a conquest and a retreat at the same time.

Competing Aspects

A second principle that could not be violated in traditional realistic painting concerns projective aspects. As I have said, one way of representing the conception of a three-dimensional body on a plane surface consists in rendering its appearance from a given angle. Many civilizations felt no need for keeping the station point identical for the whole of an object or an arrangement

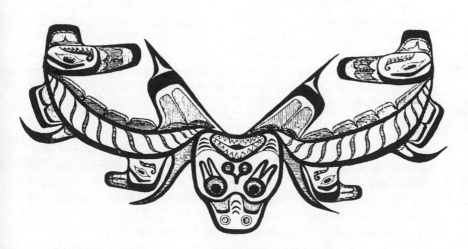

Figure 108

of objects in a scene, because the underlying visual conception was not bound to any particular aspect but referred to the object "as such." Since the intention, however, was to reproduce things as correctly and clearly as possible, certain rules for the combination of projective aspects had to be observed. The most characteristic aspects had to be chosen. They had to be combined in an organically correct way—for example, head and neck had to be placed symmetrically between the shoulders. The difference of aspect had to respect organic and perceptual subdivision—that is, a frontal eye could be put into a profile head because it represented a relatively independent entity, whereas a frontal nose or mouth was not acceptable in a profile face. Furthermore, a body, or part of a body, could be represented only once. There could be either a side view or a front view of one and the same object, but not both together. A side view from the left could not be combined with a side view from the right of the same thing.

Violations of these rules are found occasionally, even at fairly primitive levels. In children's drawings the combination of a frontal nose with a profile nose may occur at stages of transition from one form of representation to another. Genuine examples of this kind are found here and there as local inventions of limited range, often for playful, decorative purposes. Thus the American Indians solved the problem of how to present the characteristic side view and the frontal symmetry of an animal at the same time by splitting up the body into two side views, which were combined in a symmetrical whole and kept precarious contact with each other by sharing either the middle line of the back or the head or by cohering at the tip of the nose or the tail (Figure 108). Morin-Jean has shown that very similar forms, which he interprets as "monsters with double body and single head," occur in Oriental decorative art, on Greek vases and coins, and again on Romanesque capitals. All these examples, however, are fanciful exceptions from the general rule.

Modern art resembles early forms of representation in that it also combines views from several angles in the same whole, but it does so in a characteristically different way. The modern artist is heir to a period that had come to identify an object with its pictorial projection. The correctness of the projection seemed to guarantee the validity of the image. Later, in the nineteenth century, such representation was found to be one-sided, subjective, accidental—which at first was a cause for applause, later for apprehension. Although the fleeting images aptly reflected the passing and superficial experiences that had become typical for much Western living, the world represented by these images was alarmingly unsubstantial. Thus artists came to expose the fact that man, in his relationship to reality, had been sentenced to catching nothing but glimpses. None of these glimpses could stand for

the whole by itself, nor would all of them add up to anything better than a
bewildering agglomeration of contradictory views. As the artists were strug-
gling to recover the stable world of the innocent eye, they resorted to the
child's or the Egyptian's procedure, with the difference that, for example, in
a child's drawing of a glass of water (Figure 109*a*) the combination of side
view and top view in a symmetrical pattern expresses the solid completeness
of a trustworthy reality, whereas in Picasso's rendering of a saucepan (Figure
109*b*) front view and side view, roundness and angularity, left tilt and right
tilt, all coincide in a clashing contradiction. By uniting the front and the
side of a head, the artist made the picture more complete and therefore more
reliable; but he also forced together the placidity of the full face and the
dynamic directedness of the profile without suggesting an organic synthesis
of the two. His subject was the tension created by the fusion of the incompatible.

Figure 109

I must disagree with a current theory according to which the multiplicity
of projective views as such produces a dynamic effect. It has been suggested
that this method of representation requires the beholder to fly on the wings
of his mind from one perspective view to the other or to find himself at different locations simultaneously. This theory would seem to be incorrect
psychologically because it is based on the assumption that a picture creates
in the observer the illusion of finding himself in the spatial position required
by the projection represented in the picture. This is seldom true. Surely, in
viewing an Egyptian relief, the observer does not seem to perform a ninety-
degree swing when the eye passes from the profile head to the frontal chest
of a figure. Nor did the Egyptians conceive of a simultaneity of various
standpoints. Instead their pictures were as independent of any fixed point
of view as the visual conception they represented. When it comes to perspective art, it is true that we feel uncomfortable when looking at the photograph
of a baroque fresco painted to be seen overhead on the ceiling of a room.

Nevertheless we can view such a picture without the illusion of lying on our backs and looking upward. The same holds for less radical examples. Although, strictly speaking, a perspective picture is, and should look, "right" only from the one station point in which the artist found himself when he painted it, we nevertheless examine it freely from all directions and distances without being disturbed in the least by the fact that the perspective does not change in correspondence with the displacement of our point of observation. This occurs because the observer does not delude himself to the point of including himself in the space of the picture. Rather, he looks into the picture space from some location in his own separate environment. Therefore it is not surprising that, for example, the combination of a front view and a side view as such produces no dynamic effect or tension whatsoever. As long as the formal segregation of the units is clear enough, they will be seen simply as things of different orientation even though they may belong to one and the same object physically. Tension can occur only after it is created by visual means. When different views are fused into one pictorial unit, tension arises from the visual contradiction of one thing being one and another at the same time. The tension is strongest when the two views are fused most intimately, as, for example, in Picasso's head of a bull (Figure 110), in which

Figure 110

front and side appear within the same contour as an inseparable perceptual whole. In summary, the dynamic effect is not the result of either imaginary movements of the observer in relation to the picture or of the painted object in relation to the observer; instead, it is the result of the tension created by visual contradictions in the pictorial pattern itself.

Reduced Representation

Two examples—projective realism and certain aspects of modern art—have been cited to show how and why artistic form may deviate from elementary visual conception. A third phenomenon, to which earlier references have

been made, should now be discussed more explicitly—the tendency to limit
the representation of objects to a minimum of structural features. A typical
example would be a child's drawing. It is true that such limitation often
means a "stripping to the essentials," so that the omissions make it easier
rather than more difficult to identify the image. It is also true, however, that
when only few features of the object are taken over, there is more freedom
to simplify and enrich the composition independently of what the object
might demand and thus to produce a pattern that is difficult to identify
for anyone not familiar with the particular style of representation. The
procedures are variously described as geometric, ornamental, formalistic,
stylized, schematic, symbolic, and an enumeration of examples makes for
strange bedfellows. They can be found in early or primitive stages of artistic
development—that is, in the work of children, African and Australian
tribesmen, or American Indians—but they are also present in the Byzantine
style of Christian art, in Western modern art, in the products of schizophrenics, in so-called "doodles," and in the large realm of ornament and
decoration. The variety of these manifestations is such that at first glance
it seems hopeless to look for a similarity of psychical impulse that might
correspond to the similarity of form.

The patterns that result when representation is limited to few features
of the object are often simple, regular, symmetrical. Offhand there would
seem to be no compelling reason for this. Shape may be made more complicated by omissions. Instead, when the object releases its grip on the process
of representation, the tendency to simple form seizes the opportunity. Before
this psychological explanation was envisaged, the tendency to simple form
was rather puzzling to theorists. In the past century they were inclined to
account for it by pointing to regular shapes in nature that man was supposed
to have imitated—the disk of the sun, the symmetrical build of plant,
animal, and man himself. As an extreme example, Worringer cites an an-
thropologist who undertook to show by means of snapshots that the pattern
of the cross was derived from the shape of flying storks. Obviously, this
approach supplies no satisfactory answer, since it cannot explain why man
should have picked the regularly shaped percepts among the immensely
more frequent irregular ones. Occasionally the simple form of an image can
be derived in part from the medium in which it was executed—for example,
in basketry—but nothing like a generally valid answer derives from this
observation. In keeping with the previously reported psychological findings,
I adopt the hypothesis that regular, symmetrical, geometric shape results
when the tendency to simple structure is set free by a remoteness from the
multiplicity of nature. The reasons for this remoteness vary greatly, and so
correspondingly do the resulting patterns.

Children and Primitives

Why do children produce simple shape in their pictures? In Chapter IV, which deals with this question much more fully, I say that an artistic image is not merely a product of perception but also of representation, in which the process of finding form in a given stimulus repeats itself. Just as we perceive an object by organizing the raw material of the stimuli projected upon the retinas, so we represent a percept by inventing in the given medium a suitable formal pattern. It is this task of representation that accounts mainly for the simplicity of children's drawings. Although it is true that perception starts with simple over-all features (see p. 34), it cannot be denied that children acutely observe individual detail at an age at which their pictures are still limited to the bare elements. Surely children are not "remote" in the sense of lacking interest in the appearance of things around them. Their mastery of pictorial form, however, which enables them to express this interest, matures slowly. The first shapes to be acquired are the simplest ones, combined in simple figures. Gradually their visual understanding applies to more complex form, and with this increasing differentiation of the medium they become able to render subtler aspects of reality.

The products of young children are typical for the form that art takes at early stages of development, and the attempts of unskilled adults look rather similar. It is psychologically probable that, in any given culture, art grows from those same simple shapes toward more complex ones. The style of much so-called "primitive" art, however, cannot be explained by lack of skill or immaturity of concept. It often shows all the skill of eye and hand that a long tradition of craftsmanship will produce. There is a preference for symmetry and geometrically stylized form units, but the patterns thus built are anything but elementary. They clearly prove that the concept of form has reached a high level of complexity. Yet only a few basic features of objects are used for their representation. Again, as with children, it cannot be assumed for a moment that this remoteness is due to a lack of interest in the environment. In fact the primitive's acuteness of observation and faithfulness of memory are prodigiously superior to what is found in more advanced civilizations. There must be other reasons, which can be discovered by considering the functions of works of art in primitive cultures and the concepts of natural processes on which they are based.

If instead of taking it for granted that Western realism is the natural aim of all art we ask what purpose more realistic form would serve, we find that it would detract from the function of primitive images rather than support it. Typically, primitive art springs neither from detached curiosity nor from the "creative" response for its own sake. It is not made to produce pleasurable illusions. Primitive art is a practical instrument for the important business of daily living. It gives body to superhuman powers so that they may become partners to concrete intercourse. It replaces real objects, animals, or humans, and thus takes over their jobs of rendering all kinds of services. It records and transmits information. It makes it possible to exert "magic influences" upon creatures and things that are absent. Now what counts for all these operations is not the material existence of things but the effects that they exert or are exerted upon them. Modern natural science has accustomed us to thinking of many of these effects as physical events intimately connected with the make-up and behavior of matter. This view is of recent origin and quite different from a simpler concept that is found most purely in primitive science. We think that food is necessary because it contains certain physical substances our bodies absorb and exploit. To the primitive, food is the carrier of immaterial powers or forces whose vitalizing virtue is transferred to the eater. Disease is not caused by the physical action of germs, poisons, or temperature, but by a destructive "fluid" emitted by some hostile agency. It follows that, according to the primitive, the specific appearance and behavior of natural things, from which we gather information about the physical effects they are likely to have, are as irrelevant to their practical function as the shape and color of a book are to the content it conveys to us. Thus, for example, in the representation of animals the primitive limits himself to the enumeration of such features as limbs and organs, and uses geometrically clear-cut shape and pattern to identify their kind, function, importance, and mutual relationships as precisely as possible. He may use pictorial means also to express "physiognomic" qualities, such as the ferocity or friendliness of the animal. Realistic detail would obscure rather than clarify these relevant characteristics. (Similar principles of representation are found in our own civilization in the illustrations for medical treatises written before the advent of modern natural science.)

Withdrawal from Here and Now

Early stages of development make for simple shape. It is not possible, however, to turn this statement around and to assume that simple shape is always the product of an early stage. People often create elementary images, not because they have so far to go, but because they have so far withdrawn. An example may be found in Byzantine art, which was the result of a withdrawal from the most realistic style of representation the world had then seen. It is understandable that as long as realism was considered the natural climax of all artistic striving, the asceticism of early Christian art could be taken only as a deplorable symptom of decadence. The virtuosos of the late

Roman era had created the illusion of volume and depth, rendered the subtleties of color modulation, light, and texture; they had mastered foreshortening and caught the fleeting effects of gesture and facial expression. The
history of the mosaic in the first Christian centuries most dramatically illustrates the gradual abandonment of this pleasant sensuality. Art became the
servant of a state of mind that, in its extreme manifestations, condemned the
use of images altogether. Life on earth was considered a mere preparation for
life in heaven. The material body was the vessel of sin and suffering. Thus
visual art, instead of proclaiming the beauty and importance of physical
existence, used the body as a visual symbol of the spirit; by eliminating
volume and depth, by reducing the variety of color, by simplifying posture,
gesture, and expression, it succeeded in dematerializing man and world. The
symmetry of the composition represented the stability of the hierarchic
order created by the Church. By eliminating everything accidental and
momentary, elementary posture and gesture emphasized lasting validity.
And straight, simple shape expressed the strict discipline of an ascetic faith.

If the emphasis of simple form in early Christian art is understood as the
fitting expression of a remoteness from material activity and passion, its kinship with psychologically similar manifestations in very different areas will
become evident. Formalism has been described as an outstanding characteristic of the pictures produced by schizophrenics. Ornamental geometric patterns are elaborated with precision and care. Striking examples are the drawings made by the dancer Nijinsky during the years of his confinement in a
mental institution. If we inquire about the corresponding state of mind, we
find a freezing of feeling and passion accompanied by a withdrawal from
reality. A shell of glass seems to surround the schizophrenic. Life around him
appears as an alien and often threatening spectacle on a stage, which can be
watched but permits no give and take. The secluded intellect weaves fantastic cosmologies, systems of ideas, visions, and grandiose missionary projects. Since the sensory sources of natural form and meaning are clogged and
the vital passions dried up, formal organization remains, as it were, unmodulated. The tendency to simple shape operates unhampered in the void. The
result is order as such, with little left to be ordered. Remnants of thoughts
and experiences are organized, not according to their meaningful interaction
in the world of reality, but by purely formal similarities and symmetries.
There is visual "punning"—the fusion of heterogeneous contents on the
basis of external resemblance.

It is no accident that similar characteristics are found in the "doodles" of
persons whose minds are concentrated on some train of thought while the
sense of form directs the eyes and hands with no guiding idea or experience
left in control. Geometric shapes generate each other, sometimes adding up

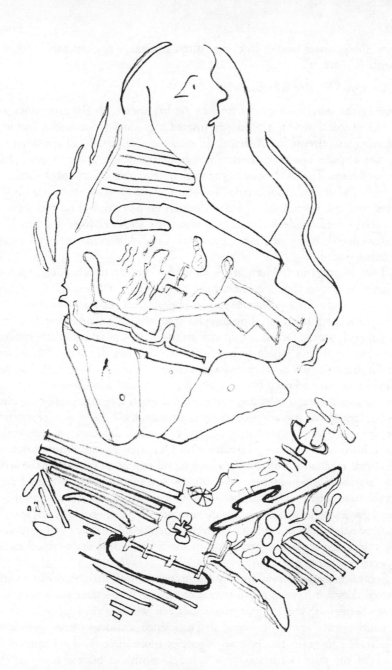

Figure III

to well-organized wholes but more often to chance agglomerations of elements (Figure III).

Geometric Shape in Modern Art

During the past few decades modern art has shown, in the representation of the physical world, a tendency toward a gradual reduction of features, reaching its extreme in "abstract" or "nonobjective" art. As in the other examples already discussed, remoteness from the object leads to geometric, stylized form. This is obvious in the work of the cubists. Some of the abstractionists (Malevich, Mondrian, Nicholson, Albers) work strictly with the ruler, and the inventions of Paul Klee can be described almost as an outgrowth of the Euclidean elements. Some artists, such as Moore and Lipchitz, prefer curved shapes of higher geometric order, but even there stylization remains evident.

The situation in modern art is somewhat similar to what happened in Byzantine art, in that our contemporaries too have renounced the skillful illusionism of their forebears. Again, withdrawal can be found as the underlying psychological cause. The complex state of affairs can be sketched only superficially; some factors are specific to the artist's position, others concern our civilization as a whole. It is well known that the Renaissance bestowed on the artist the doubtful gift of a new dignity. As a craftsman, he had fulfilled an established need in the affairs of government and Church. Now, the former useful citizen, who had endorsed and artistically interpreted the ideas and values of the community, became an outsider—the maker of cultural surplus goods to be stored in museums or used to demonstrate the wealth and refined taste of those who could afford luxuries. This exclusion from the economic mechanism of supply and demand tended to transform the artist into a self-centered observer. We can easily understand the effect of such detachment when we remember what happens when we attend a public or social gathering in which we take no interest. We hardly perceive the specific matter with which the group is actively concerned. We take in the sound of the voices, the impact of gestures—in short, the formal or "compositional" aspects of what is going on.

Such detached observation may lead to penetrating insight, because withdrawal does not have to mean retreat or refusal. A spectator steps back also to see better—that is, to gain the distance at which accidental detail drops out and essence reveals its broad shape. Science withdraws from individual appearance to grasp the primary agencies more directly. This immediate grasp of the pure essentials, for which Schopenhauer praised music as the highest of the arts, is attempted through the abstractness of the best modern painting and sculpture. The precision of geometric form aims more directly

at the hidden clockwork of nature, which more realistic styles represent indirectly by its manifestations in material things and happenings. The concentrated statement of these abstractions is valid as long as it retains the
sensory appeal of life that distinguishes a work of art from a scientific diagram.

The remoteness of modern art also manifests certain negative traits that
belong to our civilization as a whole. In comparing a highly integrated culture—for example, the European Middle Ages—with the present era, we
find that the collectively accepted body of philosophical and social ideas has
dissolved into an infinity of individual "schools." Basic principles of thought
have lost their direct impact. They have been split off from "practical life"
and made the exclusive concern of experts, philosophers, and priests. This
is a serious threat, because the main virtue of any genuine culture would
seem to be the capacity to experience the practical activities of living as
tangible manifestations of basic principles. As long as getting a drink of
water is felt—consciously or unconsciously—as obtaining sustenance from
nature or God, as long as man's privilege and fate are symbolized for him
in his labor, culture is safe. But when existence is limited to its specific material values, it ceases to be a symbol and thus loses the transparency on
which all art depends. The very essence of art is the unity of idea and material realization. I have spoken of the "overwhelming presence" of material
objects in realistic art, which obscures their metaphoric meaning. Surely
modern art is not materialistic; but some of its representatives are affected,
nevertheless, by the fatal split between idea and concrete existence. In particular there are certain "abstract" artists who have weakened their case and
cheapened their work by claiming that they were interested only in the
pleasure derived from "formal relationships." It is important to realize that
the identical mentality prevails in the auto salesman for whom a car is nothing but a marketable means of transportation and in the artist for whom
cubes and circles are only a tickle to the eye. In such examples, withdrawal
from meaning has been added to the withdrawal from the object.

The decisive point here is not whether or not the artist is consciously
intent on the symbolic representation of ideas. More often than not the
direct focusing on ideas leads to a shortcut, a neglect of the living substance
in which alone they can be realized artistically. What counts is that the
artist should be the kind of person to whom existence is the manifestation
of life and death, love and violence, harmony and disharmony, order and
disorder in whatever he sees and is and does; he should be unable to handle
the visual forces of shape or color without expressing by them the behavior
of those governing powers.

The alternative is play; for play means borrowing a life situation to use only its pleasurable aspects. It means borrowing the suspense, the thrill, and the delight of victory from fighting without accepting also the cause, the harm, and the pain. It means borrowing the pleasures of touch, warmth, and release from love without accepting the tie of the communion. It means borrowing the stimulation of sight and the easy peace of pattern without accepting the responsibility that goes with their significance. In art, just as everywhere else, play—the enjoyable privilege of the higher creatures— becomes immoral when it takes the place of the real thing.

A few words should be said here about "formalism." An artistic style cannot be accused of formalism only because it reduces representation and uses geometric form. Good modern art is anything but formalistic play. Some modern artists reduce the object to its bare essentials. Others take from it an elementary theme, which they develop to complete and sharpen it. They "orchestrate" it, enrich it by countermotifs, but they do not betray it. The formalist, instead, emancipates the medium from the content it is supposed to serve. He may allow pretty shape to gloss over drama—as, for example, Aubrey Beardsley, who represents the story of Salome and St. John through ornamental lace patterns. There is also the formalism of the disciples and imitators, who adopt a style neither required by nor congruous with their own experience.

Not all formalism springs from immaturity, shallowness, or irresponsibility. A deep-seated one-sidedness of the creator's outlook and needs may impose a pattern upon the object that narrows its nature unduly and thus distorts it. In some of van Gogh's late works, the violence of his diseased mind transforms the world into a conspicuous tissue of flames, so that the trees stop being trees and the houses and farmers become calligraphic brush strokes. Rather than submerging in the content, form steps between the beholder and the theme of the work. Certain artists today are compelled by a fear of surrender to force the exuberance of life into a strait jacket of geometry. Then formalism may be the expression of tragic human limitation. The art expression of schizophrenics carries formalism to a pathological extreme.

Ornament

What is an ornament?

Is it to be defined as a visual pattern that does not represent objects? Obviously not, because many ornaments do not consist of pure forms but use plants, animals, human figures, ribbons, knots. There is hardly any object in this world that has not appeared in ornaments. On the other hand, modern art has given us nonrepresentational patterns that are not ornaments. An abstract painting by Kandinsky and a square yard of wallpaper differ from each other in principle.

It seems more promising to attempt a distinction based on purpose or function. Shall I say that the work of art proper serves to represent and interpret a content whereas ornament does nothing of the sort but instead simply makes things look attractively opulent? There are several objections to this description. First of all, there cannot be a pattern that represents nothing. Any shape or color has expression; it carries a mood, shows the behavior of forces, and thus depicts something universal by its individual appearance. Therefore every ornament must have a content. Its content, however, is affected by its function. An ornament is almost always a part of something else. It is an attribute meant visually to interpret the character of a given object or situation or happening. It sets a mood; it helps define the rank and *raison d'être* of a tool, a piece of furniture, a room, a person, a ceremony.

Ornament is not limited to making things look pleasurable. This is but one of its functions, even though our present civilization—significantly enough—has come to consider it the only one. When ornament is applied to a living room, its subject matter and pattern may be suitably chosen to represent harmony, peace, healthy abundance, physical perfection. In a dance hall strong colors and aggressive shapes in active movement may be chosen in accordance with the stimulating effect of jazz, alcohol, dance rhythm. Pleasure is obtained because the character of the ornament fits the needs of the people in the given situation. But ornament serves also to explain to the eyes the nature of a church, a palace, a courtroom, a cemetery. It distinguishes youth from old age, a football player from a professor, a cocktail party from a board meeting. Being a part of something else, the ornament is specific in nature—that is, its content is limited to the particular character of its carrier.

Such a limitation is inadmissible in the work of art proper. Whereas the ornament is a part of the world in which we live, the work of art is an image of that world. For this reason the work of art must fulfill two conditions. It must be clearly separate from the world, and it must validly represent the total character of the world. The work of art is either quite independent of its environment, as, for example, in the neutral setting of a museum, where in contemplating the work we forget what is around it, or, as in a stage performance, it is the center and climax of a place designed to make us receive the view of the world that is represented in the work. As a representation and interpretation of reality, it cannot be one-sided and valid at the same time. The particular slant that the style of the work gives to the world view refreshes and deepens our concept of the whole rather than limiting it.

From this difference of function it also follows that the economy of the work of art is determined internally by the statement it presents, whereas the economy of the ornament is determined externally by the carrier it serves. Therefore, repetition is proper in the ornament; in the work of art even the exact replica of a part always goes with a difference of function. A work of art cannot say anything twice; ornament may apply a uniform character to a surface of any size.

Regularity and simplicity of shape result necessarily from the one-sidedness of content in ornament. The more limited the content, the fewer structural features are needed to express it; and, as I said earlier, the number of structural features determines the degree of simplicity. In the work of art, regularity of shape is used with great caution, because nature, which art undertakes to interpret, is characterized by the complex interaction of many forces. Reduction of complexity in the work of art is likely to produce a deadening effect: too much weight is given to order with not enough living substance to be ordered, whereas in ornament such one-sidedness is not only admissible but indispensable.

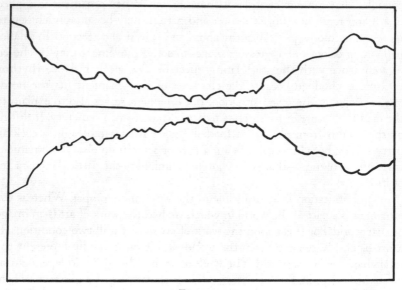

Figure 112

The interaction of many structural features breaks up the simplicity of shape and the regularity of arrangement. Thus strict symmetry is as rare in the work of art as it is frequent in ornament. Figure 112 gives the main outlines of a landscape by Ferdinand Hodler representing mountains reflected in a lake. The picture is completely symmetrical around a horizontal axis and almost symmetrical around the central vertical. By turning nature into ornament, the artist has obtained a chilly preponderance of order. William Hogarth was aware of this danger when he wrote: "It may be imagined that the greatest part of the effects of beauty results from the symmetry of parts in the object, which is beautiful: but I am very well persuaded this prevailing notion will soon appear to have little or no foundation." He said it was a constant rule of composition in painting to avoid regularity. It is true that, even in works in which an over-all symmetry is in keeping with the subject, its severity is always mitigated by enlivening deviations.

An exception that confirms the rule is the frequent use of strict symmetry and repetition for the purpose of obtaining a comic effect. Symmetrically arranged action occurs in comedy on the stage. As an example from literature, the humorous opening scene in Flaubert's novel *Bouvard et Pécuchet* may be cited. In this scene two men of the same profession walk at the same moment to the same park bench from opposite directions and in sitting down discover that they both have the habit of inscribing their names in their hats. The use of twins, the repetition of situations, the constant mannerisms in the behavior of a person, are all favorite "ornamental" devices in comedy because they uncover mechanical order—that is, lifelessness—in life, which is precisely what Henri Bergson has described as the business of all humor.

If we look at an ornamental design as though it were a work of art, the one-sidedness of its content and form makes it look empty and silly. If a work of art is used as an ornament, it will overstep its function and disturb the unity of the whole it has been asked to serve. There are imaginative craftsmen with whose products nothing is wrong except that they are presented as painting or sculpture when they would make excellent wallpapers or fountain figures. On the other hand, a good piece of sculpture, placed in the corner of a living room for decoration, may distort the whole setting by becoming a powerful center to which everything else must submit; a Beethoven symphony, when misused by alleged music lovers as a background for conversation, will take revenge by noisily breaking the rules of polite company.

A correction is necessary. Thus far, in order to drive my point home, I have described the difference between the "work of art" and the "ornament" as a dichotomy. As most dichotomies, this one is too much of a simplification. First of all, the term "work of art" has been used here only reluctantly and for lack of a better one, because it gives the misleading impression that ornament is less—or not at all—artistic. Actually there is only a difference of degree in the way a silver spoon, a baroque façade, or a painting by Watteau expresses the philosophy of life around the year 1700. An uninterrupted scale leads from the simplest ornamented tool to the full-fledged work of art, and along that scale there is gradual change in the three characteristics I have discussed: (1) the part of a whole becomes a self-contained whole; (2) one-sided representation becomes more and more complete; and (3) simple, regular form becomes more and more complex.

The amount and kind of representation ornament carries is dependent on the function of the object it serves. The simple form of a refrigerator, which is nothing more than a technical instrument for keeping food cool, will represent nothing more than cleanliness and the functions of solidly containing and protecting things. A spoon or a bowl participates in the social, philosophical, and religious implications of food received and enjoyed in company, and therefore should properly contribute by its appearance to making these overtones explicit. The buildings of a bank or a church should look their parts. In our civilization the handling of ornament betrays the decay and confusion of values. Some things are assigned values they do not have. The inherent value of others is no longer understood, and therefore inappropriate values are attached to them. The dwelling of an insurance company is considered a temple or a palace; the bathtub, having lost the high symbolism of its function that Pilate's washing bowl still possessed, is equipped with the lion feet of a throne. And "functionalism," in its disconcerting honesty, reveals that to modern man a house is nothing but a container of bodies, and a chair a support of the human anatomy.

In the arts our self-contained works of painting and sculpture are the products of a gradual—but probably not final—emancipation. My assertion that works of art must offer a "complete" image of the world applies to such isolated works. But paintings and statues can also be, in varying degrees, parts of a larger setting, and their place in the context will determine the amount and kind of representation they must contain. If we take an altar piece of the fourteenth century or an Egyptian stone figure out of its setting and treat it in a museum as a complete work, it reveals limitations of content and form that it must possess to be a part of a whole. When the emancipation of art started in the Renaissance, it began to interfere with the sure sense for the relation between the character and the function of the work. The mobile easel painting was a declaration of independence that tempted the mural painters. So much completeness and weight were given to wall paintings—for example, in Raphael's *Stanze* in the Vatican—that it was difficult to tell whether they were meant to sustain the walls of the room or whether the room was meant as a mere viewing box for the pictures. On the other hand, an element of "interior decoration," which dilutes the substance, can be found even in the works of some great masters, and only toward the end of the nineteenth century did art regain the uncompromising intensity that fitted its independence.

Architecture is instructive here. A building is a work of art, but at the same time it fulfills a specific function as a practical object in our life space. For this reason it is different in form from a piece of abstract sculpture. It expresses a *Weltanschauung,* and at the same time not only admits but favors strict symmetry and other devices of simple form. The regularity of shape reflects the specific role of the building as a solid, lasting instrument of protection and as a man-made, inorganic object, to be distinguished from nature and man—that is, from the other elements of the "complete" total scene.

The story of ornament is thus simply one aspect of the story of artistic form. Wherever integrated form exists, it is impossible to separate the shape of an object "itself" from the ornament "added" to it. The leaves are not an ornament of the tree. What is painted on a vase is no more and no less a part of the object itself than the shape given to it by the potter. The distinction becomes possible only when a split has occurred between the function of the object and the meaning of the form applied to it. In the last analysis the distinction is a symptom of art's having become an ornament of life rather than being a form of living.

One more aspect of this split is the artificial and harmful distinction between applied and pure—or fine—arts. The "designer" is prevented from realizing that to give form to an object means more than to make it pretty or "functional." He is driven to ignore the fact that he is responsible for significant representation in a similar if more limited way than the "artist." In turn, the painter and sculptor are compelled constantly to try for the supreme task of creating a valid image of the world—a frightening restriction, which certainly contributes to producing a state of restless anxiety in many of our artists. Human nature is not made to function always at the highest pitch, and the skill, discipline, and imagination that are needed to accomplish the deepest artistic revelation are better acquired under the more leisurely conditions of less engaging tasks. It is well known that even Renaissance artists did not object to designing jewelry, clothing, fountains, pageants, thus training their capacity for creating significant form but saving the substance of their deepest experience for the rare climax of their endeavors. Remnants of this procedure are found today where the healthy instinct of artists has remained relatively unimpaired; but when Matisse designs tapestries or Picasso paints on dishes, they risk having their products sternly scrutinized as "works of art" by unwise connoisseurs who complain about slightness and frivolity.

Reality and Form

Ornament has been discussed as one of the artistic areas in which patterns of regular, geometric shape appear. I began with the hypothesis that such shape results when the tendency to simple structure is set free by some kind of remoteness from the multiplicity of nature. Remoteness expresses itself by limiting the representation to particular features of reality—a limitation that is necessary with ornament because it serves to sustain the character of a specific object.

There is, then, a polarity between multiplicity of reality and simplicity of form in the sense that by withdrawing from one of these poles we approach the other. This polarity, however, should not be thought of as obtaining between world and man or object and subject. It is not a question of the rational mind approaching irrational matter. The polarity is found in both mind and nature. In both we observe constancy and change, repetition of the equal and diversity of the individual, the necessity of law and the irrationality of accident, the regularity of intended structure and the irregularity of its realization.

The cognitive faculties of the mind, of which artistic creation is one, search for order; but whereas science distills the order of law from the multiplicity of appearance, art uses appearance to show order in the multiplicity.

Order in nature can be discovered only when the capacity for grasping order is developed in the mind. The first stages of this process can be found in the art of children. Primitive art shows that the complexity of order in nature is represented only to the extent to which it is understood.

In exposing itself to the multiplicity of reality, the order-seeking mind faces an adventure. The attitude toward this enterprise lies always somewhere between two extremes. One extreme is the complete surrender of the quest for order to multiplicity for the sake of mere consumption; this is defeat by an excess of experience, exemplified artistically by illusionism. The other extreme is the complete withdrawal from multiplicity, which is defeat by an excess of order, exemplified artistically in the empty patterns of the schizophrenic. All styles of art seem to lie somewhere between the danger zones of these two poles. A strong need for order produces that predominance of relatively simple form that is found in the "classic" styles. Byzantine art is an example. A leaning toward the protean variety of nature makes for the complex form found in the "romantic" styles, of which projective realism is an example. Whatever the position of a work of art between the two poles, it must draw its lifeblood from the one and its wisdom from the other.

Imagination

When patterns of shape and color are considered as form—that is, as images representing some content—the question of artistic "invention" or "imagination" comes up, because it is by means of this gift that the artist creates form. Imagination is sometimes misunderstood as the invention of new subject matter. In that view an imaginative artist is one who creates situations of which no one else has thought before or which have never existed or never could exist. Actually the achievement of artistic imagination could be described more correctly as the finding of new form for old content, or—if the handy dichotomy of form and content is not used—as a fresh concept of an old subject. The invention of new things or situations is valuable only to the extent to which they serve to interpret an old—that is, universal—topic of human experience. In fact artistic imagination reveals itself most strikingly in the presentation of common objects and well-worn stories. There is more imagination in the way Titian paints a hand than in hundreds of surrealist nightmares depicted in a dull, conventional manner.

Imaginative form does not spring from the desire to offer "something new" but from the need to revive the old. It springs from the original view that an individual or culture will take spontaneously of the inner and outer world. Rather than distorting reality, imaginative form reaffirms the truth. It is the unsought result of the attempt to reproduce an experience as accurately as possible.

Imagination is indispensable, because a subject itself does not offer the form needed to represent it. Form must be invented; and since no form invented by someone else will fit an artist's own experience, he himself has to do the inventing. An impressive example can be found in the drawings of young children. When children start to experiment with shape and color, they are faced with the job of inventing a way in which the objects of their experiences can be represented in the given medium. Occasionally they are helped by watching other children's work, but essentially they are on their own. The wealth of original solutions they produce is all the more remarkable because their subject matter is most elementary. Figure 113 shows representations of the human figure copied at random from drawings by children at early stages of development. Certainly these children were not trying to be original, and yet the attempt to put down on paper what he sees makes each of them discover a new visual formula for the old subject. Every one of these drawings, which could easily be multiplied by the hundreds, respects the basic visual concept of the human body—as witnessed by the fact that it is understood by the beholder—and at the same time offers an interpretation that distinguishes it from the other drawings.

It is evident that the object itself dictates only a bare minimum of structural features, thus calling for "imagination" in the literal sense of the word—that is, the activity of making things into images. If we examine the drawings more closely, we find broad variations in many formal factors. The considerable differences in absolute size do not show in Figure 113. The relative size of parts—for example, that of the head in comparison with the rest of the body—varies considerably. Many different solutions are

Figure 113

found for the subdivision of the body. Not only the number of parts, but also the placing of border lines varies. Much detail and differentiation are in some, little in others. Round shapes and angular shapes, thin sticks and solid masses, juxtapositions and overlappings, all are used to represent the same object. But a mere enumeration of geometric differences does not do justice to the individuality of these drawings that is apparent in their over-all appearance. Some of the figures look stable and rational, others are carried away by reckless action. There are sensitive ones and crude ones, simple ones and subtly complex ones, plump ones and frail ones. Every one of them expresses a way of living, of being a person. The differences are due partly to the stage of development, partly to the individual character of the child, partly to the purpose of the drawing. Together these pictures demonstrate the abundant resources of pictorial imagination that are found in the average child until lack of encouragement, unsuitable teaching, and an uncongenial environment disperse them quickly enough in all but a fortunate few.

If so much imagination is displayed in the young child's rendering of the human frame, it is not surprising to find it immensely enriched in the adult artist's representation of life and nature. The artistic concept of an object or event is much more like the invention of a musical theme than like the activity of a photographic camera. It consists in the creation of a visual pattern that can be described as the final result of a whole series of embodiments. The abstract core of Michelangelo's *Creation of Adam* is, let us say, the interplay of an active and a receptive principle. This theme is embodied in the shape of a life-giving power that animates matter. On the next level of concretization is the story from the book of Genesis. This story must be made visual, which means making images of God, Adam, the setting, the action. For example, the Biblical motif of the breath of life is translated into a pictorially more concrete one: Adam raises his arm to meet the outstretched arm of God, through which enlivening energy seems to be conveyed. Finally, the scene must be adapted to pictorial representation in a plane of given proportions. At each of these levels, imagination is needed in order to invent a translation of one stage into the next. Let me hasten to say that I am not trying to describe the sequence of events that occurred in Michelangelo's mind. The creative process never takes place in any simple order, from the universal to the specific or the other way round. Its trail cannot be read off from the finished work. Whatever the sequence of steps, however, the process must have necessarily involved the above-mentioned tasks for the artist's imagination.

The solutions the artist chooses depends on such factors as who he is, what he wishes to say, in terms of what medium he is thinking. Van Gogh seizes upon the converging furrows of a field to obtain an intense display of energy through a subject that would have evoked calmer patterns in a serener artist. Grünewald, the colorist, invents for the theme of the Resurrection a gigantic orange aureole that glows in the black sky and contains the figure of Christ composed of moving reds and yellows.

A successful artistic solution is so compelling that it looks like the only possible realization of the subject. Different renditions of the same theme must be compared before the role of imagination can be truly appreciated. Systematic accounts of the various ways in which a particular subject has been represented have been given much too rarely. A recent example is Rudrauf's analysis of Annunciation pictures as "variations of a plastic theme." He shows how differently the famous encounter has been interpreted, depending on which moment of the event the artist chose and how his imagination distributed active and passive function, dominance and submission, and so on. Historic surveys, which follow a given theme through the ages, are more frequent. Among other things they show how occasionally an artist hits upon an image that embodies some basic subject with a spellbinding validity. The same story, the same composition, or the same posture lives on for centuries as an indelible contribution to man's visualization of his world.

La Source

Some of the wealth of imagination that goes into a masterwork can be apprehended by analyzing one such work of art in some detail. The chosen picture may easily give the impression of offering little more than an elementary theme presented in an obvious manner. La Source, painted by Ingres at the age of seventy-six in the year 1856, represents a girl standing upright in a frontal position and holding a water jug (Figure 114). At first sight it shows such qualities as lifelikeness, sensuousness, simplicity. Richard Muther notes that Ingres' nudes make the observer almost forget that he is looking at works of art. "An artist, who was a god, seems to have created naked human beings." We may well share this experience and at the same time ask: How lifelike is, for example, the posture of the figure? If we judge the girl as a person of flesh and blood, we may find that she is holding the jug in a painfully artificial way. This discovery comes as a surprise because to the eye her attitude was and is beautifully natural and simple. Within the two-dimensional world of the picture plane it presents a clear and logical solution. The girl, the jug, and the act of pouring are shown completely. They are lined up side by side in the plane with a thoroughly Egyptian need for clarity and neglect of realistic posture.

Thus the basic arrangement of the figure turns out to be anything but an obvious solution. To make the right arm take the detour around the

Figure 114

head and to "get away with it" required bold imagination. Then too the location, shape, and function of the jug evoke significant associations. Clearly, the body of the jug is an inverted likeness of its neighbor, the head of the girl. Not only are they similar in shape, but both have also one free, unobstructed flank that carries an ear (handle) whereas the other flank is slightly overlapped. Both are tilted to the left, and there is a correspondence between the flowing water and the flowing hair. This formal analogy serves, on the one hand, to underscore the faultless geometry of the human shape, but by inviting comparison it also stresses the differences. By contrast with the empty "face" of the jug, the features of the girl establish an even more conspicuous contact with the observer. At the same time, the jug openly permits the flow of the water whereas the girl's mouth is all but closed. This contrast is not limited to the face. The jug rhymes also with the body—it has uterine connotations—and again the resemblance stresses the fact that the vessel openly releases the stream whereas the lap is locked. In short, the picture plays on the theme of withheld but promised femininity.

Both aspects of this theme are developed in further formal inventions. The virginal refusal in the compression of the knees, the tight adherence of the arm to the head, and the grip of the hands are counteracted by the full exposure of the body. A similar antagonism can be found in the posture of the figure. Its over-all shape indicates a straight vertical axis of symmetry; but the symmetry is nowhere strictly fulfilled, except in the face, which is a small model of completed perfection. The arms, the breasts, the hips, the knees, and the feet are merely swinging variations of a potential symmetry (Figure 115). Similarly, the vertical is not actually realized anywhere; it merely results from the obliquities of smaller axes, which compensate each other. The direction changes at least five times in the axes of the head, the chest, the pelvis, the calves, and the feet. The straightness of the whole is made up of oscillating parts. It is the peace of life, not of death. There is in this wave movement of the body something truly waterlike, which puts the straight flow from the jug to shame. The still girl is more alive than the running water. The potential is stronger than the actual.

Looking further at the oblique central axes on which the body is built, we notice that these axes are short at the extremities and get larger toward the center. A crescendo of size leads from the head over the chest to the long expanse of belly and thighs, and the same is true for the approach from the feet over the calves to the center. This symmetry between top and bottom is enhanced by a decrescendo of pictorial "action" from the extremities toward the center. In both the top and the bottom areas there is an abundance of small units and angular breaks; there are crowding in detail and forward and backward movement in the depth dimension. This action dies down gradually as the units grow in size until beyond the gateways of the breasts and the knees all small motion is hushed, and in the center of the silent plane lies the closed sanctuary of the lap.

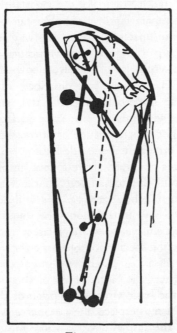

Figure 115

In the left contour of the figure from the shoulder downward, there are small curves leading to the large arc of the hip, followed again by curves of decreasing size in the calf, the ankle, and the foot. The left contour strongly contrasts with the right, which is nearly a straight perpendicular. This vertical is lengthened and strengthened by the raised right arm—a good example of the formal reinterpretation of the object, because this combined trunk and arm contour is a discovery, a new line, not foreseen in the basic visual concept of the human body. The right contour explicitly states the vertical that is only implied in the zigzag of the central axis. It embodies complete rest and perfect geometry, and thus fulfills a function similar to that of the face. The body, then, lies between pure statements of the two principles it unites in itself: the perfect calm of its right contour, and the undulating action of the left.

The natural symmetry of the body is replaced by a polarity of rest and motion. The invented symmetry of top and bottom, which I described earlier, contradicts organic build and in fact is checked by the over-all outline of the figure, which is a slim, tilted triangle formed by the raised elbow, the left hand, and the feet as corners. This triangle establishes a new, oblique central axis, which is quite weak and yet relieves the plumb line of the right contour of some of its rigidity by making it the slanted deviation from the axis of the triangle (compare Figure 74b). The tall triangle, which stands on a pointed corner, is in unstable balance. Its sway subtly adds to the life of the figure, without disturbing the basic verticality.

There is an oblique symmetry of the two elbows that does not coincide with, but belongs to, the triangle just described. Here is an element of angularity that is quite important in giving the "salt" of sharpness to a composition that otherwise might have suffered from the monotony of sweet curves. This slight hint at wedge or arrow shape helps to save the pattern of forces from ornamental one-sidedness.

A few of the features described above follow simply from the objective shape and construction of the human body, but a comparison of La Source with a Titian Venus or Michelangelo's David will demonstrate how little the bodies artists create have in common. The shape and posture patterns of organic form are most elusive. They are precise in their over-all framework of axes but rarely prescribe specific contours or colors. To make an image of these patterns, it is necessary to invent and impose upon them a compositional scheme that reflects the "intentions" of the artist and at the same time does not violate the basic visual conception of the model object. The remarkable fact about a masterpiece like La Source is that in looking at it we sense the effect of the formal devices whose meaning makes it such a complete representation of life and yet we may not be conscious of these devices at all. So masterfully are they blended into a whole of great over-all simplicity, and so organically is the compositional pattern derived from the subject, that we seem to see simple nature at the same time that we marvel at the depth and richness of the experience it conveys.

Visual Information

There is no such thing as the faithful copying of physical reality. As far as the human body is concerned, nature does not commit itself in its visual appearance to any particular pattern that can be correctly copied. Throughout the history of art, sculptors have used hundreds of different arrangements of planes to represent the human head, no one of which can be called more correct than the other. Every sculptor knows this fact from experience; any reader who does not believe it is invited to get some clay and a patient friend as a model and find out for himself that the natural object has a definite structural skeleton of axes but is elusive in the specific shape of surfaces. The same is true for color.

For this reason plaster casts, shadows on the wall, or photographs can be said to have shape only in a rough, over-all sense. They are shapeless for two reasons: because the contour or color of their units are often ambiguous, and because these units do not add up to configurations simple enough to be comprehensible to the eye. The surface formation of plaster casts is spongy and noncommittal; and if a photograph is examined for the clearly defined relationships found in paintings or sculpture, the picture seems to evaporate like an apparition.

We might think that mechanical recording by photography had super-seded the human draftsman where exact reproduction is required; but this is true only within limits. Photography is indeed more authentic in the rendition of a street scene, a natural habitat, a texture, a momentary expression. What counts in these situations is the accidental inventory and arrangement, the over-all quality, and the complete detail rather than formal precision. When pictures are to serve technological or scientific purposes—for example, illustrations of machines, microscopic organisms, surgical operations—the preference is for drawings or at least for photographs retouched by hand. The reason is that pictures give us the thing "itself" only by telling us about some of its properties—the characteristic outline of a bird, the color of a chemical, the number of geological layers. A medical illustration is meant to distinguish between smooth and rough texture, to show the relative size and position of organs, the network of blood vessels, the mechanism of a joint. A technological picture must give exact proportions and angles, the concavity or convexity of a given part, the difference between what is in front and what in the back, the distances between units. These properties are all we wish to know. This means, not only that the better picture is one that leaves out unnecessary detail and chooses telling characteristics, but also that the relevant facts must be unambiguously conveyed to the eye. This is done by means of perceptual factors, some of which are discussed in this book—for example, simplicity of shape, orderly grouping, clear overlapping, distinction of figure and ground, use of lighting and perspective to interpret spatial values. Precision of form is needed to communicate the visual characteristics of an object.

A draftsman charged with producing a faithful likeness of an electric clockwork or a frog's heart must invent a pattern that fits the object—exactly as the artist must do. And since producing a likeness means nothing but bringing out the relevant traits, it is not surprising that the draftsman must understand what these traits are. Biological, medical, or technological training is needed to make a usable reproduction of an object. Such knowl-edge will suggest to the artist an adequate perceptual pattern to be found in the object and applied to the picture. All reproduction is visual interpre-

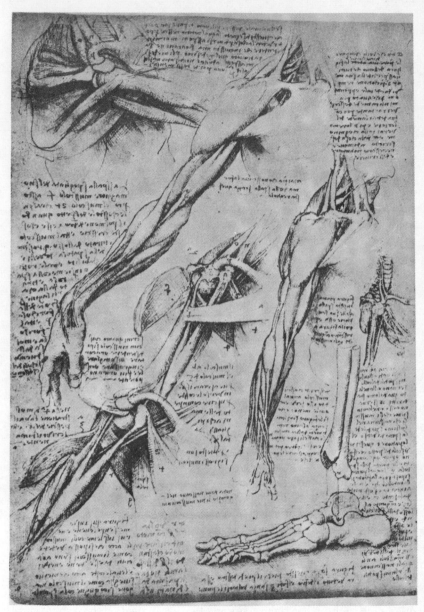

Figure 116

tation. The interpretations of the uninformed draftsman, based on nothing but what he can see at the moment, are likely to be wrong or vague. Leonardo da Vinci's scientific drawings are remarkable because he thoroughly understood the build and function of the things he was depicting and at the same time knew how to organize complex perceptual patterns with the greatest clarity (Figure 116).

The relationship between intellectual knowledge and visual representation is frequently misunderstood. Some theorists talk as though an abstract concept could be directly rendered in a picture; others deny that theoretical knowledge can do anything but disturb pictorial conception. The truth would seem to be that some abstract propositions can be translated into visual form and as such become a genuine part of a visual conception. Leonardo's statement "The neck has four movements, of which the first consists of raising, the second of lowering the face, the third of turning right or left, the fourth of bending the head right or left" does not in itself determine an image; but someone can use this bit of theory to look for the mechanisms of the four movements in the human body and thus articulate his visual concept of the neck.

The study of anatomy is valuable for the artist because it permits him to acquire a visual concept of things that cannot be seen directly but help to shape what can be seen. The human body is like a Christmas stocking stuffed with objects whose shapes make for bulges but cannot be discerned clearly because the bag smooths over the contours and hides everything that is not turned outward. Thus the shape of the bag is likely to look chaotic unless a previously acquired visual concept of what is inside makes the external marks meaningful. It then becomes possible to invent a pattern that interprets the outside in keeping with the inside. A person's observations at a given moment are always influenced—helped or hampered—by what he has seen and thought and learned before. All capacities of the mind should coöperate in the making of a picture, whatever its purpose.

Since representing an object means showing some of its properties, it follows that at times the purpose can be achieved best by greatly deviating from its "photographic" appearance. This is most evident in diagrams. For example, the pocket map of subway lines issued by the London Transport Corporation gives the needed information with the utmost clarity and at the same time delights the eye through the harmony of its design (Figure 117). This is achieved by renouncing all geographic detail except for the pertinent topological properties—that is, sequence of stops and interconnections. All roads are reduced to straight lines; all angles to the two simplest: ninety degrees and forty-five degrees. The map leaves out and distorts a great deal, and just because of this it is the best possible picture of what it wants

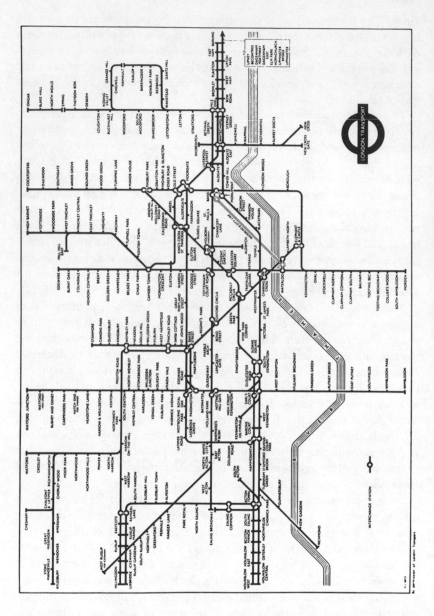

Figure 117

to show. As another example, Leonardo suggests: "When you have represented the bones of the hand and you wish to represent above this the
muscles which are joined with these bones make threads in place of muscles.
I say threads and not lines in order to know what muscle passes below or
above the other muscle, which thing cannot be shown with simple lines. . . ."
Here nothing but the points of attack and the crossings in space is to be
given. Rendition of the size and shape of the muscles would distract and
obstruct the view.

All this is very similar to what happens in art; the artist also does not try
to present the object "itself" but only some of its properties. If a person
actually approaches a human body or a tree with no other motive than to
copy "it"—and it is doubtful that before the nineteenth century anyone
has actually tried to, although almost everyone asserted that this was all he
was doing—he will be caught by accidental suggestions of shape and color
found through piecemeal observation. The result will be one of those ugly
wraiths of reality that do not belong to either science or art. The scientific
or technological drawing is made to transmit perceptual characteristics in
order to give information about corresponding physical traits of the things
depicted. The artist uses the same perceptual characteristics for the different
purpose of permitting the beholder to experience the expressive qualities of
a pattern of visual forces. The map maker may use blue and red to distinguish
the locations of water and land. A painter may do the same to produce a
tension between cold and warm.

There is a rule that the expression conveyed by any visual form will be
only as clear-cut as the perceptual features that carry it. A clearly curved
line will express the corresponding swing or gentleness with equal clarity;
but a line whose over-all structure is confusing to the eye cannot carry any
meaning. An artist may paint a picture in which a ferocious tiger is easily

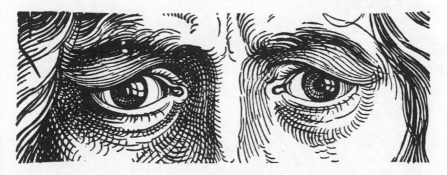

Figure 118

recognizable; but unless there is ferocity in the colors and lines the tiger will look taxidermic, and there can be no ferocity in the colors and lines unless the pertinent perceptual qualities are brought out with precision. Figure 118 is taken from a Dürer woodcut that shows Christ's face crowned with thorns. Notice that the perceptual definition of each element in itself and its relationship to the whole, as to direction, curvature, brightness, spatial position, give the eye the precise expression of anguish, which rests on such features as the heavy lid overhanging the staring pupil. Not often does artistic form offer such a simple weave of simple elements; but however complex the pattern of color, mass, or contour, it must in its own way have the precision of Dürer's lines to deliver its message.

IV   GROWTH

Recent progress in the field of the psychology of perception makes it possible to describe the artistic process more adequately. In the past an oversimplified concept of this process was based on a double application of what is known in philosophy as "naïve realism." According to this view, there is no difference between the physical object and its image perceived by the mind. The mind sees the object itself. Similarly, the work of the painter or the sculptor is considered simply a replica of the percept. Just as the table seen by the eye is supposed to be identical with the table as a physical object, so the picture of the table on the canvas is simply a repetition of the table the artist saw. At best the artist is able to "improve" reality or to enrich it with creatures of fantasy by leaving out or adding details, selecting suitable examples, rearranging the given order of things. As an example, Pliny's famous anecdote, so widely quoted in Renaissance treatises, may be cited. The Greek painter Zeuxis, unable to find any one woman beautiful enough to serve as a model for his painting of Helen of Troy, "inspected the maidens of the city naked and chose out five, whose peculiar beauties he proposed to reproduce in his picture."

The manipulations ascribed to the artist by this theory may be called "cosmetic," because in principle they could be performed just as well on the object itself. There is no notion of any basic difference between the world of reality and its image in paint or marble.

The approach was not basically changed by what optics and physiology contributed to a better understanding of the process of vision. It became clear that the physical object could no longer be identified with the image received by the eye; but the role of the physical object was taken over by its equally physical projection, and the conviction prevailed that a visual experience was identical in all its properties with the picture projected upon the retinae. Just as the retinal image of the table was complete in all its detail and distorted in size and shape by perspective, so the subjective percept of the table was assumed to be mechanically complete and perspectively deformed.

This theory encountered puzzling contradictions in the field of the arts. If spontaneous perception corresponded to the projective image, it was reasonable to expect that naive pictorial representation at early stages of development would tend toward completeness and perspective distortion. Modifications of the elementary experience would not be expected to occur until later when the maturer mind became free to elaborate the perceptual raw data. The opposite, however, was found to be true. Representation started genetically with highly simplified geometric patterns, and realism was the late and laboriously accomplished product of such sophisticated cultures as Hellenism and the Renaissance.

Why Do Children Draw That Way?

The early drawings of children show neither the detail nor the perspective deformations to be expected. What is the explanation? Since it was taken for granted that the drawings do not correspond to what the children actually see, a reason for the deviation had to be found. For example, it was suggested that children are technically unable to reproduce what they perceive—just as they cannot hit the bull's-eye with a gun because they lack the concentrated glance and the steady hand of an adult marksman, so their eyes and hands do not have the skill to hit the right lines with a pencil or brush. Now it is quite true that the drawings of young children show incomplete motor control. Their lines sometimes steer an erratic zigzag course and do not meet exactly where they should. Much of the time, however, the lines are accurate enough to indicate what the drawing is supposed to be like, particularly if many drawings of the same kind are compared. Moreover, at an early age the former imprecision of the stroke gives way to an exactness that is more than sufficient to show what the child is trying to do. There can be no doubt that none of these drawings is an unskillful attempt at projective realism. They all clearly try to do something else. The reader is invited to put a pencil in his mouth or between the toes of one of his feet and copy a realistic picture of a human ear. The lines may turn out to be so crooked as to be totally unrecognizable; but if the drawing is at all successful, it will still be basically different from the usual way in which the child draws an ear as two concentric circles. Thus lack of motor skill cannot explain the phenomenon.

Others have maintained that children make straight lines, circles, and ovals because these simple shapes are easier to draw. This is perfectly true, but does not indicate what mental process induces the children to identify the complex objects of reality with the very different geometric patterns.

Neither can lack of interest or careless observation be cited. I have referred earlier to the sharpness of children's observation. Whoever has seen the expression of breathless fascination in their eyes or the concentration they devote to their art work will agree that the explanation is unsatisfactory. It is true up to a certain age that if the child is asked to draw a man he will pay little attention to the particular man put in front of him as a model. This behavior, however, does not prove the child's incapacity or unwillingness to observe his environment; instead, it is due simply to the fact that fresh information is neither needed nor usable for what, in the opinion of the child, the drawing of a man is supposed to contain.

Then there are explanations that sound convincing but are really little more than a play with words, such as the assertion that children's pictures look the way they do because they are not copies but "symbols" of real things. The term "symbol" is used nowadays so generously that it can serve indiscriminately whenever one thing stands for another. For this reason it has no explanatory value. There is no way of telling whether the theory is right, wrong, or no theory at all.

The Intellectualistic Theory

The oldest—and even now most widespread—explanation of children's drawings is that since children are not drawing what they are assumed to see, some mental activity other than perception is responsible for the modification. It is evident that children limit themselves to representing the over-all qualities of objects, such as the straightness of legs, the roundness of a head, the symmetry of the human body. These are facts of generalized knowledge; hence the famous theory according to which "the child draws what he knows rather than what he sees." In substituting intellectual knowledge for sensory perception, the theory follows the kind of thinking that Helmholtz popularized in the 1860's. Helmholtz explained the "constancy" phenomena in perception—that is, the fact that we see objects according to their objective size, shape, color—as the effect of unconscious acts of judgment. According to him, persons obtain a "correct idea" of an object's actual properties through frequent experience; since the actual properties are what interests them for practical purposes, they come to overlook their own visual sensations and to replace them unconsciously by what they know to be true. In a similar intellectualistic vein children's drawings have been described by hundreds of investigators as representations of abstract concepts.

It is a strange theory indeed; for it is well known that a main characteristic of the mind at early stages of its development is its thorough dependence upon sensory experiences. To the young mind, things are what they look like, sound like, move like, or smell like. Of course children also think and solve problems. They also generalize because their biological interest, like that of all creatures, is in the typical rather than in the unique; but this thinking, problem solving, and generalizing goes on largely within the perceptual sphere itself rather than at the level of intellectual abstractions. For example, the child learns how to keep his upright body in balance without formulating any abstract rules on the subject. He learns to distinguish men from women without isolating their distinctive traits by induction. Abstract intellectual concepts referring to concrete facts are likely to be very few in children, considering how rare they are in adults of our Western culture. An example of such a concept might be the fiveness in the statement "a hand has five fingers." The visual concept of a hand usually contains the radial spreading out of fingers without specification of their number, and in a picture of the hand the correctness of the number is usually ascertained by counting. Here, then, a visual fact is known mainly or exclusively by means of the intellect, which is called upon for the purpose of correct picturing. Another example: my memory image of my uncle John may not contain the information on what side he parts his hair; but I may remember from a conversation the words "Uncle John parts his hair on the right side," and in drawing a portrait of him from memory I shall supply by conceptual knowledge what my visual knowledge fails to offer.

We need only mention such examples to realize how untypical they are. It is also significant that they refer to facts that are visually undistinguished, such as numbers above three or four or the difference between right and left. Most of the time man, child, and animal rely on visual knowledge. Parents are taller than children, men wear pants, a face has two eyes above the mouth, the human body looks symmetrical from the front—all these facts are known visually, even though words also may be available to express them. There is certainly no evidence that young children possess the rather advanced intellectual concepts necessary to think abstractly of symmetry, proportion, or rectangularity. According to the intellectualistic theory, the child, in drawing the picture of a human head, relies on his knowledge of the words "a head is round" and draws the roundness rather than a head. But even if the child possessed the intellectual concept of roundness, the theory would fail to answer the question "Where did he derive the circular shape by which roundness can be adequately represented?"

The theory has been applied not only to children's drawings but to any kind of highly formalized, "geometric" art, particularly that of primitive peoples. And since it could not be very well asserted that all art was derived from nonvisual concepts, the theory led to the contention there existed two artistic procedures that were different from each other in principle. Children, Neolithic painters, American Indians, and African tribesmen worked from intellectual abstractions; whereas Paleolithic cave dwellers, Pompeian muralists, and Europeans during and after the Renaissance represented what they saw with their eyes. This absurd dichotomy was one of the main drawbacks of the theory, for it obscured the essential fact that well-defined form, which is so prominent in the work of many primitives, is indispensable and exactly of the same kind in any "realistic" representation that deserves the name of art. A child's figure is no more a "schema" than one by Rubens—it is only less differentiated.

On the other hand, the theory neglects the fact that perceptual observation contributes to even highly stylized work. When a South Sea Islander paints the sea moved by the wind as a rectangle striped with oblique parallel lines, essentials of the model's visual structure are rendered in a simplified but entirely un-"symbolic" manner. And, as I have pointed out, Albrecht Dürer's highly naturalistic studies of hands, faces, and birds' wings are works of art only because the innumerable strokes and shapes form well-organized, even though complex, patterns that interpret the subject.

It will be apparent now that the formula "The child draws what he knows rather than what he sees" would be invalid even if the word "knowledge" had a connotation different from what the promoters of the theory meant and mean by it—if it referred to visual rather than to intellectual knowledge. Even then the theory would be misleading, because it would still assume between perceiving and knowing a dichotomy that is alien to the perceptual and the artistic processes. It is in the very nature of these processes that every particular act of seeing involves the grasping of over-all features—that is, of generalities. Conversely, all visual knowledge, as remote as it may be from any individual percept, requires the concrete realization of certain structural features. The indivisible unity of visual perceiving and visual knowledge is basic for the processes I am discussing. Therefore any theory that attempts to account for the "geometric" styles of representation by asserting that they spring from a procedure different in principle from that of so-called realistic art is a misinterpretation.

They Draw What They See

The intellectualistic theory would hardly have monopolized the writings on the subject for such a long time if another theory had been available as an alternative. To work out a better explanation it was necessary: first, to revise the conventional psychology of perception; second, to become aware of the conditions imposed on artistic representation by the particular medium in which it occurs.

The first point requires only recapitulation of what I have said before.

Vision as experience differs in two important ways from "photographic" projection. It does not register the complete set of individual detail contained in the retinal image. Evidence has been given to show that perception does not start from particulars, which are secondarily processed into abstractions by the intellect, but from generalities. "Triangularity" is a primary percept, not a secondary concept. The distinction between individual triangles comes later, not earlier. Doggishness is perceived earlier than the particular character of any one dog. If this is true we can expect early artistic representations, based on naïve observation, to be concerned with generalities—that is, with simple, over-all structural features. Which is exactly what happens.

Another distinction between retinal image and visual experience concerns perspective. The image created by the lenses of the eyes shows the projective distortions of a photograph, whereas in vision not much influence of distance on size and shape is observed. Most objects are seen approximately in their objective shape and size: a rectangular suitcase looks rectangular, and distant persons in a room look no smaller than those close to the observer. It is quite difficult for many persons to visualize the working of perspective, even when it is demonstrated to them with a yardstick. Recently an intelligent and sensitive young college student, to whom I tried to show the oblique shape of a box on the table, finally hid her face in sudden terror and exclaimed: "It is true—how horrible!" If perspective plays so small a part in vision, the same can be expected to happen in early stages of art, which is exactly what we find.

Children and primitives draw generalities and undistorted shape precisely because they draw what they see. But this is not the whole answer. Unquestionably children see more than they draw. At an age at which they easily tell one person from another and notice the smallest change in a familiar object, their pictures are still quite undifferentiated. The reasons must be sought in the process of representation.

In fact, as soon as we apply our revised notion of visual perception, a peculiar difficulty arises. I said that perception consists in the formation of perceptual concepts, in the grasping of integral features of structure. Thus, seeing the shape of a human head means seeing its roundness. Obviously roundness is not a tangible perceptual thing. It is not materialized in any one head or in any number of heads. There are shapes that represent roundness to perfection, such as circles or spheres. Even these shapes stand for roundness rather than being it, and a head is neither a circle nor a sphere. In other words, if I want to represent the roundness of an object such as the head, I cannot use the shapes actually given in it but must find or invent a shape that will satisfactorily embody the visual generality "roundness" in the world of tangible things. If the child makes a circle stand for a head, that circle is not given to him in the object. It is a genuine invention, an impressive achievement, at which the child arrives only after laborious experimentation.

Something similar is true for color. The color of most objects is anything but uniform in space or time; nor is it identical in different specimens of the same group of things. The color the child gives to the trees in his pictures is hardly a specific shade of green selected from the hundreds of hues to be found in trees. It is a color that matches the over-all impression given by trees. Again we are not dealing with an imitation but an invention.

The Medium

The circle and the sphere represent the structural features of roundness most purely by their curved boundaries and centric symmetry. The same task can be accomplished, more or less perfectly, by various patterns. The one chosen will depend upon the medium. For example, a pencil creates objects by circumscribing their shape with a line. A brush, which creates broader spots, may suggest a disk-shaped patch of color. In the medium of clay or stone the best equivalent of roundness is a sphere. A dancer will create it by running a circular path, spinning around his own axis, or by arranging a group of dancers in a circle. In a medium that does not yield curved shape, roundness may be expressed by straightness. Figure 119 shows a snake pursuing a frog as represented in a basketry pattern by the Indians of British Guiana.

Figure 119

A shape that expresses roundness best in one medium may not do so in another. A circle or disk may be the perfect solution in the flat picture plane. In three-dimensional sculpture, however, circle and disk are combinations of roundness and flatness and thus imperfect representations of roundness. A black-and-white apple becomes "colorless" when transferred from a monochromatic lithograph to an oil painting. In a painting by Degas a motionless dancer is a suitable representation of a moving dancer, but in a film or on the stage a motionless dancer would not be in movement but paralyzed.

Furthermore, the term "medium" refers not only to the physical properties of the material but to the style of representation used by a specific culture or individual artist. A flat-looking patch of color may be a human head in the essentially two-dimensional world of Matisse; but the same patch would look flat instead of round in one of Caravaggio's strongly three-dimensional paintings. In a cubist statue by Lipchitz a cube may be a head, but the same

cube would be a block of inorganic matter in a work of Ródin. Figure 120
shows Picasso's drawing *The End of a Monster.* The way in which the
head of the monster is drawn serves in other works by the same artist to
represent undistorted, nonmonstrous shape (compare the bull of Figure 110).
There is no contradiction in this fact. A pattern that produces a monster in
a relatively realistic picture may stand for "straight" anatomy in a work that
applies the same manner of distortion to everything.

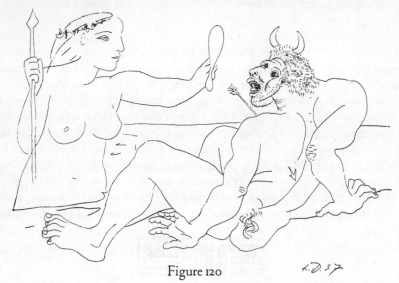

Figure 120

Representation never produces a replica of the object but its structural
equivalent in a given medium. Apart from other reasons, this is true because
replication is possible only if the object is duplicated in its own medium.
Anywhere else there are considerable differences between model and image.
Some of these are so common that we are hardly aware of them. We do not
notice, let alone resent, the fact that most images are smaller or larger than
the things they stand for. We accept without questioning a flat picture for
a round body or a bunch of lines for a solid object. This is not an esoteric
convention thought up by artists but common usage everywhere in life.
Scale models, line drawings on blackboards, or road maps deviate most
strongly from the objects they depict. The young child spontaneously discovers and accepts the fact that a visual object on paper can stand for an
enormously different one in nature, provided it is its structural equivalent
in the given medium. I shall presently demonstrate the unerring logic and
consistency of the child in this matter.

The psychological reason for this striking phenomenon would seem to be,
in the first place, that in human perceiving and thinking similarity is not

based on piecemeal identity but on the correspondence of essential structural features; secondly, that an unspoiled mind spontaneously understands any given object according to the laws of its context.

It takes a great deal of "spoiling" before we come to think that representation is not only an imitation of the object but also of its medium, so that we expect a painting not to look like a painting but like physical space, and a statue not like a piece of stone but like a living body of flesh and blood. This unquestionably less intelligent concept of representation, far from being natural to man, is a late product of the particular civilization in which we happen to have lived for a while.

Representational Concepts

Earlier I spoke of "perceptual concepts," by which I meant the over-all structural properties that are grasped in vision. Now I must consider also "representational concepts"—that is, the conception of the form by which the perceived structure of the object can be represented with the properties of a given medium. Representational concepts find their external manifestation in the work of the pencil, the brush, the chisel.

The formation of representational concepts, more than anything else, distinguishes the artist from the non-artist. Does the artist experience world and life differently from the ordinary man? There is no good reason to think so. He must be deeply concerned with—and impressed by—these experiences. He also must have the wisdom of finding significance in individual occurrences by understanding them as symbols of universal truth. These qualities are indispensable, but they are not limited to artists. The artist's privilege is the capacity to apprehend the nature and meaning of an experience in terms of a given medium and thus make it tangible. The non-artist is left "speechless" by the fruits of his sensitive wisdom. He cannot congeal them in adequate form. He can express *himself,* more or less articulately, but not his experience. In the moments in which a human being is an artist, he finds shape for the bodiless structure of what he has felt. "For rhyme can beat a measure out of trouble."

Why do some landscapes, anecdotes, or gestures "ring the bell"? Because they suggest, in some particular medium, significant form for a relevant truth. In search of such telling experiences, the artist will look around with the eyes of the painter, the sculptor, the dancer, or the poet, responding to what fits his form. On a walk through the fields a photographer may look at the world with camera eyes and react only to what will "come" photographically. The artist is not always an artist. Matisse was once asked whether a tomato looked to him when he ate it as it did when he painted it. "No," he replied, "when I eat it I see it like everybody else." The ability to capture the "sense" of the tomato in pictorial form distinguishes the response of the painter from the frustrating, shapeless gasping with which the non-artist reacts to what may be a very similar experience.

The formation of adequate representational concepts makes the artist. In this sense I would answer in the affirmative the old question whether Raphael would have been an artist if he had been born without hands. It cannot be maintained, however, that the representational concept always precedes the actual realization of the work. The medium itself is a powerful source of inspiration. It often supplies form elements that turn out to be usable for the expression of experience. There is nothing illegitimate about a rhyme suggesting a content, and there are great artists—for example, Paul Klee—of whom it is tempting to say that their ideas sprang primarily from the medium. But what counts is not the chronology of steps in the process of creation. If in the final product a valid content has found adequate form, the goal has been attained.

Perhaps it is necessary to point out again that by using the term "concept" I am not subscribing to the intellectualistic theory of the artistic process. Neither perception nor representation in a given medium is based on intellectual abstraction. Nothing but our particular one-sided tradition suggests that concepts are formed only by the intellect. All the cognitive instruments of the mind operate by grasping over-all features of a phenomenon or a group of phenomena through form patterns of a medium. The medium may consist of the stock of "perceptual categories" or the shape patterns of a means of representation or the abstractions of the intellect. The word "concept" refers to an operation that may occur in any kind of cognition; it does not reduce all cognition to intellectual processes.

The nature of representation is illustrated most simply and clearly in the drawings of young children. For this reason, this chapter will deal in detail with the development of their work. Throughout the analysis, however, the true subject will be the growth of artistic form in general, even though it will not be possible here explicitly to refer to the larger subject. In particular, striking similarities between the art work of children and of peoples at early stages of artistic development ("primitive art") have been demonstrated. This kind of comparison is not popular today because of a fashion of thought according to which it is more scientific to talk about differences than about similarities. Undoubtedly there are considerable differences of various kinds between the art work of the child and the adult; but it would seem that there is no way of understanding differences anywhere as long as the common ground has not been determined. In fact, I can think of no essential factor in art or artistic creation of which the seed is not recognizable in the work of children. The following investigation deals with some of these factors.

The example of children's drawings makes it particularly evident that pictorial representations cannot be described and understood simply by their distance from the object they purport to portray. Rather must they be related, on the one hand, to the experience they reflect and, on the other, to the medium in which they are done. The representation offers a structural equivalent of the experience that gave rise to it, but the particular concrete form in which that equivalent appears cannot be derived only from the object. It is also determined by the medium.

Credit is due Gustaf Britsch for having been the first to demonstrate systematically that pictorial form grows organically according to definite rules of its own, from the simplest to more and more complex patterns, in a process of gradual differentiation. Britsch showed the inadequacy of the realistic approach, which found in children's drawings nothing but charming imperfection and which could deal with the phases of their development only in terms of increasing "correctness." Being an art educator, Britsch did not avail himself of the psychology of perception, but his findings support and are supported by the newer trends in that field. Like many pioneers, Britsch seems to have carried his revolutionary ideas to the opposite extreme. As far as can be determined from the writings that have been published under his name, there is little room in his analysis for the influence of the perceived object upon pictorial form. To him the development of form was a self-contained mental process of unfolding, similar to the growth of a plant. This very one-sidedness makes his presentation all the more impressive; and as I try to describe some phases of formal development as an interplay of perceptual and representational concepts, I acknowledge that I am proceeding from the base laid by Britsch.

Drawing as Motion

The eye and the hand are the father and mother of artistic activity. Thus far I have said a great deal about the influence of the eye but only little about that of the hand. Drawing, painting, and modeling are a part of human motor behavior, and they may be assumed to have developed from two older and more general kinds of such behavior—physiognomic and descriptive movement.

Physiognomic movement is the component of bodily activity that spontaneously reflects the nature of the given personality as well as that of the particular experience at the given moment. The habitual firmness or weakness, confidence or timidity of a person is expressed in his movements. At the same time his bodily behavior will reveal whether he is interested or bored, happy or sad at this particular minute.

Descriptive movements are deliberate gestures meant to represent perceptual qualities. We may use our hands and arms, often supported by the entire body, to show how large or small, fast or slow, round or angular, far or close something is or was or could be. Such gestures may refer to concrete objects or events—such as mice or mountains or the encounter between two people—but also figuratively to the bigness of a task, the remoteness of a possibility, or a clash of opinions. It seems permissible to assume that the activity of deliberate artistic representation has its motor source in descriptive movement. The hand that traces the shape of an animal in the air during a conversation is not far from fixating this trace in the sand or on a wall.

Gestures often describe the shape of objects by their outlines, and it is for this reason that representation by outline seems to be the simplest psychologically and most natural technique for making an image by hand. The filling of a surface with paint or the modeling or carving of an object involves movements that may lead to the desired shape but are not in themselves an imitation of that shape. They serve visual representation more indirectly than the drawing of outlines, which in its beginnings is little more than recorded gesture.

In fact the child begins his pictorial activities by making lines. To what extent this is apparent in the resulting product depends on the tool. Pencil scribbles look like lines. Brush scribbles look less so; but even if the first effort consists in smearing the content of a medicine bottle on the bathroom wall, the result must be described as lines because it is brought about by linear, one-dimensional strokes.

The first scribbles are not intended as representation, but rather as presentation—that is, they involve the exciting experience of bringing about something visible that was not there before. This interest in the visible product for its own sake—the earliest signs of which may be found in chimpanzees' whitewashing their cages with lumps of white clay—remains alive in all art.

There is need for abundant movement in children, and thus drawing starts as gamboling on paper. Shape, range, and orientation of the strokes are determined by the mechanical construction of arm and hand as well as by the child's temperament and mood. The visible effect, however, soon attracts his attention. Among the things he learns immediately is the important fact that lines can add up to patches—in other words, that one-dimensional motion may produce two-dimensional masses. This basic trick may be put to little use for a while, once representation—with its emphasis on contour—has set in, but the art of daubing comes back as the "painterly" approach, particularly in the work with crayons and brushes.

The Primordial Circle

To see organized form emerge in the scribbles of children is to watch one of the miracles of nature. The observer cannot help being reminded of another process of creation, the shaping of cosmic whirls and spheres from amorphous matter in the universe. Circular shapes gradually appear in the clouds of zigzag strokes. At first they are rotations—traces of the corresponding arm movement. They show the smoothing or simplification of curves that always comes with motor training. Any manual operation arrives after a while at fluent motions of simple shape. Horses will turn the familiar corner of the barnyard gate in a perfect curve. The rounded paths of rats running angular mazes and the beautiful spirals described by a swarm of pigeons in the air are further examples of such motor skill. The history of writing shows that curves replace angles and continuity replaces discontinuity as the slow production of inscriptions gives way to rapid cursive. The lever construction of the human body favors curved motion. The arm pivots around the shoulder joint, and subtler rotation is provided by the elbow, the wrist, the fingers. Thus the first rotations indicate organization of motor behavior according to the principle of simplicity.

The same principle also favors the priority of circular shape visually. The circle, with its centric symmetry, which does not single out any one direction, is the simplest visual pattern. We know that perception spontaneously tends toward roundness when the stimulus gives it leeway to do so. The perfection of circular shape attracts attention. For example, the roundness of the pupil makes the animal eye one of the most striking visual phenomena in nature. A dummy eye on the wing of a butterfly simulates the presence of a strong adversary, and in reptiles, fish, and birds elaborate camouflage devices hide the revealing disks of the pupils. Experiments by Charlotte Rice have shown that young children often pick the circles from a collection of different shapes even though they have been asked to look for diamonds. The perceptual preference for the simplicity of round shape expresses itself genetically in the priority of circles in children's drawings.

As visual control begins to dominate the motor impulse, the unruly rotation changes to a single, more or less well defined outline, clearly understandable to the eye. To be able to make—all by himself—something so clear, so orderly, and perfect must be an extraordinary experience for the child. In fact he tries it again and again, working with evident pleasure and concentration and producing a great number of what adults may dismiss as "repetitions." The circle, with its simple variations, offers probably as many opportunities for exciting experimentation to the child as the female body does to Matisse.

Line, the prime element of the child's work, must be considered a tremendous abstraction by the realist. "There are no lines in nature," he points out. Lines are indeed highly abstract if we view drawings merely in comparison to "photographic" reality. However, if we understand representation to be the creation of a structural equivalent rather than a mechanical duplication, and if we remember that line is produced by a motor act in a pictorial medium, we find that the one-dimensional trace is the eminently concrete and direct rendering of perceived shape.

The handling of line is full of adventure. It soon reveals its double character. A line may be a self-contained visual object, which is seen as lying on top of a homogeneous ground (as indicated in schematic section in Figure 121*a*). But as soon as a line or a combination of lines embraces an area, its character changes radically and it becomes an outline or contour. It is now the boundary of a two-dimensional surface that lies on top of a throughgoing ground. The line's relationship to the neighboring surfaces has ceased to be symmetrical. It now belongs to the inner surface but is still independent of the outer (Figure 121*b*).

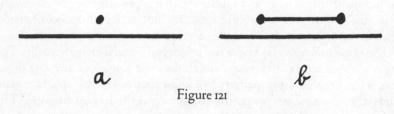

Figure 121

The inner area gives the impression of greater density; it looks more solid, whereas the ground is looser, less limited to a given, stable plane. This impression may seem to be nothing but a carry-over from our experience with physical objects, which are seen against the empty space of their surroundings. Experiments suggest, however, that it is more likely to derive from physiological factors underlying the perceptual process itself, quite independently of previous experience. These experiments have shown that the area within the contour offers greater resistance to the appearance of a visual object projected upon it with gradually increasing strength than does the outer ground—that is, it takes stronger light to make the object barely visible inside the contour. Other experiments have proved that visual objects will shrink in size when their image falls on an area of the retina upon which an outline figure had been projected earlier. Thus the perceived density or cohesiveness of the surrounded area does not seem to be due to mere assumptions based on past experience.

To the grown-up artist the motor act that produces the drawing is merely a means to an end. In the child the derivation of drawing from gesticulation can still be discerned, for the child continues for a few years to count the motor act as part of the representation. Figure 122 shows a man working in the garden, as drawn by a four-year-old girl. The whirl at the right depicts a lawn mower, not only because the rotating lines render the characteristic

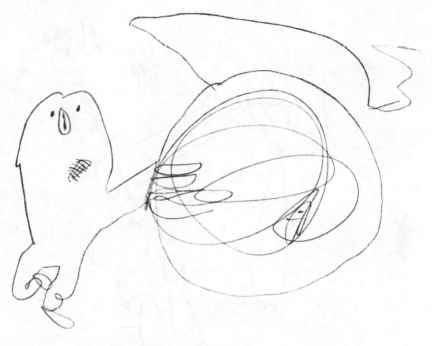

Figure 122

motion of the machine visually, but because the child's arm did so during the drawing. In the same way the sequence in which different parts of an object are drawn is significant for the child even though in the picture nothing of it shows. For example, at early stages the figure is often drawn first and then later dressed with suitable coats and pants. Feeble-minded and weak-sighted children in particular are sometimes satisfied with the mere time connection, in the act of drawing, of items that belong together. They do not bother to render this connection visually on paper, but spread the eyes, the ears, the mouth, and the nose of the face over the paper in almost random disorder.

There is no reason to assume that the child discovers the shape of the circle mainly by imitating round objects he has observed. The tendency to simple shape in visual and motor behavior is likely to play a leading part in the process. Even so, all perceptual experience interacts, and as the circle emerges on paper it establishes contact with the similar shape of objects perceived in the environment. Neither does all drawing spring from the desire to portray things; nor are only round objects portrayed by means of the circle.

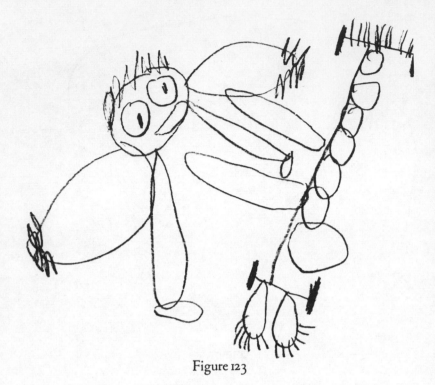

Figure 123

Once the child has, during the early explorations of the new medium, hit upon the idea that the things he is making can be used as pictures of other things, the circle serves to represent almost any object at all, such as a human figure, a house, a car, a book—even the teeth of a saw, as may be seen in Figure 123, a drawing by a five-year-old. It would be mistaken to say that the child neglects or misrepresents the shape of these objects, because only to the eyes of adults is he picturing them as round. Actually, intended roundness does not exist before other shapes, such as straightness or angularity, are available. At the stage of the circle, shape is not yet differentiated at all. The circle does not stand for roundness, but only for the more general quality of "thingness"—that is, for the compactness of a solid object, which is distinguished from the nondescript ground.

The Law of Differentiation

We are dealing here with a first example of what I shall call the law of differentiation. According to this law, a perceptual feature will be rendered in the simplest possible way as long as it is not yet differentiated. The circle is the

Figure 124

simplest possible shape available in the pictorial medium. Until shape becomes differentiated, the circle does not stand for roundness, but for any
shape at all and none in particular. In adult thinking and representation also
objects are often represented by dots, circles, or spheres when their actual
shape is unknown or irrelevant to the purpose. This is true for our conception
of the smallest particles in nuclear physics as well as for the notions of the
Greek atomists. Spheres, disks, and rings figure prominently in early theories
about the shape of the earth and the universe, not so much on the basis of
observation as because unknown shape or spatial relationships are represented
in the simplest way possible.

At any stage of human thinking the law of simplicity will make a conceived shape remain as undifferentiated as the object for which the shape
stands will permit it. A parallel from another area of psychology may be
found in the development of language. Apart from exclamations the early
speech of children consists mostly of nouns. It would be erroneous to conclude from this that the child is more interested in objects than in happenings. Rather do these nouns represent "one-word sentences" that stand for
questions, demands, and reports at a stage at which the verbal statement has
not yet been differentiated into several different words. Person, object, and
action are still represented as an undivided entity through one word.

The early circles, then, precede the portraying of specific shape. As the
next step in the development from the simple to the more complex, basic
combinations of circles may be mentioned. Figure 124 is an example of how
the child experiments with placing circles concentrically or a number of
small ones into one larger. "Containing" is probably the simplest spatial
relationship between pictorial units that the child learns to master. At the
most elementary level, two concentric circles may be used to represent an
ear with its hole or a head with its face. Later elaborations of the container
theme serve to show people in a house or train, food on a plate, bodies surrounded by dress.

Concentric circles do not yet involve differentiation of shape or direction.
A short step leads to sunburst patterns, in which straight lines or oblongs
irradiate from a central circle or a combination of concentric circles. The pattern may be used as a free design (Figure 125a); at various levels of differentiation it may recur as a flower (b), a tree with leaves (c), the headdress of an
Indian (d), a pond surrounded by plants (e), a tree with branches (f), a head
with hair (g), a hand with its fingers (h), the sun with a core of fire or a
lamp with its bulb in the center (i), a running man (k). Here is a good illustration of how a formal pattern, once it has been acquired, will be used—
more or less identically—to describe different objects of corresponding structure. For example, Figure 125i, the inner circle painted red, the outer yellow,

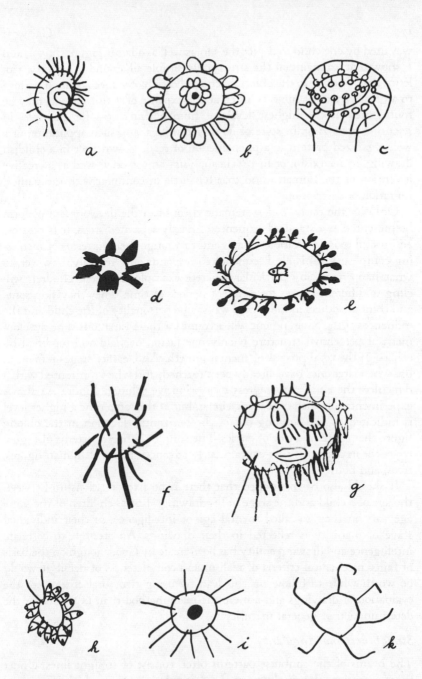

Figure 125

was used by one child to depict the sun as well as a lamp. Figure 125*g*, *h*, and *k* show that, to maintain the structurally simple all-around symmetry, violence may be done to the object. Such application of a once acquired pattern to a great variety of subjects, often at the expense of verisimilitude, may be found even at the highest levels of human thinking—for example, in scientific theorizing. In spite of its shortcomings, any such application of a well-organized pattern to a phenomenon of reality—whether in a childish drawing, in Marxism, or in psychoanalysis—must be viewed as a creative invention of the human mind that has little in common with mechanical imitation or description.

Only for the purpose of systematic theory can the development of form be presented as a standard sequence of neatly separated steps. It is possible and useful to isolate various phases and to arrange them in terms of increasing complexity. This ideal sequence corresponds only roughly, however, to what happens in any particular concrete example. Different children will cling to different phases for different periods of time. They may skip some and combine others in individual ways. The personality of the child and the influences of the environment will account for these variations. The development of perceptual structure is only one factor, overlaid and modified by others, in the total process of mental growth. Also, earlier stages remain in use when later ones have already been reached; and when confronted with a difficulty, the child may regress to a primitive solution. Figure 124 shows experimentation with concentric circles, but at the same time a higher level is indicated by the singling out of the horizontal direction in the oblong figure that contains a row of circles. The simple sunburst patterns of Figure 125 occur in drawings that contain fairly advanced forms of human figures, trees, and houses.

It should also be mentioned that there is no fixed relationship between the age of a child and the stage of his drawings. Just as children of the same age vary in their so-called mental age or intelligence, so their individual stage of maturity is reflected in their drawings. An attempt to correlate intelligence and drawing ability has been made by Goodenough on the basis of fairly mechanical criteria of realism and completeness of detail. It would be worth while to follow up this lead by using structural criteria for the evaluation of drawings and a more adequate method than I.Q. tests for the determination of general maturity.

Straightness and Angularity

The beams of the sunburst patterns often consist of straight lines. Under these conditions the singling out of a particular direction, which is involved in the conception of the straight line, is compensated by the symmetrical distribution of many lines covering all directions equally. In this sense the sunburst does not yet go much beyond the stage of the circle. It should also be noticed that single straight lines are rarely used to represent solids. They generally serve as appendages of an outlined figure. Rays are attached to the central circle, or arms and legs are attached to the body. Kerschensteiner, who examined a large number of children's drawings, claims never to have found a "stick man," whose trunk consisted of a straight line. This, he says, seems to be an artifact of adults. Apparently a drawing must contain at least one two-dimensional unit in order to convey the solidity of "thingness" in a way satisfactory to the child. Oval oblongs are used early to combine solidity with "directedness"—for example, in the representation of the human or animal body.

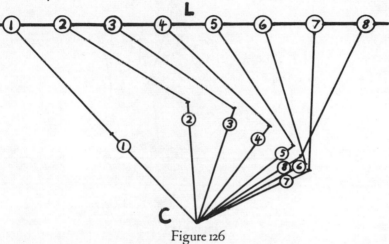

Figure 126

The straight line is essentially a product of man, created because of its mechanical advantages in building and its visual simplicity. Delacroix notes in his journal that the straight line, the regular serpentine, and the parallels, straight or curved, "never occur in nature; they exist only in the brain of man. Where men do employ them, the elements gnaw them away." The human body does not contain straight lines, and to produce one in a drawing we must go through a complex motor process. Figure 126 schematically indicates the intricate changes of speed, angle, and direction that are necessary if a jointed lever (pivoting around point C) is to trace a straight line (L) at even speed. To produce a reasonably straight line is difficult for the child. The fact that nevertheless he uses it so often shows how greatly he values its visual simplicity.

Straight lines are rigid and stiff when compared with curved ones. For

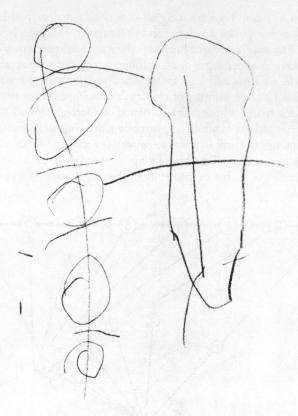

Figure 127

Figure 128

Figure 129

this reason the straight legs, arms, or fingers of early drawings are sometimes misinterpreted as symptoms of a rigid personality or as means for expressing a momentary sensation of "freezing up"—for example, in fear. Such diagnoses should be considered only when straightness continues to dominate beyond the stage at which rounded lines have been or should be mastered. Curved lines are visually less simple than straight ones. (I am not speaking here of circular or oval contours.) As long as "directedness" is undifferentiated, it is represented by the straight line as the simplest available structure. The adult, peeping from his own world into that of the child, must keep in mind that straightness assumes its specific meaning only when non-straightness has been acquired.

Misinterpretations of early stages in terms of later ones are frequent in the history of art. Wölfflin warns that the "rigidity" of archaic representations must not be judged as though later *"Formmöglichkeiten"* (resources of form) had already been known at the time. "All effects are relative. The same form does not mean the same thing at all times. The meaning of the vertical in classical portraits differs from that in the portraits of the primitives. Here it is the only form of representation; there it is set off from other possibilities and thus acquires its particular expression."

The same is true for the earliest way of showing difference of direction. The adult, particularly when he is a child psychologist, is tempted to interpret outstretched arms (Figure 129) as a gesture of despair, a declaration of bankruptcy. Actually they are nothing but the visually most clear-cut representation of the fact that there is a difference of direction between the arms and the body from which they issue. As long as difference of direction is undifferentiated, it is rendered in the structurally most simple form—as a right-angular relationship. Figure 127 shows a four-year-old's experimentation with the newly acquired device in its combination with circle and oblong.

The vertical-horizontal relationship goes a long way in refining the child's pictures of human figures, animals, and trees. The simple "dog" of Figure 128 is built entirely in this spatial system. Figure 129, *Mother and Daughter,* illustrates the consistency with which an intricate theme is subjected to a given law of form. The over-all construction of the two figures clings strictly to the two main directions, and the design of dress, socks, and shoes, as well as the teeth and the dignified wrinkles on the forehead that distinguish the mother from the daughter, obey the law with equally severe visual logic. Many an artist would have reason to envy the incorruptible discipline imposed by the child upon reality and the clarity with which he interprets an involved subject. The drawing can also serve to show how earlier stages survive when higher ones are already attained. To represent the hair the child has fallen back to the disorganized motions of the scribble stage, using half-controlled zigzag and spiral forms. Circles and sunbursts appear in cheeks, eyes, and the mother's right hand, and the right arm seems to indicate the transition from rectangular relationship to the higher level of bent shapes, which is not yet attained otherwise. Finally, Figure 130, copied from a more complex crayon picture in color, will demonstrate how one and the same form device—the vertical-horizontal T pattern—is used ingeniously to render two very different things: the neck and body of the girl and the traffic-light pole. Only a large number of examples could give an idea of the inexhaustible wealth of formal inventions that children draw from the simple vertical-horizontal relationship, every one of them surprisingly new and at the same time faithful to the basic concept of the object.

Like all pictorial devices, the vertical-horizontal relationship is at first worked out within isolated units and applied later to the total picture space. In early drawings an internally well-organized figure may float in space, totally unrelated to other figures or the picture plane. In Figure 130 the entire drawing, including the rectangular boundaries of the sheet of paper on which it is made, is spatially integrated. The uprights of figures, trees, and poles are seen in relation to the horizontal ground. The picture has become

Figure 130

a visual unity, in which each detail holds its clearly defined place in the whole.

Obliqueness

Once the child has attained visual mastery of the simplest angular relationship, he becomes able to tackle the more complex problem of oblique directions. At first the diagonals are added to the vertical and horizontal. Later more subtle angular relations are explored. The right angle now becomes a specific case, with specific meaning. The example of this development may be used to discuss a more general question. Why exactly does the child's drawing ability grow from stage to stage? As mentioned before, Britsch, who tended to neglect the representational aspect of art, seems to have thought of structural differentiation as a spontaneous, internally motivated process, similar to the growth of a plant. At the other extreme is the more familiar view according to which the child's pictures will become more faithful as his manual skill and power of observation increase. The first may be called an "introverted" theory, the second an "extroverted" one. It seems necessary to combine them to a less one-sided description. The activity of drawing in itself may well contain an incentive to differentiation. It is not absurd to assume that a hypothetical person who never saw anything of the world except his drawing paper would nevertheless proceed from simpler to more complex "designs," motivated solely by the results of his formal experimentation. A child will not proceed to the rendering of oblique relationships before he has fully mastered the vertical-horizontal stage, unless premature complexity is imposed upon his work by art teachers or other authorities. On the other hand, it can easily be observed that children grope for higher stages of differentiation because they are dissatisfied with the limitations of the lower ones. For a while they will keep the human figure within the vertical-horizontal scheme, untroubled by the fact that this allows no distinction between a running person and one standing at rest. Later the ambiguity of his work becomes unsatisfactory to him. He wishes to make a distinction in his picture where there is one in the objects he is portraying. Motion, in particular, is of such vital importance to the child that he derives

Figure 131

great pleasure from being able to make things run or move. Thus differentiation is greatly enhanced by the child's urge to overcome ambiguous representation. One by one these ambiguities occur to him as they enter the range of his growing visual comprehension. The same phenomenon can be observed in the history of art.

Oblique relationships are applied gradually to everything the child draws, and help to make his representation richer, more alive, more lifelike, and more specific. This can be seen by a comparison of Figures 131 and 132. They are traced from two drawings made by the same child—one about a year earlier than the other. Figure 131 shows two separate details of the earlier drawing; Figure 132, a part of the later. The earlier tree and flower are done with the limited means of vertical-horizontal angularity—clearly and consistently. But the later tree is more interesting to the eye; it looks more like a tree, and the constant application of oblique angles conveys the impression of a live, growing thing. In the earlier giraffe the main relationship between body and neck is still rendered by a right angle. There is the beginning of obliqueness in the legs, but it looks as though this refinement is due not so much to the girl's observation of the animal as to lack of space. As often happens, her spatial planning had been insufficient, so that by the time she arrived at the legs she found that she had to squeeze them in sideways if they were not to cross the base line of the ground. A year later the animal walks freely in a more lively, more specifically giraffelike attitude. The differentiation not only applies to the directional relationship between separate parts but makes also for a more subtle rendering of shape. Undulating

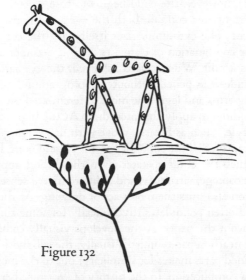

Figure 132

ground has replaced the straight line. From the point of view of the later drawing, the earlier is stiff and schematic. But it must be realized that within the universe of the earlier drawing there was not yet any room for stiffness, and also that the later stage could not have been truly mastered if the earlier had not preceded it.

The Fusion of Parts

Throughout the early stages differentiation of shape is accomplished mainly by the addition of self-contained elements. For example, the child proceeds from the earliest representation of the human figure as a circle by adding straight lines, oblongs, or other units. Each of these units is a geometrically simple, well-defined form. They are connected by equally simple directional relationships, at first vertical-horizontal, later oblique. The construction of relatively complex whole patterns is made possible by the combination of several simple ones. This does not mean that at the early stage the child has no integrated concept of the total object. The symmetry and unity of the whole and the planning of proportion show that—within certain limits— the child shapes the parts with a view to their final place in the total pattern. But the analytic method makes it possible for him to deal at every particular moment with a simple shape or direction.

Some children carry this procedure to highly intricate combinations, building the whole on a hierarchy of detail, which reveals careful observation. The result is anything but poor.

After a while, however, the child begins to fuse several units by a common, more differentiated contour. Both the eye and the hand contribute to this development. The eye familiarizes itself with the complex form that results from the combination of elements until it becomes able to conceive of the whole as a unit. When this is achieved, the eye safely controls the outline as it guides the pencil without stopping around an entire human figure, including arms and legs. The more differentiated the conception, the more skill is required to apply this procedure. At the highest levels, masters of the "linear style," such as Picasso, move with unswerving precision along a contour that captures all the subtleties of muscle and bone. But considering the basis on which the child operates, even the earliest applications of the method require courage, virtuosity, and a differentiated sense of shape.

Contour fusion also suits the motor act of drawing. At the scribble stage, the child's hand often pendulates rhythmically for some time without lifting the pencil from the paper. As he develops visually controlled form, he begins to make neatly separate units. Visually, the subdivision of the whole into clearly defined parts makes for simplicity; but to the moving hand, any interruption is a complication. In the history of writing, there was a change from the detached capital letters of monumental inscriptions to the fluently connected curves of the cursive script, in which the hand was allowed to win over the eye for the sake of speed. Similarly the child, with increasing facility, favors the continuous flow of line. Figure 133, a horse, drawn by a five-year-old boy, has the elegance of a businessman's signature. The extent to which the individual draftsman permits the motor factor to influence shape depends considerably on the relationship between spontaneously expressed temperament and rational control in his personality. (This can be shown convincingly in the graphological analysis of handwritings.)

The two fishes (Figures 134 and 135) are taken from drawings made by one child at different times. In the earlier picture only a first hint of fusion can be observed in the jagged fins. Otherwise the body is constructed out of geometrically simple elements in vertical-horizontal relationship. Later the

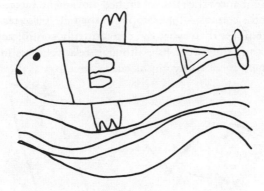

Figure 134

Figure 135

entire outline is given in one bold, uninterrupted sweep. It will be seen that this procedure enhances the effect of unified movement, favors oblique direction, and smooths corners—for example, in the tail. It also tends to produce shapes more complex than what the eye can truly control and understand at this stage; thus the earlier fish, although relatively less interesting and sprightly, is more successfully organized.

Figure 133

The snowball fight of Figure 136, drawn even later by the same child, shows how the experimentation with more differentiated shape enables the child after a while to modify the basic static shape of individual body units. Movement is no longer limited to the relative spatial orientation of different parts, but the trunk is bent in itself. At this stage, the child copes more convincingly with figures sitting on chairs, riding horseback, or climbing trees. Even beyond the bending lies the deformation of shape that is employed in foreshortening. This final differentiation, however, is so sophisticated that it is rarely accomplished spontaneously, except in the simple cases of circles, squares, or rectangles.

The transition from a combination of constant elements to one internally structured unit has parallels in other activities of the mind. In language, for example, it marks the psychological difference between the English method of declension, which adds prepositions to unchangeable nouns, and the more complex Latin way of inflecting the noun within its own body. Primitive thinking conceives of soul, passion, or disease as separate entities added to, or subtracted from, the unchangeable unit of the body or mind; whereas more highly differentiated reasoning describes them as fused with or produced by the internal functioning of the body or mind itself. In our time we are witnessing the transition from more primitive "atomistic thinking," which interprets natural phenomena through interrelations between constant elements, to the gestalt conception of integrated whole processes. The musician might be reminded of the change from the melodic sequences of

Figure 136

constant tones, different from each other only in duration and pitch location, to the harmonic system of internally changeable chords, which have developed from the vertical combination of elements.

Size

Like the other factors that have been discussed, size is at first undifferentiated. The law of differentiation will make us expect that size relationships are represented first in the structurally simplest way—that is, by equality. In fact the units of a pictorial context are conceived of as equal in size until a need for differentiation arises. Keeping this in mind, we shall not ask the traditional question: "Why do the size relationships in some representations not correspond to reality?"; rather we shall ask: "What makes children arrive at giving different sizes to the objects in their pictures?"

Perceptual identity depends relatively little on size. The shape and orientation of an object remain unimpaired by a change of size. It is a mere "transposition," in the musical sense of the word. Just as, within broad limits, it makes no difference to most listeners in what key a piece of music is performed, so a change of visual size often remains unobserved. A more direct parallel can be found in what musicians call "augmentation" or "diminution": a theme remains recognizable even though the speed of its presentation—that is, its temporal size—is changed. The basic irrelevance of visual size is shown most strikingly by the fact that we are usually unaware of the constant perspective change of size in the objects of our environment. As far as images are concerned, nobody protests against an inch-high photograph of a human being or against a gigantic statue. A television screen looks small in the living room, but we need only to concentrate on it for a while and it becomes an acceptable frame for "real" persons and buildings.

Therefore it is not surprising that the need for "correct" size relationships in pictures is weak. Even in the mature art of medieval book illustrations, castles and people are frequently of about the same size. In the pictorial statement "Man walks toward house" the two objects carry equal weight as long as there is no reason for distinction. If, for example, the man is to stand in the doorway or look out of a window, he must become smaller than the building; but even then the size difference does not generally go beyond what is needed to make the relative function of man and building visually clear. No attempt is made to match the real difference in size. Figure 137 is taken from one of the tapestries at the cathedral of Angers illustrating the Revelation of St. John. In the scene of the earthquake the human figures are drawn at a scale that would make them considerably taller than the build-

Figure 137

ings. In this way even the faces of the figures who are almost completely hidden by the collapsing buildings are large enough to hold their own visually against the buildings. In the interest of unity and coherence, artists tend to keep size intervals small. The more equal in size pictorial units are, the more compellingly are they grouped together by the rule of similarity of size. It is almost impossible to establish a direct visual relationship between a human figure and a high building if both are drawn to scale; either the figure becomes a tiny appendage of the house, instead of playing the role of a partner in a relationship between two objects, or the whole statement has no visual unity. Where such great size differences are desirable, artists generally connect the large and the small units of their compositions by others of intermediate size, thus bridging the gap.

The psychological and artistic aspects of size have little to do with metrically correct replication. It seems safe to say that differences in size are very rarely introduced for the sake of faithful imitation only. They appear when functional relations of a spatial, emotional, or symbolic nature require it. Psychologically this is a good example of what Piaget means by his thesis "Space is topological before it is Euclidean." Early spatial conceptions deal with qualitative relationships rather than with measurements.

Figure 138

The child, then, starts with the undifferentiated phase, in which sizes are equal. This is true even for the size relationship of parts within one and the same object, although differentiation imposes itself first in these closely knit functional contexts. Figure 138 gives a particularly pure example. Head, trunk, and limbs are equivalent parts, still undifferentiated in size. Usually the phenomenon is less obvious, but Lowenfeld has drawn attention to the many examples in which a face is as big as a car, a house is no taller than a child, hands are no smaller than heads, or flowers reach to the hips of a person. He interprets such representations in the traditional way by assuming that proportions would be "correct" unless some other factor interfered. This factor he believes to be the subjective value attributed by the child to certain objects, which therefore are drawn "too large." He asserts, for example, that in a drawing, *Horse Bothered by Flies,* the fly is given roughly the size of the horse's head because of its importance for the child. If, instead of thinking in adult terms, we consider the genetic process, the fact that the fly is drawn *smaller* than the horse is what requires an explanation.

True, the history of art offers examples of importance being expressed by size. In Egyptian reliefs persons in authority, such as gods, kings, or parents, are often at least twice as large as their inferiors. In the early drawings of children, however, such an explanation can be applied only with caution. For example, they frequently contain human figures with very large heads. It seems natural to speculate that this is true because the head is the most important part of the body. Looking at another person means looking mostly at his face; in our own bodies we localize the "self" in our heads, somewhere between the eyes. Also, the face contains so many important organs that it takes plenty of space to accommodate them. On the other hand, however, it must be remembered that the head is the leftover from the original circle, from which the more differentiated human figure was developed by secondary additions. This process lingers on in the child's concept for some time. He starts his drawing by making a large circle, often placed in the middle of the paper, so that the "hindmost is left to the devil"—condemned to squeezing into whatever space remains. As long as size is undifferentiated, it is often handled arbitrarily. Just as at the stage of undifferentiated shape, the circle—holding the field without competition—is drawn less carefully than later when it is to be distinguished from other shapes, so undifferentiated size often results in things being drawn indiscriminately large or small because the difference does not yet count. Under these conditions it is difficult in any particular picture to be sure that an object has been made large because of its importance.

The factor of size is connected with that of distance. The need for a simple and clear picture requires the child neatly to separate visual objects from each other. They must not be allowed to mingle, because this would greatly complicate the visual structure. When young children are asked to copy geometrical figures that touch each other or overlap, they typically eliminate such contact and leave space between the units. At the undifferentiated stage there is a standard distance, which—from the realistic point of view—looks sometimes too small and sometimes too large, depending on the subject matter. For the sake of clarity the distance is always ample, even where a close connection is to be represented. Hence the overlong arms that reach from object to object, bridging over the required large distance. Contact between parts of an object is accomplished rather early—for example, arms and legs attached to the body—but the closeness or superposition of different objects remains visually uncomfortable for some time.

The Misnamed Tadpoles

Perhaps the most striking case of misinterpretation due to realistic bias is the case of the "tadpole" figures, called *hommes têtards* by the French writers and *Kopffüssler* by the Germans. The popular view is that in these very frequent drawings the child leaves out the trunk entirely and erroneously attaches the arms to the head or the legs. Figures 139 and 140, drawn by four-year-olds, show some of these mysterious creatures. Various theories have been offered. The child was believed to overlook or forget the body or even to "repress" it for reasons of modesty. If we look at the genetic process, we discover that no such explanation is pertinent, because in these drawings the trunk actually is not left out.

Figure 139

It will be recalled that at the earliest stage the circle stands for the total human figure, just as it stands for so many other complete objects. Later, shape is differentiated through the addition of appendages. For example, in Figure 141, an eight-year-old boy's drawing of a church, the original circle is still clearly discernible. In the human figure the original meaning of the circle is gradually limited by the additions. There are essentially two types.

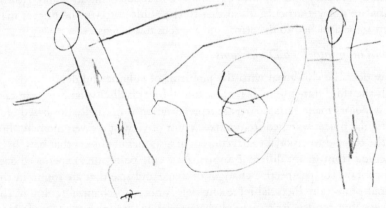

Figure 140

In Figure 139 the circle functions as an undifferentiated representation of head and trunk. Therefore the child is entirely consistent in attaching legs and arms to it. Only to adults does the picture look as though something had been left out. The circle is often extended to an egg-shaped oblong, which may contain the features of a face in its upper part or indications of clothing in the lower. Figure 140 illustrates the other type. In the center is a house with two fish in it, at the right a cowboy, and at the left a cow. The cowboy has one stomach, and the cow has two. These stomachs are useful

for our purpose, because they show that here the two parallel vertical lines
are an undifferentiated representation of trunk and legs whereas the circle
has become limited to being a head. The arms are attached where they belong—to the verticals. The double function of the line as self-contained unit
and as contour (see page 168) is not yet clearly differentiated. The two

Figure 141

verticals are contours (trunk) and self-contained units (legs) at the same
time. It may be added that a similar lack of differentiation of shape is often
evident in the way other parts of the body are represented. The features of
the face may be drawn as a single circle, contained in the larger circle of the
head, before they split up into eyes, nose, and mouth; and in Figure 138 the
limbs are not yet articulated, so that to the adult observer the fingers may
seem to be attached to the arms, and the toes to the legs.

Translation into Two Dimensions

How does the child deal with the problems of volume and depth—that is,
with the third dimension? It may be useful for this discussion first to restate
a few points made earlier. Artistic representation is normally not based on a
particular object watched from a fixed point of view at a given moment, but
on the three-dimensional visual concept of a species of objects that have been
observed from many different angles. As a rule perceptual experience does
not contain the perspective changes of shape and size that are found in the
retinal projection. Pictorial representation is not a mechanical replica of the
percept, but renders its structural characteristics through the properties of a
particular medium. The young mind has a spontaneous awareness of, and
obedience to, the formal requirements of the medium. When representation
is limited to two-dimensional projections, the simplest and most characteristic aspect is chosen for each object or part of object.

In the early work of children, space exists only within the two-dimensional
picture plane. In this plane, things can be large or small, close together or far
apart, to the left or to the right. The third dimension is still undifferentiated—that is, nothing in the picture distinguishes between a flat and a
voluminous object or between depthlessness and depth. The spatial qualities

of a dinner plate are not treated differently from those of a football, and all things lie at the same distance from the observer. At the undifferentiated stage, space is represented in the simplest way—that is, two-dimensionally. But this type of representation does not have the meaning of flatness to the child. The distinction between flat and deep does not yet enter. Flatness exists only in a three-dimensional universe.

In fact originally even the projective aspect is undifferentiated. Three-dimensional bodies are not represented the way they look from a particular point of observation. The early circle is not a front view or a side view or any two-dimensional projection at all. It is the pictorial equivalent of the round object; and its contour does not represent the one-dimensional horizon line that delimits a perspective view, but stands for the entire outer surface of the body.

A good way of getting to understand how children represent space is by reading E. A. Abbott's fantastic novel *Flatland*. Flatland is a two-dimensional country in which, compared with our own world, everything is reduced by one dimension. The walls of houses are mere outlines of plane figures; but they serve their purpose, because in a flat world there is no way of penetrating a closed outline. The inhabitants are geometric shapes. Their bodies too are satisfactorily bounded by a line. A visitor from three-dimensional Spaceland makes a nuisance of himself by telling them that their houses are open: he can see them inside and outside at the same time. He also proves that he can touch a Flatlander's intestines, producing a shooting pain in the Square's stomach. To the Flatlanders their houses are neither closed nor open at the top, because they have no such dimension; and their intestines are kept properly invisible and untouchable by the surrounding contour line.

Those who assert that children draw open houses and X-rayed stomachs behave like the inopportune Spacelander. They are unaware of the admirable logic with which the child adapts his pictures to the conditions of the two-dimensional medium. It is not enough to say that children draw the inside of things because they are interested in it. With all their interest they would be horrified by the picture of a man with an open stomach. The point is that in the two-dimensional medium the inside of a flat figure stands for the inside of a solid, which is covered all around by the contour line. Therefore the food piled up in the stomach (Figure 142) is visible even though the stomach is neither open nor transparent. The outside observer can make use of a dimension that does not exist within the medium. The drawing of the house is neither a transparent front view nor a section. It is the two-dimensional equivalent of a house. The rectangle stands for cubic space, and its outline for the six boundary surfaces. The figure stands inside, completely surrounded by walls. Only a gap in the contour could provide an opening.

If the child could be explicit about these things he would answer the usual objections to his procedure in the same way we would if a visitor from a fourth spatial dimension told us that our houses and bodies were open because he could see their insides and outsides at the same time. Closedness is not an absolute fact, but can be defined only with regard to a particular set of dimensions. The child discovers the most convincing solution of the insoluble artistic problem—how to represent the interior of a closed object. The child's invention lingers on through the ages, so that even in the highly realistic art of Albrecht Dürer the Holy Family is housed in a building without front wall, camouflaged unconvincingly as a broken-down ruin. And of course our modern theater stage is accepted without hesitation by those who accuse the child of "X-ray pictures."

Figure 142

As indicated in Figure 142, pictures of this kind present hair as one row of lines, all touching the contour of the head. This is quite correct in that the circular head line stands for the complete surface of the head, which is thus shown as being covered with hair all over. Yet there is in this method an ambiguity, which derives from the fact that the child uses it inevitably for two different and incompatible purposes at the same time. Obviously the face is not meant to lie inside the head, but on its outer surface; and the two oblique lines represent arms, and not an open cape hanging down from the shoulders and surrounding the entire body. That is, the two-dimensional units of the drawings are equivalents of solids and/or two-dimensional aspects of the outside of solids, depending on what is needed. The relationship between flatness and depth is undifferentiated, so that by purely visual means there is no way of telling whether a circular line stands for a ring, a disk, or a ball. It is because of this ambiguity that the method is used mostly at very primitive levels (for example, in the art work of the Australian aborigines) and is quickly abandoned by the Western child.

The process is well illustrated by the results of an experimental study by Clark, in which children of different ages were asked to make a picture of

an apple with a hatpin stuck horizontally through it and turned at an angle
to the observer. Figure 143*d* illustrates the position in which the children saw
the model. Figure 143*a* shows the earliest solution of the problem. It is logical
in that the pin goes uninterruptedly through the inside of the circle, which
stands for the inside of the apple. But it is ambiguous in that the straight line

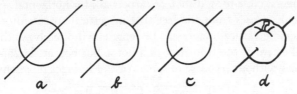

Figure 143

inevitably stands for a one-dimensional object (pin) and not for a surface.
At the next stage, *b*, the child makes a first concession to projective representation by showing the center part of the pin hidden in the apple. (To the
younger child this would be the picture of two pins touching the apple at
the outside.) But the contour of the circle still stands for the entire surface of
the apple, as shown by the fact that the pin does not go beyond the contour.
At *c* the contour has become the horizon line, and the area of the circle is
the front face of the apple. With some refinement of shape, this leads to the
realistic solution, *d*. This picture is spatially consistent, but at the sacrifice
of the striking visual clarity with which the essentials of the three-
dimensional conception were rendered through the properties of the two-
dimensional medium at the earliest stage, *a*. The differentiation between
two-dimensional and three-dimensional form has been achieved, but only
through the suspect trick of making the picture plane appear as an image
of three-dimensional space. (Compare here the earlier discussion of how to
draw a pond with trees.)

Everything in the Plane

The representation of three-dimensional volume is a late stage, and not much
of it is accomplished spontaneously by the child. He may use shading to
indicate the roundness of a ball or a simple foreshortening of the turned face.
A tangible development can be found only in the depicting of geometrically
simple bodies, such as houses, boxes, tables, because here parts that differ in
spatial orientation are clearly distinguished from each other as rectangular
side faces. The problem of "aspects" has been discussed before and therefore
needs to be considered now only genetically. The pictorial difficulty with
which the child has to come to grips is the fact that only two of the three
spatial dimensions can be represented directly in the picture plane. He can
use the vertical dimension of his plane to distinguish between top and

bottom and the horizontal for right and left and thus obtain what I shall call "vertical space" (elevation). Or he can use his two dimensions to show the directions of the compass in a ground plan, which produces "horizontal space" (Figure 144). Upright objects, such as human beings, trees, walls, table legs, appear clearly and characteristically in vertical space, whereas gardens, streets, table tops, dishes, or carpets ask for horizontal space. Additional difficulty arises from the fact that in vertical space only one among the innumerable vertical planes can be represented directly, so that the picture can take care of the front face of a house but not, at the same time, of the side faces without recourse to some trick of indirect representation.

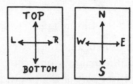

Figure 144

In the early drawings of children the spatial orientation of planes is still undifferentiated. In accordance with the law of differentiation, all planes are given the simplest possible orientation—the one that coincides with the picture plane. The usual mistake of judging products of an undifferentiated stage from the adult standpoint of accomplished differentiation has been commonly made here too. We read that the children "deform" shape by "folding over" things that belong to different orientations, and that they do so out of negligence or special "interest" in certain aspects of the objects. Actually, "folding over" can exist only in a three-dimensional world.

It has been pointed out earlier that unless we evaluate the child's procedure from the point of view of projective realism, we find that he uses the one strictly logical way of conforming to the conditions of the two-dimensional medium. In passing, it may be mentioned that the highly sophisticated and realistic technique of the motion picture has recaptured some of the striking effects of elementary representation. By decomposing the visual world into a succession of partial views, the film has been able, for example, to go back to the principle that the units of a visual statement are basically of equal size. If a person is shown watching a butterfly, a close-up shot may make the insect as large as the person. Similarly, a change of the camera angle will make the screen picture switch from vertical to horizontal space, so that the spectator may see a side view of people sitting at the dinner table and, a second later, a top view of the food. This procedure is "justified" realistically through the succession of the shots in time, which, in theory, allows a change of distance or angle. In the actual experience of the spectator, however, these changes of the observation point are not clearly perceived as such. Essentially, he accepts things as being presented at such a size and angle as fits them best without worrying whether or not such visual correctness is "true to nature." In much modern art, of course, all realistic pretense has been frankly dropped: objects are being given the size and angle required by the visual purpose.

Boxes in Three Dimensions

In one sense, the accommodation of all necessary surfaces in the picture plane is the most satisfactory solution. On the other hand, lack of differentiation leads to ambiguity. There is no way of showing by this method that the legs and the top of a table lie in differently oriented planes. At a certain stage of their development children begin to feel the need for representing the depth dimension. In drawing the picture of an angel the child may be disturbed by the fact that a circular halo stands upright instead of lying on the head. Differentiation becomes necessary; but the question is how to accomplish it. When five-year-old children are forced experimentally to face the question of how to represent a stick or disk inclined toward the observer, they say: "One cannot draw that!" and explain that they would have to pierce the paper with the pencil. Some hit on the clever idea of drawing the object in the normal view and then tilting the paper in the appropriate direction. A little later in life they find—or are taught—the trick of showing depth by oblique orientation.

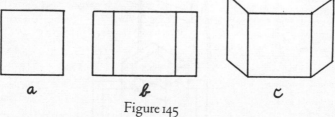

a   *b*   *c*

Figure 145

At an early stage, cubic bodies are drawn as quadrilaterals (Figure 145*a*). These rectangles (or squares), it will be remembered, are not representations of front faces, but two-dimensional equivalents of the three-dimensional cubes. The need for a more complete picture, which will show, for example, the side entrance of the house, produces a differentiation by which the original rectangle is limited to being the façade, and one or two side faces are added to it (Figure 145*b*). The side faces are drawn as regular rectangles in accordance with the fact that perspective distortions are not seen spontaneously. Even when children are made to see foreshortenings, they generally take the sane view that these distortions do not count. Piaget reports that when he showed a seven-year-old boy a tilted disk and asked him to draw it, the child made an ellipse but commented: "It goes like this; one would say it is not round, but it is round anyway."

The spatial ambiguity of the drawing dissatisfies the child after a while and makes him welcome the effect of oblique orientation (Figure 145c). This effect is not based on an arbitrary convention. It will be shown later that obliquity produces genuine perception of depth. Nevertheless it is an indirect procedure in that the missing third dimension is replaced on paper with a distortion of two-dimensional shape. Occasionally we find examples of early stages in which an object is tilted as a whole without being distorted in itself. Figure 146 is taken from a Persian miniature, which shows a prince sitting on his throne. There is a rug under the throne, and a canopy held up by poles is suspended above it. The rug shares the vertical-horizontal orientation of the ground floor, but the throne is placed obliquely upon it, and the canopy is rectangular but tilted at again a different angle. Evidently this was the artist's way of trying to show that throne and canopy were not flat on the ground, and that in addition they were at different distances above the floor. Similar solutions, in which the object remains unchanged but is tilted as a whole, are now and then produced by children.

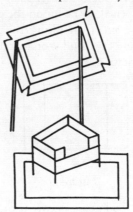

Figure 146

This procedure is hardly suitable, however, when only a part of the object is to be shown as tilted in depth. Then the distortion of shape becomes inevitable (Figure 145c). It can be seen that this stage does not come about simply as the result of "better" observation of nature, but mainly as a way out of a dilemma that arises in the picture.

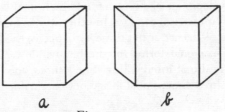

Figure 147

Sometimes only one side face is added to the front wall. At the higher stage this leads to Figure 147*a*. The use of both side faces, however (Figure 147*b*), satisfies elementary visual thinking better because the symmetry of the whole is maintained. To present one side and to leave out the other is disturbingly illogical. At the stage of differentiated orientation in space, Figure 145*b* leads to Figure 145*c* and to Figure 147*b*. The latter occurs in children's drawings and also in Western medieval painting (see Figure 148*a*, a detail from a Spanish nativity of the fourteenth century). Realistically inclined art historians have puzzled over such cases of "inverted perspective." Why would anyone make the vanishing lines diverge rather than converge as they do in nature? It will be evident that we are dealing here not with an inversion of central perspective observed in nature, but with the logical differentiation of the stage of Figure 145*b*. Actually this type of representation has several visual advantages. Not only does it maintain the symmetry of the whole and expose both side faces to the observer, but it also produces a top face with two obtuse angles in front. In this way the top face broadens toward the back and embraces objects that are put upon it with a kind of semicircular contour. Compare this with the "correctly" drawn Figure 148*b*, which is less three-dimensional and less complete, because it hides the side faces, and which squeezes the baby into a converging pattern. Figure 149 shows the compositional advantages of the "inverted" method in a painting by Picasso.

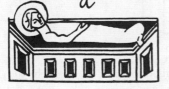 

Figure 148

The pattern indicated in Figure 150 is sometimes found in representations of architecture—for example, in Persian and Chinese paintings. It is possible, and indeed probable, that this is usually a rendering of an actually hexagonal unit. But psychologically it would also be plausible to think of it

as a further development of Figure 147*b*, which in this way would be furnished with a symmetrical top face. In other words, Figure 150 might serve
to depict a cube. Whether or not this ever happens, the frequency of hexagonal and semihexagonal forms (of the bay-window type) in some styles
of architecture is also of interest here. The slanted side faces afford, in front
view, a clearly three-dimensional image not obtainable with the cube.

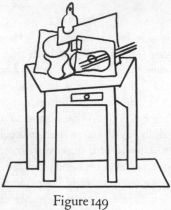

Figure 149

Figure 147*b*, as already mentioned, must not be interpreted as an inversion
of central perspective. Figure 147*a* is also a much earlier form than central
perspective, because it does not yet involve size differentiation according to
distance. The front edges are no larger than the back edges. Size differentiation according to distance does occur in the drawings of older children to
the extent that human figures, houses, or trees may be drawn smaller with

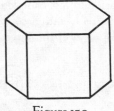

Figure 150

increasing distance from the spectator. This differentiation is fairly simple,
because it requires only a transposition of size. It leaves shape untouched.
When applied within one and the same object, however, the principle leads
to the convergence of parallels and the corresponding distortion of rectangles
and squares. This is so radical a transformation of the object that it does not
occur spontaneously in children's work. It is a product of training, limited
to specific cultural conditions.

Many other forms of pictorial differentiation lie essentially beyond the reach of the child. Examples can be found in the history of art. Two of them will suffice here. In the so-called "painterly" style, line loses its double function. It ceases to be used as contour and is limited to the representation of actually linear objects. Venturi describes the growing aversion during the Renaissance to what Vasari calls "the hard and cutting" outline. Solid objects are conceived as volumes rather than through their boundaries, and the "dry manner, full of profiles," is replaced with the juxtaposition of masses. As a second example, "aerial perspective" may be cited, that is, the differentiation of color, detail, and sharpness in relation to distance.

Educational Consequences

The preceding detailed analysis of the growth of form in the drawings of children fulfills its purpose only if its wider implications are evident. It has been undertaken mainly for two reasons. In the first place, there seems to be no more striking demonstration of the fact that pictorial representation cannot be understood merely in relation to the realistically conceived model object. I have tried to show how form develops within its medium and according to the conditions of the medium. Misinterpretations are inevitable if the picture is considered a more or less correct replica or derivative rather than a structural equivalent of the object in terms of the medium. This holds true, not only for the work of children, but for all art including the realistic.

In the second place, it seemed useful to describe how pictorial form develops organically from the simplest to increasingly complex patterns. Thus the process of growth gives further evidence of the tendency to simplicity, which was demonstrated earlier in visual organization. Step by step, the maturing mind requires greater complexity, but the higher stage can be reached only by way of the lower ones. The mastering of a given stage creates need and readiness for the next. The mind proceeds at the rate at which it can comprehend, and at any point of the rising path it is handling a medium that seems fitting and natural. Willful interference with this process creates disturbance. The old-fashioned teacher who imposes on his student advanced tricks of the trade is just as guilty as the new-styled primitivist who admonishes the child: "This is a nice picture, but we do not make noses in second grade!" The art student who copies the manner of an admired teacher will be in danger of losing his intuitive sense of right and wrong by wrestling with a form of representation that he can imitate but not master. His work, instead of being convincing and congenial, is puzzling to him. He has lost the honesty of the child, which every successful artist preserves and which gives the simplest possible shape to any statement, complicated as the result may be objectively. Arnold Schönberg, the composer of some of the most intricate music ever written, told his students that their pieces should be as natural to them as their hands and feet. The simpler they seemed to them, the better they would be. "If something you have written looks very complicated to you, you do well to doubt its genuineness right away!"

The formal features already discussed are derived from the cognitive functions of the mind: the sensory perception of the outer world, the elaboration of experience in visual and intellectual thinking, and the conservation of experience and thought in memory. Considered from this angle, pictorial work is a tool for the task of identifying, understanding, and defining things, investigating relationships, and creating order of increasing complexity. More commonly psychologists have been using art work for a different purpose. They have studied it—particularly in mentally disturbed or diseased individuals—as a manifestation of a person's social attitude, his mood and temperament, the equilibrium or disequilibrium of motivational forces, his fears and desires. These studies have opened a promising field of research, likely to be of great value for the understanding of both art and the human personality.

Until now there has been little coördination between the two approaches. Some investigators have examined pictorial form as though it was detached from the vital aims of living, whereas others have treated art as a diagnostic tool without giving attention to the perceptual and representational factors. Because of the youth of the enterprise, such one-sidedness may be necessary and useful, except for the misinterpretations resulting from it. It is true that a complex whole cannot be understood without an analysis of the factors that are integrated in it. Understanding will not get beyond a first stage, however, unless a more comprehensive view is taken. General psychology has paved the way. It is well known by now that such cognitive functions as intelligence, learning, or memory cannot be dealt with apart from the total structure of wishes, needs, attitudes. "Personality" has been shown to manifest itself in the individual's way of perceiving the world. On the other hand, the range of a person's outer experiences and the level of intelligence are considered in their effect upon his or her over-all attitude.

The need for such integration may be illustrated by an example, chosen at random, among many to be found in the literature on the subject. In a book on art education Herbert Read comments on a drawing of a girl who is a little less than five years old. A tiger is represented very simply by a horizontal stroke for the body and two verticals for the legs. The lines are crossed with short stripes, meant to depict the tiger's skin. Read speaks of the "wholly introvert, inorganic" basis of the picture. The child, he says, has given no regard to whatever image of a tiger she may have had; she has created "an expressive symbol which corresponds not to her perceptual awareness or conceptual knowledge of the tiger. . . ." The picture is a typical example of the horizontal-vertical stage, at which the average child will represent an animal in just this way. Very often no differentiation between organic and inorganic shape is possible at this level; straight lines stand for both. Pictures of this kind are meager in content, not because the child is unable or unwilling to observe and to use his observations, but because the elementary stage of representation does not permit him to use much of what he has seen. Whether or not this particular child is a withdrawn introvert cannot be determined on the basis of his drawing and his age alone. Introversion may retard differentiation of form, but undifferentiated form in itself does not suggest introversion. The same drawing could come from a noisy extrovert, passionately interested in the way animals look and behave.

The perceptual and representational characteristics already discussed are more universal—because they are more elementary—than most pictorial effects of "personality." The development of pictorial form relies on basic properties of the nervous system, whose functioning is not greatly modified by cultural and individual differences. It is for this reason that the drawings of children look essentially alike throughout the world, and that there are such striking similarities among the early art products of different civilizations. A good example is the universal occurrence of circular, concentrically arranged figures, to which Jung has applied the Sanskrit word "mandala." It is found in Eastern and Western art, in Egypt as well as in the drawings of children or American Indians. Jung refers to this pattern as one of the archetypes or collective images that appear everywhere, because the collective unconscious, of which they are a part, "is simply the psychic expression of identity of brain structure irrespective of all racial differences." The reader will recognize the mandala as a form of the sunburst pattern, which was found to be characteristic for an early stage of differentiation. The universal occurrence of the pattern in children's drawings would seem to be sufficiently explained by the need of the young mind for visual order at a low level of complexity. At the same time such patterns are able to symbolize deepest insights into the nature of the cosmos as they are intuited and shaped by the unconscious and the conscious mind. This demonstrates the unity of the mind, which needs and creates the same forms in the outermost layers of sensory perception and in the hidden core, from which dreams and visions originate.

Visual symbols cannot be studied adequately without consideration of perceptual and representational factors. The psychoanalyst who assumes that the child starts his art work with circles in remembrance of his mother's

breasts, which were the first important objects of his experience, neglects the
elementary visual and motor conditions that favor the circle. Early symbols,
like the sun wheel or the cross, reflect basic human experiences by means
of equally basic pictorial form. There is no point to engaging in a priority
struggle as to what came first, the content or the form.

Modern art education is profiting from the methods and findings of psychology, but to now there has been one-sided emphasis on art as an expression of emotions, conflicts, needs, and so on. For this reason something like
a monopoly has developed for technical tools that foster the spontaneous
stroke, the impulsive flash, the raw effect of amorphous color, and interfere
with the precision of visually controlled form. Broad brushes and dripping
easel paints compel the child to create a one-sided picture of his state of
mind, and the possibility cannot be excluded that the kind of picture he is
permitted to make may, in turn, influence the state of mind he is in. Unquestionably the modern methods have given an outlet to aspects of the
child's mind that were crippled by the traditional procedure of copying
models with a sharpened pencil. But there is equal danger in preventing the
child from using pictorial work for clarifying his observation of reality and
for learning to concentrate and to create order. Shapeless emotion is not the
desirable end product of education, and therefore cannot be used as its mean
either. The equipment of the art room and the mind of the art teacher should
be comprehensive and variable enough to let each child act as a whole person
at any time.

The Birth of Form in Sculpture

The principles of form development I have discussed are based on elementary psychological factors, and therefore can be expected to apply not only
to drawing and painting but to other artistic media as well. For example, it
would be interesting to study the growth of form conception in theater
direction and choreography. In the history of styles as well as in the development of the individual director or choreographer, are there early compositional forms, distinguished perhaps by symmetrical arrangements and
preference for frontal and rectangular spatial orientations or groupings according to simple geometric figures? Can differentiation be shown to proceed
stepwise from these to more and more complex conceptions? In architecture
it would be possible to show the changes from simple circular and rectangular plans to more intricate ones, the gradual breaking up of the unified
block and wall, the deviation from the symmetrical façade, the introduction
of oblique orientation and curves of increasingly high order.

Here I shall merely sketch the development of spatial conception in sculpture. An investigation of this kind ought to be undertaken for the work of

children, but hardly any usable material is available at this time. Photographic reproductions, always a poor material for the study of sculpture, are particularly unsatisfactory for the unpolished surfaces of the children's clay work. Also, the mechanical difficulties of the three-dimensional media make it harder for the child to produce the form he has in mind. Therefore it will be necessary to choose examples from the history of adult art. What follows here is highly tentative, little more than a group of conjectures and suggestions.

It might be supposed that physical bodies are more easily represented in sculpture than on paper or on canvas, because the sculptor works in volumes and therefore is not faced with the problem of how to render three-dimensional objects in a two-dimensional medium. Actually this is true only to a limited degree, because the lump of clay or the piece of stone presents the sculptor with three dimensions only materially. He still has to acquire the conception of three-dimensional organization step by step, and it might well be maintained that the task of mastering space is more difficult in sculpture than in the pictorial arts because of the added dimension. When the child works out his first circle in drawing, he has not mastered two dimensional space but merely annexed a bit of territory on paper. He must go through the slow process of differentiating the various angular relationships before he can be said to be truly in command of the formal possibilities in the medium. Similarly, modeling a first ball of clay does not mean the conquest of three-dimensional organization. It merely reflects the most elementary kind of form concept, at which neither shape nor direction is differentiated. If we may judge by analogy with what happens in drawing, the "primordial ball" will represent any compact object—a human figure, an animal, a house.

I do not know whether this stage exists in the work of children, nor have I found any example in the history of art. The nearest to it would seem to be the small Paleolithic stone figures of fat women, the best-known of which is the "Venus of Willendorf." These figures, with their round heads, bellies, breasts, and thighs, look indeed as though they had been conceived as combinations of spheres modified to fit the human shape. We may wonder whether their obesity is to be explained only by the subject matter—symbols of motherhood and fertility, preference of prehistoric man for fat women—or also as a manifestation of early form conception at the spherical stage.

Sticks and Slabs

The simplest way of representing one direction, corresponding to the straight line in drawing, is by means of a stick. A stick is of course always a three-dimensional object physically; but just as the breadth of the pencil or

Figure 151

brush stroke does not "count" in early drawing and painting, so the stick in sculpture is the product of one-dimensional conception, counting only as to its orientation and length. Good examples can be found among the terracotta figures done on Cyprus and at Mycenae during the second millennium B.C. (Figure 151). The bodies of men and animals—legs, arms, snouts, tails, and horns—are made of sticklike units of roughly identical diameter. Stick elements are found also in the small bronzes of the Geometric period in Greece, around the eighth century B.C. Children make sausagelike sticks for their clay and plasticine figures. Probably this stage exists universally at the beginnings of modeling.

The regression to one-dimensional sticks demonstrates that the mastery of volume in earlier, spherical forms is only apparent. The early sphere does not involve the employment of all directions but of no direction at all. The stick shows that the sculptor has learned to cope with one.

To describe further differentiations we need two descriptive terms. The spatial dimensions of an object refer either to its own shape ("object dimen-

sions") or to the pattern it makes in space ("spatial dimensions"). Thus a
ring is sticklike, or one-dimensional, as an object but two-dimensional as a
pattern in space.

The simplest combination of sticks leads to patterns of two spatial dimensions—that is, arrangement within one plane (Figure 152*a*). Later the third
dimension is added. Patterns are arranged in more than one plane. In the
simplest stage these planes are parallel or meet at right angles (*b*). Further
differentiation of orientation produces the bending and curving of sticks, to
the most complex twisting (*c*) and oblique connections between units in two
or three dimensions (*d*). The length of the units is probably at first undifferentiated, just as we have found it in drawing (compare Figure 138), and
only gradually distinctions of length are worked out.

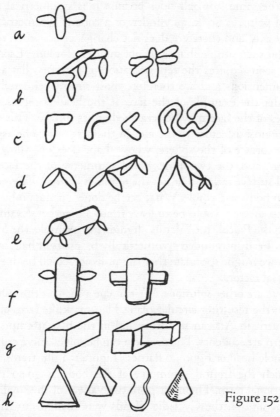

Figure 152

In the foregoing only one object dimension was used. Figure 152*e* illustrates examples in which the diameter is differentiated. The trunk is made
thicker than the legs. That is, each unit still has only one object dimension

in itself, but a second is introduced by the relation between units of different thickness. In Figure 152*f* there are two object dimensions within the individual, slab-shaped unit. In the cubic forms of *g* the third object dimension becomes an actual part of the visual conception rather than being only present physically. Finally, in *h* there is differentiation of shape within the two-dimensional or three-dimensional unit. It will be understood that the variations of orientation and size indicated for the first dimension in *a–e* apply also to bodies of two or three object dimensions.

Probably even this simplified survey of steps reads confusingly enough. It indicates how much more complex the development of form becomes by the addition of the third dimension.

Some of the stages mentioned require more detailed treatment. A ball looks the same from all sides because it is symmetrical in relation to one central point. A stick, a cylinder, or a cone is symmetrical in relation to a central axis, and therefore does not change aspect when rotated around the axis. But such simple shapes are not sufficient for long. Especially, the human figure soon requires the representation of patterns that are symmetrical in two dimensions and are therefore most simply rendered on a flat surface. Consider the example of the face. If the head is represented by a sphere, features of the face may be scratched on its surface. This solution, however, is quite unsatisfactory to the eye. In the first place, one aspect is singled out on the surface of the sphere, whose shape does not allow for any such distinction; also, the two-dimensional symmetry of the face is rendered on a curved surface rather than on the required flat one. The same is true for the human body as a whole. What can be done? In the problem of the face. the simplest answer would be to leave it out altogether. Examples can be found among the Paleolithic "Venus" figures. For example, the Willendorf woman has her head surrounded symmetrically by plaits of hair, but there is no face. Again we might speculate that this omission could be due, partly or wholly, to formal factors.

There are other solutions. We can cut a slice off the sphere and make the face on the resulting circular plane. Flat, masklike faces of this kind are not infrequent in African sculpture and in the first attempts at portraiture by Western art students. The problem can be solved more radically by reducing the whole head or figure to flatness. Figure 153 illustrates an Indian figurine in which the frontal symmetry of the body is given the simplest, two-dimensional form. The most primitive variety of the small stone idols found in Troy and on the Cycladic Islands were made from rectangular slates of marble and shaped like a violin. Even where the front and the back views have developed considerable relief, there is not yet a side view that can be considered a part of the concept. In the same culture are combinations of two- and one-dimensional form; for example, the trunk of the body is a flat, frontal shield, whereas head and legs have the vaselike, undifferentiated roundness of an earlier stage.

Figure 153

Some parts of the body do not fit into the frontal plane: noses, breasts, penes, feet. One solution of this problem can be found in the head of the baby, held by the figure to the left in Figure 154. The head is wedged like the blade of an ax—nothing but nose, so to speak, with the eyes scratched in laterally.

At the stage of rectangular connections noses and breasts, for example, stick out perpendicularly from the frontal plane. Figure 155a shows the section of a flat head with the nose protruding at a right angle. When, in the course of further differentiation, this pattern is smoothed to more organic shape (Figure 155b), we arrive quite logically at the curious birdlike heads of Figure 154. I cannot tell whether this stage occurs typically in all early sculpture, but the statuettes from Cyprus certainly correspond to what we would expect psychologically.

Figure 154

The strict frontal symmetry of primitive sculpture is abandoned gradually. Even in Egyptian and early Greek art, however, symmetry is still evident to such an extent that Julius Lange described it as the basic law of sculptural composition in these archaic styles.

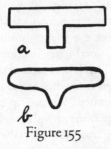

Figure 155

As in drawing, the differentiation of the figure comes about not only by the addition of units to the main base but also through internal subdivision. In Figures 153 and 154 clothing is represented by scratched-in lines. At the same time these early figures show how subdivision develops from scratching to a more sculptural, three-dimensional procedure. The scratched-in lines, remnants of the technique of drawing, are replaced with moldings. Ribbons are applied to the surface in order to outline the eyes. In the archaic Greek statues of young men (sixth century B.C.) such ribbons are used, for example, to mark the border line between the belly and the thigh. Angular steps, rather than mere dividing lines, distinguish the protruding chest from the stomach. These moldings become gradually smoother and fuse with the ground plane; the scratched-in lines develop into cavities representing such things as the mouth or the hollow of the eye. From a combination of separate units a continuous relief evolves gradually. Figure 156 illustrates this development by two schematic sections.

Figure 156

The ground plane tends to disappear materially. But even at the most differentiated level, the need for unity requires that the shape of the figure conform to a common visual plane. The sculptor Hildebrand has suggested that we imagine a statue placed between two parallel panes of glass, one in the front and one in the back. It should then be possible to see the statue as a series of layers parallel to the glass. In particular Hildebrand asked that the outermost points should clearly establish the imaginary frontal plane as a base from which the rest of the figure could be understood. We may find that this principle fits the relief better than the round figure, and we may perhaps prefer Michelangelo's saying, "A good statue can be rolled down hill without damage"; yet the fact remains that the organization of a piece of sculpture should enable the eye to see a unified boundary.

The stage of vertical-horizontal space relationships has been described by the Egyptologist Schaefer in his law of rectangularity, which, he says, holds for the art of "all peoples and individuals who have not been influenced by the Greek art of the fifth century." According to this law, the basic plane is perpendicular to the observer's line of sight, and all other planes are parallel with, or at a right angle to, this base. Occasional exceptions are obliquely bent arms or legs.

The Cube and the Round

The flat figure, of which the Cycladic marble idols served as examples, conceives the human body by two object dimensions. A further step of differentiation adds the third object dimension and presents the body as a cubic block. In addition to the front and the back planes there are now two side views. The visual construction of the figure out of four main views, which lie at right angles to each other, was first formulated as a law for archaic Greek sculpture by Löwy. It applies more generally to sculpture of early stages. The psychological reasons for this procedure can be described as follows. First, the complexity of roundness is reduced to the simple rectangularity of the cube. Second, the complex continuity of the whole is interpreted as a combination of relatively self-contained, simple parts. Third, the variety of aspects is reduced to the four that are the perceptually simplest: the symmetrical views of front and back and the two profiles. Finally, the sculptor can concentrate at any particular moment upon a relatively closed partial composition, which he can survey without changing his point of observation. He may work first on the front view, later on the side view, and so forth. The combining of the views is left to a secondary phase of the process.

The independence of the four views is most strikingly illustrated by the winged bulls and the lions that served as gatekeepers of Assyrian palaces (Figure 157). Viewed from the front, such an animal shows two symmetrical front legs standing still. The side view has four legs walking. This means that from an oblique point of observation we count five legs. But such adding up of unrelated elements violates the intended concept. The important thing for the Assyrians was the completeness of each view in itself.

Every beginner in the art of sculpture finds that the cubic concept imposes itself upon his work. When he tries to abandon it in favor of the kind of roundness that was achieved during the Renaissance, he has to overcome the Egyptian in himself. Furthermore, he will be tempted constantly to finish one aspect of the work as it appears from a given point of observation, only to discover that when he turns his figure the horizon of his previous view is no longer valid as a boundary. In consequence he will find himself with unexpected breaks and ridges and with incomplete planes that shoot into outer space instead of turning around the figure. The capacity to think of the total volume as a continuous whole marks a late mastery of three-dimensional space. It would be a mistake to assume that this had been accomplished already in the shaping of the primordial ball. Rather did it take the reduction to the one-dimensional stick and the gradual differentiation by way of flat and cubic bodies to arrive at the genuine roundness of Michelangelo's or Bernini's figures.

Figure 157

In baroque sculpture the subdivision into well-defined aspects is abandoned, and sometimes it is impossible to find one main view. Every aspect is an inseparable part of constantly changing form. Emphasis on oblique foreshortening prevents the glance from stopping. From any point of observation, planes lead beyond the given view and demand an endless change of position. The screw is the underlying structural pattern, which is applied most simply in the bands of pictorial reliefs that spiral around the Roman columns of Trajan or Marcus Aurelius. A characteristic example is Michelangelo's Christ in Santa Maria Sopra Minerva in Rome. Every segment of the figure is set obliquely against the next, so that at any given aspect the frontality of one of the segments is counteracted by the obliqueness of the others. This adds up to a screwlike rotation of the whole body. According to Lomazzo, Michelangelo advised his students to make their figures "serpentlike."

Needless to say, the style of such figures is not more artistic than the simpler cubes of the Egyptian or African carver. It is merely more complex; and although the richness of the unending symphonic flow may enchant the educated eye, there is also the danger that the artist will lose control and end with visually incomprehensible multiformity or amorphous imitations of nature. This danger threatens least when the artist has gradually arrived at complex form through the organic sequence of stages, never going beyond what his eye has learned to organize and being accustomed to accepting nothing he cannot master. The danger is greatest when a highly differentiated style, whether it is realism or cubism, is sprung upon the unprepared student. There are no short cuts on the road to the refined manifestations of a late culture that constitute the art of our day.

Of other late stages of complexity, I shall mention only one. Throughout the history of sculpture there is a clear distinction between the solid block and surrounding empty space. The figure is bounded by straight or convex planes, and the holes that detach arms from the body or legs from each other do not impair the compactness of the main volume. In the next chapter there will be an opportunity to show how the introduction of concave form draws space into the realm of the figure. The block begins to disintegrate, until in our century we find sculpture that surrounds empty space in addition to being surrounded by it.

V   SPACE

A line drawn on a piece of paper does not seem to lie *in* the plane but on top of it. The empty environment does not border the line—the way two floor tiles border each other—but continues underneath without interruption. This was demonstrated in Figure 121. The thicker the line, the more striking the phenomenon. In fact the line is only a special example of a patch of color; it is the limiting case in which the area of the patch approaches zero. As a rule a patch of color lies on top of the empty ground, not in it. Figure 158 illustrates this in Paul Klee's painting *The Script*.

The Plane Splits Up

Obviously the effect is not the result of conditions in the physical object, but arises in the beholder psychologically. Why does it occur? If the line were seen as lying within the plane, the paper surface would be interrupted, broken by an insert. When the line is seen as lying on top, the surface remains intact. There is a third possibility. The Klee picture, for example, might be seen as a white surface into which various shapes had been cut with scissors; through the cutouts we would see blackness underneath. Then too the white plane would be broken.

The second version produces the simplest structure, for an unbroken surface is simpler than a broken one. This suggests that the observed effect may occur in order to produce the simplest pattern obtainable under the circumstances. There is in a plain surface a tendency to maintain its integrity. If the intruder consists in nothing but a small dot, it is likely not to be seen at all. This is one way of solving the problem, but it is feasible only when the stimulus is very weak. A line or patch cannot be erased in this manner. Only one avenue of freedom is open—the third dimension. To the image on the retina it makes no difference whether the line lies in the plane or slightly in front of it. Thus the perceived surface is free to thrust the intruder forward, just enough to gain completeness. The total pattern splits within the depth dimension. One part of it—the line, or lines, or patches—appears at a near level, whereas the ground, empty and uninterrupted, lies a little further away from the observer.

Figure 158

The tentative generalization to be drawn from this example is that a surface pattern will look three-dimensional rather than two-dimensional when this makes for the simpler structure. Since the simplification occurs by means of splitting up the pattern, we recognize it as a special example of what has been described as subdivision. We earlier found that a figure will subdivide into several units within the frontal plane if this results in the simpler organization. It seems now that the same rule holds for the depth dimension.

Actually the situation is somewhat more intricate in that subdivision itself introduces a new complexity, a step away from the simplicity of the un-divided whole. That is, in order to avoid one complication another is toler-ated. In order to avoid the interruption of the frontal surface, the splitting of the pattern into more than one depth level is accepted. The reason for this preference is unknown. We must assume for the time being that the break in the depth dimension produces a simpler situation than that in the frontal plane.

The line or patch is distinguished from its surroundings by brightness and color. This difference determines the boundary. If we now consider out-line figures, which are produced by nothing but a contour, we find that they too tend to appear in front of the ground plane. Figure 121b showed that the areas of such figures seem to lie on top of a throughgoing ground.

We might wonder why a circular outline figure is not seen as an empty ring suspended in front of the plane rather than as a disk. This, it seems, would solve the problem of interference in a way that would require a smaller transformation of the flat physical stimulus pattern. Actually this solution would be the simpler one, but it presupposes that the inside and the outside of the figure are seen as belonging to the same homogeneous plane. Such a homogeneity does exist for the physical stimulus. The same white paper is inside and outside the circle. But it has already been pointed out that, for physiological reasons, the inside of the figure does not appear quite like the outside. The inside is relatively more dense and solid; the outside, loose and penetrable like empty space. The inside resists intrusions more strongly, and figures seen at a place where an outline figure had earlier been fixated shrink in size. Psychologically, then, there is considerable dissimilarity between the inside and the outline area, a fact that interferes with the ring solution. More densely textured surfaces tend to lie closer to the observer, as I shall demonstrate below.

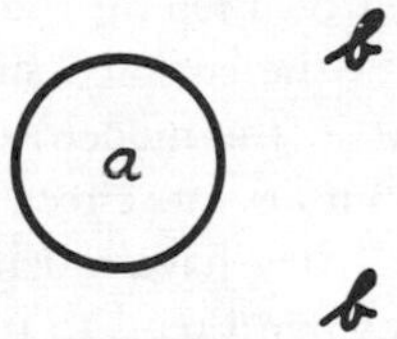

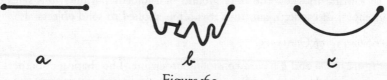

Figure 159

In Figure 159, then, *a* tends to be seen as a surface that lies on top of the throughgoing ground plane *b*. This involves peculiar psychological problems. Any point of area *a* lies closer to the observer than any point of *b*. This difference of location in depth, however, is not brought about by any process originating in the point itself; it is induced by remote control through the contour. Therefore the surface we see inside the contour is also produced by remote control. Now in theory this surface could assume any one of an infinite number of shapes, just as the straightness of a drumhead is only one of the innumerable shapes we could obtain if, instead of the skin, we draped a tablecloth over the drum. Yet we see the surface in the circle as straight (Figure 160*a*) and not as curved in the manner of the sections *b* or *c*. The straight plane is the simplest one by which the circle can be filled, and I shall show later that with any change of the contour the inner surface changes accordingly, always assuming the simplest available shape.

Figure 160

The simplest surface is often, but not always, the smallest one available. This tendency toward the smallest surface exists not only in visual perception, but also in physics, as has been demonstrated by experiments designed to solve Plateau's problem: to find the surface of smallest area bounded by a given closed contour in space. If we dip wire contours into a soap solution, the resulting soap film will show the smallest possible surface.

Since the inner surface is induced by the contour, the strength of the phenomenon at any given point can be expected to depend on such factors as the distance of the point from the contour. The larger we see the pattern, the weaker the influence of the border line upon the inside will be, and the effect will decrease toward the center with increasing distance from the outline. The relative size of the figure in comparison to other forms surrounding it will probably also be of importance. A comparison of line drawings by Rembrandt with those of Matisse or Picasso will show that in the older master solidity is obtained by keeping the outlined units relatively small. Also Rembrandt reinforces the enclosed surfaces by inner design, such as folds of clothing, whereas in the modern drawings the units are often so large that the contour all but loses its effect. The border-line character of the Matisse contours is weak; they have much of the quality of independent lines. The bodies look loose, and tend to reveal that they are nothing but pieces of empty paper surface. The drawing lies like a transparent web of lines on the ground. The three-dimensional effect is reduced to a minimum. Of course this is not due to negligence or incapacity. Whereas the older artists wished to stress solid volume and clearly discernible depth, the modern ones want to dematerialize objects and minimize space. The modern drawings are meant as lightweight products, obvious creations of man, figments of imagination, rather than illusions of physical reality. They are meant to stress the surface from which they spring.

What has been said here about outline drawings is true also, though to a lesser extent, of homogeneous patches of color. Their inner surfaces too are determined by the shape of their boundaries. The difference of color will more effectively resist identification with the surrounding ground, but an unmodulated stretch of color will tend to look loose and empty and to coincide in depth with the adjoining planes. In the older paintings this effect is reserved for the representation of empty space, such as in the gold ground of Byzantine mosaics, the blue ground of Holbein portraits, the skies of landscapes; in modern paintings it is often applied to solid objects also.

The Sharing of Contours

In Figure 159, *a* and *b* have a common border line. The sharing of borders is always uncomfortable. In the two hexagons of Figure 161 an urge to pull apart is evident. Under special conditions the separation can actually be seen to happen. When the control of the stimulus over the organizing forces in the brain is weakened, for example, by the exposure of dim figures for a

split second, it is sometimes found that a pattern like Figure 162*a* is rendered
by the observer as one like *b,* showing a tendency to give each unit its own
contour. When young children were asked by Piaget to copy geometric
designs in which circles or triangles touch each other, they often eliminated
the contact in their reproductions. In an ability test developed by Rupp,
people were asked to draw a honeycomb pattern (Figure 163*a*). They often
made the hexagons independent of each other by leaving space between them
(*b*), and even emphasized the interstices by shading the figures (*d*); or
they introduced overlapping, which damaged the shape of one figure in
order to free its neighbor (*c*).

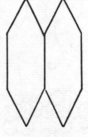

Figure 161

In the examples cited, contours were shared by equal partners, none of
which could claim preference. This is not true in Figure 159. Here *a* is a compact, coherent figure of simple shape bounding an area of relatively high
density, whereas *b* is an endless plane of loose substance. Under such conditions the ambiguous function of the common border can be eliminated. The
circular figure is strong enough to snatch the border away from *b* and to
monopolize it as its own contour. The outline is seen as belonging to *a* but
not to *b*.

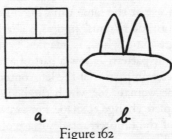

a   *b*

Figure 162

This leaves the plane *b* in a predicament since it ends where *a* starts, but
without border—a visually paradoxical situation. A satisfactory solution is
found as *b* appears to continue unbroken under *a;* it is no longer in need of
a border line. This analysis shows that the splitting of the pattern into two

levels serves a double purpose. It avoids the interruption of the outer surface
and eliminates its dilemma of ending without having an end.

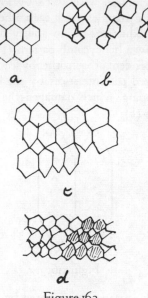

Figure 163

The ambiguity of the common contour is aggravated by the fact that,
although physically unchangeable, the contour almost always assumes a
different shape, depending on whether it is seen as belonging to the one or
the other of the two adjoining surfaces. For example, the line in Figure 159
is convex when related to the inner surface and concave in relation to the
outer. These two versions of shape are incompatible—an object cannot be
seen as convex and concave at the same time. Figure 164a, vaguely reminis-
cent perhaps of the prehistoric "Venus" figures, is characterized by a number
of protrusions. In Figure 164b, which is adapted from a detail of Picasso's
painting *La Vie,* the same pattern—now a part of a larger whole—has lost
most of its figure character. In particular the left contour has now been taken
over by the body of the woman, for which the body of the man serves as
ground. There is a complete change of shape. For example, the protrusion on
the left is now a part of the uninterrupted surface of the man's chest, and
therefore looks as little like an outgoing wedge as the elbow and the breast
of the woman did in Figure 164a.

Perhaps the example of Figure 165, derived from a painting by Braque, is
even more instructive. The shape of the profile line changes entirely, depending on which face it is seen to belong to. What was empty becomes full;

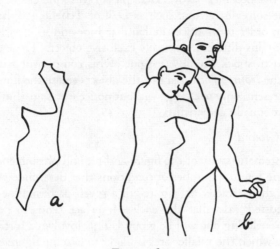

Figure 164

Figure 165

what was active becomes passive. Examples of this kind can be found every-where. Some surrealist artists, such as Dali or Tchelitcheff, have used the technique in order to produce the familiar hide-and-seek tricks, by which a picture contains different, mutually exclusive objects. These compositions are designed to shock the observer out of his complacent trust of reality. Painted in the *trompe l'oeil* manner, the objects create the illusion of being materially present, only to change without notice into something completely different but equally convincing.

Figure and Ground

The first systematic study of the figure-and-ground phenomenon was made by Rubin. He found a number of conditions that determine which surface will assume the character of "figure" in a given pattern. One of his rules, already discussed, says that the enclosed surface tends to become figure whereas the enclosing one will be ground. This involves a further principle, according to which the smaller area is likely to become figure under certain conditions. In Figure 166 the narrower stripes or sectors are seen as lying on top. If we try to produce the inverse view, we experience a strong resistance in the pattern. It should be noted, however, that this principle holds only when the larger units are placed in such a way that they can form a con-tinuous ground that is endless or of simple outline. In Figure 167 the situ-ation is reversed. The smaller elements form a continuous pattern that lies under the larger ones. In general the laws of perspective imply that larger objects are seen nearer to the observer. In Figure 166 the double function of the contour lines makes effective the rule of "similarity of location," accord-ing to which the lines that lie closer together will be grouped together.

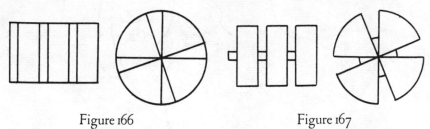

Figure 166   Figure 167

I have already pointed out that when surfaces are empty, the contour lines produce differences of density and spatial position, and that internal texture will reinforce the effect of the contour. Figure 168*a* shows that texture en-hances the figure quality of the disk, whereas in *b* the enclosing environ-ment tends to lie in the foreground so that a circular hole appears in the center. In the Matisse print (Figure 169) the relatively empty body of the

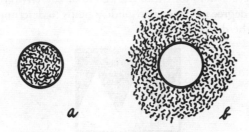

Figure 168

Figure 169

woman looks like a hole torn into the tissue of the environment. Thus it seems that the degree of density or solidity helps to determine the position of a surface in the depth dimension.

Figure 170

The texture effect is one among several factors influencing the figure-ground phenomenon that at the present time can be only described but hardly related to more general principles from which they may derive. This is true for the role played by top-and-bottom orientation. In Figure 170 the white part is generally seen as lying in front. If the drawing is turned upside down, the opposite occurs. In other words, the lower section tends to lie in front. This confirms an earlier observation: that space in the frontal plane is "anisotropic," that is, that the lower half and the upper half are not of equal weight. Thus far, however, there is no convincing theory that would account for these observations. The suggestion has been advanced that in patterns like Figure 170 the observer is simply applying his experiences of daily life, where solid objects at the bottom are known to lie in front of the empty sky. For the same reason, textured objects are seen as figure. Such an explanation sounds plausible, and is in line with the kind of theorizing we have inherited from earlier generations of psychologists and philosophers. Again and again the reference to past experience, however, has been found to be little more than a convenient "stand-in," which had to give way when causes for the phenomenon in question were discovered in the perceptual situation itself. Therefore caution suggests that we think of our observations in daily life, present or past, as belonging among the figure-ground situations that are in need of explanation rather than supplying this explanation.

Our theoretical knowledge is even less satisfactory when the effect of color and brightness is considered. It seems fairly well established that the colors on the short-wave side of the spectrum, mainly blue, make a surface look farther away from the observer than those on the long-wave side, mainly red. There is also some indication that the protruding colors look denser, firmer, more solid, so that conceivably the above-mentioned tendency of denser texture to promote spatial nearness may be relevant here. One experimenter has suggested that the brighter surface may more often supply the ground. Further evidence is lacking.

Other observations permit us to tread on more familiar ground. Often the figure-and-ground versions that can be obtained from a pattern differ as to their simplicity. In the magic banister of Figure 171 the contradiction between the right and the left sides of the drawings makes it impossible to obtain a stable image. But in this fluctuation we rather vividly experience the effect of the various perceptual factors. In *a* both versions yield symmetrical patterns. For most people the convex columns are more often seen as figure, because, according to one of Rubin's rules, convexity tends to win out over concavity. But in *b* the concave units clearly prevail, because they give the picture more symmetry. The general rule asserts that the figure-ground version that produces the simpler total pattern will prevail. For example, the more simply the interstices between figures in a picture are shaped, the more likely they are to be seen as positive patterns rather than as borderless pieces of ground.

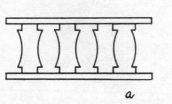
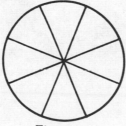

Figure 171

Simplicity is effective, not only in the shape of a pattern itself, but also in the spatial orientation of the pattern. The two Maltese crosses in Figure 172 are identical except for their orientation to the framework of the visual field. Under these conditions the cross whose main axes coincide with the vertical and horizontal coördinates of the visual field more easily becomes the figure, whereas the other more often vanishes into the shapeless ground.

Figure 172

Of particular practical interest for the artist is the fact that convexity makes for figure, concavity for ground. Figure 173*a* has a disposition to look

Figure 174

like a hole in the plane, although both *a* and *b* are enclosed areas and are thus more likely to have figure character. The phenomenon varies somewhat,

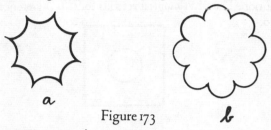

a

Figure 173   *b*

depending on what part of the pattern holds the observer's attention. If he looks at the bulges, *a* will be more clearly a hole, and *b* a solid patch on top of the ground. The opposite effect is usual when he fixates the pointed angles between the bulges, because their narrowness makes for figure character. Jacques Lipchitz's drawing *Prometheus Strangling the Vulture* (Figure 174) contains white areas in whose contours concavities predominate. The contradiction between the solidity of the flesh suggested by the subject matter and the perceptual emptiness of the white spaces suggested by the concavities and the lack of texture enhances the conflict that the drawing is meant to convey.

Depth Levels

The terms "figure" and "ground" are suitable only as long as we are dealing with an enclosed, homogeneous pattern in an equally homogeneous, endless environment. But conditions are rarely so simple. Even in most of our elementary examples more than two levels were involved. For example, in Figure 172 the cross appears on a ground that is not endless but circular and lies in turn as a disk on top of the surrounding empty plane. The disk is ground for the cross but figure for the surrounding surface. This is awkward terminology. It seems more adequate to speak of patterns distributed over a number of depth levels, the figure-and-ground pattern being the special case of a two-level configuration.

When there are more than two planes, the above-mentioned rules must be amended. We should expect that in Figure 175 the enclosed circle would lie as figure on top of the square, which in turn would rest on the ground plane. Instead we tend to see a square with a circular hole in it. This seems to be due to a principle of economy, according to which the number of depth levels in a given pattern is as small as conditions permit. If the circle produces a disk that lies on top of the square, the result is a three-level distribution, whereas the perforated square makes for a total of only two levels. This leaves us with a smaller number of planes—that is, with a numerically simpler pattern. We conclude that when the perforation (interruption) of the square is weighed against the three-level arrangement, the former represents the simpler solution. The physiological reasons for this preference have not been investigated.

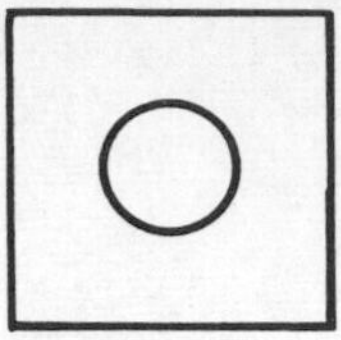

Figure 175

A somewhat more complex example may further illustrate the point. Figure 176 is a woodcut by Hans Arp. The perceptual factors are balanced against each other in such a way that several spatial conceptions are equally possible. We may see a four-plane arrangement (Figure 177*a*): a pyramid, consisting of a small black patch on top, a larger white one underneath, this resting in turn on a black patch, and the whole lying on an endless white ground. Figure 177*b* illustrates a three-plane solution, in which a white ring lies on a black patch. Two two-plane solutions are given in *c* and *d:* a large black ring with a black patch in the center lies on a white ground; or everything white lies in front, and a black background is seen through the cutouts. The principle of economy would of course favor a one-plane solution as the simplest (*e*); but this would involve a series of interruptions, which are avoided by a three-dimensional conception. The only solution that has the advantage of avoiding all interruptions is the pyramid (*a*), which is also favored by the rule of enclosedness. The pyramid, however, requires the largest number of planes. If brightness makes for ground character, *c* would tend to dominate; but the two narrow bridges contained in the white ring would enhance the figure character of the central white figure (*b* or *d*). Finally, similarity of color would tend to group all whites as against all blacks in two separate planes (*c* or *d*).

It will be seen that the various perceptual factors may work with, and against, each other. In Arp's woodcut the powers of these factors are proportioned in such a way that the result is fluctuating and ambiguous. This effect is welcomed by some modern artists—for example, by Picasso and Braque in their cubist pictures—because it undermines the material solidity of the visual world. The older masters, who wished to enhance solidity, preferred compositions that, although not forgoing the counterpoint of antagonistic factors, added up to a system of clearly defined dominances. There was no doubt as to the particular location of each unit in the system of depth planes. It would be tempting to chart, with the section method of Figure 177, the

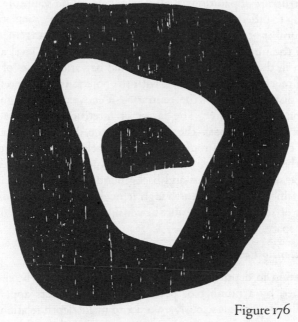

Figure 176

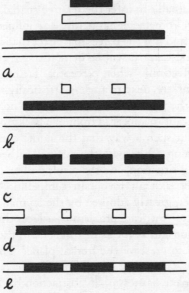

Figure 177

spatial structure of paintings, sculptural reliefs, round sculpture, or buildings belonging to different style periods. We should find characteristic differences in the number of levels employed as well as in their arrangement. We could examine the number of objects assigned to each depth level and their distribution in the frontal plane. There would be various types of depth relief: the total relief might be concave, with the objects in the center lying at the greatest distance, or—on the contrary—a convex relief might build up a protrusion in the center. The factor of interruptedness versus coherence could be studied in both the frontal and the depth dimensions. In some works a continuous, "chromatic" scale of levels would lead from the front toward the back, whereas in others there would be large intervals, for example, between foreground and background. Such an analysis is likely to yield significant results even though it neglects the volume of objects and the slant of surfaces, which must be considered in any more comprehensive study of space.

Application to Painting

The location in depth of frontally oriented surfaces has been shown to be determined by a number of perceptual factors. Artists apply these rules, intuitively or quite consciously, in order to make depth relationships visible, and there is no other way of representing space than by making the eye grasp it directly. It is true that knowledge of the subject matter will often allow the beholder intellectually to infer the relative spatial position of objects in a painting; but such knowledge has hardly any influence on the perceptual effect of the picture, and it is the perceptual effect that conveys the expressive meaning of the work. Later it will be demonstrated that knowledge determines the spatial effect only when perceptual factors are absent or ambiguous. Such situations are next to useless artistically, because in them the spatial structure of the visual field is overruled by nonperceptual agents. If a human figure is meant to appear in front of a background, the total pattern must be organized in such a way that the figure comes to the fore, quite apart from its meaning. Otherwise the eye will either contradict or fail to support the intended situation, and the result will be confusing or feeble.

Actually it is not difficult to obtain compelling depth with pictorial means. This art, often greatly admired by the layman, is easily acquired by any student. The more intricate problem that faces the artist is how to preserve the frontal plane and at the same time obtain the desired depth. Why is the artist anxious to preserve the frontal plane? The degree of intended three-dimensionality varies all the way from the deep vistas of the baroque painters to the complete flatness of an abstraction by Mondrian. No intention and no skill, however, will ever make the depth effect truly complete, except on the faraway ceiling of a church or in combination with stage tricks. In the physical space of the observer the picture remains a flat surface. Therefore, instead of attempting an illusion that is condemned to be incomplete, the painter deliberately emphasizes the presence of the frontal plane and obtains the richness of the double composition already discussed. Among the means by which this is accomplished we are concerned here with those related to the figure-ground phenomenon. If the painter would enlist all available factors to give figure character to the foreground scene and ground character to the back, he would easily obtain a strong depth effect but his picture would fall apart. Instead, he undertakes the difficult task of balancing the influences of the various factors in such a way that the unity of the frontal plane is preserved. Figures 169 and 174 demonstrated how Matisse attempted to solve the problem by giving strong texture to the ground, and Lipchitz by drawing concave contours. An instructive example can be found in van Gogh's well-known *L'Arlésienne*. In this painting the seated woman has all the texture and is enclosed by an empty ground. Strong counterfactors were needed to keep the picture from splitting. For shape, this is achieved by concave boundaries. If we concentrate on the right arm of the woman to the isolation of the rest, the arm looks almost like a dark hole cut in the canvas. In the context of the total composition the woman clearly holds the front but, at the same time, remains sufficiently related to the ground.

Figure 178

Aubrey Beardsley's drawing *Madame Réjane* (Figure 178) may be used as an exercise to determine the factors that tend to make the figure-ground relations ambiguous almost everywhere in the picture. In contrast, Figure

Figure 179

179 presents a particularly successful solution of the problem. Dominance of the women is assured by their narrow shapes and essentially convex outlines. The figure character of the two large clothes bundles is enhanced by the texture effects of the folds. On the other hand, the dark interstices are so narrow and enclosed that they impose themselves almost, but not quite, as positive figures in their own right. The subdued figure-ground effect, although defining the spatial situation with masterful precision in every detail, permits a playful alternation of dark and bright, meaningful and meaningless shape, which fits the decorative purpose and preserves the surface of the cup.

Painters take care to verify the shape of interstices by forcing their eyes to reverse the spontaneous figure-ground effect. This requires training, because the naïve observer sees such areas as shapeless parts of the underlying ground. He pays no attention to them, and finds it difficult and unnatural to do so. When individuals being tested were asked to copy the pattern of Figure 180 as accurately as possible, many reproduced the shape and size of the crosses and squares quite well but entirely neglected the fact that the

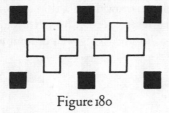

Figure 180

inner edges of the squares lie on the same lines as the outer edges of the crosses. These relations were not seen as a part of the pattern. Even in the Rorschach ink blots, in which figure-ground reversal is facilitated by structural ambiguity, positive use of the interstices is said to suggest a diagnosis of negativism, stubbornness, doubt, suspiciousness, or even paranoid trends. The artist controls such areas in order to assure the unity of the work in the frontal plane and also to enhance the subtle interplay between the positive figures and the negative, half-hidden shapes, which, within their limits, contribute to the expression of the total composition.

Frames and Windows

The function of picture frames is also related to the psychology of figure and ground. The frame as we know it today developed during the Renaissance from the façadelike construction of lintels and pilasters that surrounded the altarpieces. As pictorial space emancipated itself from the wall and created deep vistas, a clear visual distinction became necessary between the physical space of the room and the world of the picture. This world came to be conceived as endless—not only in depth, but also laterally—so that the boundaries of the picture designated only the end of the composition but not that of represented space. The frame was thought of as a window, through which the observer peeped into an outer world, confined by the opening of the peephole but not limited in itself. In our present discussion this means that the frame was used as figure, with the picture space supplying an underlying borderless ground. This trend was brought to a climax in the nineteenth century, where—for example, in the work of Degas—the frame was made to cut across human bodies and objects much more ostentatiously than ever before. This emphasized the accidental character of the boundary and therefore the figure function of the frame. At the same time, however, the painters began to reduce the depth of pictorial space and to stress flatness. Correspondingly, the picture began to "snatch the contour" from the frame, that is, to make the contour the outer boundary of the picture rather than the inner of the frame. Under these conditions the figure character of the traditional heavy frame and the spatial gap between the window in front and the pictorial world in the back became unsuitable. The frame adapted itself to its new function by either narrowing to a thin strip—a mere contour—or even slanting backward ("reverse section") and thus establishing the picture as a bounded surface—a "figure," lying well in front of the wall.

Figure 181

A somewhat similar problem exists in architecture in the perceptual appearance of windows. The original window is a hole in the wall—a relatively small area of simply shaped boundary within the large surface of the wall. This involves a peculiar visual paradox, in that a small enclosed area on a ground plane is destined to be "figure" and at the same time it is, and is meant to look like, a hole in the wall. Perhaps this is the reason why there is something perceptually disturbing about some modern windows that are mere cutouts. The naked edges of the wall around the window look unconvincing. This is not surprising if we remember that the ground is borderless because the contour belongs to the figure. A flat pattern solves the problem by having the ground continue underneath without interruption. This solution is not feasible, however, when the figure is a deep hole, which bars the continuation of the ground. Thus the wall must stop but has no boundary. There are various ways of dealing with this dilemma. One is by means of the traditional cornice. The cornice is not just decoration; it is a way of framing the window. It confirms the figure character of the opening and provides a protrusion beneath which the ground surface of the wall can end. Another solution consists in enlarging the area of the windows so that the wall is reduced to narrow ribbons or strips, both vertical and horizontal. In Gothic architecture, where the remnants of the wall are often further disguised by relief work, the typical effect is an alternation of open and solid units, neither of which is clearly figure or ground. An even more radical transformation is found in some modern architecture, where by an actual reversal of the perceptual situation the walls become grids of horizontal and vertical bars through which the inside of the building can be seen as an empty cube. The network of crossing bars, a visible counterpart of steel construction, has become the dominant figure, which possesses the contours, whereas the windows are parts of the underlying continuous and empty ground. Figure 181 schematically illustrates the three principles. A systematic analysis of the perceptual effects obtained by varying relationships of open and solid areas in architecture, including the function of doors, colonnades, and "ornamental" elements, would be enlightening for both architects and psychologists.

Concavity in Sculpture

The theory of figure and ground can be applied to three-dimensional volume, notably to sculpture. This will be attempted here only for the principle of convexity and concavity.

Even in painting and drawing, convexity and concavity are found not only in the linear contours of surfaces, but also in the two-dimensional boundaries of volumes. The human body is represented mainly through shapes that bulge toward the outside, whereas a niche in a building is concave. As far as the shape of total compositions is concerned, we find that what I called the depth relief of a picture may be concave, as in the hollow box space of a Dutch interior, or convex, as in some cubist pictures that build up from the sides toward a protrusion in the center.

Obviously, figure-ground relationships between volumes can be perceived visually only when the outer volume is transparent or empty. We cannot observe the convexity of a cherry stone in its relation to the concave inner surface of the pulp. But a statue and the surrounding space can be considered as two adjoining volumes—if indeed we are willing to consider the environment as a volume rather than mere vacancy, since the statue seems to monopolize all the figure qualities. It is the enclosed, smaller volume, and it has texture, density, solidity. To this practically all sculpture throughout the history of art has added convexity. The statue is conceived as an agglomeration of spherical or cylindrical shapes bulging outward. Intrusions into the block, and even perforations, are treated as interstices, that is, as empty space between solids that monopolize the contour surface. The interstices are shapeless ground. It is true that the sculptor, just as the painter, keeps an eye on these openings, but traditionally they play a lesser role in sculpture than they do in painting, where even the ground is part of a substantial and bounded surface.

Concavities occur now and then, particularly in Hellenistic, medieval, baroque, and African Negro sculpture. In Bernini's horseback-riding Louis XIV the sweeping locks and folds collect air in hollow pockets. In these examples, however, the concavities are subordinated to the convexity of larger units to such an extent that they contribute no more than a minor enrichment. It was only after 1910 that sculptors like Archipenko and Lipchitz, and later particularly Henry Moore, introduced concave boundaries and volumes as rivals of the traditional convexities. The effect can be predicted from what is found in patterns like Figure 173a. The cavities and holes assume the character of positive, though empty, bulges, cylinders, cones. In fact it seems not even correct to call them empty. Their inside looks peculiarly substantial, as though space had acquired semisolidity. The hollow containers seem filled with air puddles—an observation that agrees with the rule that figure character makes for increased density.

As a result the piece of sculpture reaches beyond the limits of its material body. Surrounding space, instead of passively consenting to being displaced by the statue, assumes an active role, invades the body, and seizes the contour surfaces of the concave units.

In this connection, a further aspect of all figure-ground relationships must be mentioned. I have described the phenomenon in purely static terms as to spatial location, contours, density; but from the very beginning of this book I have insisted that all percepts are dynamic—that is, are described best as configurations of forces. This holds true also for the percepts at hand. A "figure" is not just a bounded area that lies on top. It is actively outgoing. It spreads outward, pushing into and over the ground. There is some evidence that the size of interstices is often underestimated, as though the irradiation of the figure units made them look smaller than they are. The aggressiveness of convex form and the resulting compression of the ground lead to the effects indicated by arrows in Figure 182. What could be the section of a piece of modern sculpture is represented schematically in c, showing how the protruding bulges of the statue push outward whereas the surrounding space invades the concavities.

It is tempting to speculate that this daring extension of the sculptural universe may have been made possible by an era in which flying has taught us through vivid kinesthetic experience that air is a material substance like earth or wood or stone, a medium that not only carries heavy bodies but pushes them hard and can be bumped into like a rock.

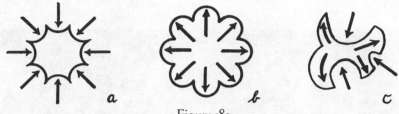

Figure 182

The expressive meaning and value of the new device are best understood if we remember that the statue was traditionally the image of a self-contained entity, isolated in a nonexistent environment and in sole possession of all activity. A comparison of Maillol's and Moore's treatment of a similar subject (Figure 183) shows that the convexity of all form in the Maillol preserves an active element in spite of the essentially passive subject matter. The figure seems to expand and to rise. In Moore's work a passive and receptive quality is obtained not only through the attitude of the woman, but even more compellingly through the hollowness of shape. In this way the figure comes to embody the effect of an outer force, which intrudes and compresses material substance. It might be said that a feminine element has been added to the masculinity of the sculptural form, if it is understood that the implied sexual symbolism is only a particular aspect of the much deeper and more universal theme of activity and passivity.

It was noted that the convex statue is essentially self-contained and independent. This involves a problem for all combinations of a piece of sculpture with others of its kind or with architecture. To say that the problem has never been solved successfully would be an obvious exaggeration. But is it too daring to assert that groups of human figures, unless they were fused in one block, have never gone much beyond rows of isolated units or the kind of loose grouping achieved by dancers or actors? Is it not true that a more intimate relationship between architecture and sculpture than that of the statue surrounded by a cube of space or placed in front of a wall was achieved only when the building provided the cavity of a niche or apse?

The use of concavity in modern sculpture seems to permit a more complete fitting of one unit to another. For example, a family group by Henry Moore shows a man and a woman sitting next to each other and holding an infant. Hollow abdomens make the two seated figures into one large lap or pocket. In this shadowed cavity space seems tangible, stagnant, warmed by body heat. In its center the suspended infant rests safely as though contained in a softly padded womb. Concavity dovetails with convexity.

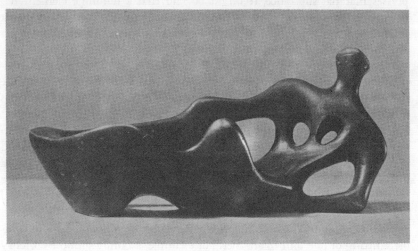

Figure 183

Figure 184

The admission of the empty volume as a legitimate element of sculpture soon led to works in which the material body was reduced to a shell surrounding a central volume of air. Thus far no sculptor seems to have created hollow interiors that could be viewed only from the inside like a room. Moore's *Helmet,* an empty head, would offer to a mouse-sized visitor the most radical experience now available of the use of surrounding concavity in sculpture.

Once the material body of the statue has become a boundary of space, it can be further reduced and thus made more transparent. Lipchitz has experimented with metal strips, and Moore has occasionally replaced solid surfaces by layers of string. These strings not only create boundaries, but also interpret shape through linear directions, as the lines of the grain do in some wood sculpture. Curiously enough, Moore thus applies the theoretical recipe of another English artist, William Hogarth, who in his *Analysis of Beauty* recommended the interpretation of volumes through similar systems of lines. Hogarth actually said, "Hollow forms, composed of such lines, are extremely beautiful and pleasing to the eye; in many cases more so than those of solid bodies." Moholy-Nagy has pointed in this connection to the skeletons of certain technological constructions, for example, in zeppelins and radio towers.

Architecture has taken more readily to concave shape, partly because it was not bound by the imitation of organic bodies and partly because it had always been concerned with hollow interiors. Any interior, whatever its shape, is of course a cavity; more specifically, spherical halls (like the dome of the Pantheon), vaults, niches, and tunnels have concave surfaces. The portals of medieval churches convey their receptive function by a frame slanting inward toward the opening. Figure 184 shows how the seventeenth-century baroque architect Borromini used the counterpoint of convexity and concavity to animate architectural form. Above the hollow round of the courtyard wall lies the cupola, whose protruding bulges are in turn compensated on a smaller scale by the receding niches in the lantern. Outer space seems to react to the vigorous expansion of the building by nipping playfully into the compact solid here and there.

Depth by Overlapping

The theory of figure and ground refers to a limited kind of spatial relationship between frontal planes. It is necessary to go further. In Figure 185 we notice, first of all, different degrees of subdivision within the two-dimensional plane. In *a* the simple arrangement of square and circle makes for a strongly unified total pattern. The centers of square and circle coincide, and the diameter of the circle is equal to the side of the square. A maximum of subdivision is shown in *e*. The over-all symmetry of pattern *a* has given way to a loose combination of two units, which do not touch each other and are symmetrical in themselves.

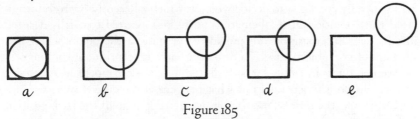

a   *b*   *c*   *d*   *e*

Figure 185

Examples of superposition are shown in *b, c,* and *d*. All three tend to impair the unity of the whole by splitting into two subunits. It will be observed, however, that among the three this tendency is least pronounced in *c*, because here the center of the circle lies on a diagonal of the square and coincides with one of its corners. This creates symmetry around the diagonal axis and strengthens the unity of the whole.

Subdivision as dependent upon the relative simplicity of the whole and the parts has already been discussed. Now we must consider the dynamic aspects of such relationships. There is little tension in either *a* or *e*. In *a* the two units fit each other so well in location, size, and shape that no conflict arises; in *e* all contact, and therefore much opportunity for conflict, has been eliminated. But in the intermediate figures, and particularly in *b* and *d*, tension is noticeable. Square and circle show a tendency toward changing their locations in the direction of one of the two extreme solutions, that is, of either coinciding or tearing apart.

Within the two-dimensional plane there is no way of eliminating the tension by either improving the marriage between square and circle or obtaining a divorce. There remains, however, the "avenue of freedom" already mentioned. The two units cannot change places within one and the same frontal plane, but the retinal projection of the pattern does not prevent them from moving apart in the third dimension. In fact it can be seen that whereas square and circle have no clearly defined spatial relationship in *e*, the two figures in *b, c,* and *d* tend to lie in front of or back of each other. Thus again an escape into three-dimensional organization serves to simplify the pattern by separating parts that badly fit each other. The same effect can be observed in Figure 45 (page 61).

As long as the contours touch or cross but do not interrupt each other, the spatial effect is not strong. In Figure 186, however, the contour of one of the units is blocked at the two points of intersection whereas that of the other continues. In 1866 Helmholtz observed that the resulting spatial

situation is determined essentially by what happens at the points of intersection. "The mere fact that the contour line of the covering object does
not change its direction where it joins the contour of the one behind it,
will generally enable us to decide which is which." Recently Ratoosh formulated this condition in mathematical terms and asserted that it is decisive
in all cases. "Interposition can provide a cue only at the points where the
outlines of two objects meet." The object with the continuous contour will
be seen as lying in front. Ratoosh also said, "What happens at one point
of intersection is independent of what happens at the other." In accordance
with this rule, the unit whose contour is interrupted holds the back position
in Figure 186*a,* whereas in *b* conflicting conditions produce a correspondingly
ambiguous situation, each unit overlapping the other at one place and being
overlapped by it at the other. An instructive example (*c*) has been contributed by Gibson. Here both spatial versions could produce a complete rectangle in the back and a broken one in front; yet the unit whose contours
continue uninterrupted at the point of intersection is seen in front.

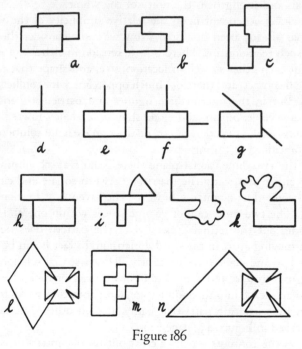

Figure 186

It is quite true that the factor of "consistent shape" is the decisive one in
most cases, but it seems unlikely that what happens at two independent
points should be the only factor to determine the spatial situation of the

whole pattern. Already in the somewhat related Figures 186d–g we notice that what happens at the points of intersection depends on the context. In d and e the interrupted line shows no desire to continue underneath the obstacle. In f there is a weak tendency to three-dimensionality, directly related to the fact that the two interrupted lines are not independent of each other but can be seen as parts of an angular whole. In g, where the rule of consistent shape strengthens the connection between the two lines, they clearly fuse into one line that continues under the square.

Of course Figures 186d–g do not meet Ratoosh's condition, but h and i do. According to the rule, the contradictory conditions at the points of intersection should create spatial ambiguity, as in b. Instead there is no trace of three-dimensionality. If someone asserted that these examples have no bearing on the problem at hand because there is no superposition, he would be begging the question, because the problem consists precisely in finding out under which conditions the perception of superposition occurs. Figure 186h could very well be brought about by two interlocking cutouts of the shape k.

It is probably true that when the Helmholtz-Ratoosh condition acts in the same direction at both points of intersection, it cannot be overruled to the extent of clearly creating the opposite spatial relationship in the pattern. Figures 186l–n, however, show that patterns can be constructed in which the unit whose contours are interrupted tends to lie on top. Admittedly the effect does not work along the common contour, but even there three-dimensionality is absent rather than active in the sense predicted by the rule. The reason is that here the pattern with the interrupted contours is a complete, simply shaped figure that neither demands nor admits additions.

We conclude that the rule of consistent shape as applied to the points of intersection probably refers to the most powerful factor in determining overlapping, but that the law of simplicity must be applied to the pattern as a whole and not just locally if a generally valid prediction is to be obtained.

In Figure 187, a tracing from Paul Klee's line drawing The Vigilant Angel, the spatial locations of the various planes are clearly established by what happens at the intersections, except for area b; to some observers area b may not lie compellingly on top of a and c while continuing under the cover of d to the left, for reasons that the reader is invited to analyze by himself.

Overlapping is of particular value in creating a sequence of objects in the depth dimension when the space conception of the picture relies on contour rather than on volume or light. For some painters space is realized best through a continuous series of overlapping objects, which lead the eye like steppingstones from the front to the back. As an example, Figure 188 gives the main outlines of Mary Cassatt's Boating Party, in which all objects are made to lie within a scale, from the man and his arm with the oar to the child, the mother, the stern of the boat, the water, and the coastline. Even the sail, which is placed outside the scale, is assigned a place in it by means of the rope. The space-building role of superposition in Chinese landscape

Figure 187

painting is well known. The relative location of mountain peaks or clouds is established visually in this way, and the volume of a mountain is often conceived as a skeleton of echelons or slices in staggered formation. The complex curvature of the solid is thus obtained through a kind of "integral" based on the summation of frontal planes.

Figure 188

It should be noted that indicating what a pattern must be like—either at the points of intersection or elsewhere—so that superposition will occur, is merely a description of the necessary conditions and not an explanation of why the three-dimensional effect occurs. The usual explanation is that we see depth in flat pictures because we apply to them our experiences with solids in physical space. We know what the spatial relationship of objects is when we see them as overlapping. This theory is not as satisfactory as it sounds, because our perception of physical space also needs explanation, and we shall discover soon that this is not a simple task. It seems preferable to adopt a theory that is in line with the principles we have found useful before. Just as in the case of the elementary figure-ground situations, the three-dimensional effect of overlapping seems to occur when the total pattern thereby becomes simpler. If one unit prevents an adjoining unit from assuming a simpler shape indicated in its appearance, completion of the imperfect shape is made possible by a splitting of the pattern into two frontal planes, which lie at different distances from the observer. Thus an interrupted contour calls for its continuation, which can be achieved only when the interrupted figure is seen as going on under the other.

The effect is strong enough to overrule actual physical differences of distance. We can draw the units of a pattern on different glass plates and arrange them in front of each other so that an observer sees the total pattern through a peephole. Kopfermann has shown that if plate *a* (Figure 189) is observed from a distance of about 80 inches and *b* lies about one inch in front of *a,* the observer does not see their combination according to the physical facts; instead, the larger triangle is seen as overlapping the smaller (*c*). This happens even though the observer readily perceives the correct physical situation when two unconnected items are shown on the two plates.

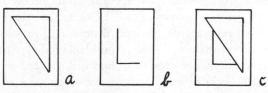

Figure 189

Overlapping is most compelling when it is supported by an actual difference of physical distance between the planes. On the theater stage the space between two overlapping buildings looks more convincing when they are put on different wings, and the presence of actual depth differences in the foreground enhances the effect of painted superpositions on the backdrop. Pictorial superpositions are more effective on a projection screen than on paper or on canvas, because in a painting or drawing the visible flatness of the ground plane will counteract the three-dimensionality of the pattern.

However strong the observer's impression may be that the interrupted figure is completed by continuing behind the back of the front figure, the interruption always remains present and visible. It always exhibits a tension between the units: they show an urge to tear apart and become free of each other. An indirect manifestation of this tension can be demonstrated by experiments in which observers are asked to reproduce from memory a picture they have observed for a short while. Overlappings in the picture are often eliminated in the reproductions, that is, the tendency of objects to steer clear of each other has its way when the direct control of the stimulus is absent. Examples of how the tension of interference is used artistically have already been discussed.

Distortions Create Space

The depth dimension is defined to the eye by more than the superposition of figures. Visual objects are also seen to have slant and volume in depth. When and why does this happen?

Figure 190 tends to lean backward, away from the observer. This tendency is weak in a drawing on paper, stronger on a projection screen or when luminous lines are exposed in a dark room. What makes the figure deviate from the plane in which it is located physically? Most people can also see it as lying in the paper plane. Then we notice that the figure does not look so much like a pattern in its own right as like a distortion of another pattern— a square (or rectangle). Geometrically we are dealing with a rhomb or diamond. Perceptually it is more adequate to speak of a twisted square.

What exactly is a distortion? Not every deviation from a given shape is a distortion. If I clip a corner from a square and add it at some other place of the outline, a change of shape results but no distortion. If I enlarge the entire square, I get no distortion. But if I look at the square or at my own body in a curved mirror, I do get it. A distortion always involves the impression that some mechanical push or pull has been applied to the object, as though it had been stretched or compressed, twisted or bent. In other words, the shape of the object (or part of the object) as a whole has undergone a change of the relationships between its spatial dimensions.

Distortion always involves a comparison of what is with what ought to be. The distorted object is seen as a digression from something else. How is this "something else" conveyed? Sometimes it is given only by knowledge. Alice's long neck is perceived as a distortion, whereas the stem of a flower is not. When the peasant at his first visit to the zoo said of the giraffe, "There is no such animal!" he compared it with some vague norm of animal shape. Mongol eyes may look distorted to Caucasians, but so do Caucasian eyes to Mongols. In all these examples the distortion is not in the given shape itself, but arises from the interaction between what is seen now and memory traces of what was seen before. Such distortions are of limited use to the artist, because expression that relies on something that cannot be perceived directly by the eye is always weak. The artist rarely relies on knowledge alone. But what else is there to rely on?

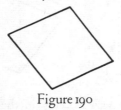

Figure 190

In the rhomb of Figure 190 a twisted square is directly given to the eye, not because we have seen squares before, but because the shape of the square is actually perceivable in the rhomb. When and how does this happen? The first condition that must be fulfilled is that the "norm" figure must be of simpler shape than the perceived one. A square is symmetrical around four axes and has right angles. The rhomb has no right angles and, in its present orientation, no symmetry. It is less simple. But the condition is not sufficient. If the rhomb is turned until it becomes a diamond with two symmetry axes, the geometrical shape of the figure remains unchanged; yet the distortion has weakened or disappeared. Stretching a square along one of its axes will result in a rectangle; but a rectangle does not normally look like a distorted square.

The visual identity of a pattern is determined mainly by its structural skeleton. A square is characterized by two axes of equal length crossing at right angles. If the square is stretched along one of the axes, the skeleton is changed by an addition that cannot be perceived in the resulting rectangle as a separate structural feature. In the rhomb the situation is different. If we think of the square as having movable hinges at the corners, the change of shape can be said to have been obtained by a double, partial rotation (Figure 191), one upward (*a*) and a longer one toward the left (*b*). This adds up to a distortion that is obliquely directed and therefore does not coincide with the axes of the square. Also the distortion is of relatively simple structure, applied to the square as a whole. It seems possible to describe the rhomb as the resultant of two relatively simple structures: the square and the twist. Under such conditions, as an earlier discussion showed, subdivision of the whole into the two substructures is likely to occur. Indeed, the pattern, when conceived as lying in the frontal plane, looks like "a square with a twist." We are now ready to formulate the conditions under which a distortion occurs: The shape of a visual pattern A is seen as distorted if we can obtain it by applying to a pattern (B) that is simpler than A a change of shape (C) that is also simpler than A, takes place along axes not coincident with those of B, and does not eliminate the axes of B.

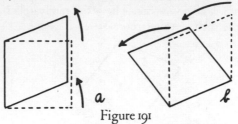

Figure 191

If the rhombic figure is seen as lying in the frontal plane, it exhibits tension like a stretched rubber band. It shows the desire to "leap back" to the shape of the square. Nothing can be done within the frontal plane to relieve this tension; but there is the "avenue of freedom" in the third dimension. Let us reduce, for a moment, the rhomb to its four corner points and imagine that they were four stars in a dark sky. Obviously each star could lie at any distance on the line that connects the observer's eyes with the star (dotted lines in Figure 192). Thus the four stars could form a quadrilateral in any one of an infinite number of differently oriented planes. If we saw them in a frontal plane, as we do with the constellations in the sky, we should perceive the familiar rhomb (Figure 192a). But there exist two planes inclined in such a way that the stars would form a perfect square (one of them is indicated in b). Thus by a tilt in the third dimension the tension would be

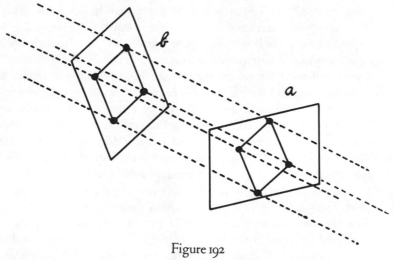

Figure 192

eliminated. The pattern would have notably increased in simplicity, and yet nothing would have changed in the stimulus configuration projected upon the retinae. This suggests the hypothesis that the three-dimensional effect occurs because it eliminates the tension of the distortion and thereby makes the figure simpler without interfering with the projective pattern.

It should be observed that the improvement is obtained at a price. The frontal position of the rhomb is given up for the tilted position of the square. A tilt is less simple than frontality, so that we have gained and lost simplicity at the same time. Therefore, when three-dimensional perception occurs, we must assume that undistorted shape in a tilted position makes for a simpler total situation than distorted shape in frontal position.

A Brain Model

To this point I have used the frontal (two-dimensional) pattern as the base of operations. I have tried to answer the question of what properties such a pattern must possess in order to exhibit a tendency toward tilting in three-dimensional space. This approach serves to determine what kinds of pictorial figures in drawing or painting will produce the effect. But it would be mistaken to assume that in the psychophysiological process of vision there is a similar priority of the two-dimensional pattern. Yet this is often done, for the following reason. Regardless of whether we look at an object that is physically flat or voluminous, frontal or tilted, perception is always based upon the images of the object projected upon the retinas by the lenses of the eyes. It is true that the retina is a two-dimensional surface—not a level plane because it is a part of the inner surface of the eyeball and therefore spherically curved rather than flat. But it is a surface nevertheless, and all images on it are as two-dimensional as a picture painted on the bottom of a bowl. Consequently it is often asserted that all vision originates from two-dimensional projections. This is a misconception. The shape of the retinal image would be of influence only if there was interaction between the processes of stimulation that occur within the surface. An analogy will illustrate this point. Think of a row of telephone booths, in each of which a person is talking. If the spatial vicinity of the booths would make for interaction, so that every listener at the receiving end would hear a jumble of all six messages, then indeed the spatial arrangement of the booths would have to be seriously considered. But since no such interaction exists, it makes no difference whether the booths are placed closely together in a straight or curved row or whether they are miles apart. This, as far as is known, is the situation of the retinal receptors, the rods and cones. Each of these many small single receptors or groups of receptors is stimulated independently by one point of the image. Given this isolation of the messages, the retinal receptor is nothing but a transition station at which light is transformed into nerve impulses. The spatial dimensions of the resulting percepts will be affected by neither the fact that all these transformer stations lie in a common surface nor by the shape of that surface.

Interaction in the field as a whole can be assumed to exist in that part of the brain upon which the optical nerve projects the retinal stimulations. It is the section of the cerebral bark that is known as the visual cortex. This organ represents the physical counterpart of visual experiences. Every characteristic of what we see must be expected to have its equivalent there. Since vision has three dimensions, there should be three dimensions in the cortex. These dimensions must not necessarily be spatial in nature, nor must all spatial relations in the percept have an exact replica in the brain. Yet for our purposes it is convenient to assume that this is true. According to Köhler and Emery, "Few would support the notion that objects which appear at different distances from [the observer] are represented by processes on different levels within the cortex, some nearer the surface and others lower. Yet, from a pragmatic point of view, there seems to be no serious harm in operating with a mental picture which presupposes precisely this topological representation of the third dimension in the visual brain."

We picture the visual cortex as a three-dimensional field, in which the stimulations arriving from the retinas are "let loose." They are isolated as they arrive, and in principle they are free to assume any spatial configuration, flat or voluminal, frontal or tilted. There is no priority for any one. But the stimulations will be limited in their freedom by one important condition: they cannot deviate from the projective pattern established on the retinas. To illustrate the situation, I shall resort to the ingenious instrument by which the Chinese do their arithmetic, a frame of parallel wires with beads, the abacus. At the risk of being blacklisted by every respectable physiologist, I shall think of the visual cortex from now on as a three-dimensional abacus, in which the stimulations are represented by beads. Figure 193 shows the

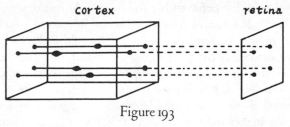

Figure 193

model with a stimulus pattern of four dots. By the projective pattern established on the retina, the dots are here arranged in our example in such a way that in a frontal plane they will form a square. But in principle they are not bound to do this. The four beads may slide freely along their wires, forming any kind of quadrilateral in any one of an infinite number of planes or indeed not lying in any common plane at all, as indicated in Figure 193. If they prefer a particular arrangement, some principle of organization must account for it.

This principle is familiar to us. We shall expect the beads to assume the location that makes for the simplest figure. That is, unless particular conditions prevent it, they will lie in a common plane, and in the example of Figure 193 the plane will be frontal.

Some theorists are willing to admit that there is need for a psychological explanation when a figure drawn on a piece of paper and observed perpendicularly looks as though it were tilted backward. But they do not realize that there is just as much to explain when the figure appears in frontal position. It is true that in the physical world the figure lies in a frontal plane. But we cannot take for granted that this should have an influence on the process of vision. If among the innumerable planes available in the abacus the figure chooses a frontal one, this may or may not have something to do with the physical situation. And if it has, we must explain how such an influence is possible. This problem will be discussed later.

What has been said here about plane figures allows us also to cope with solids. Figure 194a consists of three parallelograms. If each of them assumes a tilted position, which transforms its shape into a square, we shall see the total pattern as a cube in three dimensions rather than as the much less simple flat and irregular hexagon in the frontal plane. Figure 194a is seen as a projection of a cube. But not all such projections will make us see a cube. In Figure 194b the effect is considerably weaker because the symmetry of the frontal figure gives much stability to the two-dimensional version. And

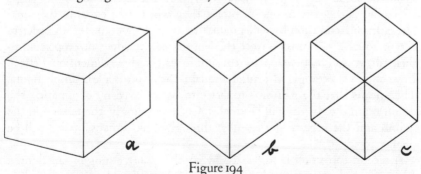

Figure 194

most observers will find it difficult to see c as a transparent version of b. These examples illustrate the rule formulated by Koffka in his pioneer investigation on the subject. "When simple symmetry is achievable in two dimensions, we shall see a plane figure; if it requires three dimensions, then we shall see a solid." Slightly rephrased, the principle asserts that whether a pattern is seen as two-dimensional or three-dimensional depends on which of the two versions produces the simpler pattern.

Two corrections must be introduced here. Neither Figure 190 nor 194a looks quite satisfactory. In the three-dimensional view, Figure 190 is too tall. When it is slightly shortened (Figure 195a), a double improvement is obtained. The three-dimensional effect is more compelling, and the resulting

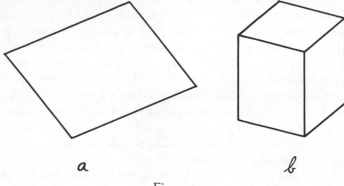

a　　　　　　*b*

Figure 195

tilted pattern looks more convincingly like a square. Similarly, if the same treatment is given to Figure 194a, the three-dimensional effect is stronger and the resulting pattern is a better cube. A glance at the abacus will show that this is to be expected. If a pattern is turned away from the frontal plane, its tilted edges will be stretched. The amount of the elongation will depend upon the angle of the tilt. Consequently, if in the frontal version all edges are equal, as they are in our examples, they will not be equal in the tilted plane. Equilateral rhombs will produce rectangles, not squares. In order to obtain squares, we must correct the lengths of the edges in proportion to their tilt. It is also obvious why this improves the three-dimensional effect. If we obtain a rectangle instead of a square, the result is a less simple figure. This means that the gain in simplicity to be achieved by eliminating the distortion in the rhomb will be smaller. Correspondingly, the tension in the rhomb and the urge to get rid of it through three-dimensionality will be smaller too.

A second correction is suggested by another shortcoming of our figures. Although each rhomb consists of two pairs of parallel edges on paper, they all look slightly wrong in the three-dimensional version. They seem to diverge toward the back, so that the shape of the resulting squares does not appear regular. This is a puzzling situation. Our basic assumption that every characteristic of the visual experience will have its counterpart in the cortical model requires us to conclude that the abacus of Figure 193 is not drawn correctly. The wires must not run parallel, but diverge toward the back, so that the distances between beads increase as they slide on. Then parallel frontal lines will diverge in any tilted plane, the amount of divergence depending upon the angle of the tilt. And in order to become parallels in the tilt, frontal lines must converge. Figure 196 shows how a frontal trapezoid could thus be transformed into a rectangular figure by inclination of the plane.

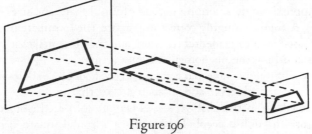

Figure 196

What is the reason for this curious asymmetry in the cortical model? An evolutionist might be willing to explain it as a device that makes the organism better fitted for survival, because this distortion in the brain tends to compensate the distortions of shape and size in the projective retinal images produced by the lenses of the eyes. In the projections the size of any object decreases with its distance from the observer. The brain, by producing the opposite effect, would tend to restore a useful correspondence between physical and psychological shape and size.

Whatever the explanation of the phenomenon, Figure 197 shows that if in the rhombs the paired edges are made to converge somewhat, the spatial effect is enhanced and regular squares or cubes are perceived.

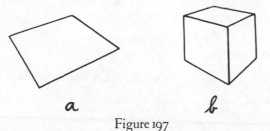

a   *b*

Figure 197

It will be noticed that the patterns with converging edges (Figure 197) create three-dimensionality in a more compelling way than those with parallel edges (Figure 195). The reason is that convergence introduces an additional element of distortion in the frontal plane; therefore the gain in simplicity obtained by three-dimensional perception and the tension toward such simplification are correspondingly greater.

Simple Rather Than Truthful

Patterns like those of Figure 197 can be obtained by photographing squares or cubes at oblique angles. It was mentioned above that in the three-dimensional version these patterns often assume the shape of the physical objects of which they are projections. This has induced psychologists to formulate the phenomenon as follows. In spite of retinal distortions, objects are seen approximately according to their physical shape and size (constancy principle). Although roughly correct in practice, the formulation is misleading. It is based on a coincidental criterion, and therefore makes it impossible to understand how the phenomenon comes about.

Suppose a luminous trapezoid is set up on the floor of a dark room at some distance from the observer and in such a way that it produces a square-shaped projection in the observer's eyes (Figure 198). If the observer looks at the figure through a peephole he will see a frontal square, because it is the simplest figure obtainable for the projective pattern. As for the physical object, he sees the wrong thing, that is, the constancy principle does not hold in this case. We may conclude that correspondence between what exists in physical space and what is seen will occur when the shape of the fore-shortened physical object happens to be that of the simplest figure of which the projective pattern can be seen as a distortion. Fortunately this occurs quite frequently. In the man-made world, parallels, rectangles, squares, cubes, and circles are frequent, and in nature also there is a tendency toward simple shape. But when the shape of objects is irregular—as, for example, in mountains—their projections may not look like distortions of simpler figures. Then constancy of shape breaks down, and three-dimensional perception must rely on other factors.

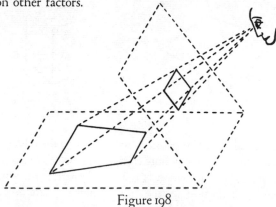

Figure 198

The principle illustrated in Figure 198 serves practical purposes on the theater stage and in architecture. It is often desirable to create the impression of greater depth than is available physically. If a stage designer builds a regular room with level floor and right-angular walls (Figure 199*a*, ground plan), the spectator will receive the projective pattern *b* and consequently see the room approximately the way it is (*c*). If, however, the floor slants upward, the ceiling downward, and trapezoidal walls converge toward the back (*d*), the physical slant will add up with the projective slant and projection *e* will result. Owing to the larger size difference between the frontal opening and the back wall, a much deeper cubic room will be seen (*f*).

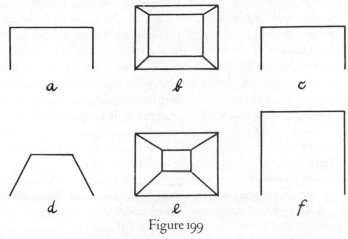

Figure 199

This contradicts the principle of constancy, but corresponds exactly to what the principle of simplicity would make us expect. A striking example can be found in the Palazzo Spada in Rome. When Francesco Borromini rebuilt the Palazzo around 1635, it was his intention to have a deep architectural vista tapering off in a vaulted colonnade. As an observer stands in the courtyard and looks into the colonnade, he sees a long tunnel, flanked by columns and leading to an open space in which he notices the large statue of a warrior. But as soon as he walks into the colonnade he experiences a strong sensation of seasickness, caused by a loss of spatial orientation. Borromini had only a limited site at his disposal, and the colonnade is actually short. It measures about twenty-eight feet from the frontal to the back arch. The front arch is almost nineteen feet high and ten feet wide. The back arch is reduced to a height of eight feet and a width of about three feet. The side walls converge, the floor rises, the ceiling slants downward, and the intervals between the columns diminish. As the observer reaches the statue of the warrior, he is surprised to find it quite small.

There are other examples. St. Mark's Square in Venice is ninety yards wide at the east end, but only sixty-one at the west. The lateral buildings, the Procuratie, diverge toward the church. Thus standing in front of the church on the east side and looking at the 192-yard-long piazza, the observer finds the vista much deeper than from the west side. Medieval architects had the practice of enhancing the depth effect in churches by making the sides converge toward the choir and gradually shortening the spacings of the columns.

The opposite device tends to maintain regular shape against the distorting influence of perspective and to shorten apparent distance. This is true for the quadrangle formed by Bernini's colonnades on St. Peter's Square in Rome and Michelangelo's square in front of the Capitol. Both converge toward the approaching observer. According to Vitruvius, the Greeks increased the thickness of columns at the top in relation to that at the bottom with increasing height of the columns. "For the eye is always in search of beauty, and if we do not gratify its desire for pleasure by a proportionate enlargement in these measures and thus make compensation for ocular deception, a clumsy and awkward appearance will be presented to the beholder." Plato mentions a similar practice of the sculptors and painters. "For if artists were to give the true proportions of their fair works, the upper part, which is farther off, would appear to be out of proportion in comparison with the lower, which is nearer; and so they give up the truth in their images and make only the proportions which appear to be beautiful, disregarding the real ones." During the Renaissance, Vasari said, "When statues are to be in a high position, and there is not much space below to enable one to go far enough off to view them at a distance, but one is forced to stand almost under them, they must be made one head or two taller." If this is done, "that which is added in height comes to be consumed in the foreshortening, and they turn out when looked at to be really in proportion, correct and not dwarfed, nay rather full of grace."

Ames has recently demonstrated discrepancies between physical and psychological space. In the best-known of these experiments (Figure 200) the observer looks through a peephole (o) into a room that seems to have normal rectangular shape ($e\ f\ c\ d$). The actual plan of the room is $a\ b\ c\ d$. The room is constructed in such a way that it gives the observer a retinal image identical with that of a rectangular room. For this purpose walls, floor, and ceiling are appropriately slanted and deformed. Mysterious things happen in such a room. A person standing in p is perceived as being in q, and therefore looks like a midget in comparison to another person standing in r. A six-foot man in p looks smaller than his young son in r. There are two windows in the back wall. The face of a person looking through the window at the left appears much smaller than a face in the right window.

The phenomenon is puzzling only if we forget that, for a man who looks with one eye through a peephole, vision depends mainly upon the projective

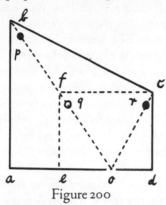

Figure 200

pattern on his retinae. Whether this pattern comes from a deformed or a rectangular room or from a photograph of either does not make the slightest difference. If the deformed room is seen as rectangular, this needs no more and no less of an explanation than the fact that a physically rectangular room is seen as what it is. The explanation, as I have suggested it, is the same for both conditions. The projective pattern represents a distortion of a hollow cube, and consequently this simplest available shape is obtained in three-dimensional perception.

Incomplete Three-Dimensionality

In the foregoing discussion only two kinds of spatial situation have been considered: the two-dimensional projection in the frontal plane, and the three-dimensional orientation in which the visual object assumes its simplest shape. In practice, however, distortions are hardly ever completely eliminated. The size compensations in statues and columns would be unnecessary if the eye of the beholder completely corrected perspective distortions. Psychologists have found that when we look at a tilted object we see a shape that is a compromise between the two extremes of the "real shape" on the one hand and the frontal projection on the other. When looking into a church or along railway tracks, we see the rows of columns converge toward the altar, and the rails as not parallel. The convergence is not so strong as it would be in a frontal projection; the angles in a photograph show a much stronger inclination. But neither is there total compensation. Correspondingly, differences in depth are seen somewhat smaller than they are.

The amount of compensation that occurs depends on several factors. First of all, depth perception is enhanced by stereoscopic vision based on the co-operation of both eyes as well as on other conditions, which I shall mention later. The more accurately depth is perceived, the more completely shape distortion will be compensated. If we look with both eyes at real physical space or through a stereoscope, the depth effect will be strong. In a picture drawn in perspective it will be weaker. The attitude of the observer also makes a difference. Whereas the "man in the street" has a difficult time convincing himself that he sees the rows of buildings slanting toward each other, an art student who has been trained in projective drawing can more readily do so. There is also some evidence that the type of space representation practiced in a given culture will have an influence on the population. Thouless found that Indian students, who are less familiar with perspective representation, saw tilted objects more nearly in their "real" shape than British students.

A further and most important factor derives from the projective pattern itself. We found that the spatial conception depends upon the relative simplicity of the two- and three-dimensional patterns. One condition that always works in favor of flatness is the frontality of orientation. Three-dimensional solids must always appear in oblique orientation relative to the observer, and obliqueness is less simple than frontality. This condition, then, will always counteract the elimination of perspective distortion. Furthermore, the frontal projection is often of such simple shape that it strongly asserts its influence. When we look from the entrance door of a church toward the altar, the projective pattern we receive is symmetrical. This symmetry will reduce depth perception, just as the symmetrical pattern of Figure 194*b* is less readily seen as a cube than *a*. If we look at the interior of the church from an oblique position, three-dimensionality increases. A stage set appearing

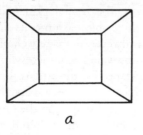
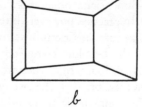

a   *b*

Figure 201

to the audience as a symmetrical pattern (Figure 201*a*) will yield less depth than an asymmetrical one (*b*). In paintings and drawings, the compensation of distortions is never complete, because the eyes see the flatness of the pictorial plane, which counteracts the tendencies toward three-dimensionality in the picture. Artists either enhance or avoid the symmetry of the frontal pattern, depending upon whether their particular style shuns or favors the depth effect. Finally, in sculpture it should be noted that the objective shape of a statue is always quite complex, so that the incentive to undo perspective distortion cannot be expected to be as strong as it is, for example, for an obliquely perceived regular cube.

Past Experience and the Muscle Sense

Why do I see the top of my desk as a rectangle, even though the projective images my eyes obtain of it are all kinds of irregular trapezoids? The usual answer is that I know its real shape from past experience. How helpful is such an explanation?

Obviously all knowledge, past or present, about the shape of objects must ultimately derive from the senses. But the senses have no direct knowledge of "real" shape. All the eyes can rely on are the projective retinal patterns, and these offer a bewildering variety of figures, depending upon the angle and distance. How, then, do we succeed in picking the "right" shape out of this multitude? It certainly cannot be maintained that I see the rectangular shape more often than the others, because in order for me to do so my line of sight would have to meet the surface of the object perpendicularly.

Since mere frequency does not hold the answer, it is sometimes maintained that the correct shape is the statistical average of all the different aspects obtained from the object. That is, if we should add up all the irregular trapezoids, they would crowd around the rectangle as a medium value. This theory does not require that the rectangle is often or, indeed, ever seen directly. But it does presuppose that all aspects are distributed around the "correct" one in an exactly symmetrical fashion, so as to compensate each other's irregularities. This is quite an assumption, considering even the large number of observations that constitute my experience with the object or with this kind of object.

But there is another, more basic objection to the theory, which makes it unnecessary to weigh the argument just presented. For the theory implies that what is seen originally is two-dimensional, frontally oriented projective patterns, among which one is somehow selected. But this is pure fiction. There is no evidence from man or beast, young or old, that anyone's vision ever started with such projections. Persons who were born blind and later acquired vision are reported at first to have great difficulty in identifying shape—but nothing indicates that these people see flat projections. The theory seems to derive from the misapprehension that all perception is based on the flatness of the retinal image. Instead, the facts indicate that whenever a person looks at an object such as a desk top he sees, not a frontal trapezoid, but more nearly a rectangle tilted in space. The more naïve the observer, the more true this is. Special training can influence vision in the direction of flatness. But even then distortion is always compensated to some extent, so much so that the Renaissance painters had to invent special devices in order to obtain pure projections.

Thus, what needs to be explained is that shape in three-dimensional space seems to be immediately given everywhere. What is the cause of space perception? Commonly it is attributed to such factors as convergence, binocular parallax, and accommodation. Convergence refers to the fact that the angle at which the lines of sight of the two eyes meet depends on the distance of the object from the observer. Psychologists have maintained that the turning of the eyeballs, which occurs in convergence, is experienced through the degree of tension in the muscles that hold the eyes in their sockets. Secondly, there is binocular parallax, that is, the fact that the two eyes receive different projective images from any object because they look from different station points. The closer the object, the more different the two projections will be, which again offers an indicator of distance. Finally, accommodation refers to the curvature of the eye lenses, which must adapt themselves to the distance of the object in order to produce a sharply defined image on the retinas. The muscular experience of the flattening of the lenses or the visual perception of the blur might again be considered indicators of distance. There are other such factors.

The efficiency of these indicators has been overestimated. It is true, however, that, at least within the narrow distance of a normal-sized room, binocular vision greatly enhances the depth effect. We have only to compare a photograph or realistic painting with what we see when looking at things in physical space or through a stereoscope. But the point to be made here is that it is not enough to show that the mind has instruments for gauging degrees of distance. The question that needs to be answered is: What makes us experience space in the first place? A thermometer indicates the temperature visually by the length of the mercury column, but it does not give us the experience of warm and cold.

Some lucid pages on this matter have been contributed by the philosopher Merleau-Ponty. The psychologists, he says, talk about perceptual depth as though it were "breadth seen in profile," that is, three-dimensionality objectively given, at which the observer happens to look from an unfavorable station point; so that nothing remains to be explained but how the observer manages to perceive distances correctly in spite of his unfortunate location. Instead, what must be accounted for is the presence of three-dimensionality itself.

Since experience presents us with the accomplished fact, we must look to the corresponding brain processes for an explanation. It is for this reason that I have introduced the admittedly hypothetical brain model. It permits us to explain two- and three-dimensionality as deriving from the tendency to simplest shape, for which we have found so much evidence elsewhere. It permits us to predict the spatial effect for a given projective pattern. Whether the same kind of reasoning can also be used to explain the effect of such things as convergence and binocular parallax will be discussed later.

In addition to the indicators of space just mentioned, reference is often made to the sense of touch. We do not perceive depth and volume by vision alone. We walk through space, we handle objects with our fingers, and the information we get in that way—so the argument goes—is much more reliable than that obtained by vision. Whereas the eyes depend on distorting projections received from distant things, our body directly touches the objects themselves and deals with them in three-dimensional space. It literally gets "first-hand" information. Thus kinesthetic experiences are supposed to register depth and volume in their correct dimensions and to help amend the mistaken notions of the eyes.

This view is the basis for many attempts to explain visual (and auditory) phenomena as derivations from kinesthetic perceptions. But it seems untenable to me, because touch connects the mind no more directly with the physical world than vision. It is true that there is physical distance between the eyes and a cigar box they see, whereas the hands are in immediate contact with it. But the mind does not profit from what happens out there. It depends entirely upon the sensations aroused in the sense organs. As our hands explore the cigar box, the so-called "touch spots" are stimulated, independent of each other, in the skin. The touch image of a surface, a shape, or an angle must be composed by the brain, just as the visual image arises from the multitude of retinal stimulations. Neither is physical size or distance given directly to touch. All the brain receives is messages about the muscular extensions and contractions that occur when a hand reaches out or around a corner. As I walk through a room, my brain is notified of a series of leg motions following each other in time. No space is contained in any of these sensations. In order to experience space kinesthetically, the brain must create it in itself from sensory messages that are not spatial. That is, the same kind of task exists for kinesthesia as it does for vision, except that how this is accomplished seems immensely more difficult to understand—so much so that, to my knowledge, no psychologist has tried to give the answer. There is no question but that the sensations deriving from the organs of touch, muscles, joints, and tendons greatly contribute to our awareness of space. But whoever tries to avoid the problems of vision by referring to kinesthesia gets himself from the frying pan into the fire.

Experiments have been made to show that if an observer knows, or assumes he knows, the size of an object, his knowledge will determine how large and how far away he sees it. But this has been possible only when the pertinent perceptual factors had been carefully eliminated. A luminous disk in a dark room appeared closer and smaller when it was thought of as a Ping-pong ball, larger and farther away when thought of as a billiard ball. The projective pattern fitted both interpretations equally well. But no knowledge of what the object is like would change its size or distance if these were determined by perceptual factors. The distorted room (Figure 200) has been used to demonstrate that we see the kind of room we are accustomed to see, whatever its real shape. But no assumption about the rectangularity of rooms will produce the effect unless the room is carefully constructed in such a way that the projective pattern represents a distortion of a regular cube. The experiment shows also that a fact as well known and as biologically important as the size of the human body is simply overruled by the principle of perceptual simplicity. One reason why this happens is that there is nothing in the visual image of a human being that requires a given size. The image offers no resistance to a mere transposition of size.

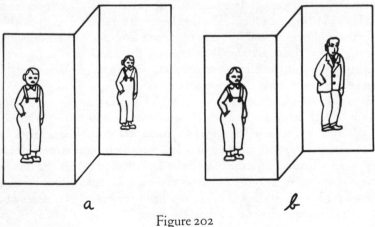

Figure 202

Among the experiments that make it difficult to keep insisting that depth perception is simply a matter of knowledge and experience is one by Carol and Julian Hochberg (Figure 202). The screen is a reversible figure—that is, either its left or its right panel may be seen as lying in front. If we watch such a pattern, the two versions alternate. The experimenter can add up the total time for which each of the two panels is seen in front. What will happen if drawings of human figures are added? In Figure 202*a* the theory of past experience would predict that the left panel will appear nearer more of the time because we know that the larger figure is generally the closer. On perceptual grounds, the same outcome would be expected, because the larger object tends to lie in front whether it is a boy or a rectangle. The outcome was as expected, but since both theories predicted the same thing the experiment could not decide in favor of either. The situation is different in *b*. Here the theory of past experience suggests that the panel with the boy will be seen in front more of the time, because when father and son appear equal in size the father must be farther away. Perceptually we would expect neither panel to be favored, because the two objects are of identical size—which is what happens.

In what way does this psychological controversy serve the artist? He is likely to profit little from the assertion that space perception is based on past experience. In his work he is not much concerned with what people know about the subject matter. His craft has taught him that all knowledge must be translated into visual appearance, and that the amount and kind of spatial effect he achieves depends on what shapes, sizes, orientations, colors he uses. The present chapter is concerned entirely with the same problem.

Objects Create Space

So far we have considered the shape and orientation a pattern will assume in itself. But space is created not only within a narrow pattern. Any visual shape will cast its influence beyond its own reach and, to some extent, will articulate the emptiness around it.

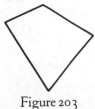

Figure 203

The trapezium of Figure 203 establishes a definite angular deviation from the frontal plane through the convergence of its edges. It is a double deviation, composed of two tilts: one turning the pattern backward like a drawbridge, and the other turning it sideways like a door. This inclination has the consequence of producing on the flat piece of paper a spatial environment, which has a vertical and a horizontal dimension and a definite range of depth. The outline pattern and the frontal plane are seen spontaneously as related to this spatial environment in either of the following two ways. Version I: The trapezium is a flat rectangle lying on level ground; the observer looks down on it at an oblique angle. An airfield is seen in this way when the pilot observes it from above. In this example the orientation of the trapezium coincides with that of horizontal plane *b* in the spatial framework *ab* (Figure 204). The frontal plane *f* is tilted in relation to the framework—that is, the observer himself assumes the tilt. Version II corresponds to what happens if we turn Figure 204 in such a way that *f* assumes a vertical position. Now the spatial framework *CD* is in line with the frontal plane and the observer. The horizontal ground *d* runs parallel with the observer's line of sight. In consequence the trapezium is no longer in a level position, but rises obliquely from the ground, on which it rests with one of its lower edges. Also, instead of assuming rectangular shape it now looks like one side of a truncated pyramid standing in the desert.

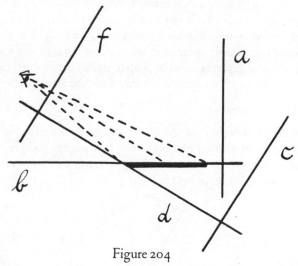

Figure 204

From the point of view of simplicity, both versions have their pro and con. In version I the position of the pattern is in line with the spatial framework. But pictorial space and the frontal plane of the observer meet at an oblique angle. In version II the frontal plane and the framework fit together, but now the pattern rises obliquely and has trapezoidal shape even in the third dimension. I said earlier that both versions occur spontaneously in vision. For example, photographs sometimes give the impression of tilted and pyramidally converging buildings rather than making the beholder feel that he is looking obliquely at perpendicular and rectangular walls.

Figure 203 must be considered a special case in that it produces a horizontal ground plane most readily. This occurs when and because the two points in which the two pairs of edges converge lie on the same horizontal line. What happens when this condition is not fulfilled (Figure

205)? In version I the theory of perspective tells us that the figure will be either a trapezium lying on a horizontal ground or a rectangle on an appropriately tilted ground (the way it might look from a lopsided airplane). In version II the pattern rises obliquely from the horizontal ground and may be seen as rectangular, like a billboard bent backward by a storm. We find that version II of Figure 205 produces a simpler solution than that of Figure 203, and we should thus expect that it would more readily occur—a prediction the reader may put to test.

Figure 205

The main point to be noted here is that of all the innumerable spatial frameworks that could be constructed around the patterns in theory, only very few occur spontaneously in perception: those that produce the simplest possible conditions in regard to the pattern and the observer.

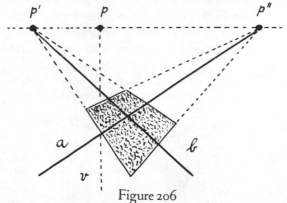

Figure 206

These patterns do more than merely establish the main directions of the spatial framework. According to the rules of perspective, they also define the place from where the observer is looking. For example, in version I of Figure 203 the pattern can be seen as a rectangle only if the observer stands on vertical line v passing through point p (Figure 206), with his eyes at the level of that point. Point p is obtained by perspective construction. To what extent this rule is also compelling psychologically could be investigated by experiment if we asked observers to find "the right point of observation" in front of such a pattern.

Furthermore, the pattern determines the main axes of the world of objects in the picture (*ab*). In our particular example this world is obliquely oriented with regard to the frontal plane. Thirdly, it also establishes the range of space, that is, the location of the horizon. The more convergent the edges of the pattern, the lower the eye level of the observer must be if he is to see a rectangle. The lower the eye level, the lower the horizon. In other words, the more convergent the edges, the narrower the range of the ground. For Figure 206, the horizon is defined by points *p, p', p"*. The fact to be noticed here is that among all the theoretically available ranges of depth the pattern spontaneously creates the one that allows it to assume the simplest shape.

What has been demonstrated for flat figures can be applied to solids. The cubic body in Figure 207 is constructed by reference to the vanishing points *a* and *b,* which establish the horizon. In an empty environment such a figure will create around itself a spatial framework determined by the same two vanishing points. If such an environment is actually drawn perspectively, there will be no trouble as long as the two spatial frameworks coincide. If, however, the horizon of the environment differs from that of the body, one of three things can happen: (1) The environment, or ground, establishes the spatial framework of the whole picture. In this event the solid conforms by assuming distorted shape and oblique orientation. (2) The solid establishes space. In this event the solid has regular cubic shape, and the environment conforms by becoming distorted. (3) The whole splits apart into two independent spatial systems. Both the solid and the ground exhibit regular shape but do not fit into the same space. In general the environment will impose itself so that the first condition prevails; but probably the other conditions can also be obtained by variations of the perceptual factors.

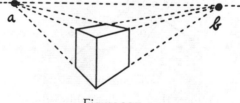

Figure 207

Here again it should be noted that generally perspective drawings like Figure 207 are perceived as pictures of right-angular bodies placed on level ground, although in principle such a drawing may represent an infinity of variously distorted and obliquely oriented bodies. The eye spontaneously sees it as a projection of the simplest possible body—in our example a cubic solid—by allowing it to establish around itself in malleable empty space the one environment that fits its own framework.

The shape and spatial position of visual objects thus depend upon the spatial properties of their environment. This has been demonstrated by experiments of the kind indicated in Figure 198. The luminous trapezoid on the floor will be seen as a right-angular figure in frontal position if its retinal projection is right-angular and the room completely dark. But if the ground floor is sufficiently visible, a trapezoid is seen, because the small enclosed pattern yields to the slant of the larger plane, to which it is perceptually related. The reader is asked to predict what will happen when the figure on the floor is rectangular or triangular.

The environment does not always impose its spatial framework on the enclosed patterns. This will be apparent to anyone who has ever watched a movie or television show from a side seat.

Wertheimer used lantern slides to project a picture upon an irregular ground, such as a heap of boxes rotating on a turntable or a blanket in wavy motion. In order to adapt itself to the ground, the picture would have to split up into innumerable pieces of accidental shape and orientation. Instead, it tends to detach itself and to lie in mid-air on a frontal plane. This split of the whole situation into two separate spatial systems permits the picture to maintain simple shape and orientation.

Pyramidal Space

On the preceding pages I have made statements like "The trapezoid appears as a rectangle." The reader may have looked at the drawings and said to himself, "Well, it does and it doesn't." Here is a crucial problem.

All perceived space ranges somewhere between two extreme situations. At the one extreme, it is equal to its projection upon a two-dimensional surface. The world is flat and lies in a frontal plane. Consequently objects located at different physical distances are as different in size as their retinal projections. Obliquely placed objects are distorted in a way that again corresponds to their retinal projections. In a picture all sizes, shapes, and angles look exactly as they are drawn. At the other extreme, space looks infinitely deep. All physically parallel lines run parallel. All physical objects have their real shape and relative size. In a picture converging lines are now seen as parallel, the horizon lies in the infinite, and distortions of shape and size are fully compensated. Neither of these two extremes ever completely materializes. For reasons that have been discussed, we always perceive an in-between situation, whose exact position between the two poles in any given example depends upon the perceptual conditions and the attitude of the observer.

Psychologists have assumed that size and shape can be seen correctly only if perceived space is an exact replica of physical space, that is, if it meets the condition of extreme situation number two. Under all other conditions percepts were supposed to be misleading, to a degree that depends, as Gilinsky has asserted recently, upon the perceived depth of total space. Accordingly, when a person reported correct observations, the psychologists assumed that he either saw undistorted, infinite space ("complete constancy") or that he corrected his faulty impressions by an estimate based on intellectual figuring ("I see a parallelogram, but it actually must be a square.")

What really happens in perception seems to be less simple. Let us again walk into a church and look through the aisle toward the altar. What do we see? The interior has depth—probably somewhat less than it ought to have. Do the rows of columns look parallel and the columns equal? Yes and no. Vanishing lines converge toward the altar, but at the same time all columns are of equal size and stand on parallel tracks. All this is seen directly, not derived from some calculation.

In theory this sounds paradoxical, in practice we notice no contradiction. When looking at a painting done in the Renaissance tradition, we see the size of foreground and background figures as alike and unlike at the same time. The size difference is obvious, but the figures are also spontaneously equal with regard to the total space that they help to constitute and in which they appear. If their equality could be understood only by intellectual figuring, it would be all but unusable artistically. But what is the solution of the paradox?

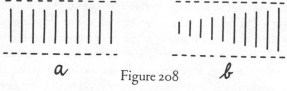

a   Figure 208   *b*

What makes objects look alike in size? It is the fact that, with regard to size, they have identical relations to the spatial framework. The bars in Figure 208*a* are seen as equal because they occupy equal amounts of space in the framework indicated by the dotted parallels. In *b* they are unequal for the corresponding reason. This observation is true in Euclidean space, in which the parallel postulate holds ("Through any point not on a given line one and only one line can be drawn parallel to the given line"). But space does not have to be Euclidean. We are accustomed to thinking of the world as an infinitely large cube whose space is homogeneous, in that things and the relationships between them do not change when their location does. But now imagine one side of the cube shrinking to the size of a point and thus moving from infinity to a finite distance. The result will be an infinitely large pyramid. (It should be understood that I am not talking about an interior of pyramidal shape contained in the usual "cubic" world of our reasoning, but of a world which is pyramidal itself.)

Such a world would be non-Euclidean. All the usual geometric criteria would hold, but they would lead to startling results. Parallels issuing from the side that had shrunk to a point would diverge in all directions. Objects would be of equal linear size if their distances from the peak were proportional to their sizes. An object moving toward the peak would shrink without becoming smaller and slow down while maintaining a constant speed. If an object changed its spatial orientation, it would change its shape and retain identity of shape at the same time.

Our visual world is of this pyramidal kind, since distortions are never fully compensated. It is of less simple structure than a cubic world, but not so complex that the eye could not master it. A few simple principles govern the whole consistently. And just as the mathematician, if he wants to deal with non-Euclidean space, does not have to translate it first into Euclidean space, visual perception orients itself in pyramidal space correctly and directly without need for the intellect to translate the findings into what they would mean in a homogeneous world. I said earlier that things are seen as identical when they have identical relations to the spatial framework. There is no reason to assume that our eyes can establish such references to the framework only under the simplest conditions, namely, when it is right-angular. Gibson has pertinently remarked, "Scale, not size, is actually what remains constant in perception."

There are what might be called "Newtonian oases" in perceptual space. Within a frontal plane, space is approximately Euclidean; and up to a few yards of distance from the observer, shape and size are actually seen as unchangeable. It is from these areas that our reasoning has taken a simplified conception of visual space. But even in the rest of the pyramidal world the relations of shape and size to the framework are perceived so directly that it is all but impossible for the naïve observer to "see in perspective"; because seeing in perspective means perceiving the inhomogeneous world as a distorted homogeneous one, in which the effect of depth appears as the same kind of crookedness that we observe when a twisted thing is seen in a frontal plane.

It is true that at a great distance human figures and objects often look not just small but too small. What counts under these conditions, however, is probably not so much the distance itself as the fact that the continuity of the spatial framework is interrupted. If we look along railroad tracks, the rails converge but nevertheless continue as perceivable parallels up to the horizon. The same is true for the size of individuals in a continuous crowd or for the trees of a forest. But when we look down from an airplane, the interval between ourselves and the ground is almost unstructured. Therefore the distance looks shorter, and consequently things on earth appear smaller.

Similarly, the frame of a window is seen as adjoined by the distant landscape outside. No visible objects define the distance between the window
and the vista, and three-dimensional perception is reduced.

The spatial framework is constructed exclusively by the objects we see.
The edges of walls or roads will do the job best. The increasingly small units
of texture on a surface perform a similar service. But, as our examples have
shown, the framework is often quite fragmentary. Nothing structures empty
space between the skyline and the moon, and therefore the moon looks no
farther away than distant things on earth. And when we glance across the
Grand Canyon we find, with distress or delight, that there is no way of
pinning down the distance of the panorama.

The Underlying Principle

The factors that promote flatness or depth are many and of various kinds.
What is common to them all? It has been suggested by Gibson that three-
dimensional space is created by perceptual gradients. What is a gradient?
And why does it create space?

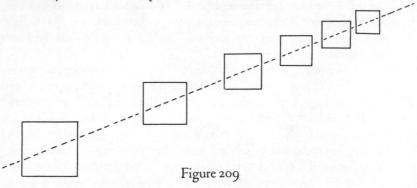

Figure 209

A gradient may be defined for our purposes as the gradual increase or
decrease of some perceptual quality in space or time. For example, oblique
parallelograms contain a gradient of location, in that the slanted figure lies
at an evenly changing distance from the normal axes of the horizontal and
vertical. Obliquity, then, must be defined as a gradient of location or distance
if we are to understand its fundamental importance in depth perception.
Figure 209, which exemplifies a number of perceptual gradients, indicates
obliquity by a dotted line deviating from the horizontal. At the same
time the figure contains a gradient of size. The squares get consistently
smaller, and the intervals between the squares also become gradually smaller.
In consequence, a fairly strong depth effect results.

The regularity of the pattern greatly contributes to the effect. If the units,
instead of being all squares, varied in shape—if, furthermore, they were

distributed in a less regular order and the intervals between them decreased less consistently—three-dimensionality would be less compelling. A photograph of rocks strewn over a field offers an example. The gradients will still be present, since the size of the units decreases in an approximate order from the bottom of the picture toward the top. There also will be an over-all decrease of intervals and some obliquity of relative location. But depth will be less convincing for the following reason.

Gradients enhance depth when they are seen as distortions. A distortion is seen when the pattern represents an over-all deviation from a simpler pattern clearly visible in the distorted one. Figure 209 appears as a distortion of a horizontal row of squares of equal size. If the angle of obliquity were less clear-cut, if irregular differences of shape made the gradual decrease of size less obvious, and if the decrease of intervals were less even, the deviation from a simpler pattern would be less obvious. Or, to put it in other words, the distortion imposed upon the whole would be less simple.

Further gradients could be introduced to make the depth effect in our pattern even stronger. If texture were added to the squares or to the ground on which they rest, in such a way that the textural units were largest at the bottom of the picture and became increasingly smaller, this would contribute an additional gradient of size. It makes no difference in principle whether we use a highly regular texture, such as checkerboard floors, coffered vaults and ceilings, or wallpaper designs—devices that serve in painting and architecture to enhance the depth effect—or the irregular surface structure of fields, rocks, or water. What counts is not that the texture is "natural," but that it conveys the perceptual gradient of size. In fact the artificial gradients are more effective than the natural ones, because their regular patterning shows the change of size more clearly. Realism as such is no contributor to depth.

This is most obvious in the case of color, brightness, and sharpness. So-called aerial perspective, first described by Leonardo da Vinci, produces a gradient of color by making objects paler with increasing distance from the observer. In nature the phenomenon is due to the increasing body of air through which objects are seen. Aerial perspective is effective, however, not because it is natural, but because it produces a perceptual gradient. It can be used at small distances, where the influence of the air is negligible. Gradients of paleness are fully effective in abstract art, where no representation of physical space is intended.

The same is true for sharpness. In physical space we see near objects more neatly defined than distant ones. In painting, the same effect serves to enhance depth—because it involves a gradient, not because it is natural. In photography the range of focus produces a zone of sharp definition and increasing blur with distance from that zone. The larger the focal length and the aperture of the lens and the smaller the distance at which the camera is focused, the narrower the range of sharpness will be. In a portrait the nose may stand out more sharply than the ears. The steepness of the gradient will determine the strength of the depth effect.

In paintings the zone of greatest definition is generally in the foreground. This establishes the foreground as the zero level or base of distance. All other distance levels are seen as deviations from it. In photography there is no such tradition. The zone of sharpness is put wherever the purpose of the picture requires it. In motion pictures the focus shifts freely during a given scene with the changing distance of the most important object. Thus the spatial base can be established at any distance within the third dimension, and a double gradient of blur makes all other levels deviate from this base toward the back and toward the front. In this way a secondary center of spatial composition is created somewhere in the perspective pyramid.

A similar use of light will be described in the next chapter. One way in which light produces depth is by means of brightness gradients. Maximum brightness appears at the level nearest to, or coincident with, the location of the light source. Thus brightness also establishes a key level of spatial distance, which does not have to be in the foreground. Rembrandt put it at any place of the pictorial space that suited him. From this base a gradient of decreasing brightness pervades space, not only toward the back and the front, but also sideways. Light creates a spherical gradient expanding in all directions from a chosen base in space.

The pioneers of the motion pictures were quick to discover that a "traveling" camera obtains more depth. The same effect is observed if we watch the landscape from a moving train or car. The apparent movement of objects varies in proportion to distance. It is fastest at close quarters, comes to a standstill along the horizon line, and increases again in the opposite direction. Objects above the horizon, such as buildings on a hill, clouds, or the sun, will travel with the observer, whereas everything between the horizon and the foreground speeds backward. In this way motion applies a consistent distortion of relative location to the entire visual world. Perceptually this violent distortion of shape is transformed into the simpler image of a world of rigid shape that moves as a whole in a kind of rotation. The same phenomenon has been studied recently for single objects by Wallach. In these experiments observers watched the shadow of an object that was rotating behind a screen. Two things could happen: Either the object could be seen as not rotating at all but as changing its shape in a rhythmical sequence; or an object of rigid shape would be seen turning around its axis. The results suggest that what happens depends on which solution yields the simpler total structure.

The general principle involved cannot be stated by saying that vision is three-dimensional when, and only when, perceptual gradients are perceived. Both implications of this statement are incorrect. In a triangle any two sides converge, that is, produce a gradient of distance or size. But no depth effect results, unless it is induced by additional perceptual factors. On the other hand, overlapping of shape and binocular parallax produce a strong depth effect without the benefit of gradients. The gradients in the triangle do not produce depth, because a triangle is not normally perceived as a distortion of another, simpler figure. Overlapping and binocular parallax do produce depth because they yield simpler patterns three-dimensionally than two-dimensionally. We conclude that gradients make for depth when and because they represent perceptual distortions, and that distortions do so because their compensation in the third dimension produces the simplest available patterns.

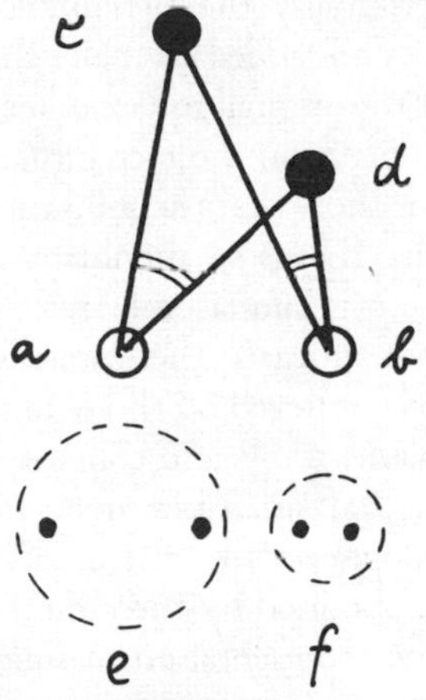

Figure 210

A word of explanation must be added about binocular parallax. Figure 210 offers an illustration. If the two eyes (*a* and *b*) look at the same two dots (*c* and *d*) they will receive different images, because the angles at which they see them are of unequal size. The images are indicated in the dotted circles *e* and *f*. Either image by itself would tend to appear in the frontal plane (unless other perceptual factors intervened). But when they are perceived together, the different distances between the dots will be an obstacle to fusion. Only in the third dimension can a difference of slant compensate this difference of distance and thereby permit the fusion of the two patterns in one image. Thus the contributions of the two eyes are united in the simplest possible way.

When both eyes look at a drawing or painting, the images they receive are identical. This favors a two-dimensional percept in the frontal plane. If the artist wishes to obtain the impression of depth, he must counteract this tendency to flatness by other perceptual factors. Inspection with one eye will reduce the depth of physical space and increase that of pictures.

Frontality and Obliquity

What was found in the drawings of children will have made it clear that the pictorial representation of space cannot be understood as a reproduction of what the draftsman has observed in physical reality. Pictorial space is discovered primarily in the pictorial surface. It evolves from the conditions of the two-dimensional medium as a result of visual experimentation with the lines and shapes and colors available to the artist.

Figure 145 characterized the early stages. The square-shaped pattern, it will be remembered, is originally the two-dimensional equivalent of the cubic solid. Later, side faces are added to make the picture more complete. This limits the function of the original square or rectangle, which now stands for the front face of the cube. Soon the rectangular side faces begin to look unsatisfactory. They do not show that the solid turns around the corner into the depth dimension. Why this is so should by now be apparent. Figure 145*b* looks flat, not because it is "unnatural," wrongly drawn, but because a rectangular pattern does not appear as the distortion of a simpler figure. No inherent tension desires to be relieved by three-dimensional conception. The figure lies in the frontal plane, stable and content.

This changes when the draftsman hits upon making the side faces oblique. The slanted parallelograms are seen as distortions of rectangles. A simpler figure can now be obtained by three-dimensional perception. Thus the principal device for the representation of solids has been acquired.

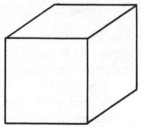

Figure 211

Figure 211 epitomizes a method of spatial representation found everywhere at an early stage of development. Children discover it, and rarely go beyond it unless helped by adults. It is found in the amateur work of "primitive," "Sunday" painters. It serves for the representation of cubic objects in the European Middle Ages as well as in the art of India and China. Whoever assumes that drawings look the more convincing the more closely they resemble the appearance of physical objects might well be surprised to find that such a pattern is accepted so spontaneously and universally as an image of a cube. For it deviates rather violently from the projection of the physical solid.

If a physical object exhibits one of its side faces, the observer must be looking at it from some lateral point of view. Under such conditions all sides, including the front face, must look distorted. There is either a frontal square—then the object is looked at perpendicularly, and no side or top face should be visible; or the sides that extend into depth are visible, in which case there can be no frontal square. Figure 211 would be obtainable only as the projection of a highly irregular, asymmetrical hexahedron, which would contain no right angles and no parallel sides.

This is true also because in the projection of a physical cube the receding sides would converge with increasing distance. Thus in order to yield the parallels of Figure 211, the sides would have to diverge physically. In other words, our pattern is a monster from the point of view of realistic representation. And yet it has been accepted as the image of a cube throughout the ages.

The solution of the puzzle lies in the fact that the pattern is not copied from nature, but has grown in the medium of representation. It is not a projection of a physical body, but rather its simplest equivalent in three-dimensional pictorial space. It combines a side view with a front view, preserving the original regular square, to which slanted sides have been added secondarily. These produce regularly shaped side faces in the third dimension. The structure of a cube is rendered in some of its essential features. The objective characteristics have been preserved as far as possible. The figure has a right-angular front and parallel edges of equal size. Distortions have been limited to the minimum necessary for the three-dimensional effect.

This method, applicable to the representation of any regularly shaped object as well as to an architectural setting as a whole, I shall call "frontal perspective." In frontal perspective one side of the solid lies in a frontal plane. All lines meant to recede perpendicularly to the frontal plane (orthogonals) are drawn at an oblique angle, which is constant throughout the picture. Thus parallels remain parallel even in the third dimension. This feature is known as the isometric method. Our cube is done in frontal-isometric perspective.

There are considerable advantages in this procedure. It employs the simplest perceptual structure and orientation available, and therefore is most easily acquired and understood. It presents the pictorial space as tuned to the framework of the observer, in that one side of the object lies parallel to the picture plane; therefore the others, although drawn obliquely, are meant as running parallel to the observer's line of sight. For this reason the world in the picture is experienced as a direct continuation of the observer's own space. The observer is in line with the world of the picture, which appears as a stable, relatively motionless setting. Furthermore, frontal-isometric perspective keeps the distortion of shape at a minimum. All frontally oriented surfaces maintain their objective size relations, regardless of their distances from the observer. (The front face of the cube is no larger than the back face.) Receding edges also can be kept to their objective length or shortened in a constant proportion, for example, reduced to one-half. Because of this objectivity the method is preferred, not only by the naïve draftsman, but also by mathematicians, architects, and engineers, who are in need of drawings from which the three-dimensional size and shape of solids, buildings, or machines can be reconstructed with complete exactness.

Finally, it should be noted that frontal perspective enhances the depth effect because distortions are more compelling when the frontal framework is explicitly present in the pattern itself rather than being only implied by the right-angular picture plane. The frontal square of the cube serves as the base or zero level from which the oblique sides deviate energetically.

Any setting laid out in frontal perspective tends to impose a corresponding framework upon the action that takes place in it. Figures may be deployed in frontal rows or perpendicularly along the observer's line of sight. This makes for a flat and static scene, better suited for pageants and ceremonial displays than for dramatic happenings.

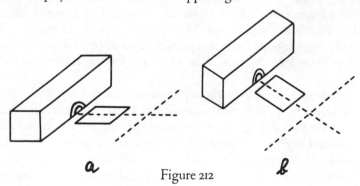

a   Figure 212   b

For these and other reasons the painter may strive for a framework whose main axes traverse the picture space obliquely. This can be partly achieved without changing the method of perspective by shifting the emphasis from the front side to the receding planes (Figure 212a). Although the construction is unaltered, the structure is now much less simple psychologically. The façade is transferred to the third dimension, and by this shift of accent the front view is changed to an oblique side view.

Under these new conditions the now subordinate frontal surfaces tend to become a disturbing remnant of a no more appropriate framework. Clinging to frontality is out of place in an arrangement whose dominant orientation is oblique. Therefore this direct attachment to the picture plane is cut, and we arrive at the perspective system illustrated in Figure 212b. Now both axes run diagonally. Right angles and horizontals have disappeared. Only the verticals keep the picture space anchored to the spatial framework of the observer.

Such angular-isometric perspective is most clearly illustrated in the Japanese woodcuts of the eighteenth century. The observer, instead of being directly related to the pictorial world, peeps into it obliquely. Things would go on totally independent of him, if the vertical dimension did not maintain its full frontality. This inconsistency comes out most clearly in the human figures, which are neither foreshortened nor seen from above as the spatial construction would require, but meet the observer's line of sight perpendicularly in their full extension—a reminder that here, just as in other perspective systems, we are not dealing with an imitation of nature but with an invented pattern, developed gradually from the perceptual conditions of representation in the two-dimensional medium.

The undistorted verticals help also to maintain the necessary connection between the tilted cube of the pictorial world and the frontal picture plane. It would be worth while to study the other compositional means by which the Japanese artists keep the angular picture from becoming an accidentally tilted peep show. They succeed in obtaining from the oblique world a projection that is satisfactorily balanced with regard to the vertical and horizontal axes of the frame.

Toward a Unification of Space

Because of its obliquity, angular space is highly dynamic. It generally stresses one diagonal at the expense of the other, so that the scene seems to cross the visual field like a train entering at front left and leaving at back right, or vice versa. There is, then, a basic asymmetry in this kind of angular space. Symmetry, which had been lost when obliquity became dominant, can be recovered, however, at a more complex level by a method of perspective that incorporates but compensates obliquity.

In Figure 213 the one-sided frontal-isometric construction is complemented by its mirror images. By such a procedure the various obliquities can balance each other, and over-all symmetry and frontality become obtainable. Since we are accustomed to the principle of central perspective, we are tempted to

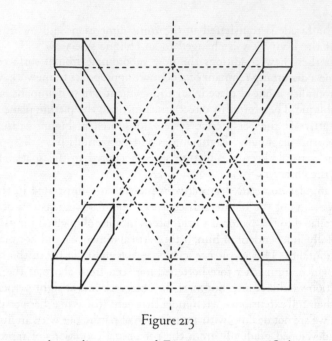

Figure 213

misinterpret the earlier system of Figure 213 as a unified space concept. Instead, it must be realized that we have here essentially a combination of several self-contained spatial constructions. This is less obvious when they are used symmetrically, as in Figure 213, where corresponding receding lines meet in a common vertical or horizontal, as indicated by the dotted lines. In the literature these lines are sometimes called "vanishing axes," a term that tends to create the misleading impression that the receding edges were drawn—in the spirit of central perspective—with the common axis as the meeting ground in mind. Actually these vanishing axes are only by-products of the symmetrical arrangement. The main difference between this procedure and the later invention of central perspective is not that the earlier method uses a vanishing axis instead of a vanishing point. There is a fundamental difference in concept. Central perspective recaptures a unity of space, which was lost at the moment when the orthogonals began to run in more than one direction. In Figure 213 there are four different directions for parallel receding edges and planes, whereas central perspective unites all directions. For this reason the assertion that the Roman wall paintings of the Pompeian type were done in central perspective is incorrect, not only in reference to the geometric construction, but more importantly with regard to the underlying concept.

The illusion that we are dealing here with unified space is dispelled in asymmetrical compositions. They make it clear that there is a separate spatial system for each object in the picture, and indeed even for different parts within the same object. Figure 214, which reproduces the main contours of a silver relief done in Germany around the year A.D. 1000, shows the effect of this atomization.

Figure 214

Figure 213 indicates that by combining spatial units of different orientation the systematic use of converging edges imposes itself. Convergence is a violent distortion of shape, particularly remote from naïve experience. An informal use of convergence may occur now and then as an imitation of effects observed in nature, but the device becomes compelling only when units of different orientation are fused into one. Dotted lines in our drawing show how the combination of any two adjacent units will produce trapezoidal patterns. The introduction of convergent shape removes the main perceptual obstacle to a new unification of space by means of central perspective.

The history of European painting in the fourteenth and fifteenth centuries, culminating in the discovery of central perspective around 1430, offers the fascinating spectacle of the human mind groping for the solution of a visual problem by means of all its faculties, the intuitive power of perception as well as the reasoning power of the intellect. The development occurs in logical steps. Whenever visual exploration has acquired a new principle it is canonized as a rational formula, which in turn serves to define and solidify the basis for further experimentation with the eyes. Hardly any other event in the history of art shows more clearly that the division between artistic intuition and rational insight is artificial and harmful. The two interfere with each other only when a formalized recipe is made to replace visual judgment. But when, as in central perspective, both coöperate in the solution of an artistic problem, the rational principle springs naturally from experience and clarifies the conquests of vision. Art educators who wonder about the most productive way of putting intellectual insight to constructive use might profitably study the integration of all mental capacities in the historic struggle for the unification of space. They will find examples for the artistic inspiration that derives from a new principle as well as for the paralyzing effect of a formula that replaces visual imagination with a recipe.

The atomized space concept can be illustrated by the following quotation from Cennino Cennini, who published his treatise on the technique of painting in the late fourteenth century: "And put in the buildings by this uniform system: that the moldings which you make at the top of the building should slant downward from the edge next to the roof; the molding in the middle of the building, halfway up the face, must be quite level and even; the molding at the base of the building underneath must slant upward, in the opposite sense to the upper molding, which slants downward." This description could fit a picture done in central perspective; the formal features mentioned by Cennini are not derived from the reference of the total structure to a common center, however, but belong to separate areas of the picture, in which the slant of recession assumes different directions.

Trouble arises where the separate spatial constructions meet. Often these places can be left empty or hidden, but when the artist must commit himself he is faced with differently oriented units clashing with each other and producing awkward seams, which reveal the patchwork.

This kind of situation arises often—not only in painting—when the mind is engaged in solving a problem: there are well-organized parts, the whole is still in pieces, but a tension in the direction of the solution is already felt. Shortly before the time of the discovery of central perspective, painters took the decisive step for some limited area of the picture. Convergence ceased to be merely a combination of two different directions. It was understood as the focusing of any number of lines in a common point. The lines of a checkered floor or a vault were represented as a family of converging beams. But the focus was not yet valid for the whole picture. This held true until around the middle of the fifteenth century in Italy, when, for the first time in the entire history of art, the decisive discovery was made. One simple principle took control of the entire composition and oriented every receding line or plane toward a common center. Unity of space had been reëstablished.

Central Perspective

The dramatic impact of this event can be understood only by remembering that central perspective represents the coincidence of two completely different principles. On the one hand, it is the culmination of the centuries-old effort to reintegrate pictorial space. In this sense it is simply a new solution of a problem that had been solved in different ways by other cultures. It is no better or worse than the two-dimensional space of the Egyptians or the system of parallels in an oblique cube employed by the Japanese. Each of these solutions is equally complete and perfect, different from the others only in the particular concept of the world it conveys.

Considered in this way, central perspective is a strictly intrapictorial matter. It is a product of visual imagination, a method of organizing the shapes available in the medium. It reflects reality, but is no more directly connected with the conception of it than the systems developed by other cultures. We do not have to look at nature for guidance or confirmation. Central perspective is a new key to solving the problem of spatial organization within the world of the wall or canvas.

But at the same time central perspective is also the result of a completely different procedure. It is what we get when we set up between our eyes and the physical world a vertical plate of glass, on which we trace the exact contours of the objects as we see them through the glass. In this sense central perspective is the product of a mechanical copy of reality. In principle neither knowledge of the geometrical formula nor effort of pictorial organization is needed to obtain this result. Anyone will get it as long as he faithfully traces the contours he sees.

As Ivins has pointed out, it is no mere accident that central perspective was discovered only a few years after the first woodcuts had been printed in Europe. The woodcut establishes for the European mind the almost completely new principle of mechanical reproduction. Until then any reproduction was a product of creative imagination. But the print is a mechanical replica of the wooden matrix. The tracing on the pane of glass is just such a replica. It is a mechanical print made from the matrix of nature. It creates a new, scientific criterion of correctness. All human arbitrariness is excluded. The tracing is an objectively exact copy of reality.

It was a dangerous moment in the history of Western thought. The discovery suggested that the product of successful human creation was identical with mechanical reproduction and, in consequence, that the truth about reality was to be obtained by transforming the mind into a recording device. The new principle did away with the creative freedom of both perception and representation. Consider the drawing machines constructed by Albrecht Dürer, which were the tangible realization of the new conception of artistic creation (Figure 215). The draftsman stared with one eye through a peephole, which secured an unchangeable point of observation. A given view of the object at a given moment took the place of the totality of experiences,

Figure 215

accumulated, sifted, judged, and organized during a lifetime, which were
formerly the "model" of the artist. And even this given view was not to be
ordered, judged, and understood by the draftsman, but to be copied, detail
by detail, as it projected itself on the glass.

In theory this was the capitulation of the human mind to a standard of
mechanical exactness. In practice, fortunately, artists neither used the machine nor subscribed literally to the conception that had created it. Artistic
imagination was as strong and active as ever, and the world to be represented
continued to be an image conjured up by the inner eye in the reclusion of
the studio, unfettered by what appeared at any given time and place. Even
when, more than three hundred years later, the machine made its reëntry
in greatly perfected form through the invention of photography, it was
imagination that engaged the service of the machine, not the machine that
expelled imagination.

Similarly, the geometric formula could not keep the artists from their task
for more than the few years during which it dazzled their eyes by its novelty

and efficiency. It was no more than an abstract scheme of composition, which had to take second place whenever the eye disagreed with what the formula decreed to be correct. And violations of perspective, which became apparent to the layman only in the work of Cézanne, were committed more subtly by the masters from the moment the rule had been set.

We must not, however, underestimate the fact that the principles of mechanical imitation and geometric construction, although mitigated in practice by the intuition of the masters, became and remained the standards of judgment in theory. The artist had to fight them in himself as well as in his patrons and critics. They contributed to an all-time low of popular visual culture in the nineteenth century, and even in the modern movement pro-voked a violence of dissension that diverted much creative energy to the cult of extravagance.

Symbolism of the Focused World

The "lifelikeness" of central perspective is of little importance to us today. Rather are we interested in its characteristics as a medium of representation and expression.

If compared with the isometric method, it is found to produce the stronger depth effect. This is because convergence adds to the distortion of the object and thus strengthens the need for compensation. On the other hand, a focusing perspective deviates much more from the objective properties of shape and size and thus is not suitable to produce pictures of physical objects from which these can be reconstructed. To build a house or a machine from a drawing done in focusing perspective is possible but complicated. Even if frontality is preserved for one side of the object—as it often is—the angle at which a receding line deviates from the frontal base depends not only upon the shape of the object to be represented, but also upon the location and distance of the object relative to the vanishing point. Thus it becomes difficult to tell the contributions of the two factors apart. The same is true for the length of the receding edges and planes. The closer the object lies to the vanishing point, the more foreshortened are its receding parts.

Perceptually and artistically this means that central perspective violates the basic concept of the object more strongly than other methods of space representation. For this reason it is structurally complex, and can be con-ceived by the human mind only after a long process of refinement. Also, as I have shown in Chapter III, it has the paradoxical effect of emancipating the artist, by the very truthfulness of its distortions, from the objective cor-rectness of shape and size, and thus breaks the ground for the freedom of modern art.

For the first time in the history of the pictorial arts, central perspective creates the image of a world that has a center. Of course any picture delimited by a frame of symmetrical shape has a center, and compositions have always been grouped around a central motif furnished by the subject matter. But the new center of the Renaissance system is independent of both. Space itself converges toward a center. Isometric space is homogeneous. It gives no preference to any one location. Focusing perspective establishes a base, from which activity irradiates and to which all existence is referred.

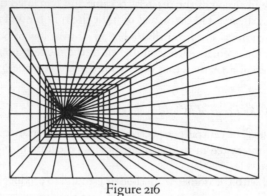

Figure 216

The simplest case is illustrated by Leonardo's *Last Supper* (Figure 105). Here the centers of the frame and the scene coincide with that of space. The lines of the walls and the ceiling converge toward the figure of Christ. The result is complete harmony, symmetry, stability, and a minimum of depth. Compare this with Figure 216. Here high tension results from the fitting together of two patterns that fight each other. The rectangular frame sets a center that is ignored by the spatial system, and the radial symmetry of space is negated by the frame. Yet a solution of the conflict is obtained. The irregularities of pressure created in the various areas by the asymmetry of the whole compensate each other. Strong compression at one side is balanced by much breathing space on the other. As distinguished from a world in which the law of the whole harmonically determines everything down to the smallest detail, we have here the image of another world in which a life center with needs, demands, and values of its own challenges the law of the whole and in turn is challenged by it. The theme of such a composition is the search for a more complex law, which permits contradictory ways of existence to get along with each other. The price of unity and harmony has been raised. Dramatic conflict has been introduced into the image of reality. It will be seen that such a conception could suit neither the philosophy of a Taoist nor the doctrines of the medieval Church. It did suit a period in the history of Western thought in which man took his stand against God and nature, and the individual asserted its rights against authorities of any kind. The exciting discord that we usually consider the main theme of modern art is sounded here for the first time.

Figure 217

Eccentricity to the second degree results when the center of the scene does not coincide with that of space. For example, in one of Tintoretto's representations of the Last Supper (Figure 217), painted some sixty years after Leonardo's, the focus of the room, as established by the lines of the table, the floor, and the ceiling, lies in the upper right corner. But the center of the story is the figure of Christ (encircled). The eccentricity of space indicates that the law of the world has lost its absolute validity. It is presented as one mode of existence among many other, equally possible ones. Its particular "slant" is revealed to the eye, and the action that takes place in this framework claims its own center and standards in defiance of the ways of the whole. Individual action and governing authority have become antagonistic partners enjoying equal rights. In fact here the figure of Christ holds the center of the frame, as far as the horizontal dimension is concerned, so that by deviating from the demands of the surrounding world the individual approaches a position of absolute validity—a turnabout that most characteristically reflects the spirit of the new age.

Considering form alone, we may describe the same phenomenon by saying that central perspective makes for a richer compositional pattern. The two-dimensional conception of space, as in Egypt, limits the main axes essentially to the horizontal and vertical directions. Isometric perspective, when used frontally, adds a system of oblique parallels and, in its angular version, replaces the horizontals with a second system of oblique parallels. The complex relationship between the stable pattern of the verticals and horizontals and the diagonals that cross them in the third dimension presents the eye with a more intricately organized whole. Central perspective tops the simpler systems by overlaying the verticals and horizontals with a sunburst of radii, which introduces an infinity of angles and intervals. In angular-central perspective a second sunburst, centered at the same level as the first, further enriches the composition (cf. Figure 207).

It will be understood that, in order to simplify the presentation, I have considered only the patterns that result from lines and surfaces meant to run parallel with or perpendicularly to the frontal plane in physical space. Any object deviating from this basic location will create its own systems of parallels in isometric perspective, its own focused beams in central perspective. Add to this the less regular shapes contributed by human figures, trees, mountains, and you begin to approach the complexity of the work of art.

Focusing produces a powerful dynamic effect. Since the distortions of the receding shapes are compensated only in part, all objects appear compressed in the third dimension. This experience is particularly strong because the compression is seen not only as an accomplished fact but as developing gradually. At the periphery, as Figure 216 shows, distances are large, and the decrease of size occurs in small steps and at a slow speed. As the eye moves toward the center, neighboring lines approach each other faster and faster, until an almost intolerable degree of compression is reached. This effect is exploited in those periods and by those artists who favor a high pitch of excitement. In the baroque style even architectural vistas are subjected to this dramatic procedure. In Piranesi's etchings the long façades of the Roman streets are sucked into the focus of space with a breathtaking crescendo. Among modern artists, van Gogh favored strong convergence; and an example by Henry Moore (Figure 218) shows how the objectively static theme of two rows of sleepers in an underground tube acquires through perspective contraction the dramatic impact appropriate to the representation of an air-raid shelter. Other artists avoided the effect of receding lines. Cézanne used them rarely, and when they did occur he often underplayed their effect by modifying them in the direction of the horizontal or vertical.

Photographic Perspective

The strength of the visual experience obtained by perspective focusing depends mainly on three factors: the angle of convergence, the extent to which the distorted object is visible, and the distance of the observer from the picture. Photographers have had occasion to give this subject much thought. The angle of convergence depends upon the distance of the camera from

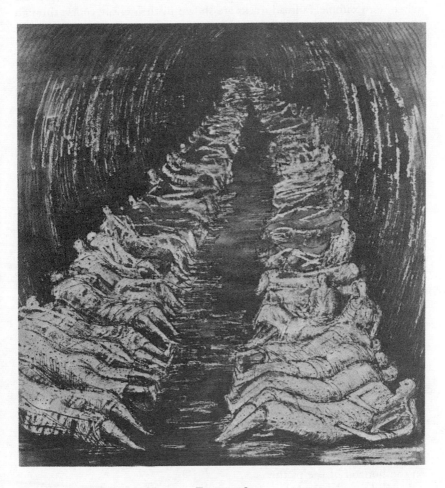

Figure 218

the object. The closer the object, the larger will be the size differences caused by different distance from the camera—hence the enormous feet and hands in snapshots taken from too close quarters, and the steeply climbing contours of buildings.

As for the second factor, convergence will obviously be more impressive when, for example, railroad tracks are shown in their entire course through the visual field rather than only in smaller sections. In photography the extent to which an object appears depends partly upon the distance of the camera. The farther the camera is away, the more of the object shows up in the picture. Then too, there is the angle of the lens, which varies with its focal length. A long-focus lens will show a limited section of the visual field from considerable distance and thus lessen the perspective effect on two accounts. A short-focus lens will cover a wide range from a short distance. This produces maximum convergence. Some film directors, such as Orson Welles, have used wide-angle lenses to obtain the dramatic effect of baroque paintings. Photographed in this way, walls will converge steeply, near objects will look much larger than distant ones, and an actor taking a few steps toward the camera grows into a towering apparition.

Convergence also depends upon the angle at which an object is photographed. When the camera's line of sight meets a surface perpendicularly, there is no distortion at all. But as the angle deviates from ninety degrees, foreshortening and convergence increase. In the 'twenties the Russian film directors showed that a human figure acquires the power of a pyramid-shaped monument by being photographed from below at a steep angle.

Perspective distortions are transformed into recession most completely when the projective angle at which the picture was taken equals that at which it is viewed. Apart from minor aberrations, no lens produces a "wrong" perspective, whatever its distance from the object. But when a picture is taken at close quarters, the spectator, in order to duplicate the projective angle, may have to be closer than comfortable vision permits. Viewed at a normal distance, such a picture shows strong convergence. Under opposite conditions the picture may look flat. In textbooks of perspective, care is taken to point out that the distance of the spectator should equal that between the principal vanishing point and the vanishing point for diagonals on the horizon of the picture.

It will be understood that the preoccupation with a "correct" perspective effect makes sense only when a duplication of everyday vision in physical space is intended. In the artistic practice of painters, photographers, and film directors, the correct amount of convergence depends entirely upon the expression and meaning to be conveyed. We have seen that distortion serves as a useful and legitimate instrument for artistic purposes.

Infinity in the Picture

One further change in the concept of space brought about by central perspective needs to be mentioned here. In a child's drawing, an Egyptian mural, or a Greek vase painting, space means nothing beyond the relations of distance, direction, and size between objects. Spengler has pointed out that the Greeks did not have a word for "space"; they spoke only of location, distance, extent, and volume. In medieval paintings there are arrangements of objects, frequently closed off by mountains or walls, that, although three-dimensional, also point in no way beyond the spatial relationships within the scene. Isometric perspective differs radically from these procedures by presenting space as an entity of its own, expressed in the system of oblique parallels to which all objects must conform. This all-inclusive medium of space does not stop at the picture frame. The parallels point beyond it, and objects are often seen to continue under the frame that cuts across them. Thus endlessness of space is indicated by isometric perspective, but as a fact that is essentially beyond the concern of man because it is referred to the areas outside of the picture. The question is, as it were, left open.

In Chinese landscapes infinity of space appears within the picture as the aim of the line of sight but beyond the reach of the eye. In central perspective, infinity paradoxically assumes a precise location in finite space itself. The vanishing point, as the top of the spatial pyramid, lies at a given distance but also represents infinity. It is within reach and unreachable at the same time, just as the limit in mathematical calculus. All pictorial objects are made to contain in their shape a visible orientation toward infinity, and infinity appears at the very center of tangible space. The presence of the infinite in any definition of the finite has been described as a characteristic of modern European thinking by Spengler.

Most painters have intuitively concealed the ambiguous meaning of the vanishing point by not allowing the converging lines actually to meet. Either the sight of the horizon is blocked by some object, or the crucial area is left empty, or the point lies outside the boundaries of the picture. Its specific location is indicated by the total perspective construction, but it remains itself unreached. The wisdom of this procedure can be realized when occasionally a composition is seen in which the actual clash of the receding lines reveals the paradox to the eyes.

Finally, it should be observed that central perspective locates infinity in a specific direction. This makes space appear as a pointed flow, entering the picture from the near sides and converging toward a mouth at the distance. The result is a transformation of the simultaneity of space into a happening in time—that is, an irreversible sequence of events. The traditional world of being is redefined as a process of happening. In this way central perspective foreshadows and initiates a fundamental development in the Western conception of nature.

De Chirico and the Cubists

The expressive properties of perspective are particularly apparent where it is not used to produce realistic space but freely modified for the purposes of the particular effect to be obtained. Striking examples can be found in the surrealist architectural landscapes of Giorgio de Chirico. Figure 219 is taken from a painting, *The Lassitude of the Infinite*. The mysterious, dreamlike quality of what at first glance looks like a straight realistic composition is

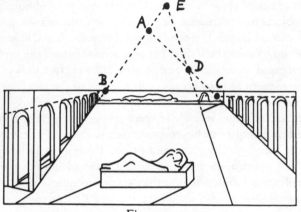

Figure 219

obtained essentially by deviation from perspective rules. The setting as a whole is drawn in focused perspective, whereas the statue rests on an isometric cube. Owing to this conflict between two incompatible spatial systems, the statue seems like an apparition, projected upon the ground rather than materially resting on it. At the same time the pedestal of the statue, with its simpler, more compelling structure, tends to make the convergences appear as actual distortions, rather than as projections of receding parallels. The setting has little strength to resist such an attack, because it is full of internal contradictions. The edges of the square meet far above the horizon in *A*. Thus either the world comes abruptly to an end and the empty universe begins beyond the small railway train and tower in the background, or, if the background is accepted as the horizon, the square, which ought to converge there, appears as immensely stretched sideways—a magic expanse, created where none could be and therefore all the emptier. In consequence the two colonnades seem to have been moved apart by the flat abyss. Or, if the eye accepts the shape of the square, the colonnades, which converge at points on or slightly below the upper margin of the picture (B, C), shrink paradoxically but look quite normal when viewed in isolation of the rest of the setting, except for the frontal arch at the extreme left, which strangely adapts itself to the flight of the receding facade. Finally, the shadow of the right colonnade produces two more vanishing points (D, E) incompatible with the others. Thus a number of inherent inconsistencies create a world that looks tangible but unreal, and changes shape depending upon where we look and which element we accept as the basis for judging the rest.

The same dreamlike unreality pervades another of de Chirico's paintings, *Melancholy and Mystery of a Street* (Figure 220). At first glance the scene looks solid enough, and yet we feel that the unconcerned little girl with the hoop is endangered by a world that is about to crack along invisible seams or to drift apart in incoherent pieces. Again a roughly isometric solid—the wagon—denounces the convergences of the buildings as actual distortions. Furthermore, the perspectives of the two colonnades negate each other. If the one to the left, which confirms the horizon as lying high up, is taken as the basis of the spatial organization, the one to the right pierces the ground. Under the opposite condition the horizon lies invisibly somewhere below the center of the picture, and the rising street with the bright colonnade is only a treacherous mirage guiding the child to a plunge into nothingness.

In these paintings by de Chirico, the combination of incompatible spatial constructions concerns a few relatively large areas that make up the whole. In the work of the cubists the same principle has often been applied to a large number of small units. Being of geometrically simple shape and thus indicating a specific orientation and direction, each of these elements refutes the spatial frameworks set up by its neighbors. If isometric and central perspective show the inventory of the world ordered by one supreme law, the spatial concept of the cubists implies that there is no other order than the mutual balancing of individual "slants," each pointing its own way.

We encountered incompatible elements also in frontal perspective, but they were fitted together carefully to reproduce the image of the physical solid by visual means derived from the two-dimensional medium. The undistorted frontal square of the cube (Figure 211) was not meant to—and did not—clash with the receding side faces originating in a different spatial framework. De Chirico too created the impression of physical completeness and solidity, for the purpose of slyly undermining the beholder's trust in reality. Deformity was presented as physically existent. This remained the formula of the surrealists. They used every device of illusionistic painting to give their creations the shocking material presence of dream monsters.

It is necessary in art to distinguish between the translation of real things into the form of a style and the presentation of unreal things as real. Figure

Figure 220

120 demonstrated that a given shape will produce a monster in one context and a real animal in another. Whether an object appears as a familiar or an imginary thing, as "straight" or distorted, is not determined by a comparison with the physical world, but by the artistic context in which it is presented. Certain drawings and paintings by Picasso or Henry Moore show—and probably are meant to show—abstract artifacts exhibited in a real world. We do not see the stylized image of a real woman, but a real piece of modern sculpture depicted as standing in real space. Discrepant principles of representation either explode the unity of the work or give the character of strangeness to those elements that are made to conform to the standards of a dominant environment. In Seurat's *Grande Jatte* the impressionist texture of minutely varied color spots and the realistically irregular distribution of objects stand against the geometrically simplified contours of the figures. Since the latter yield to the standards of the rest, we see the petrified statues of Parisian citizens mysteriously displayed under suburban trees like the stone images on Easter Island.

Poets, says Marianne Moore, should present "imaginary gardens with real toads in them." The cubists took pains to secure the reality of their toads. They did not wish to show unreal creatures in real space. Rather they presented things that were real but decomposed, because their components had to obey the laws of heterogeneous systems of space crossing each other irregularly. This could be shown only by the disintegration of space itself. If the cubist figures, guitars, and tables do not look like realistic hunks of interpenetrating crystals, it is because the spatial independence of the units is revealed by effective visual means. The cubists use, among other devices, the superposition of objects that render each other transparent and the fading out of objects into the neutral ground of the picture. The psychological effect becomes evident if we remember that the same means are used in motion pictures to represent discontinuity of space. If the scene shifts from the living room to the hotel lobby, the room will fade out into spacelessness— that is, for a moment pictorial space gives way to the physical surface of the screen, after which the opposite process introduces the new space of the lobby. Or, in a lap dissolve, both scenes appear for a moment as overlaying each other, thereby indicating their spatial independence to the eye. But whereas in the conventional film story, fade and dissolve represent only leaps within homogeneous and orderly space, experimental films and modern paintings use them for their attempts to obtain an integration of discordant orders.

VI   LIGHT

If an event or thing is experienced frequently and we have learned to react to it smoothly, our reasoning and feeling are not likely to remain actively concerned with it. And yet it is the most common and elementary matters that reveal the nature of existence with powerful directness.

The Experience of Light

Light is one of the revealing elements of life. To man, as to all diurnal animals, it is the condition for most activities. It is the visual counterpart of that other animating power, heat. It interprets to the eyes the rejuvenating life cycle of the hours and the seasons. It is the most spectacular experience of the senses, an apparition properly celebrated, worshiped, and implored in early religious ceremonies. But as its powers over the practice of daily living become sufficiently familiar, it is threatened with falling into oblivion. It remains for the artist and the occasional poetical moods of the common man to preserve the access to the wisdom that can be gained from the contemplation of light.

The artist's concept of light is influenced by the general human attitude and reaction in two ways. First, practical interest subjects the phenomena of light to selective attention. It eliminates from awareness whatever is common and does not call for action. An outbreak of fire or the sudden darkness brought about by an eclipse are readily observed, and the observation reverberates in emotion. But the play of maple leaves with the rays of the sun or the delicate scale of brightness and shadow that defines the roundness of an apple must be brought back to the eyes by a need to find meaning in the inconsequential.

Second, the artist's concept relies on the testimony of the eye, which deviates substantially from the scientist's view of physical reality. Even facts of common knowledge do not easily replace the evidence of direct observation. Four hundred years after Copernicus, the sun still moves across the sky. In fact, not even the ancient geocentric doctrine of the sun's continuous rotation around the earth has ever been adopted by the eye. The sun still is born in the east and dies in the west; and his rise and fall, his increase and decline of radiant strength, hardly compatible with the theory of rotation, symbolize the path of the hero as convincingly as ever. Perhaps our eyes have by now accepted the view that the world does not end where the vault of the sky touches the horizon, and perhaps some day it will be our daily experience actually to see the earth, and ourselves with it, rotate beneath an immobile sun.

Physicists tell us that we live on borrowed light. The light that brightens the sky is sent through a dark universe to a dark earth from the sun over a distance of ninety-three million miles. Very little of this agrees with our perception. To the eye, the sky is luminous by its own virtue and the sun is nothing but its brightest attribute, affixed to it and perhaps created by it. According to the book of Genesis, the creation of light produced the first day, whereas the sun, the moon, and the stars were added only on the third. In Piaget's interviews with children, a seven-year-old asserted that it is the sky that provides light. "The sun is not like the light. Light illuminates everything, but the sun only where it is." And another child explains: "Sometimes when the sun gets up in the morning, he sees that the weather is bad, so he goes to where it's good." Since the sun appears as nothing but a shiny object, light must reach the sky from somewhere else. Driver, in his comment on Genesis,.says: "It seems thus that, according to the Hebrew conception, light, though gathered up and concentrated in the heavenly bodies, is not confined to them; day arises, not solely from the sun, but because the matter of light issues forth from its place and spreads over the earth, at night it withdraws, and darkness comes forth from its place, each in a hidden, mysterious way." This is more clearly expressed in the Lord's question to Job: "Where is the way where light dwelleth? And as for darkness, where is the place thereof, that thou shouldst take it to the bound thereof, and that thou shouldst know the paths to the house thereof?"

Instead of being an effect transmitted from one object to another, light appears here as a self-contained phenomenon or as a quality inherent in the objects themselves. "Day" is a bright thing, often thought of as an accumulation of white clouds, which arrives from the beyond and moves over the vault of the sky. In the same way the brightness of objects on earth is seen basically as a property of their own rather than as a result of reflection. Apart from special conditions to be discussed below, the luminosity of a house, a tree, or a book on the table does not appear to the eye as a gift from a distant source. At the most the light of the day or a lamp will call forth the brightness of things, as a match ignites a pile of wood. These things are less bright than the sun and the sky, but not different in principle. They are weaker luminaries.

Correspondingly, darkness is seen either as the extinction of the object's inherent brightness or as the effect of dark objects hiding bright ones. Night is not the negative result of withdrawn light, but the positive arrival of a dark cloak that replaces or covers the day. Night, according to children, consists of black clouds, which move close together so that none of the white can shine through. Some artists, such as Rembrandt or Goya, at least part of the time, show the world as an inherently dark place, brightened here and there by light. They happen to endorse the findings of the physicists. But the prevailing view throughout the world seems to be and to have been that light, although originally born out of the primordial darkness, is an inherent virtue of the sky, the earth, and the objects that populate it, and that their brightness is periodically hidden or extinguished by darkness.

To assert that these are children's and primitives' misconceptions eradicated by modern science would mean closing our eyes to universal visual experiences, which are reflected in artistic presentations. Knowledge has made us stop talking like children, ancient chroniclers, or Polynesian islanders. Our image of the world, however, is all but unchanged, because it is dictated by compelling perceptual conditions that prevail everywhere and always. Even so, we have trained ourselves to rely on knowledge rather than on our sense of sight to such an extent that it takes the accounts given by the naïve and the artists to make us realize what we see.

Relative Brightness

Another discrepancy between physical and perceptual facts is revealed by the question: How bright are things? It has often been observed that a handkerchief at midnight looks white, like a handkerchief at noon, although it may send less light to the eyes than a piece of charcoal under the midday sun. Just as in shape and size, the theory of the phenomenon has been obscured by the habit of psychologists to speak of a "constancy of brightness" or to assert that objects tend to be seen "as bright as they really are." The term "constancy" simplifies the facts unduly, and it is difficult to understand what could be meant by "real brightness," considering that experience offers nothing but a variety of illuminations, none of which can claim absolute validity.

Physically, the brightness of a surface is determined by its reflecting power and the amount of light that hits the surface. A piece of black velvet, which absorbs much of the light it receives, may, under strong illumination, send out as much light as a dimly lit piece of white silk, which reflects most of the energy. Psychologically, there is no direct way of distinguishing between reflecting power and illumination, since the eye receives only the resulting intensity of light but no information about the proportion in which the two components contribute to this result. If a dark disk, suspended in a dimly lit room, is hit by a light in such a way that the disk is illuminated but not its environment, the disk will appear brightly colored or luminous. Brightness or luminosity will appear as properties of the object itself. The observer cannot distinguish between the brightness of the object and that of the illumination. In fact he sees no illumination at all, though he may know that the light source is in action or may even see it. If, however, the room is made brighter, the disk will be seen to become correspondingly darker. In other words, the observed brightness of an object will depend upon the distribution of brightness values in the total visual field. Whether or not a handkerchief looks white does not depend upon the absolute amount of light it sends to the eye but upon its place in the scale of brightness values seen at a given time. Leon Battista Alberti said: "Ivory and silver are white, which, when placed near swan's down, seem pale. For this reason things seem very bright in painting when there is a good proportion of white and black as there is from lighted to shadowy in the objects themselves; thus all things are known by comparison." If all the brightness values in a given field are changed in the same proportion, each value is seen to remain "constant." But if the distribution of brightness values is changed, each value changes accordingly and there is no constancy.

The phenomenon of glow illustrates the relativity of brightness values. Glow lies somewhere in the middle of a continuous scale that extends from the bright sources of light (sun, fire, lamps) to the subdued luminosity of everyday objects. One of the conditions—not the only one—for the sensation of glow is that the object must possess a brightness value well above the scale established by the rest of the field. Its absolute brightness may be quite low, as we know from Rembrandt's famous glowing gold tones, which shine through the dust of three centuries. In a blacked-out street a piece of newspaper glows like a light. If glow were not a relational effect, realistic painting would have never been able convincingly to represent the sky, candlelight, fire, and even lightning, the sun, and the moon.

An object may approximately retain its apparent brightness in two different ways. Either the illumination will be seen as changing while the object remains more or less what it is, as can be observed in a concert hall when the lights are dimmed or brightened; or the brightness level of the whole field will be transposed in such a way that the experience roughly duplicates another one, which occurred at a different level. For example, a landscape painting may seem satisfactorily to reproduce the bright summer light. In the first condition, an over-all change of the setting is observed, which, however, does not necessarily affect the individual object. In the second, no difference may be observed either in the field as a whole or in any particular object contained in it.

Such transpositions of the field do occur within certain limits. They are caused partly by mechanisms of adaptation in the eye. The pupil enlarges automatically when brightness decreases, thus admitting a greater amount of light. The receptor organs of the retina also adapt their sensitivity to the intensity of the stimulus. We presumably underestimate the brightness difference between two situations, once the initial contrast effect has worn off. We may get so accustomed to the dimness of the light in a room that after a while we perceive it no more than we do a constant odor. It is also well known that we can immerse ourselves in an old painting to such an extent that we are surprised to find how dark the apparent whites in the picture are if we compare them with a piece of paper. Thus a certain amount of actual transposition takes place.

Again, as in three-dimensional space, it must be emphasized that spontaneous identification and other direct comparisons are possible not only when conditions are perceived as identical. Just as in pyramidal visual space, objects at different distances from the observer can be seen as equal in size because they have identical relations to the surrounding framework, so the brightness values of two objects (or the same object) at different intensity levels may be seen as alike because they have the same relation to the brightness scales of their fields. Such relational perception is quite spontaneous but does not prevent the observer from realizing that the objects "actually" do not look alike if he forces himself to examine them in isolation from their framework. If I compare an envelope on the window sill with one lying in the back of the room, I do not have to rely on knowledge or intellectual calculation to realize that they are both the same white. I see it directly and spontaneously because I see each envelope in relation to the over-all brightness of its environment. But at the same time I can just as clearly see that the one is brighter than the other if I force myself to perform the kind of reduction that was formerly practiced by realistic painters. This difference of attitude has frequently puzzled experimenters and their subjects, who were asked to say whether two things seen under different lighting conditions were identical. They could either see things in their context ("naïve attitude") or abstract them to some extent from it ("objective attitude"), but often felt uncomfortable about the ambiguity of the request. The eye is "intelligent" enough to see the snow in a Brueghel landscape as white while realizing at the same time how different it is from the dazzling sensation on a ski range.

Illumination

The term "illumination," which has slipped into the discussion, needs to be examined with some care. At first thought it might seem as though illumination must be involved whenever we see anything, because unless light falls on an object it remains invisible. This, however, is the reasoning of the physicist. The psychologist and the artist can speak of illumination only if and when the word serves to name a phenomenon that is directly discerned by the eyes. Is there such a thing, and under what conditions is it observed?

An evenly lighted object shows no sign of receiving its brightness from somewhere else. Its luminosity, as I said before, appears as a property inherent in the thing itself. The same is true for a uniformly lighted room. It even seems justifiable to say that a theater stage viewed from the darkened house does not necessarily give the impression of being illuminated. When the light is evenly distributed, the stage may appear as a very bright world, a large luminary. But illumination is something else.

I look at the small wooden barrel that contains my tobacco. Its cylindric surface displays a rich scale of brightness and color values. Next to the left contour there is a dark brown, almost black. As my glance moves across the surface, the color gets lighter and more clearly brown, until it begins to become paler and paler, approaching a climax at which whiteness has all but replaced the brown. Beyond the climax the color reverts back to brown.

But this description is correct only as long as I examine the surface inch by inch or, even better, if I scan it through a small hole in a piece of paper. When I look at the barrel more freely and naturally, the result is quite different. Now the whole object is uniformly brown. On the one side it is overlaid with a film of darkness, which thins out and disappears while an ever thicker layer of brightness begins to replace it. I find that over most of its surface the barrel shows a double value of brightness and color, one belonging to the object itself and another, as it were, draped over it. This happens although the eye receives one unitary stimulation from each point of the object. Psychologically, the unity is split up into the two layers. Here is a new phenomenon, which requires a name. The bottom layer will be called the object brightness and object color of the barrel. The top layer is the illumination.

Thus the psychological and artistic definition of illumination has no necessary reference to an actual light source. There may be a light source physically, but no illumination is perceived, as in an evenly lighted object, or illumination may be seen but no corresponding light source, as in a photograph or realistic picture made of the barrel. What counts is the visual split observed in the image itself.

The top layer, which was called illumination, is a transparent film. The color and brightness of the object shine through it. A few remarks on transparency will enable us to take the next step. A thin fabric allows the skin to shine through. What is the psychological cause of this phenomenon? It does not require that two objects actually lie on top of each other, because a painter can obtain it by using only one tone, a mixture of the skin and the fabric colors. In any event, the eye receives only one color and brightness value from each point. If we look through a small hole in a paper screen, we see no transparency at any point but only a unitary color mixture.

Figure 221 shows an example of transparency. The white beam of light covers the black numbers. Actually a uniform gray is sent to the eyes by the areas of the numbers shared with the white beam. And if we concentrate narrowly on these areas, we see in fact an undivided gray. But when the pattern is viewed as a whole, these same areas are split into black superposed by white. The reason is easily deduced from the principle of simplicity. The subdivision of the flat design into two different spatial layers is to be expected because it yields the simpler structure. Instead of seeing four black units plus three gray ones and four white ones, all oddly shaped and separated, we

Figure 221

obtain three-dimensionally two coherent black patterns of relatively simple shape and one uniformly white triangle. To make this simplification possible, the grays must split into a combination of black and white, the proportion of the two components being determined by the brightness values of the surrounding, nontransparent pattern.

It follows that the painter, in order to obtain transparency, must shape the fabric and the body in such a way that the splitting of the color values makes for the simpler total figure.

The setup of Figure 221 can be reversed. In Figure 222 a dark transparent bar is seen as lying on top of a white rectangle. A similar effect can be obtained by having the shadow of a ruler fall on a piece of paper. A shadow is a layer (or volume) of darkness seen as lying upon or in front of an object and as having brightness and color values different and distinguished from those of the object itself.

Figure 222

It should be observed that the existence of brightness and color values belonging to the object itself is purely psychological. It seems that a medium value or common denominator of the various values exhibited by the object assumes that role. This concept is reflected in the pictorial practice—found, for example, in medieval painting—of giving the object a uniform local color and brightness, to which darkness is applied on the one hand and the whiteness of highlights on the other. Only the technique of the impressionists in the nineteenth century radically ignored the perceptual distinction of object values and illumination values by presenting any surface as a sequence of graded nuances and leaving to the eye the task of separating the properties of the object from those of illumination.

Patterns like those of Figure 223 *a* and *b* tend to show only a small illumination effect or none at all. If a distinction of figure and ground occurs, both units are seen as part of the object itself. This is different in the case of gradual transitions (*c* and *d*). Here darkness or brightness or both often appear as immaterial films imposed upon the solid and homo-

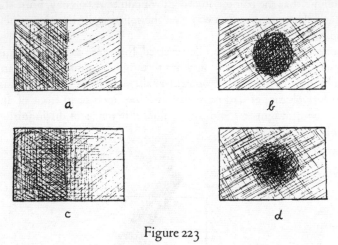

a   *b*

c   *d*

Figure 223

geneous surface of the object. This was first demonstrated by Hering. "A small shadow, thrown upon the surface of one's writing paper, appears as a casual spot of blurred grey superimposed upon the white paper. Under normal circumstances the white paper is seen *through* the shadow. There is no suggestion that it forms in any way a part of the genuine color of the paper. If, now, a heavy black line is drawn around the shadow so as to coincide exactly with its outline a striking change may be observed to take place. The shadow ceases to appear as a shadow and becomes a dark gray spot on the surface of the paper, no longer a casual spot superimposed upon the paper but an actual part of the color of the paper."

Light Creates Space

The presence of the shading suggests a splitting of the pattern into a ground of uniform brightness and color and an applied film of graded density. Since we are dealing here with gradients, the facts discussed in Chapter V will make us look for three-dimensional effects. Figure 223 *c* and *d* indeed shows such tendencies. The rectangle may be seen as turned obliquely toward depth or as exhibiting a cylindrical curvature, either convex or concave, and the dark round spot may either recede or protrude. The phenomenon is necessarily weak because the evenly colored background contradicts and therefore counteracts three-dimensionality, and so does the fact that the contour neither converges nor curves. Under somewhat different conditions, however, shading becomes a decisive factor for the perception of volume and depth.

In an experiment performed by Gehrcke and Lau a wooden, whitewashed cone, whose base had a diameter of about five inches, was viewed from a distance of thirteen yards. The cone was placed sideways with its vertex toward the observer, whose line of sight coincided with the main axis of the cone. When the cone was lighted evenly from all sides the observer saw no cone, but only a flat white disk. The cone became visible when the light fell from only one side. Evidently a three-dimensional view could provide no improvement of structure as long as the lighting was even. But with lateral illumination, perception of a cone simplified the pattern in two ways. First, it provided a homogeneously white surface, detached from the unevenly distributed shading. Second, it transformed the shades of gray into aspects of three-dimensional orientation, just as in linear perspective the convergence of contours is seen not as a property of the object's shape but as an effect of its placement in depth. In both, the three-dimensional version eliminates the distorting feature from the object and attributes it to its spatial properties. The perception of this feature serves to create space, and because of its translation into spatial properties the observer is all but incapable of seeing it in itself, as an attribute of the object. In fact naïve observers are unaware of such shadows, or at least do not "count" them; as a rule they do not mention them even when asked to give a carefully detailed description of what they see. The same holds true for unevenly illumined rooms, in which a gradient of brightness extends from the strong light near the source to the darkness of the far corners. As every painter and stage designer knows, such illumination greatly enhances the depth effect and is not perceived primarily in itself but as an aspect of distance.

In Figure 224 shading produces the depth effect more readily than in Figure 223, because the circular shape of the outline lends itself to the three-dimensional conception of a spherical solid. It will be observed that the effect is stronger in *a* than in *b*. The asymmetrical distribution in *a* produces a more disturbing distortion and thus makes its elimination more urgent; *b* yields a completely symmetrical pattern in the second dimension. When we considered shape, we found that in order to be effective a distortion must run counter to the axial framework of the simpler figure from which it deviates.

In Figure 223 *c* and *d* the shape of the pattern permitted but did not ask for three-dimensional perception. It was the shading that induced the effect. This is different in Figure 225. The combination of two sharply separated areas of homogeneous brightness promotes neither the shadow effect nor three-dimensionality (Figure 223 *a* and *b*). In fact if we force ourselves to see Figure 225 as a flat, V-shaped pattern, it appears as asymmetrically colored; light gray on the left, dark gray on the right. But the distorted shape promotes three-dimensionality; and, given this lead, the asymmetrical coloring greatly strengthens it. It is possible now to see a corner-shaped object, evenly colored in itself but overlaid by shading, which appears as an aspect of spatial orientation.

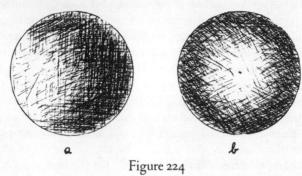

a   *b*

Figure 224

Shading, then, can serve to convey volume and depth with the means of the two-dimensional medium. The resulting spatial effect depends strictly upon the distribution of brightness values. Apart from the influence of the contour, a spherical object results from Figure 224 because the gradient irradiates in all directions from one highest spot. The degree of darkness of any given spot determines its angular deviation from the tangential plane that we can imagine to touch the sphere at the point of the highest light. The steepness of the gradient determines the degree of curvature, and all spots of equal darkness assume the same angular deviation from the zero level.

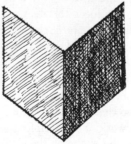

Figure 225

In large objects or rooms the degree of darkness will also determine the distance from the high spot. In order to create the impression of evenly increasing distance, the scale of darkness values projected upon the retinas must progress at a particular rate, which derives from the laws of perspective in pyramidal space—-just as in the animation process of the cartoon film, the effect of a car moving away from the observer at a constant speed is achieved by gradually decreasing the speed of its movement across the frontal picture plane. A discontinuity of the brightness gradient will produce either a sudden change of spatial orientation or a leap over an interval in the depth dimension. When a dark object in the foreground is seen next to a bright background, the distance between the two planes is made more visible by the large difference in brightness. A similar effect is obtained by a bright object in front of a dark foil.

In the representation of an object of complex shape, the contours and the distribution of brightness often coöperate to produce the spatial relief. Areas of similar spatial orientation are correlated visually by their similar brightness. The closer they come to meeting the incident light perpendicularly, the brighter they appear. We know that units of similar brightness are grouped together in perception. Thus a grouping by similarity of spatial orientation is obtained indirectly. Parallel surfaces are knitted together by the eye at whatever place of the relief they may occur, and this network of relations is a powerful means of creating spatial order and unity. Whereas a fly walking across an object would experience nothing but a bewilderingly irregular sequence of ups and downs, the surveying eye organizes the whole by correlating all spatially corresponding areas.

The neat analogy of brightness and spatial orientation is interfered with by cast shadows because they may darken an area that would be bright otherwise and by reflections that light up dark places. Also differences in local brightness will interact with the lighting scheme. In sculpture, dirt spots on the marble or irregularities of brightness in the grain of the wood will often distort shape by being misinterpreted as effects of shading.

We are here again meeting the problem that arises because the eye cannot directly distinguish between reflecting power and strength of illumination. Roger de Piles, a French writer of the seventeenth century, writes, in a discussion of what he means by *claro-obscuro:* "*Claro* implies not only anything exposed to a direct light, but also all such colors as are luminous in their natures; and *obscuro,* not only all the shadows directly caused by the incidence and privation of light, but likewise all the colors which are naturally brown, such as, even when they are exposed to light, maintain an obscurity, and are capable of grouping with the shades of other objects." The painter or stage designer can produce the effect of illumination with the brush, just as he can create depth by converging lines. On the other hand, illumination may produce object brightness, just as depth makes railway tracks converge. The experiment with the disk that seemed to be of brighter color because it alone was struck by light is easily reproduced on the stage. Also the effect of illumination can be compensated by appropriate shading so that the roundness of volume becomes invisible. This principle is used in camouflage. "In innumerable animals, belonging to groups as diverse as caterpillars and cats, mackerel and mice, lizards and larks, countershading forms the basis of their coloration. Such animals are colored darkest above, lightest beneath, with graded tones on the flanks. . . . Viewed under diffused lighting from the sky such animals seem to lack solidity." A recent fad in interior decoration prescribes that the walls containing the windows be painted a shade brighter than those struck by the light. In this way the effect of illumination and contrast is partly compensated.

It seems that if the eye is to segregate illumination from object brightness, two conditions must be fulfilled. First, all brightness values due to illumination must add up to a visually simple, unified system; and similarly the pattern of dark and bright colors on the surface of the object must be reasonably simple. Second, the structural patterns of the two systems must not coincide. If the first condition is not satisfied, there will be confusion; if the second is not, there will be deception—that is, the perceptual split between the two systems will differ from the physical split.

Examples of confusion can be found in photography when lights are not properly blended. The simplest method of producing a comprehensible distribution of brightness values consists in using only one light source. But often more than one source is present, which may be desirable to avoid an excessive darkness of shadows. Several lights may add up to an even illumination, or each of them may create a clearly self-contained distribution of brightness values. The over-all result may convey visual order. But the light sources may also interfere with each other by partly increasing or reversing each other's effects. This will make the shape of objects as well as their spatial interrelations incomprehensible. If several light sources are to cooperate, the photographer will endeavor to organize them in a hierarchy by giving one of them the leading part of the "motivating source" and producing clearly weaker countereffects through the others.

I said earlier that a judicious distribution of light serves to give unity and order to the shape of a complex object. This is just as true for the totality of objects assembled in a painting or on a stage, because whatever appears in a frame is really nothing but one large object, of which all the particular ones are parts. Painters, such as Caravaggio, have sometimes used strong lateral light to simplify and coördinate the spatial organization of their pictures. Roger de Piles has said that if objects are disposed in such a way that all the lights are together on one side and their darkness on the other, this collection of lights and shades will hinder the eye from wandering. "Titian called it *the bunch of grapes* because the grapes, being separated, would have each its light and shade equally, and thus dividing the sight into many rays, would cause confusion; but when collected into one bunch, and becoming thus but one mass of light, and one of shade, the eye embraces them as a single object."

The spots of greatest brightness establish one spatial direction as being that of the light; and when space as a whole is pervaded by a gradient of illumination, the eye is guided toward a center of light, which may or may not be actually visible. For just as in linear perspective the vanishing point is indicated by the converging lines yet may not be present itself in the picture, so the strength and location of a source of light may be perceived indirectly through its effects. Cast shadows often act like pointed fingers. When the shadows of various objects are projected upon the horizontal ground, their main axes meet in a point of the ground exactly underneath the light source; and if a point on the contour of the object is connected with the corresponding point on the contour of the shadow, the resulting line is directed toward the light source. For example, in Figure 229 three corner points of the cube are represented in the shadow, and the connecting lines are seen to converge at the location of the light source.

Shadows

Shadows may be either attached or cast. Attached shadows directly overlie the objects by whose shape, spatial orientation, and distance from the light source they are created. Cast shadows are thrown from one object upon another, or from one part upon another of the same object. By means of a cast shadow one house reaches across the street to touch its opposite number, and a mountain may darken the villages in the valley with an image of its own self. Thus cast shadows equip objects with the uncanny power of sending out darkness. But this symbolism becomes artistically active only when the perceptual situation is made comprehensible to the eye. There are two things the eye must understand. First, the shadow does not belong to the object on which it is seen; and second, it does belong to another object, which it does not cover. Often the situation is understood by reasoning but not easily by vision. Figure 226 indicates the outlines of the two main figures of Rembrandt's *Night Watch*. On the uniform of the lieutenant we see the shadow of a hand. We have no difficulty in determining that it is cast by the gesticulating hand of the captain, but to the eyes the relationship is not at all obvious. The shadow hand has no meaningful relation to the object on which it appears. It may look like an apparition from nowhere, because it acquires meaning only when related to the captain's hand, which is some distance away, not directly connected with the shadow, and, because of its foreshortening, quite different in shape. Only if the beholder while looking at the shadow brings into play a clear awareness, conveyed to him by the picture as a whole, of the direction from which the light is falling and if the projection of the hand evokes its objective three-dimensional shape, can the hand and its shadow be truly correlated by the eyes. Of course Figure 226 is grossly unfair to Rembrandt by singling out two figures and showing one shadow in isolation from the impressive display of light of which it is a part. Nevertheless it seems justified to say that shadow effects of this kind strain the capacity for visual comprehension to its limit.

Figure 226

Lesser masters have overstepped this limit all too frequently, misguided by models, which they copied mechanically; and in photography puzzlingly spotted surfaces are often encountered. Thus cast shadows are to be used with caution. In the simplest cases they are directly connected with the object from which they derive. For example, the shadow of a man meets his feet on the ground; and when the ground is even and the rays of the sun fall at an angle of about forty-five degrees, the shadow will produce an undistorted image of its master. This duplication of a living or dead thing by an object that is tied to it and that imitates its motions and at the same time is curiously transparent and immaterial has always attracted attention. But even under optimal perceptual conditions, shadows are far from being spontaneously understood as an effect of lighting. It is reported that the tribesmen of western Africa avoid walking across an open square or clearing at noontime because they are afraid to "lose their shadow," that is, to see themselves without one. But their knowledge that shadows are short at noon does not imply understanding of the physical situation. When asked why they are not equally afraid when the darkness of the evening makes shadows invisible, they reply that there is no such danger in darkness, because "at night all shadows repose in the shadow of the great god and gain new power." After the nightly "refill" they appear strong and big in the morning—that is, daylight feeds on the shadow rather than creating it.

Human thinking, perceptual as well as intellectual, seeks the causes of happenings as near to the place of their effects as possible. Throughout the world the shadow is considered an outgrowth of the object that casts it. Here again we find that darkness does not appear as absence of light but as a positive substance in its own right. The second, filmy self of the person is identical with or related to his soul or vital power. To step on a person's shadow is a serious offense, and a man can be murdered by having his shadow pierced with a knife. At a funeral care must be taken to avoid having a living person's shadow caught by the lid of the coffin and thus buried with the corpse. Again I say that such beliefs must not be ignored as superstitions, but accepted as indications of what the human eye spontaneously perceives. The sinister appearance of the ghostly darker self in the movies, on the stage, or in surrealist painting keeps exercising its visual spell on people who have studied optics in school; and Jung uses the term "shadow" for "the inferior and less commendable part of a person."

As to the soberer properties of cast shadows, it should be noted that they create space around the object. Figure 227 shows that the rectangle *a* lies flat on a frontal plane or at least creates no articulate space around itself. In

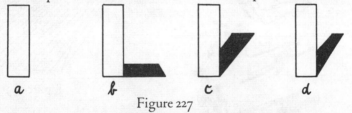

a   b   c   d

Figure 227

b there is a clearer detachment from the ground, partly because of the contrast created by the black bar and partly because the obliqueness of the small edge advocates depth. But on the whole, *b* shows much less three-dimensionality than *c* or *d,* for the reason that the rectangular pattern formed by the bar and its shadow is simple and stable and can hardly be improved by a different version. In *c* the three-dimensional version eliminates an oblique angle and allows the black bar to be seen as a complete rectangle. In *d* the shadow converges—an additional distortion, which makes three-dimensionality even more desirable. In other words, the solid and its shadow function as one object, to which the rules for the spatial appearance of objects apply. Figure 228 shows how effectively shadows create space.

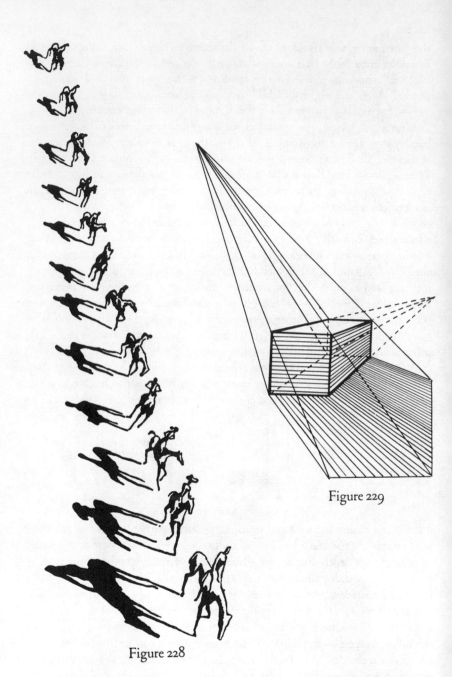

Figure 228

Figure 229

A word about the convergence of shadows. Since the sun is so far away that within a narrow range of space its rays are practically parallel, its light produces an isometric shadow projection—that is, lines that are parallel in the object are also parallel in the shadow. But a shadow is subject to perspective distortion just as any other perceived thing, and therefore will be seen as converging from its base of contact with the object when it lies behind the object and as diverging when it lies in front of it. In addition, a near source of light, such as a lamp or a fire, will produce a pyramidal family of rays and consequently a shadow of divergent physical shape. This objective divergence will be either increased or compensated by perspective, depending upon the position of the shadow in relation to the observer.

Figure 229 shows that illumination adds the effects of another pyramidal system to those resulting from the convergence of shape. Just as the shape of the cube is distorted because its physically parallel edges meet in a vanishing point, so the shape of its cast shadow is distorted by conforming to another focusing point, which is created by the location of the light source. Illumination also distorts the homogeneous local brightness of the cube by darkening parts of its surface with attached shadows. In both perspective and illumination the structure of the distorting system is simple enough in itself to be distinguished by the eye from the constant properties of the object. The result is a twofold visual subdivision. Both the shape and the local brightness of the object are distinguished by the eyes from modifications imposed upon it by spatial orientation and illumination. It should be emphasized here that these deformations are not, as some psychologists seem to believe, just a nuisance, eliminated by the mechanism of vision in the interest of more effective orientation. Instead, they are of the highest value in defining the shape and the spatial orientation and location of the object. Without them we should hardly perceive space at all. These deformations do not escape awareness only to provide us with a constant and stable image of our environment, but because, and to the extent to which, they are seen as indicators of spatial characteristics. Illumination considerably adds to this source of information. Light not only makes us see *that* there are objects around us, but also how they are shaped, in what direction they are turned, and how far away they are from us and their neighbors.

Light is successful in performing this vitally important task in pictures even when what we see is not familiar to us from physical space in everyday life. What counts is not familiarity but adherence to the aforementioned structural conditions. When these conditions are satisfied, even pictures that most violently run counter to our daily experience will create visual space convincingly. This is true, for example, for the negatives of photographs, which present a paradoxical world of luminous objects partly darkened by black light. They define three-dimensional shape with some clarity, except for the kind of cast shadow that destroys rather than conveys space.

Painting without Lighting

In everyday experience light is thus invaluable as an indicator of space, but usually does not enter awareness as a visual phenomenon in its own right, or at least is not counted as an integral property of the world of things. It is, therefore, not surprising that at early stages of the visual arts light is not represented. In the pictures of young children, brightness values serve only to mark differences within the object itself. Dark hair may be set off against a light face. Light sources, such as the sun or a lamp, are often shown as sending out rays, but no indication is given that it is these rays that make objects visible. The same is true for early Egyptian painting. On Greek vases figures are detached from the background by a strong brightness contrast, but these differences appear as the result of object brightness, not of illumination. Literary sources indicate that in the course of the centuries Greek painters learned the use of shadows, and the results of these discoveries can be seen in the Hellenistic wall pictures or the Egyptian mummy portraits around the second and first century B.C. Here the chiaroscuro was handled with a virtuosity not rediscovered until the late Renaissance.

As the need to convey the roundness of solids arises, shading is introduced, later complemented by heightening. In physical space these effects are produced by illumination. But the use of shading does not originate necessarily from the observation of nature, and certainly is not always used in accordance with the rules of illumination. Rather we can assume that after having worked for a while with the perceptually simpler means of line contour and homogeneously colored surfaces, the painter will discover the spatial virtues of unevenly distributed brightness. The perceptual effect of gradients becomes apparent to the eyes. Dark shading will make the surface recede toward the contours. Highlights will make it protrude. These variations are used to create roundness, and do not necessarily imply a relation to a light source. Often the distribution of "shadows" follows different principles. Shading may issue from the contour all around the pattern, and give way gradually to lighter values toward the center. In the symmetrical compositions of medieval painters the figures at the left often have their highlights on the left side, whereas those on the right have them on the right side; or in the laterally foreshortened faces the larger half may always appear bright, the narrower dark. Thus by adapting itself to requirements of composition and shape, brightness is often distributed in a way that would be termed "incorrect" if judged from the point of view of illumination.

The same is true when brightness differences are used to detach overlapping objects from each other. In Greek vase paintings the figure-ground effect is enhanced simply by using contrasting homogeneous object colors (Figure 179). But when a depth interval between objects of nearly identical brightness is to be shown, shading is often introduced. As Figure 230 indicates, the brightness contrast obtained in this manner serves to enhance the overlapping, and there is no need to justify the result as an effect of illumination. In fact Schaefer-Simmern has pointed out that a genuine pictorial conception of illumination can develop only after the formal properties of shading have been mastered. Following a lead by Britsch, he gives examples from Eastern paintings and European tapestries in which the principle of Figure 230 is applied to overlapping scales of rocks, buildings, and trees. To speak here simply of "shadows" is to overlook the main pictorial function of the device.

Figure 230

Such an interpretation of shading and contrast becomes particularly compelling when we find that even after the art of rendering illumination realistically has been acquired, some painters will use brightness values in a way that is not derived from the rules and, at times, even contradicts them. Carpenter has pointed out that Cézanne separated planes in space "by a gradual lightening or darkening of the further plane where the two overlap." Using an example similar to that of Figure 231, he showed that Titian had the same technique. Particularly striking are the darkening of the buildings next to the sky and the brightening of the castlelike structure in the back, which is thereby set off against the roofs. Carpenter also demonstrates that Cézanne sometimes darkened the ground behind a light figure and rounded a cheek in a portrait by applying a gradient of darkness, which is an "abstract" use of the perceptual device rather than the rendition of an effect of lighting. Illustrations from Filippino Lippi and Rembrandt are

Figure 231

given to prove that Cézanne here too was following a tradition. "There is always a battle between light effect and form in painting; and the course of European painting from Giotto to the Impressionists represents a gradual victory of the former over the latter. Cézanne turns his back on the final phase of this trend and, while looking forward to the future, he also looks back to the firm traditions of the past."

Goethe once drew his friend Eckermann's attention to an inconsistency of lighting in an engraving after Rubens. Most objects in the landscape were seen as illumined from in front and therefore as turning their brightest side toward the observer. In particular, the bright light falling on a group of laborers in the foreground was set off effectively against a dark foil. This contrast was achieved, however, by means of a large shadow, which fell from a group of trees toward the observer, in contradiction to the other light effects in the picture. "The double light," comments Goethe, "is indeed forced and, you might say, against nature. But if it is against nature I will say at the same time that it is higher than nature. . . ."

The Symbolism of Light

During the early Renaissance, light was still used essentially as a means of modeling volume. The world is bright, objects are inherently luminous, and shadows are applied to convey roundness. A different conception is observed for the first time in the *Last Supper* of Leonardo, whom Wölfflin has called the father of chiaroscuro. Here the light falls as an active power from a given direction into a dark room, applying strokes of brightness to each figure, to the table top, and to the walls. The effect is pitched to the highest key in some of the paintings by Caravaggio, who prepares the eyes for the electric spotlights of the twentieth century. This sharply focused light animates space with directed motion. It sometimes tears up the unity of bodies by tracing the border lines of darkness across the surfaces. It stimulates the sense of sight by playfully disfiguring familiar shape and excites it by violent contrast. A comparison with Hollywood movies is not entirely out of place, because here just as there the impact of the dazzling rays, the dance of shadows, and the secret of darkness give tonic thrills to the nerves rather than nourishing the mind by the symbolism of light.

The symbolism of light, which finds its moving pictorial expression in the work of Rembrandt, probably goes as far back as the history of man. I mentioned earlier that in perception darkness does not appear as the mere absence of light but as an active counterprinciple. The dualism of the two antagonistic powers is found in the mythology and philosophy of many cultures— for example, China and Persia. Day and night become the visual image of the conflict between good and evil. The Bible identifies God, Christ, truth, virtue, and salvation with light, and godlessness and the Devil with darkness. Interpreted to the eyes by the symbolic use of daylight in church architecture and of candles in the religious service, this tradition remained alive through the centuries. It stirred up resonance in the mind of Rembrandt.

The religious symbolism of light was, of course, familiar to the painters of the Middle Ages, and the pictorial effects of illumination had been studied in theory and practice since the Renaissance. But the gold grounds, halos, and geometric star patterns—symbolic representations of the divine light—appeared to the eye as little more than shiny attributes; on the other hand, the correctly observed light effects of the fifteenth and sixteenth centuries were essentially the products of curiosity, research, and *gourmandise*. Rembrandt personifies the final confluence of the two sources. Divine light is no longer an ornament but the realistic experience of radiant energy, and the sensuous spectacle of highlights and shadows is transformed into a revelation.

Rembrandt's pictures typically present a narrow, dark scene, into which the beam of light carries the animating message of a beyond, unknown and invisible in itself but perceivable through its powerful reflection. As the light falls from above, life on earth is no longer in the center of the world but at its dark bottom. The eyes are made to understand that the human habitat is nothing but a valley of shadows, humbly dependent upon the true existence on the heights.

When the source of light is located inside the picture, the meaning changes. Now the life-giving energy establishes the center and the range of a narrow world. Nothing exists beyond the corners to which the rays reach. There is a *Holy Family* by Rembrandt in which the light seems to originate in the brilliantly lighted book from which Mary is reading, because the candle itself is hidden. The light of the Bible reveals the sleeping child in the cradle, and the listening Joseph is dwarfed by his own towering shadow, which is cast on the wall behind and above him. In another painting by Rembrandt, the light, again hidden, brightens the body of Christ, which is being taken down from the cross. The ceremony is performed surreptitiously in a dark world. But as the light falls from below, it heightens the limp body and imparts the majesty of life to the image of death. Thus the light source within the picture tells the story of the New Testament—that is, the story of the divine light transferred to the earth and ennobling it by its presence.

Rembrandt's pictures illustrate and use the twofold effect of light on the objects struck by it. The objects are seen as passively receiving the impact from an outer force, but at the same time they become light sources themselves, actively irradiating energy. Having become enlightened, they hand on the message. The hiding of the candle is a means of eliminating the passive aspect of the happening—the illuminated object becomes the primary source. In this way Rembrandt enables a book or a face to send out light without violating the demands of a realistic style of painting. By this pictorial trick he copes with the central mystery of the Gospel story, the light that has become matter.

How does Rembrandt obtain his glowing luminosity? I have already mentioned some of the perceptual conditions. An object appears luminous not only by virtue of its absolute brightness, but by greatly surpassing the brightness level established in the rest of the field. Thus the uncanny glow of rather dark objects comes about when they are put in an even darker environment. Furthermore, luminosity results when brightness is not perceived as an effect of illumination. To this end, shadows must be eliminated or kept at a minimum. And the strongest light must appear within the limits of the object. It is not difficult to find in Rembrandt's work examples that approximately duplicate the effect of the psychological experiment with the suspended disk. He frequently places a bright object in a dark field, keeps it almost free of shadow, and partly lights the objects around it. Thus in a *Wedding of Samson* Delilah is enthroned in front of a dark curtain as a pyramid of light, and the reflection of her splendor is seen on the table and the people around her. Similarly in a *Toilet of Bathshebah* the body of the woman is singled out by a strong light, whereas the environment, including the two maids who minister to her, remains in the dark. In general terms, it might be said that glow occurs at the place of the light source or when there is more brightness in a given spot than is warranted by the structure of the light distribution in the whole field. In the latter event the bright spot does not correspond to the brightness value required by the total pattern at that particular place, thus establishing a self-contained and isolated light system of its own.

Glow is also associated with a lack of surface texture. Objects appear opaque and solid by means of texture, which establishes the boundary surface. A glowing object does not stop the glance by such an outer shell. Its limits are not clearly defined for the eyes. In Katz's terms, it has "film color" rather than "surface color." Light seems to originate within the object at an indefinite distance from the observer. Brightness that looks strong in comparison with the environment will tend to eclipse surface texture; and a lack of texture will favor the effect of glow. Rembrandt enhances luminosity by giving little detail to the places of highest brightness. The indefiniteness of the outer surface endows his glowing objects with a transfigured, immaterial quality.

In styles of painting that do not conceive of illumination, the symbolic and expressive moods of brightness and darkness are rendered through properties inherent in the objects themselves. Death may appear as a figure clothed in black, or the whiteness of the lily may depict innocence. When illumination is represented, light and shadow tend to assume the task of producing these moods. An instructive example can be found in Dürer's engraving *Melencolia*. Traditionally the melancholic was given a black face, because it was assumed that a darkening of the blood—the word "melancholy" means literally "black bile"—was responsible for a depressed state of mind. Dürer places his melancholy woman with her back against the light so that her face is in the shadow. In this way the darkness of her face is at least partly justified by the absence of light. For the realistic painter this method has the advantage of giving an object the degree of brightness that suits his purpose without interfering with its "objective" appearance. He can make a white thing dark without suggesting that it is dark in itself. The procedure is used constantly in Goya's etchings. In the movies also back lighting serves to give a figure the sinister quality of darkness. The uncanny sensation obtained in this manner is partly owing to the fact that the dark figure is not present positively as a solid material body with observable surface texture, but only negatively as an obstacle to light, neither round nor tangible. It is as though a shadow were moving in space like a person.

Illumination also helps to distribute emphasis in accordance with the desired meaning. An object can be singled out for attention without having to be large or colorful or situated in the center. Similarly, secondary parts of the scene can be subdued at will. All this without "surgical interventions," which would alter the inventory of the scene itself. Light can be made to fall on, or be withheld from, any object. It can be handled independently of the scene to which it applies. A given arrangement of dancers on the stage can be interpreted to the audience in different ways depending upon the scheme of lighting. Rembrandt uses this means of interpretation constantly without being much concerned about a realistic justification of the effect. In the aforementioned *Descent from the Cross* brilliant light falls on the fainting Mary, whereas the bystanders next to her remain relatively dark. Or we see Samson's hands brightly lighted as they explain a riddle to the wedding guests, while his face is kept in the dark because its contribution is secondary. In his representations of the Potiphar story Rembrandt translates the accusing words of the woman into visual language by throwing the strongest light on the bed (Figure 232).

As I pointed out earlier, there is a fundamental difference between a style of painting in which objects are conceived essentially by their contours, and in which shading is added to convey three-dimensional relief, and a style in which illumination is applied to the picture as an over-all principle. Shad-

Figure 232

ing is an attribute of the individual, self-contained object, whereas illumination supplies a common substratum from which objects, or parts of objects, emerge as from a dark lake to be brought to existence by light. In the latter event, objects are intimately connected with the material medium of the dark ground, and there is often no clear boundary between them. They are not defined by their contours—that is, by the areas farthest from the observer. They become visible by being brought to light. The light takes hold of them by their convexities, and spreads over their surfaces from their centers. The object reaches as far as it is illumined. Wölfflin has described this difference of approach by distinguishing between the "linear" and the "painterly" style. In the painterly concept the object does not have a stable, constant nature, defined only by its own shape. It is evoked by an outer principle, and the resulting appearance is a joint product of the shape of the object and the effect of light upon it. The result is accidental in the sense that there is no necessary, immutable relation between the two components. The light is made to fall the way it does, but the object could look quite different under different conditions. This means that illumination adds to the momentary, fleeting character of the pictorial event—a quality also produced by perspective, which orients objects in an accidental direction and applies changeable distortions of shape to them. This representation of life as a "passing scene" is brought to a climax in the art of the nineteenth century.

Particularly when the shadow is so deep that it provides a foil of black nothingness, the beholder receives the compelling impression of things emerging from a state of nonbeing and likely to return to it. Instead of presenting a static world with a constant inventory, the artist shows life as a process of appearing and disappearing. The whole is only partly present, and so are most objects. One part of a figure may be visible while the rest is hidden in darkness. In the film *The Third Man* the mysterious protagonist stands unseen in a doorway. Only the tips of his shoes reflect a street light, and a cat discovers the invisible stranger and sniffs at what the audience cannot see. The frightening existence of things that are beyond the reach of our senses and that yet exercise their power upon us is represented by means of darkness.

It is often asserted that when objects are partly hidden, "imagination completes" them. Such a statement seems easily acceptable until we try to understand concretely what is meant by it and we compare it with what happens in experience. No one is likely to assert that imagination makes him actually see the whole thing. This is not true; if it were, it would destroy the effect the artist tried to achieve. What happens is that the visible object is seen as incomplete—that is, as a part of something larger. Our knowledge of what things look like is not primarily responsible for this reaction. If nothing but the head of a figure is visible, knowledge not only will not complete the picture but it will not even make it look incomplete. The effect comes about only if the visible shape is such as to indicate a simpler pattern that could be achieved if the given one were continued. Just as a circular line with a gap looks incomplete and suggests completion, without, however, bringing completion about, so a fragment of a face, if suitably "cut," will call for a completion of its symmetry but neither accomplish it itself nor make the observer do it "by imagination." On the other hand, a fragment of reasonably simple shape will not look incomplete even though we may know that it is. The phases of the moon are a good example: we see a crescent, not a part of a disk.

The shape suggested by the tendency to continuation is often not very explicit. We see that the object goes on beyond the borders of the visible but, instead of demanding closure, dwindles away into the empty dark ground. Far from being necessarily a shortcoming, this indefiniteness creates the emergence of the object from the world of nothingness and disappearance into it, in keeping with the meaning to be conveyed.

In Modern Art

The perceptual experience of illumination presupposes, as I said earlier, a subdivision by which the appearance of an object is seen as a composite of the brightness and color values inherent in the object itself and those imposed upon it by a source of light. I also showed that this distinction is brought about psychologically when it leads to the simpler total pattern. The optical stimulus that reaches the retinas from any point of the visual field is not thus divided. It has but one unitary value of brightness and color.

There are two basic ways of representing illumination pictorially. The more naïve and genetically earlier procedure reflects the experience of the perceptual split in the technical process of painting. As I pointed out earlier, the object is given a homogeneous local color and brightness, to which light and shadow are added separately. Pure examples are found, for example, in medieval and early Renaissance painting; but the method survives even in our day. On the other hand, it is feasible to supply the eye with the kind of unitary stimulus it receives from physical space. If the painter gives each spot of the picture a suitable brightness and color value, the observer will produce the subdivision and see illumination in the picture just as he does in physical space. This second method has been followed most purely by the impressionists of the nineteenth century.

It is not easy to make the eye of the painter function like a photographic plate. Only by intense training can it arrive at "reductive vision," by which the value of each spot of the object is determined in isolation as though perceived through a small hole in a screen. Actually, in the more characteristic specimens of the impressionist style, the illumination effect thus obtained is weak. The brightness scale of these paintings is narrow. They stay within the range of the lighter tones and exclude the darker ones, so that there is little leeway for contrasts of light and shadow. Furthermore, there is little consistency of color within the individual object. Each displays an array of different hues, which are not reserved to the particular area but appear throughout the picture. Thus there is no pronounced local color, and, similarly, no specific colors are reserved to light and shadow. As an object turns toward, or away from, the source of illumination it changes to a different group of hues. There is a great variety of values in each spot, and little articulation in the picture as a whole. Such a pattern does not favor the perceptual subdivision required for the illumination effect.

In impressionist paintings the world appears as inherently bright and luminous. This is enhanced by the fact that the boundaries of objects are blurred. No contours are drawn, and the surfaces are not defined by texture. Things have no specific substance, because the only texture given is essentially that of the whole picture, the pattern of strokes on the canvas. Consequently, objects are not opaque and limited in space. Luminosity streams from their insides in all directions. The effect is particularly strong in pointillism, an extreme form of the impressionist style. Here the pictorial unit is not the represented object but the single brush stroke. The picture consists of self-contained dots, each of which possesses only one brightness and color value. This even more thoroughly excludes the concept of an external, governing light source. Instead, each dot is a light source of its own. The picture is like a panel of radiant bulbs, all equally strong and independent of each other. Equality and harmony are the only principles that keep this highly democratic assembly together.

When, after the period of the impressionists and in reaction to it, painting reverted to the well-defined object, illumination of the traditional type also returned in the work of some painters. In the more characteristic styles of modern art, however, illumination is either ignored or transformed into a completely new device. It is all but ignored in certain works of Matisse or Modigliani. Here all objects, rendered in plain local colors, are textureless and luminous. When shading is used, it often serves to render volume rather than lighting. The gradual brightening or darkening of planes, as found in Cézanne and his predecessors as a means of detaching overlapping units from each other, is widely used by the cubists for spatial organization, unrelated to illumination.

A significant reinterpretation, best observed in the work of Braque, is illustrated schematically in Figures 233*a* and *b*. Here the distribution of dark

Figure 233*a*

Figure 233*b*

and bright tones undoubtedly reproduces observed effects of light and
shadow, and is understood as such; yet it can hardly be said that we see
illumination. The object is composed of two or more homogeneous areas.
They strongly differ in color and brightness, and are divided by sharp contours. They are often flat and textureless, and their shape destroys rather
than enhances the three-dimensionality of volume. There is no one local
color, because all given colors have an equal claim to represent the object
itself. Yet enough of the illumination effect is maintained to prevent us from
interpreting what we see as the portrait of a bottle stained half dark and half
bright by an eccentric glass manufacturer. The bottle has a color, but it is
neither the one nor the other actually presented by the painter. It is the clash
of both—an unconsummated mixture. Existence is defined as an unresolved
contradiction of opposites.

The human figures in Braque's *Painter and Model* (Figure 233*b*) show
that the eternal struggle between brightness and darkness is no longer
carried out by powers that apply to the world of things but are not a part
of it. Now light and shadow are the powerful elements of the figures themselves. They are not applied to them, but constitute them. The dark self of
the woman is thin, bounded by many concavities, actively presenting the
profile of her face and stretching forth her arm. The bright woman is large,
rounded by convexities, poised in a more static frontal position, and hiding
her arm. In the man the dark self is dominant; the bright one is nothing
but a weak echo of the subordinate back contour. Both figures are tense—in
themselves as well as in their relation to each other—with the antagonism
of contrasting forces, which reflects a modern interpretation of the human
community and the human mind.

VII   COLOR

Strictly speaking, all visual appearance is produced by color and brightness. The boundaries that determine shape derive from the capacity of the eye to distinguish between areas of different brightness and color. Lighting and shading, important factors in the creation of three-dimensional shape, come from the same source. Even in line drawings, shapes are made visible only through the brightness and color differences between ink and paper. Nevertheless it is justifiable to speak of shape and color as separate phenomena. Roundness and angularity are quite independent of the particular values that make them visible. A green disk on a yellow ground is just as circular as a red disk on a blue ground, and a black triangle on a white ground is as good as its negative.

Shape and Color

Since shape and color can be distinguished from each other, they can also be compared. Both fulfill the two most characteristic functions of vision: they convey expression, and they allow us to obtain information through the identification of objects and happenings. The shape of a soaring poplar tree carries a definite expression, different from that of a birch. The color of Chianti wine has a different mood than that of a sauterne. Shape enables us to distinguish things from each other, but color also helps considerably. When looking at a black-and-white movie, we are often at a loss to identify the strange food the actors have on their plates. In signals, graphs, uniforms, color is used as a means of communication.

Shape, however, is a more efficient means of communication than color; on the other hand, the expressive impact of color cannot be obtained by shape. Shape yields an immense variety of clearly distinguishable patterns, as faces, leaves, and fingerprints demonstrate. Shape rather than color is used for writing, because it gives us signs that are easily and dependably produced and recognized even in small size; whereas if color distinctions were to serve a similar purpose, we could not safely rely on more than half a dozen values. But as for expression, the effect of a sunset or the Mediterranean blue cannot be matched by that of the most pronounced shape.

Differences in people's reactions to color and shape have been brought out in psychological experiments. In a setup used by various investigators, children were asked to select from a number of red triangles and green circles the figures that resembled a test pattern presented separately. The test pattern was either a red circle or a green triangle. Children of less than three years of age seemed more often to choose on the basis of form, whereas those between three and six picked the pattern that had the right color. The preschool children made these choices without hesitation, whereas those of more than six were disturbed by the ambiguity of the task and used shape more often as the criterion of their choice. Werner, in reviewing the evidence, suggests that the reaction of the youngest children is determined by motor behavior and thus by the "graspable" qualities of the objects. Once the visual characteristics have become dominant, the majority of the preschool children will be directed by the strong perceptual appeal of the colors. But as culture begins to train the children in practical skills, which rely on shape much more heavily than on color, they turn increasingly to shape as the decisive means of identification.

Choices between color and shape can also be studied in the ink-blot test. Some of the Rorschach cards give the observer an opportunity to base his description of what he sees on color at the expense of shape, or vice versa. One person may identify a pattern by its contour, even though the color contradicts the interpretation; whereas another may describe two symmetrically placed blue rectangles as "the sky" or "forget-me-nots," thus neglecting shape in favor of color. Rorschach and his followers assert that this difference in reaction is related to one in personality traits. The observations were originally made on mental patients. Rorschach found that a cheerful mood makes for color responses whereas depressed people more often react to shape. Color dominance indicates an openness to external stimuli. Such people are sensitive, easily influenced, unstable, disorganized, given to emotional outbursts. A preference for shape reactions goes with an introverted disposition, strong control over impulses, a pedantic, unemotional attitude.

Rorschach offered no theory on why perceptual behavior and personality are connected in this manner. Schachtel, however, has pointed out that the experience of color resembles that of affect or emotion. In both cases we tend to be passive receivers of stimulation. An emotion is not the product of the actively organizing mind. It merely presupposes a kind of openness, which, for example, a depressed person may not have. It strikes us as color does.

Shape, on the contrary, seems to require a more active response. We scan the object, establish its structural skeleton, relate the parts to the whole. Similarly, the controlling mind acts upon impulses, applies principles, coördinates a variety of experiences, and decides on a course of action. Broadly speaking, in color vision, action issues from the object and affects the person; in order to perceive shape, the organizing mind goes out to the object.

A literal application of the theory might lead to the conclusion that color produces an essentially emotional experience, whereas shape corresponds to intellectual control. Such a formulation seems too narrow, particularly if it refers to art. It is probably true that passivity of the observer and immediacy of experience are more typical for color responses, whereas active control characterizes the perception of shape. But a picture can be painted or understood only by actively organizing the totality of color values; on the other hand, we passively surrender in the contemplation of expressive shape. Instead of speaking of color responses and shape responses, we may distinguish more appropriately between a receptive attitude to visual stimuli, which is encouraged by color but applies also to shape, and a more active attitude, which is prevalent in the perception of shape but applies also to color composition. More generally, it is probably the expressive qualities (of color, but also of shape) that spontaneously affect the passively receiving mind, whereas the tectonic structure of pattern (characteristic of shape, but found also in color) concerns the actively organizing mind.

The corresponding traits of the human personality also need not be limited to the difference between affective and intellectual approach. In the first category there are not only the passions but also the inspirations that are given to us—arriving, it seems, from nowhere—as well as an openness to the outer world that impresses the mind through the senses. In the second category there is not only the intellect but also the organizing power of the mind that guides our dealings with people, situations, tasks, intuitively by means of processes occurring often below the level of conscious reasoning. Furthermore, this category comprises, as Rorschach has pointed out, the introverted mentality of the man who is wrapped up in thoughts and ideas and who tends to impose a preconceived system upon his experiences.

It would be tempting to explore these correlations between perceptual behavior and personality structure in the field of the arts. The first attitude might be called a romantic one; the second, classicist. In painting, we might compare, for example, the approach of Delacroix, who not only bases his compositions on striking color schemes but also stresses the expressive qualities of shape, with that of David, who not only conceives mainly in terms of shape, employed for the relatively static definition of objects, but also subdues and schematizes color.

Matisse has said: "If drawing is of the spirit and color of the senses, you must draw first, to cultivate the spirit and to be able to lead color into spiritual paths." He is voicing a tradition according to which shape is more important and more dignified than color. Poussin said: "The colors in painting are, as it were, blandishments to lure the eyes, as the beauty of the verses in poetry is a lure for the ears." A Germanic version of this view can be found in the writings of Kant: "In painting, sculpture, and indeed in all the visual arts, in architecture, horticulture, to the extent to which they are fine arts, design is essential, for design constitutes the foundation of taste only by what pleases by its shape and not by what entertains in sensation. The colors, which illuminate the outline, belong to the stimulation. They may animate the sensation of the object but cannot make it worthy of contemplation and beautiful. Rather are they often greatly constrained by the requirements of beautiful shape and, even where stimulation is admitted, ennobled only by shape." Given such views, it is not surprising that we find shape identified with the traditional virtues of the male sex, color with the temptations of the female. According to Charles Blanc, "The union of design and color is necessary to beget painting just as is the union of man and woman to beget mankind, but design must maintain its preponderance over color. Otherwise painting speeds to its ruin: it will fall through color just as mankind fell through Eve."

Reactions to Color

The fact that color conveys strong expression is undisputed. There also have been attempts to describe the specific moods of the various colors and to draw generalizations from their symbolic use in different cultures. But next to nothing is known about the origin of these phenomena. To be sure, there is a widespread belief that the expression of color is based on association. Red is said to be exciting because it reminds us of the connotations of fire, blood, and revolution. Green calls up the refreshing thought of nature, and blue is cooling like water. But the theory of association is no more interesting and promising here than in other areas. The effect of color is much too direct and spontaneous to be only the product of an interpretation attached to it by learning. On the other hand, there is not even a hypothesis on the kind of physiological process that might account for the influence of color upon the organism. We are on somewhat firmer ground in discussing shape. There, at least, we can relate the expression of specific patterns to that of more general properties, such as orientation in space, balance, or the geometric characteristics of outlines. We can even speculate on processes in the brain field that might account for the specific effect of certain shapes (see Chapter X).

Not so in color. It is known that strong brightness, high saturation, and hues corresponding to vibrations of long wave length produce excitement. A bright, pure red is more active than a subdued grayish blue. But we have no information on what specifically intense light energy does to the nervous system or why the wave length of vibrations should have an influence. Some experiments have demonstrated a bodily response to color. Féré found that muscular power and blood circulation are increased by colored light "in the sequence from blue—least, through green, yellow, orange, and red." This agrees well with the psychological observations on the effect of these colors, but there is no telling whether we are dealing here with a secondary consequence of the perceptual phenomenon or whether there is a more direct nervous influence of light energy on motor behavior and blood circulation. The same is true for observations by Goldstein, who found in his neurological practice, for example, that a patient with a cerebellar disease had disturbances of her sense of balance, became dizzy, and was in danger of falling when she wore a red dress—symptoms that disappeared when she wore green. Goldstein investigated the phenomenon by asking patients with similar brain defects to look at a sheet of colored paper while holding their arms stretched out in front. The arms were hidden from view by a horizontal board. When the patient looked at a yellow paper his arm, controlled by the defective brain center, would deviate about 55 centimeters from the midline. The deviation was 50 centimeters for red, 45 centimeters for white, 42 centimeters for blue, 40 centimeters for green. When he closed his eyes the deviation was 70 centimeters. Goldstein concluded that the colors corresponding to long wave lengths go with an expansive reaction, whereas the short wave lengths make for constriction. "The whole organism ... through different colors is swung toward the outerworld or withdrawn from it and concentrated toward the center of the organism."

This physical reaction is paralleled by the painter Kandinsky's remarks on the appearance of colors. He asserted that a yellow circle will reveal "a spreading movement outwards from the center which almost markedly approaches the spectator"; a blue circle "develops a concentric movement (like a snail hiding in its shell) and moves away from the spectator." Goldstein's tentative findings deserve to be followed up. It is necessary, in such experiments on the effect of hues, to make sure that the colors are identical in brightness. In an earlier investigation Pressey had people perform simple motor activities, such as a rhythmic tapping of the finger, under varying illumination. He found a decrease of function under dim light and an increase under bright light. Different hues did not change the performance.

Warm and Cold

Hardly any attempts have been made to group the expression of the various colors under more general categories. The distinction between warm and cold colors is fairly common. Artists use these terms, and references to them are also found in books on the theory of color. But sketchy remarks based on the subjective impressions of their authors offer no satisfactory material for a psychological theory. Allesch's experimental observations on this point seem to have led to inconclusive results as far as can be judged from his short references to the subject. Under these conditions it may be permissible for me to propose a theory of my own. It has not been tested experimentally, and may turn out to be quite wrong; but at least it will offer investigators a target to shoot at.

The terms "warm" and "cold" have little reference to pure hues. If they do so at all, red would seem to be a warm color, blue a cold one. Pure yellow also would seem to be cold, but this is even less certain. The two terms seem to acquire their characteristic meaning when they refer to the deviation of a given color in the direction of another color. A bluish yellow or red tends to look cold, and so does a yellowish red or blue. On the contrary, a reddish yellow or blue seems warm. My contention is that not the main color but the color of the slight deviation from it determines the effect. This would lead to the perhaps unexpected result that a reddish blue looks warm whereas a bluish red looks cold. Mixtures of two evenly balanced colors would not show the effect clearly. Green, a mixture of yellow and blue, would be closest to coldness, whereas balanced combinations of red with blue in purple and with yellow in orange would tend to be neutral or ambiguous.

It seems, however, that the balance of two colors in a mixture is quite unstable. One of them is easily made dominant over the other. This may be achieved by a subjective effort of the observer. Within certain limits he can make himself see a given orange as a red modified by yellow or a yellow modified by red. I predict that in the first version the color will look cold, in the second warm. In the same way a purple seen as a blue red will be cold and as a red blue, warm. In green both versions should produce coldness. A more important factor for the establishment of dominance of one color over the other in a mixture is the influence of other colors in the environment. The phenomena of assimilation and contrast, to be discussed later, will often stress one color at the expense of the other. In this way the instability of the mixture is greatly reduced, and thereby its "temperature" more reliably defined.

If this theory is tenable it might be extended to the expression of color in general. Perhaps it is not so much the dominant hue but its "afflictions" that produce the expressive quality. Perhaps the basic hues are fairly neutral key values distinguished by their being unique and mutually exclusive rather than by their specific expression. And it is only when a color produces a dynamic tension effect by leaning toward another color that it reveals its expressive characteristics. Pure red, yellow, and blue may be zero levels of color, slight in dynamics and therefore slight in expression; but reddishness, yellowishness, and bluishness, by drawing another color away from its own fundamental character, would produce the tension without which no expression is possible. My suggestion is admittedly incautious and justifiable only in a field of study in which theories are so scarce that an unsupported hypothesis seems better than none at all.

The situation is further complicated by the fact that the expression of color in general and its temperature in particular are influenced not only by hue but also by brightness and saturation. Therefore the expressive values of hues can be compared only when the two other factors are kept constant. For example, in the spectrum of sunlight all hues are strongly, though not equally, saturated but differ greatly in brightness. Spectral color has its greatest brightness in the yellow, from which point it diminishes continuously on both sides to the ends, that is, the red and the violet. There is some indication that a high degree of brightness tends to make a color cold and a low degree warm. Thus in order to be sure, for example, that a pure red is warmer than a pure yellow we have to compare them at equal brightness.

Saturation, or chroma, refers to the purity of a color. We can best understand its nature by remembering what is known as timbre in music. A completely pure tone would be produced by sound energy of a single wave length. The simplicity of such a sound would correspond to the simple shape of the vibration, which could be represented by a regular sine curve. In practice, however, tones are produced by mixtures of different wave lengths. The combination of the various wave lengths results in a curve of complex shape, and accordingly the tone sounds impure. In the same way a completely pure color would be produced by only one wave length of light. This condition is most nearly realized in the saturated hues of the spectrum. As colors of different wave lengths are mixed, the resulting vibration becomes correspondingly complex; and the outcome is a duller-looking color. An extreme low of saturation is obtained with colors that add up to a completely achromatic gray. Colors that produce this effect are known as complementaries. The closer the components of a mixture come to being complementaries, the more grayish the mixture will look.

The degree of saturation obtainable varies with the brightness of a color. At the extremes of highest and lowest brightness, hues are little different from mere white and black; in the medium range, a moderate number of chromatic steps leads from a highly saturated hue to a gray of the same brightness. But in this middle range, a further complication arises from the fact that the pigments used in painting and printing vary widely as to the degree of saturation attainable. For example, in a typical printing process of the present time, red is available at a higher degree of saturation than yellow or blue. Thus in judging the expressive value of colors, we must consider their saturation level. The specific effect of this factor on the "temperature" of a color has still to be established. It is possible that impurity enhances the temperature quality established by the modifying hue, making a warm color warmer and a cold one colder. Here again are need and opportunity for psychological research.

It seems remarkable that an expressive quality of color should be best described by the words "warm" and "cold," which refer primarily to experiences of temperature. Evidently there must be striking similarities between sensations in the two areas. Our language habits reveal many such similarities, but the words that we use should not induce us to assume that certain properties of color remind us of corresponding sensations in the field of temperature and for that reason are called "warm" and "cold." We hardly think of a hot bath or the effect of the summer sun when we see the dark red of a rose. Instead, the color creates a reaction also provoked by heat stimulation, and the words "warm" and "cold" are used to describe colors simply because the expressive quality in question is strongest and biologically most important in the realm of the temperature sense. Body temperature is a matter of life and death, color temperature is not. We are dealing here, not with a transfer of skin sensations to seeing and hearing, but with a structural quality common to all three of these senses.

If we attempt to analyze this quality and to speculate about its origin, we arrive at a theory that can be formulated either in a more limited or in a more generalizing way. As long as we investigate the phenomenon only in the various branches of perception, we may wonder whether stimulations by heat and light—and we may add sound as well—produce in the nervous system effects that, whatever their nature, are actually similar or identical in certain respects. But this theory, although perhaps correct, seems too narrow if we remember that we also speak without hesitation of a cold person, a warm reception, a heated debate. Since in these the stimulus is not perceptual, it must be assumed that the quality under discussion is not limited to a property of the senses.

A cold person is one who makes us withdraw. We feel the need of defending ourselves against an unwholesome power—we close up and shut the gates. We feel ill at ease, inhibited in giving vent to our thoughts and impulses. A warm person is one who makes us open up. We are attracted, willing to expose freely whatever we have to give. Our reactions to physical chill or warmth are obviously similar. In the same way, warm colors seem to invite us whereas cold ones keep us at a distance. But the properties of warm and cold do not refer only to the reactions of the observer. They also characterize the object itself. A cold person behaves as though he felt cold. He seems wrapped up in himself, on the defensive, unwilling to give, restricted, closed, withdrawn. The warm person seems to irradiate vital energy. He approaches us freely. Here again a parallel can be found in the perceived behavior of color. I have already referred to the tendency of colors of long wave lengths, such as red, to appear closer to the observer whereas blue surfaces seem to lie farther away. Allesch has noted the more dynamic effect of colors moving toward or withdrawing from the observer. The same experimenter found, in agreement with Kandinsky, that some colors seem to expand outward whereas others contract.

In evaluating these results we must keep in mind that not only the hue but also the brightness of colors contributes to the effect. According to Goethe, a dark object looks smaller than a bright one of the same size. He asserts that a black disk on a white ground looks one-fifth smaller than a white disk on black ground, and points to the familiar experience that dark dresses make people look slim. Thus when a yellow is described as expanding and advancing, it will be necessary to investigate to what extent this is due to its brightness rather than to its hue.

Expression of Colors

There seems to be general agreement that colors differ in their specific expression. Not much experimental work has been done on the subject. Goethe's vivid literary portrait sketches of the principal colors are still the best source. They convey the impressions of one man only, but they come from a poet who knew how to express what he saw. To a lesser degree this is true also for Kandinsky's somewhat disorganized and overwritten notes on the subject. Casual observations on the effect of the colors of the environment on people have been made by decorators, designers, and therapists. They are typified by the remark of "a witty Frenchman," who, according to Goethe, "pretended that his tone of conversation with Madame had changed since she changed the color of the furniture in her cabinet from blue to crimson."

Because all these descriptions are verbal, it is impossible to determine exactly to which colors they refer. Not only does the appearance of a color depend greatly upon the context in space and time; it would also be necessary to know the precise hue referred to as well as its brightness and saturation. For example, Goethe asserts that all colors lie between the two poles of yellow ("the color closest to light") and blue ("which always contains some darkness"). Correspondingly, he distinguishes the positive or active colors— yellow, red yellow (orange), yellow red (minium, cinnabar)—which produce an "active, animated, striving" attitude, from the negative or passive ones—

blue, red blue, blue red—which "fit a restless, soft, and yearning" mood. An amusing illustration of a similar point may be found in Ketcham's report on a football coach who "painted the team's dressing room blue, to give a relaxing atmosphere during the half-time intermission, but provided an antechamber in red for a more exciting background to his last-minute pep talks." It is safe to assume that different degrees of brightness and saturation contribute greatly to these effects of color.

As far as unmixed hues are concerned, there is probably some difference in expression. Red is described as passionate, stimulating, and exciting; yellow as serene and gay; blue as depressing and sad. But there is also support for my contention that the unmixed colors are relatively neutral if compared with the dynamic effect introduced by mixtures. This neutrality takes the form of indifference, emptiness, balance, majesty, serenity. Goethe finds in the pure red a high dignity and seriousness, because, according to his belief, it unites all other colors in itself. A bright landscape observed through a red glass impressed him as "awe-inspiring," remindful of the light that would spread over heaven and earth on the Day of Judgment. In keeping with its character of majestic repose, red is the color of royalty. Goethe called pure yellow gay and softly charming, and blue "a charming nothing," empty and cold, conveying a contradictory sensation of stimulation and repose.

Kandinsky says: "Of course, every color can be warm and cold, but nowhere is this contrast so strong as in red." In spite of all energy and intensity, "it glows in itself and does not radiate much vigor outwardly, achieving a manly maturity; [it is] a relentlessly glowing passion, a solid power within itself." Yellow "never contains a profound meaning [and is] akin to utter waste." It is true that Kandinsky also calls it capable of representing violent, raving madness, but here he is thinking presumably of very bright yellow, which he finds unbearable "like a shrill horn." Dark blue sinks "into the deep seriousness of all things where there is no end," whereas the lightest blue "achieves a silent repose."

The well-known controversy as to whether or not green is an elementary color has not been settled. Some maintain that it is perceived as a combination of yellow and blue; others count it with red, yellow, and blue as one of the four basic color sensations. Whatever the truth, it seems that a well-balanced green exhibits the stability found in the pure, unmixed colors. Goethe, although adhering to the former view, says that green gives "a real satisfaction" by letting the eye and the mind "repose on this mixture as on something simple. One does not want to go further, and one cannot go further." Similarly, Kandinsky finds "complete quietude and immobility" in green. There is "earthly, self-satisfied repose of rather solemn, supernatural profoundness." Absolute green, "which is the most restful color in existence, moves in no direction, has no corresponding appeal, such as joy, sorrow, or passion, demands nothing." Its passivity reminds Kandinsky of "the so-called bourgeoisie" and of "a fat, healthy, immovably resting cow, capable only of eternal rumination, while dull bovine eyes gaze forth vacantly into the world."

Characteristic for the stirring effect introduced by admixtures is Goethe's explanation of why yellow not only serves to symbolize noble serenity—yellow is the imperial color of China—but has also been used traditionally to express shame and contempt. This color, he says, is extremely sensitive to adulteration, and looks unpleasantly sulphureous when it has a greenish shade. For Kandinsky, yellow with a tint of blue "takes on a sickly color." When red is affected by blue it acquires, for Goethe, an "intolerable presence," and he suggests that the high clergy has adopted this color because "it strives irresistibly, on the restless steps of an ever advancing increase, to the heights of the purple of the cardinal."

What is the result of an affliction with yellow? According to Goethe, a yellow red produces an incredible shock and seems literally to bore itself into the organ of sight; it disturbs and enrages animals. "I have known educated people who found it intolerable when on an otherwise gray day they encountered someone in a scarlet coat." Kandinsky finds that a yellow red "arouses the feeling of strength, energy, ambition, determination, joy, triumph."

This latter description comes close to Goethe's observation that yellow, when heightened by red, grows in energy and becomes more powerful and magnificent. Red yellow is best suited to give to the eye "the feeling of warmth and delight," whereas a red blue makes us restless rather than animating us. We feel impelled to move on—to further activity by red yellow, to a place of rest by red blue. For Kandinsky, "violet, a cooled-red, both in the physical and spiritual sense, possesses an element of frailty, expiring sadness. This color is considered proper for dresses of older women, and the Chinese actually use it as the color of mourning."

Flimsy though this evidence is, it illustrates my suggestion that unmixed hues and evenly balanced mixtures tend to have a stability whose expressive impact is relatively low whereas admixtures enhance expression by introducing a strong dynamic quality. It would be tempting to pursue this analysis further and to look for the principles governing the different effects that are obtained when a warm hue is modified by a cold one or when a cold hue affects a warm one. A different result again should be obtained when one cold hue is added to another cold one. But there is no point in generalizing these differences as long as reliable experimental data are unavailable.

Color Preferences

Investigations in this area have been mainly concerned with the colors people prefer, partly because manufacturers are interested in the answers, partly because much of the work in so-called experimental aesthetics is still based on the notion that the principal function of art is to please people. I have pointed out before that, in order to arrive at some understanding of art, we may take it for granted that art, like anything else that satisfies needs, produces pleasure and that we must proceed to ask what these needs are and how they are being fulfilled. As far as our particular problem is concerned, this would require information on what people see when they look at colors and how such experiences fit their desires and standards of value.

Some studies have indicated that people prefer saturated colors to unsaturated ones; others have suggested the opposite. We are told that the colors at both ends of the spectrum—that is, reds and blues—are favored whereas the rating of yellow is normally low; the preference for blue is said to be greater in men than in women. But there is no way of evaluating these results unless we know what expressive qualities people receive from colors and how these impressions fit their needs.

Color preferences are probably related to important social and personal factors. One difficulty to be overcome in such studies is the fact that a given color will provoke different reactions depending upon its use. A color may be suitable for a man's car but not for his toothbrush. When color samples are presented abstractly in the psychologist's laboratory, there is no certainty as to the extent observers associate them with some practical application. Results may appear contradictory but be actually due to different references. If one person, consciously or unconsciously, thinks of a wall stain and another of an evening dress, their judgments are not comparable. In order to control this factor, it might be preferable not to experiment with colors "as such" but to relate them to specific objects, as is done in the field of market research. By such a method it should become possible to isolate some of the many motives that determine color preference. Social mores will express themselves in the choice of colors. If in a given culture the free manifestation of feelings is frowned upon, walls and furniture will be kept in subdued shades. It may be considered proper for young people to show their vitality in strongly colored dress but not for the old. If an evening gathering is to be a frank exhibition of personal attractions, it will call for different colors than one designed to show dignity and restraint. Cultures that stress the difference between man and woman will produce other color habits than those that favor similarity and comradeship. What is suitable for a

PLATE 2

woman to wear will depend upon whether she is considered the man's partner or his plaything. Thus, once the expression of color is reliably explored, studies of color preference are likely to yield a highly significant picture of the cultural setting.

The same is true for the reflections of the individual personality. Rorschach found that people who keep their emotions in check have a preference for blue and green and avoid red. Reactions of this kind are likely to become manifest in the way people dress or decorate their rooms. The characteristic color scheme of individual artists also could be related to the subject matter of their works as well as to what is known about their personalities. The prevailing red in Rouault's paintings clearly points to a different person than does the preference for yellow in van Gogh's work, and the change from the "blue period" to a "pink period" in Picasso's development corresponds to a change in the mood of his subject matter. If an artist limits himself to black and white, as, for example, Redon did for considerable time, the psychologist will be reminded of the "color shock" observed in the reactions of certain individuals to the Rorschach ink blots.

The Quest for Harmony

In the visual arts the expressive qualities are an important—but not the only important—object of study in the field of color. It is equally necessary to explore what might be called the syntax of color composition, that is, the rules of structural organization. The masters of painting who handled these rules with the greatest ingenuity and sensitivity seem to have done so mostly by intuition rather than by intellectually formulated principles, if we may judge from the scarcity of their remarks on this vital subject in their writings and recorded conversations.

Theorists have been concerned mostly with what is known as color harmony. They have tried to determine which assortments of colors produce combinations in which all values readily and pleasantly blend with each other. These prescriptions derived from the attempts to classify all color values in a standardized, objective system. The earliest of these systems were two-dimensional, depicting the sequence and some interrelations of hues by a circle or polygon. Later, when it was realized that color is determined by three dimensions—hue, brightness, and saturation—three-dimensional models were introduced. Lambert's color pyramid dates back to 1772. Wundt proposed a color cone, ancestor of the double cone developed in the twentieth century by Ostwald, and also a color sphere of the type later popularized by Munsell. Although differing in shape, the various models are based on the same principle. The central vertical axis presents the scale of achromatic brightness values from the lightest white at the top to the darkest black at the bottom. The equator, or the polygonal contour corresponding to it, contains the scale of hues at a medium brightness level. Each horizontal section through the solid presents all the chromatic values available at a given brightness level. The closer to the outer border of the section, the more saturated the color; the closer to the central axis, the greater its admixture with a gray of the same brightness.

Double pyramids, double cones, and spherical color solids, all agree in having their maximum girth at medium height and tapering off toward the poles. The reason is that in the medium range of brightness all colors show the greatest number of saturation steps between the pure hue and the corresponding gray, whereas a very bright or a very dark color differs little from white and black. The cone and the pyramid on the one hand and the sphere on the other imply different theories on the rate at which the range of saturation changes with changing brightness. Again, the difference between the roundness of cone and sphere and the angularity of the pyramid distinguishes between theories that tend to present the sequence of hues as a continuously gliding scale and others that emphasize three or four elementary colors as cornerstones of the system. Finally, there is a difference between regularly shaped color models, which provide space for all colors considered possible in principle, and irregularly shaped ones, which—as, for example, the Munsell color tree—accommodate only the colors obtainable with the pigments at our disposal today.

These systems are supposed to serve two purposes—to allow an objective identification of any color, and to indicate which colors harmonize with each other. We are concerned here with the second function. Ostwald proceeded on the basic assumption that "two or more colors in order to harmonize must be equal with regard to essential elements." Since he was not sure that brightness could be considered an essential element in this sense, he based his rules of harmony on either identity of hue or identical amount of saturation. This implied that all hues were consonant as long as they were equal in saturation. Even so, Ostwald believed certain hues fitted each other particularly well, notably those that faced each other in the color circle and represented a pair of complementaries. Any regular tripartition of the circle was also expected to yield an especially harmonious combination, because such triads too were complementary, that is, added up to gray when mixed at equal parts.

Munsell also based his theory of harmony on the principle of common elements. A horizontal circle around the axis of the sphere contains all the hues, equal in brightness and saturation. A vertical line combines colors that differ only in brightness. A horizontal radius groups all the shades of saturation for a color of given hue and brightness. But Munsell went further by suggesting that "the center of the sphere is the natural balancing point for all colors," so that any straight line through the center would connect harmonizing colors. This meant that two complementary hues could be combined in such a way that the greater brightness of the one would be compensated by the lower brightness of the other. He also admitted values lying on a spherical surface "in a straight line," meaning presumably on a great circle.

Now harmony is essential in the sense that all the colors of a composition must fit together in a unified whole if they are to be relatable. It is also possible that all the colors used in a successful painting or by a good painter keep within certain limits, which exclude some hues, brightness values, or saturation levels. Since we now possess fairly reliable standards of objective identification, it would be valuable to measure the palette of specific works of art and artists. What is much less probable is that the colors artists use will be found to fit in many cases any such simple rule as those suggested by the systems of color harmony.

For one thing, the interrelation of colors is strongly modified by other pictorial factors. Both Ostwald and Munsell recognized the influence of size, and suggested that large surfaces should have subdued colors whereas highly saturated colors should be used only in small patches. But it seems that even by considering this one additional factor the proposed rules of harmony would be complicated to such an extent as to make them practically useless—and size is only one among many other factors, which cannot be controlled by quantitative measurement as comfortably as size.

To mention but one of these factors—the appearance and expression of a color are modified by the subject matter. A given red is not the same color when applied to a puddle of blood, a face, a horse, a sky, or a tree, because it is perceived in relation to the normal color of the object or imbued with the connotations of the situation suggested by such coloring. A red may look pale as the color of blood, but very strong when indicating a flushed complexion.

There are, however, more fundamental objections to the principle on which the rules of color harmony are based. This principle conceives of a color composition as a whole in which everything fits everything. All local relations between neighbors show the same pleasant conformity. Obviously this is the most primitive kind of harmony, suitable at best for the so-called color schemes of clothing or rooms, although there seems to be no reason why even a dress or a bedroom should cling to a noncommittal homogeneity of color rather than setting accents, creating centers of attention, separating elements by contrast. Certainly a work of art based on such a principle could describe nothing but a world of absolute peace, devoid of action, expressing only a static over-all mood. It would represent that state of deadly serenity at which, to use the language of the physicist, entropy approaches a maximum.

A glance at music may drive the argument home. If musical harmony were concerned only with the rules of what sounds well together, it would be limited to a kind of aesthetic etiquette. Instead of telling the musician by what means he can express what, it would teach him only how to behave. Actually this aspect of musical harmony has proved to be of no permanent value, because it is dependent on the taste of the period. Effects that were forbidden in the past are welcome today. This is precisely what has happened to certain norms of color harmony even within a few decades. For example, Ostwald, commenting in 1919 on the rule that saturated colors must be presented only in small bits, asserted that large-sized surfaces of pure vermilion, as found in Pompeii, are crude, "and all the blindly superstitious belief in the artistic superiority of the 'ancient' has been unable to keep attempts at the repetition of such atrocities alive." In reading this today, we may remember a painting of Matisse in which six thousand square inches of canvas are covered almost completely and quite satisfactorily with a strong red, and conclude that the proposed norm was nothing but the expression of a temporary fashion.

But—to come back to music—the rules of theory are hardly concerned with such matters. Arnold Schönberg says, in his *Theory of Harmony:* "The subject matter of the doctrine of musical composition is usually divided in three areas: harmony, counterpoint, and the theory of form. Harmony is the doctrine of the chords and their possible connections with regard to their tectonic, melodic, and rhythmic values and relative weight. Counterpoint is the doctrine of the movement of voices with regard to motivic combination. . . . The theory of form deals with the disposition for the construction and development of musical thoughts." In other words, musical theory is not concerned with what sounds nicely together, but with the problem of how to give adequate shape to an intended content. The need for everything to add up to a unified whole is only one aspect of this problem, and it is not satisfied in music by drawing the composition from an assortment of elements that blend smoothly in any combination.

To state that all the colors contained in a pictorial composition are part of a simple sequence derived from a color system would mean no more— even though perhaps no less—than to say that all the tones of a certain piece of music fit together because they belong to the same key. Even if the statement were correct, still next to nothing would have been said about the structure of the work. We should not know what parts it consists of and how these parts are related to each other. Nothing would be known about

COLOR 339

the particular arrangement of the elements in space and time; and yet it is true that one and the same assortment of tones will make a comprehensible melody in one sequence and a chaos of sounds when shuffled at random, just as one and the same group of colors will produce a senseless jumble in one arrangement and an organized whole in another. Also it goes without saying that composition requires separations just as much as connections, because when there are no segregated parts there is nothing to connect, and the result is an amorphous mash. It is useful to remember that the musical scale is suited to serve as the composer's "palette," precisely because its tones do not all fit together in easy consonance but provide discords of various degrees as well. The traditional theory of color harmony deals only with obtaining connections and avoiding separations, and is therefore at best incomplete.

The Elements of the Scale

How much do we know about the syntax of color—that is, about the perceptual properties that make relationships between colors possible? First of all, of what kind are the elementary units of color composition, and how many of them are there? The raw material comes in continuously gliding scales. The scale of hues is best known from the spectrum of sunlight. Brightness and saturation also produce scales, which lead from the lowest to the highest degrees of these properties. The maximum number of shades of gray the average observer can distinguish on the scale between black and white is, according to some sources, about 200. It is worth noticing that the number of hues distinguishable in a spectrum of pure colors between the two extremes of violet and purplish red is apparently somewhat smaller—about 160. Chandler cites these findings, and adds: "With reference to pigment, color papers, and textiles, we shall not be far wrong if we think of 150 distinguishable hues, 200 gradations of value (brightness), and a maximum of twenty gradations of saturation, at the most favorable level of value for each hue, with fewer gradations at higher and lower levels of value." (The word "value" is used in this quotation in the sense of brightness—a common practice among artists. Such usage may be acceptable in informal studio language, which adopted it from the French painters as a translation of the word "valeur." But theorists should be expected to use specific terms when they refer to specific matters, and to reserve the more general ones for the description of correspondingly general phenomena. In the present book the term "value" is, therefore, never used in the narrow sense of the brightness scale only.)

In music the number of tones used is considerably smaller than that of the pitch levels distinguishable by the human ear. Hence the familiar assertion that the musical medium is limited to a number of standardized elements whereas the painter ranges freely through the entire continuum of colors. Now it is true that no attempt to standardize colors has had any appreciable effect on artistic composition. There have been informal recommendations as to what palette to use, what colors to avoid, but they applied only to specific schools of painting or fashions. Thus the Père Tanguy, owner of a small store that furnished the impressionists with paints, resented anyone's asking for a tube of black, because he shared the opinion of his favorite customers that "tobacco juice" had no place in a good picture. It is equally true, however, that a color composition, just as any other artistic pattern, will have a comprehensible form only if it is based on a limited number of perceptual values. This limitation is particularly evident in pictures composed of evenly colored surfaces, for example, Persian miniatures or certain paintings by Matisse. But even in a Velázquez or Cézanne containing a large number of gradations the composition is based on a relatively small number of color values. The subtler mixtures appear as secondary inflexions or variations of this fundamental scale, or they form a variety of chords in which the common elements remain discernible. Thus a tablecloth may modulate in nuances composed of dozens of hues without relinquishing its basic whiteness, or a triad of green, violet, and yellow may combine in any number of proportions and yet remain visible in every spot of the picture as the underlying key.

Such straying away from and toying with the basic tones of a composition are not so foreign to music as it seems as long as we think only of what is put down in notation. In the performances of singers and string players, in the freely elaborating improvisations and harmonizations of jazz bands, in primitive and folk music, deviating intonation, slides, and glissandi are quite common. In fact the difference between the standardized scale of the musician and the free scale of the painter would seem to be the result, not of a fundamental difference of the two media, but of practical necessities that exist in the one field but hardly in the other. A work of the visual arts is unique, executed by one individual and persisting in time. Music depends upon performance, and requires notation, transmission, coöperation of several persons, the construction of instruments—all of which presupposes limitation to what can be standardized without too much difficulty. A similar development could be expected to occur in the dance if the demand for preservation through notation should become greater. It is significant that the attempts to standardize color have come, not from artistic practice, but from needs arising in the manufacturing of pigments and the mass production of colored objects in industry.

There are, however, certain fundamental values of hue that are inherent in the psychological experience of color and therefore, like the consonance of the octave in music, play their part wherever color is perceived and employed. The debates about what has been variously called the primary, principal, primitive, or elementary colors have produced some confusion. The question of which colors can serve to produce all others by mixture has been thrown together with the totally different one of which hues are perceived as simple and irreducible. The first problem came up in the theory of color vision when Young and Helmholtz tried to prove that the sensitivity of the eye to three basic colors could account for the perception of all others. Painters were concerned with the rules governing the mixture of pigments; and the techniques of color printing and color photography required a limited number of "primaries." These problems, however, are unrelated to what happens when the eye looks at colors of whatever origin. In the spectrum of light a single wave length may produce a hue that is experienced as a mixture—for example, a reddish blue—whereas a straight red may be obtained from a superposition of a yellow and a purple filter. The fact that a white, or gray, or black may result from the combination of two or three or all colors has no bearing on its appearance, and the psychological question of whether green is simple or composite has nothing to do with the procedures by which this color is produced. In the following I am concerned exclusively with appearance.

There is no disagreement on the fact that the sensations of black, white, yellow, blue, and red are fundamental in the sense of being irreducible perceptually, although there has been some question as to whether all these colors could be produced in complete purity. Goethe, for example, believed that yellow and blue were the only colors capable of complete purity whereas red always had an admixture of yellow or blue. There is no "proof," but only the possibility of agreement in these matters, as shown clearly by the controversy about green. Some persons see green as mixed, some as simple; and nothing can be done about it except trying by demonstration to determine to what extent green shares the properties of simple colors. If, for example, a green is placed between a yellow and a blue, it will probably be found to behave differently than a red in the same position. The red will contain little if anything of the character of its neighbors, whereas any green shows blueness and yellowness, just as orange always shows the elements of red and yellow. On the other hand, it seems equally apparent that a continuous scale of hues from blue to yellow does not look "linear" but has a turning point in the pure green, whereas, for example, red shifts smoothly in a continuous change of proportion through orange to yellow. Presumably green is elementary in some ways but not in others, and I shall treat it accordingly.

When observers are asked to point out the places of the purest colors in a spectrum of light, their sensations do not strictly agree on a particular wave length. Yellow is located rather consistently in the area around a wave length of 575 millimicrons (millionths of a millimeter), and blue is close to 475. There is less agreement on green, which is seen somewhere between 512 and 530, and least on red, placed by some observers at 642, by others as high as 760. Allesch has reported that "a large quantity" of a definitely blue light may be added to a definitely red one, and the mixture will still be a pure red to some observers. For the purposes of the artist, however, pigments and lights produce colors that look sufficiently pure in an absolute sense as well as in comparison with mixtures.

What is the syntactic character of these elementary colors? They are essentially unrelatable to each other, because any relation requires a common dimension. Two objects can be related as to their size or weight, but the elementary hues have no such common dimension except that they are all pure colors. They show some difference in expression, and can also be compared as to brightness and chroma; but these colors do not fit into any common scale of hue alone. They represent fundamental qualities, which exclude each other. They can be distinguished from each other, but their company produces little tension, neither attraction nor repulsion. A scale can be established between any two of them—for example, between red and yellow—and all the mixtures on this scale can be compared and ordered as to their proportions of red and yellow, but the two pure values at the poles are unrelatable. Therefore in a pictorial composition these simple hues can never serve as a transition. They stand isolated, or appear at the beginning or the end of a sequence of color values, or mark a climax at which the sequence turns in another direction. Thus the red spots in Corot's landscapes are in contrast to, and in balance with, the colors surrounding them but not connected with them by any path. Cézanne often marks the highest point of a convexity—a cheek or an apple—with a pure red spot, or puts a pure blue in the depth of a hollow—for example, a corner of an eye. Unmixed hues can also be found at the borders of objects, where shape starts and ends. They provide the composition with places of rest, with keynotes, which serve as a stable frame of reference for mixtures. In Cézanne's late water colors, which avoid unmixed hues, the anchorless violets, greens, and reddish yellows seem to move in a constant flux with no rest at any place except in the supreme balance of the picture as a whole.

Syntax of Mixtures

Perceptual mixtures of hues fall into three main groups: those between red and blue, blue and yellow, and yellow and red. Within each of these groups it is necessary to distinguish between the mixture that keeps the two fundamentals in balance and those in which one of the fundamentals dominates. If, for the sake of simplicity, we exclude the additional hues that result from combinations with black or white—such as the shades of brown—we obtain a system of nine principal mixtures:

BLUE	violet	blue and red	purple	RED
RED	yellow red	orange	red yellow	YELLOW
YELLOW	green yellow	green	green blue	BLUE

These mixtures can serve as stages of transition between the fundamentals; but the three values in the central column, each of which evenly balances two fundamentals, show relatively high stability and self-contained-ness. They thereby resemble the fundamentals, which have the same properties to a higher degree. The other six mixtures, in which one fundamental dominates over the other, have the dynamic properties of "leading tones," that is, they appear as deviations from the dominant fundamental and exhibit a tension toward the purity of that fundamental. Just as in the key of C the B presses toward becoming C, so in the red-yellow scale a red yellow presses toward yellow, and a yellow red toward red.

In the strictest sense, mixtures are homogenous hues in which the fundamentals are completely fused. But in practice it is not possible to separate them from the juxtaposition of colors in space. Within a brush stroke, pigments will often mix unevenly so that, for example, a patch of purple may show at close inspection a streak of pure red. Similarly, a larger unit of color may appear as a mixture of various shades contained in it side by side. In this way it becomes easier to combine hues that in complete mixture would tend to add up to a gray, such as a reddish green or a bluish orange. We know that the impressionists produced some of their mixtures by the juxtaposition of separate touches. They thus avoided the decrease in saturation resulting from the actual fusion of pigments, reproduced the vibration effect of the atmosphere, and revealed to the eye the elements of color combined in the complexity of mixture. In the last analysis any picture can and should be considered as an over-all "mixture" of all the color values of which it is made.

Scales of mixtures lead the eye from one area of a picture to another and produce movement in specific directions. Thus a scale of greens may trace a linear path through a landscape. In Grünewald's *Resurrection* a large halo spreads from the head of Christ outward in all directions by gradually changing from a central yellow through orange to green like a rainbow. An evenly colored disk would show little of this centrifugal movement.

The fewer common elements colors contain, the more clearly they separate. Thus the three fundamental hues, blue, red, and yellow, are most completely distinguished from each other because they have nothing in common. Mixtures of two fundamentals are thoroughly separated from the unmixed third, for example, orange from blue, purple from yellow, green from red. Such distinction by exclusion serves to erect border lines between areas in a composition.

Colors with common elements—as, for example, green and orange, which share the yellow—are less distinct from each other, but they may be even more effectively separated by what may be called clash or mutual repulsion. This phenomenon always involves common elements. It is necessary here to consider the different roles of the constituents in a mixture. Compare the juxtaposition of a reddish yellow and a reddish blue with that of a reddish yellow and a bluish red. The first pair will be found to combine smoothly, whereas the second often seems to produce mutual repulsion. What is the difference? Both contain a common element: the red. But in the first pair the red holds the same structural position in both colors—it is subordinate. In the second pair the structural positions are reversed—red is subordinate in one color, dominant in the other. I feel that this structural contradiction often produces a conflict or clash and therefore mutual repulsion; whereas in the first pair the correspondence of structural similarity makes for a ready attraction or what is commonly called harmony.

The two pairs of colors exemplify two types of mixture. The first type (Figure 234) may be named "Similarity of the Subordinate," and refers to the following combinations:

> Yellow red and yellow blue
> Red yellow and red blue
> Blue yellow and blue red

The second type (Figure 235), "Structural Contradiction for One Common Element," refers to:

> Red yellow and blue red
> Red blue and yellow red
> Yellow red and blue yellow
> Yellow blue and red yellow
> Blue yellow and red blue
> Blue red and yellow blue

It will be seen that Figure 234 shows an arrangement in which the two mixtures of each pair lie at equal distances from—that is, symmetrically to—the pole determining the color of the subordinate. The dominants also lie at equal distances from their poles. In Figure 235 there is no such simplicity. Each pair of mixtures is placed asymmetrically in relation to all three poles. The color each pair shares lies close to its pole in one mixture (dominant) and distant from it in the other (subordinate). It would be desir-

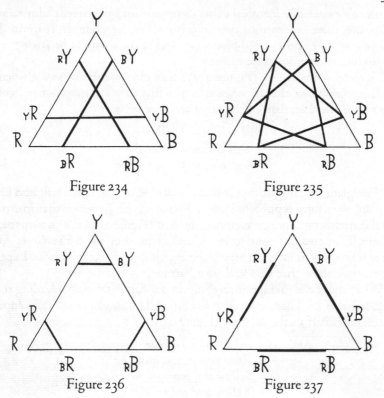

Figure 234   Figure 235

Figure 236   Figure 237

able to test by experiment my supposition that the first type produces attraction, the second repulsion. In such experiments care should be taken to use only definite "leading tones," that is, unequivocally to establish the difference between dominant and subordinate in each mixture. Although empirical evidence is missing, I will carry my speculation a little further.

What are the results of a type of grouping that may be described as "Similarity of the Dominant"?

> Yellow red and blue red
> Red yellow and blue yellow
> Yellow blue and red blue

Here again (Figure 236) each pair is placed symmetrically in relation to one pole, but this time the two mixtures lie close to that pole, that is, they share the dominant. The difference from the type illustrated in Figure 234 is that whereas similarity of the subordinate produces two essentially different colors connected by the same admixture, similarity of the dominant produces two essentially identical colors distinguished by different admixtures. The same color is torn into two different scales, for example, red into the red-yellow scale and the red-blue scale. The effect seems to be jarring and to produce some mutual repulsion.

"Structural Inversion" (Figure 237) takes place when the two elements exchange positions, that is, when the color that serves as subordinate in one mixture is the dominant of the other and vice versa:

Red yellow and yellow red
Red blue and blue red
Yellow blue and blue yellow

At first glance we might expect that the double contradiction will lead here to a doubly strong repulsion. It should be observed, however, that in structural contradiction for one common element (Figure 235) the two mixtures always lie in two different scales, whereas here they lie in the same. Also there is an element of symmetry in the exchange of structural places. Experiments may show that this leads to a harmonious relationship.

What about the juxtaposition of a pure fundamental with a leading tone that contains it? There are two possibilities. The fundamental may appear as the dominant in the mixture (Figure 238):

Blue and red blue
Blue and yellow blue
Yellow and blue yellow
Yellow and red yellow
Red and yellow red
Red and blue red

Or the fundamental may appear as the subordinate (Figure 239):

Blue and blue yellow
Blue and blue red
Red and red blue
Red and red yellow
Yellow and yellow blue
Yellow and yellow red

In both circumstances the two colors to be combined lie on the same scale. Furthermore, in the first they are essentially alike. One hue dominates the pair. But some disturbance arises from the fact that one of the colors is a pure fundamental whereas the other has an admixture. They are asymmetrical. In the second there is even more cause for a clash. The pure fundamental reappears as the subordinate in the mixture, which produces structural con-

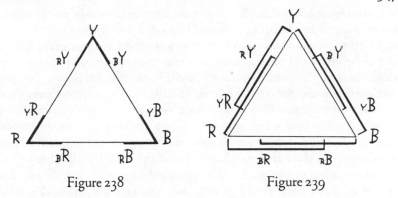

Figure 238   Figure 239

tradiction in addition to the asymmetry. Here again systematic experiments are needed to reveal the typical effect. The same is true for other kinds of combination, for example, those involving what I have called the balanced mixtures: orange, green, and red-blue.

The effect of clash or mutual repulsion is not "bad," forbidden. On the contrary, it is a precious tool for the artist who wishes to make an articulate statement in color. It can help him detach the foreground from the background, the leaves of a tree from its trunk and branches, or keep the eye from traveling a compositionally undesirable road. It is necessary, however, that the discord fit the over-all structure of the work as established by the other perceptual factors and the subject matter. If a discord occurs where shape demands a connection or if the juxtaposition seems arbitrary, chaos will result.

The Complementaries

The combination of certain colors produces achromatic white, gray, or black. Two colors, if appropriately chosen, will do so; and certain groups of three will also give the effect. When all the colors of the spectrum of white light are put together, they produce an achromatic mixture. The combination of colors can take place in two different ways, known as additive and subtractive mixtures. An additive mixture is obtained when colored lights are projected on the same spot of a screen or when dots of pigment are placed close to each other on a canvas so that the colors fuse in the eye of the observer. In psychological experiments additive mixtures are easily obtained by putting sectors of different colors on a disk, which is then made to rotate rapidly by means of a motor. If under such conditions colors add up to white or gray, they are called complementaries.

Subtractive mixture takes place, for example, when colored filters are placed on top of each other. Then colors do not pool their lights, but absorb or compensate each other. A subtractive mixture of strictly complementary colors traps all light, that is, produces black or a dark gray.

In other words, complementary colors are combinations that add up to the complete whole of whiteness or, when subtracted from each other, produce the complete nothingness of black. It can also be shown that when one color is presented, the eye tends to call up its complementary, that is, to achieve completeness. When we stare for a while at a red surface and then switch quickly to a white one, we will see a blue-green instead of white, blue-green being complementary to red—that is, the so-called negative afterimages produce the complementary of the color that has been fixated. The same effect can be produced by means of contrast. If a small gray patch is put on a red background, it will look blue-green. If the background is green-yellow, the gray patch will look violet. Goethe described the phenomenon by saying that complementary colors "demand each other." They do so because the eye demands completeness.

If we ask which colors are complementary, we encounter the usual difficulty of color identification. Color completion is a psychological, not a physical matter. It is true that the wave lengths of any two complementaries have a roughly similar ratio, about 1.25; but the only valid criterion is the report of observers, who tell the experimenter whether and when a mixture is achromatic or what hue is produced by afterimages or contrast. Now it is possible precisely to indicate the wave lengths of the colors that produce the effect for the average observer. For example, 607.7 and 489.7 millimicrons are such a pair. What we want to know for practical purposes, however, is which colors correspond to these physical stimuli; and since the laboratory equipment that will produce the proper spectral hues is rarely at hand, we must resort either to words or to pigments. This is where scientific precision ends and the Babylonian confusion starts. If, for example, we look on the chart compiled by Hiler from different sources for the name of the color corresponding to 600 millimicrons, we find that it has been described by various authors as Orange Chrome, Golden Poppy, Spectrum Orange, Bitter Sweet Orange, Oriental Red, Saturn Red, Cadmium Red Orange, or Red Orange. If we consult a chart of printed pigments, the color we see will depend on the book consulted.

Under these conditions all statements about complementary colors must remain vague. We cannot be surprised to find that the color circles, which present complementary colors in diametrical opposition, agree only roughly with each other. Figure 240 is an example of a color circle. The fact that it contains only seven color names and no actual pigments makes it more rather than less accurate. Any two points of the circumference that can be connected by a diameter indicate two approximately complementary colors.

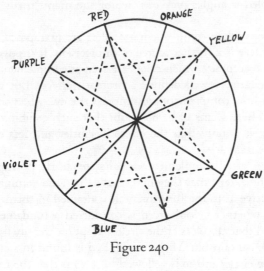

Figure 240

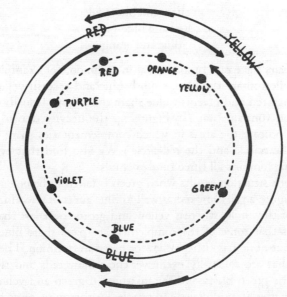

Figure 241

The two stippled triangles pick out two of the many triads that produce completion.

What happens when complementary colors are juxtaposed in a pictorial composition? Here is a further source of imprecision. It is possible to determine with some accuracy which colors are seen as complementaries because they produce relatively well defined achromatic effects. But we cannot be equally sure of how complementaries impress the eye when they appear in juxtaposition. There seems to be no doubt that such combinations play an important role; it is only that the effect is subtler and less easily pinned down experimentally.

The members of all complementary pairs are clearly distinguished from each other to the extent that they never have the same dominant. Are they mutually exclusive as to the fundamentals contained in them? The answer depends upon whether or not green is considered a fundamental color. If it is not, we find that all colors of the circle, except for the small area between red and yellow, contain blue (Figure 241). Red is found in somewhat more than half of the circle, and so is yellow. This means that the two colors of a complementary pair are never mutually exclusive, except for the three cases in which one of them is a pure fundamental:

Yellow and blue-violet
Red and blue-green
Blue and orange

All other pairs have one fundamental in common; for example, violet and greenish yellow share the blue, reddish blue and reddish yellow share the red, yellowish red and greenish blue share the yellow. Usually blue will be the common fundamental. (In Figure 241 the heavily drawn parts of the blue-circle indicate the areas in which complementaries share blue, and so for the yellow-circle and the red-circle.) We also find that every complementary pair contains all three fundamentals.

A different situation results when green is taken to be one of the fundamentals (Figure 242). Now red as well as blue are contained in a little more than half of the circle, whereas yellow and green cover less than half of it. This means that some of the complementary pairs share blue, and a few share red; but none has either yellow or green in common. There are, then, two areas that are mutually exclusive: the yellow reds and their complementaries the green blues, and the mixtures of green and yellow and their complementaries around violet and purple. Furthermore, some pairs contain all four fundamentals: for example, the yellow-greens and the violet-purples; some contain only three: for example, the reddish yellows and the reddish blues (which contain no green) and the bluish reds and the bluish greens

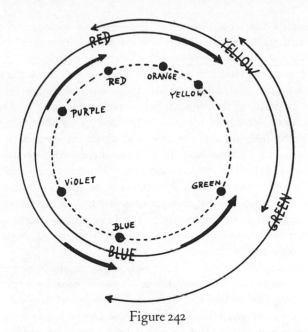

Figure 242

(which contain no yellow). No pair contains less than three fundamentals.

Four general conclusions may be drawn. (1) In all pairs of complementaries in which one color is a pure fundamental, the two colors are mutually exclusive. (2) If green is considered a fundamental, there are two areas in which pairs of mixtures are mutually exclusive. (3) In no pair of complementaries are the two colors mixed of the same two fundamentals. (4) If we think in terms of three fundamentals, all three are contained in all pairs. If green is one of the fundamentals, some pairs contain all four fundamentals, some three, but none less than three. (Some authors assert that the fundamentals form complementary pairs: red and green, and blue and yellow. Our color circle shows that this is a misleading simplification.)

Mutual Completion

The colors of any pair of complementaries thus always have a considerable amount of distinctness and at the same time contain between them all or most of the fundamentals. This makes for combinations that are both clear-cut and rich. But the present discussion has not yet described the most characteristic property of complementary colors. I mentioned earlier that mixtures of complementaries produce achromatic color and that the eye seems to strive for completion by subjectively calling up the balancing opposite of any color stimulus. Experience seems to indicate that the juxtaposition of

complementary colors gives rise to an experience of balance and completeness. The underlying kinship with white must be the reason for this. White,
however, has a peculiarly twofold quality. On the one hand, it is the supreme
fulfillment, the integration of all the richness to which particular colors can
add up. But on the other hand, it is also the absence of hue and therefore of
life. It has the purity of the innocent, who have not yet lived, and the emptiness of the dead, for whom life is over. In *Moby Dick,* Melville asks why
"whiteness refiningly enhances beauty" and stands for superiority and kingship, whereas at the same time there "lurks an elusive something in the
innermost idea of this hue, which strikes more of panic to the soul than that
redness which affrights in blood." He speaks of the ghastly whiteness of the
albinos and the dead, of white mountains, animals, and the white squall. In
a similar vein Rabelais, describing the colors of Gargantua's clothes, asks why
it is that "the lion who by his mere cry and roar frightens all animals, dreads
and reveres only the white cock."

White is completeness and nothingness. Like the shape of the circle, it
serves as a symbol of integration without presenting to the eye the variety of
vital forces that it integrates, and thus is as complete and empty as the circle.
Not so the complementary colors. They show completeness as the balance
of opposites. They exhibit the particular forces that constitute the whole.
The stillness of achievement appears as an integration of antagonistic tendencies. A painting built on a theme of complementaries may attain this
animated repose. It may do so by a composition based on a pair of extreme
opposites, a dramatic contrast, whose tension is felt in the balance of the
whole. Delacroix, in his later period, used a counterpoint of a green and a red
thereby representing life as a clash of powerful elements. But the painter
may also arrive at completeness by unfolding the spectral array of innumerable nuances. Here the variety of vital forces is displayed in many gentle
steps, and richness rather than contrast results. Instead of being divided in
large opposing camps, the colors show their total range in each spot of the
picture, add up to completeness everywhere; the result is a kind of over-all
grayness, loaded with life but serene. Kurt Badt said: "In the late works of
the great masters every particularity of feeling is extinguished by a unity of
all opposites. Such pictures have neither grace nor grandeur nor splendor.
They possess everything but are beyond any limitation. In these late works
the details dissolve, the melodies dissipate, and even the accomplishments of
middle life, namely clarity, richness, beauty of color, disappear. There remains an ultimate simplicity of effect and countereffect, of the spiritual and
the material, of surface and space, of color and line. Nothing is any longer by
itself, nothing predominant."

The eye spontaneously seeks out and connects complementary colors.

Here is a principle of grouping that refers to a somewhat more complex structure than the simple grouping by similarity of color. Just as all the reds or all the greens in a picture tend to be seen together, so complementary pairs or triads often unite in a pattern. When dealing with shape and motion, we found that not only similar elements are grouped, but also those that complete each other to a simply structured whole. This is true also in the complementary colors. When a theme of complementaries underlies the total pictorial composition, it contributes to the coherence or unity of the whole. When it appears in a limited area of the picture, it tends to be so self-contained and self-sufficient that it poses a compositional problem. Similar to perfect circular shape, which does not fit easily into a context and therefore is often given a central or frankly isolated position, the complementary pattern does not subordinate itself without difficulty to a larger color scheme. It functions best as a relatively independent subwhole or as a central core or theme around which further color values are arranged.

Compared with complementary groups, other combinations of colors, although often quite harmonious and sufficiently distinct, show a one-sidedness, which seems to call for completion. Thus a pattern based entirely on reds and yellows looks thin, in need of blue—an effect that is not necessarily undesirable. It is often used deliberately by the artist. A picture filled with nothing but blues and yellows produces a quest of red and thus a powerful tension, which may be exactly what is intended. Sometimes the need for the completing color is satisfied in another area of the picture or, in stage settings, in the color scheme of a later scene.

Since complementary colors are clearly distinct from each other but at the same time merge into a unified whole, they are particularly suited to represent volume by shading. A green object may acquire roundness by shades of purple, and inversely the reddish complexion of the human skin or a piece of fruit may be modulated by the corresponding blue. As discussed earlier, attached shadows are, and need to be, seen as a veil imposed upon the inherent brightness of the object rather than as a part of the brightness scheme of the object itself. A complementary color achieves such a segregation more effectively than a gradation of values within the range of one color. Thus, in a Cézanne still life, if one apple all shaded in greens of different darkness is compared with another that varies from bright oranges to dark blues, it is likely that the volume of the second will be found more compelling. At the same time the mutual exclusiveness of the oranges and blues is compensated by their tendency to unite as complementaries. The unity of the object is thus preserved.

The phenomenon of contrast was cited earlier as demonstrating that the eye tries to obtain what I called "completion" by subjectively calling up the complementaries of color stimuli. If contrast makes a gray surface appear in a color that is complementary to the color of its environment, it may also be expected to "correct" suitable color arrangements in the sense of making them look like more complementary pairs or triads. This would be an example of how colors define each other mutually in an organized whole. It has often been observed how evasive and fluctuating colors are, how they change under the influence of their neighbors in space and time, and how even the very same color will begin to look different when inspected for a while. Ruskin said: "Every hue throughout your work is altered by every touch that you add in other places; so that what was warm a minute ago, becomes cold when you have put a hotter color in another place, and what was in harmony when you left it, becomes discordant as you set other colors beside it." Because of this extreme instability and mutual dependence, it is not surprising that psychological experiments in which random series of isolated colors or pairs of colors were presented to observers led to chaotic results. It is significant, however, that Allesch, whose investigation brought out this ambiguity most clearly, remarks that the pregnancy or variability of any color is reduced when it is put in a context. The order of a pictorial composition stabilizes the character of each color and makes it as unequivocal as is necessary if the artistic statement is to be reliable.

Contrast is only one of the many structural devices that serve this purpose. Adaptation is another. It would be valuable to learn more about the conditions that decide when colors enhance each other's difference and when they enhance similarity. Allesch has experimented with a greenish yellow and a reddish yellow whose admixtures were so slight that when inspected separately both colors looked like pure yellows. Brought together they tended to emphasize their distinctness, looking clearly greenish and reddish and presumably producing the kind of clash already discussed as the effect of "Similarity of the Dominant." But if a third yellow of intermediate hue was placed between the two, the contrast diminished and the total arrangement showed a more unified yellow. Effects of adaptation are also observed when, for example, one strongly red patch in a painting brings out subtly red components in the colors around it.

Relationships between hues cannot be described adequately without reference to their saturation and brightness. Experiments have shown that the distinctness of color depends more upon brightness than upon hue. Liebmann found that when, for example, a red figure is put on a green background of exactly equal brightness, the boundaries become fluid, soft, colloidal. The figure-ground relationship disappears, objects look incorporeal, and there is difficulty in telling differences of distance apart. Also shape tends to melt, the points of stars disappear, triangles look rounded, rows of dots merge into uninterrupted forms. Therefore it is not surprising that painters usually reinforce different hues by different brightness. It seems that they are least reluctant to entrust distinction between neighboring areas to hue alone in the presence of what we have called clash or mutual repulsion. For example, there may be a blue-green background bordering on a reddish blue coat of approximately identical brightness and saturation. This would seem to confirm the view that the most effective distinction between hues is brought about by clash.

Matisse and El Greco

This analysis of color syntax will be concluded by a discussion of two examples. The first is taken from Matisse's painting *Luxury* (Figure 243), which shows three women in a landscape. Two of the figures are in the near foreground, the third is further back. A slight overlap connects the frontal figures and also defines their spatial relationship. The third is much smaller; but in order to tone down the difference in depth, no overlapping is used for this figure. The identical coloring also tends to place all three women in the same plane. The environment is divided horizontally into three main areas: the orange foreground with the white drapery, the green water in the center, and the background with its slightly violet sky, white cloud, and two mountains, one bluish red, the other orange. There is, then, a kind of color symmetry between top and bottom. The white garment in the nearest foreground corresponds to the white cloud in the farthest background; the orange appears in both areas, and so does the yellow of the nude bodies. The approximate center of this symmetry is indicated by the bouquet of flowers. We cannot help feeling that the small woman is spending all her surprising energy and concentration on holding the pivot of the picture in her hands. The bouquet is small, but attracts attention because its shape has the simplicity of a circle, outlined in a pure dark blue that is unique in the painting. The bouquet parallels the navel of the tall figure, thus making it clear that the center of this figure helps to establish the symmetry axis of the total composition.

The symmetry serves to counteract the depth of the landscape created by the superpositions of shape. The two whites, at the extremes of the total range of space, tend to lie in the same plane and thereby to compress the three-dimensional expanse. The orange areas do the same. The three yellow figures overlap the entire landscape and therefore lie in front of it. But they are brought back into the spatial context by the distribution of the brightness values. The two white areas, being the brightest spots in the picture, protrude most strongly—that is, they place the somewhat darker figures inside the brightness scale and in this way hold them back, enclosed between the brightest and the darkest tones.

Except for the whites and the small spots of black and blue, there are no unmixed colors in the picture. The yellow of the bodies is warmed by a reddish tinge. Yellow, established as the dominant color of the composition by the three figures, is also contained in the orange and the green, but probably absent in the sky and the bluish red mountain. Thus in the upper left corner the common color element is reduced to the red, which, however, is weak in the sky and quite faint in the figure. Essentially the colors in that area are distinct to the point of being mutually exclusive.

Just as yellow is excluded from the upper corner of the background landscape, so blue, most clearly expressed in the sky and contained in the bluish red mountain and the green water, is absent from the lower part of the picture. In other words, yellow reaches upward, blue reaches down. They meet, in balanced proportion, in the central green. The critical spot of the picture seems to be the orange mountain and its relation to its neighbor. The only clash of the picture seems to occur between this yellow red and the blue red next to it (Similarity of the Dominant). The reader may use his own judgment as to whether this conflict is justified by its role in the total composition, or whether it must be considered an unsolved remainder of the pictorial problem.

The figures and the foreground are tied together by a structural inversion of yellow and red, and so are the sky and the left mountain by inversion of blue and red. The only example of an approximately exclusive distinction occurs, as I said before, between the sky and the yellow face and shoulders. Here is also the largest interval of depth. The figures are most intimately connected with the landscape at the bottom of the picture, where yellow and, to a slight extent, red are shared. The hair of the kneeling figure even picks up the orange, and thereby makes the affinity all the more complete. In the middle ground there is greater distinction. The bodies and the water contain yellow as one common fundamental, but the reddish admixture of the skin and the blue contained in the green introduce an element of mutual exclusion. Also the black hair of the small figure and the colors of the bouquet enhance detachment. The crescendo of separation reaches its climax in the upper left corner. The spatial leap between the head and shoulders and the sky is compensated, however, by the fact that here the color relationship approaches complementarity. The colors produce maximum cleavage by furnishing the strongest distinction and at the same time bridge over the gap by the harmony of their mutual completion.

As a second example I have chosen El Greco's *The Virgin with Santa Inés and Santa Tecla* (Plate 2). The skeleton of the composition is symmetrical. The Virgin, flanked by two angels, holds the center in the upper half of the picture, whereas the two saints face each other in the lower half.

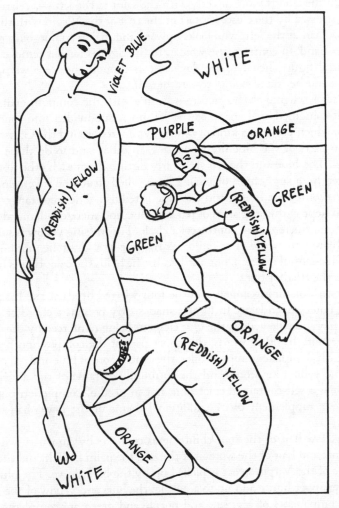

Figure 243

The basic symmetry is animated, however, by deviations, of which the following are relevant here. The attitudes of the Virgin and the child create a slanted axis. The tilt from the upper right toward the lower left connects the figures in the clouds more directly with the saint to the left—a relationship further stressed by the closer contact of the coat of the Virgin with the head of the woman at the left, who looks upward and makes an outgoing gesture with her hand. In contrast, the woman to the right is farther removed from the central figure, her eyes are downcast as though she were wrapped in thought, and her hand points toward herself.

The color scheme of the picture is in line with the compositional motif. The self-contained oval shape of the Virgin is subdivided into four main sections, which produce a kind of central symmetry around the Christ child. The two parts of the blue dress oppose each other, and so do those of the red dress. The blue and the red are clearly distinct from each other, but also connected by a suggestion of what I have called structural inversion, since the red is somewhat bluish and the blue is reddish. The color range of the Virgin is kept within the areas of red and blue, and therefore demands completion from the remainder of the color circle. The missing yellow is supplied by the hair of the child. The child has the role of a keystone, not only because of his central location, but also because he holds the color that is needed to create the triad of hues.

The two worshiping angels and the four winged heads at the base form a trio of outer appendages. In lighter shades they present a chord of green, pale purple, and pale yellow, the blue element being reinforced by the clouds of the ground. In other words, the upper part of the composition presents two roughly complete groups of color: the central core of blue and red topped off by the yellow keystone, and the surrounding frame of the angels and clouds. It is a self-contained color unit, not in need of completion but able to receive a supplement by the additional theme of the lower half of the picture.

The yellow hair of the four child angels connects by similarity with the yellow coat and hair of the woman at the left, the palm branch, and the lion. The blue of the Virgin's coat is picked up by the blue sleeve. The blue and red of the upper figure add up to a purple; the blue and yellow of the lower are the components of a green; and purple and green are complementary. Hence the easy union between the central figure and the left woman. Compare this with the clash between the orange coat of the woman at the right and the purple scheme of the Virgin. The red, dominant in both areas, is torn into the conflicting scales of red-blue and red-yellow, and the barrier created by this clash prevents the eye from gliding across the interval between the two figures.

There is enough of a golden tinge in the shadows of the yellow coat at the left to prevent a true clash between it and the orange red of the coat at the right. The eye can connect the two colors by structural inversion, just as the contact of the two frontal hands, the parallelism of the other two hands, the symmetrical shape of the two-woman group, and the peaceable-kingdom theme of the lion and the lamb all strengthen the horizontal tie. In sum, we find that in El Greco's painting shape and color combine in representing two united aspects of the religious attitude, inspiration and contemplation, receiving and digesting, dependence upon grace and freedom of will. The over-all symmetry of the work makes the contrast of the two-fold human attitude fit into the greater harmony of godhead and man, dominance on the heights and submission on earth.

VIII   MOVEMENT

Motion is the strongest visual appeal to attention. A dog or cat may be resting peacefully, unimpressed by all the colors and shapes that make up the
immobile setting around him; but as soon as anything stirs, his eyes will
turn to the spot and follow the course of the motion. Young kittens seem
completely at the mercy of any moving thing as though their eyes were tied
to it. Human beings are similarly attracted by movement; I need only to
mention the effectiveness of mobile advertising.

It is understandable that such a strong and automatic response to motion
should have developed in animal and man. Motion implies a change in the
conditions of the environment, and change may require reaction. It may
mean the approach of danger, the appearance of a friend or desirable prey.
And since the sense of vision has developed as an instrument of survival, it
is keyed to its task.

Happenings, then, attract us more spontaneously than things do, and the
prime characteristic of a happening is motion. We call the railway station a
thing; the arrival of the train, a happening. We distinguish between an
orator and his gestures. A painting or statue is a thing; the performance of
a dance is a happening. The distinction depends not only upon movement,
but also upon other kinds of change—the lobster and its getting red, the
potato and its getting tender.

Actually we do not see happenings as such, but rather we see things
undergoing change. There are exceptions, for example, when the action is
very fast. Wertheimer found in his experiments on stroboscopic motion that
what his observers perceived under certain conditions was not an object
moving from one position to another. Rather was there "pure movement,"
taking place between two objects and unrelated to both. More commonly,

however, happenings are seen as the performances of objects. The world is made up of things that are changing and others that are not.

Even the distinction between objects in action and objects at rest is not so correct and useful as it may seem. To the physicist all matter is in motion, whether it be that of a house or that of a bird in flight. But whereas in a stone wall the molecular motion remains within the limits of a given volume at a given place, there is also a displacement of the whole object in a flying bird. In the last analysis the distinction of thing and action disappears altogether, matter being nothing but an agglomeration of energy. In this simplified concept of nature, thingness and activity are but properties of patterns of forces.

Such a view is welcome and highly suggestive to the psychologist because he too finds himself compelled to describe things as patterns of forces. Thus I pointed out earlier that a visual object is a stimulation—that is, an action upon the organism that results in action within the nervous system. In the next chapter I shall insist more explicitly that any visual object is a dynamic event and that a thing at rest is one in which forces are not absent but in balance. The difference between the immobile shape of a painting or statue and the body of a dancer in motion becomes secondary.

Time and Sequence

Once this basic similarity of all visible things has been stressed, it is necessary to think of the way they differ. Certainly the performance of a dance, a play, or a piece of music creates a very different experience and conveys a correspondingly different concept of life than a picture, a piece of sculpture, or a work of architecture. We are accustomed to say that the dance occurs in time whereas the picture is outside of time.

Time is the dimension of change. It helps describe change, and does not exist without it. In a universe in which all action had ceased, there would be no more time. Similarly immobile objects give us the impression of being outside of time. Theoretically my desk persists in time while my pen is moving over the paper. But I do not perceive the desk as being busy persisting the way the pen is busy moving. At any given moment the pen is in a particular phase of its course across the paper. For the desk there is no such comparison between its states at different moments. It does not "remain the same" or "stand still." The time dimension does not apply. The story represented in the picture on the wall is not stopped in its tracks. It is outside of time. Special conditions, to be discussed soon, are necessary to make an immobile object appear as being deprived of motion or resisting it.

But is it really the experience of its being in time that distinguishes the dance performance from the picture—if by time experience we mean being aware of the fact that different phases of the dance happen at successive moments? Suppose a dancer leaps across the stage. Is it part of our experience—let alone the most significant aspect of it—that time passes during that leap? Does he arrive out of the future and jump through the present into the past? And exactly what part of his performance does belong to the present? The most recent second of it, or perhaps a fraction of that second? And if the whole leap belongs in the present, at what point of the performance before the leap does the past start?

No answer can be given. Our question turns out to be absurd. The time category does not seem to apply. Apparently the fact that different phases of the performance occurred at different moments of time is not a part of the experience. The dance, to the point to which I have seen it, is given to me as an essentially timeless whole, just as any particular leap or motion.

Slightly alarmed by this unexpected finding, we look around and find the same peculiar quality of timelessness in many other events. A car on the highway is experienced as moving in space, not through time. In a spirited conversation the argument moves along a path, one thought leading to the next in a coherent sequence. It is the logic of this process or development that characterizes the event, not the succession of elements in time. When at the end of the conversation we look at the clock, we are surprised to find that several hours have passed. A day of inspired work or an evening of concentrated reading produce the same effect. Compare these examples with others in which the experience of time is indeed significant. When you are waiting for something, the slow course of time, the succession of the minutes, is foremost in consciousness. Under such conditions you are comparing two points of time: the present and the goal point of fulfillment. The span between the two points is empty, or filled with something disorganized, uninteresting, painful. The time you are marking is not an attribute of what is happening. Rather you are concerned with time instead of with what is happening because you cannot or will not be involved. It is also significant that we are reminded of time at moments at which our occupation loses its grip on us—that is, when the conversation has run into a dead end, when our thoughts hit a block, when we are getting tired or hungry.

In other words, what distinguishes the experience of happenings from that of things is not that it involves the perception of passing time, but that we witness an organized sequence in which phases follow each other meaningfully in a one-dimensional order. When the event is disorganized or incomprehensible, the sequence breaks down into a mere succession. It loses its main characteristic; and even the succession lasts only as long as its elements are being squeezed through the gorge of the immediate presence. Beyond that point they lie scrambled in disorder. No bond of time connects them, because time cannot create order. It is order that creates time.

If we think back to an event that has no meaningful place in the sequence of past happenings, it is as unrelated to time as one isolated bright object in a dark room is unrelated to space. And if it does have its definite place, what we experience is not so much its "date" of occurrence as its belonging in an organized context.

The timelessness of events will seem less surprising if it is remembered that the past as such is never available to the mind. The percepts and feelings of yesterday are gone. They survive only to the extent to which they have left within us remnants that are present now. These traces are not identical with the original experiences, because they are continually modified by other traces, imprinted upon the mind previously and afterward. Thus the trace of a picture seen recently may be changed by that of another picture seen years ago. And the introductory measures of a dance are no longer the same after we have seen the rest of the composition. What happens while the performance is going on is not simply that new beads are being added to the chain. Everything that came before is constantly modified by what comes later.

This availability of the past for change, and the fact that the whole sequence of a past event is given to us like the motion of an object we are looking at now, is explained by the spatial character of memory. Whatever is remembered is located in the space of memory traces, has its place somewhere in the brain as it exists now, has an address rather than a date. That is, we have to understand the experience of an event, such as a dance or a piece of music, by the interaction of the traces it has left in us.

Composition in Dance and Drama

Time as such—that is, the mere succession of elements—no more represents a principle of order for a dance or play than the mere distribution of parts in space organizes a work of painting or architecture. The essential difference between the two kinds of artistic media is not that the one is based on time and the other on space, but that the sequence in which the parts of a composition are to be related to each other is prescribed by the work itself in the dance or play whereas it is not in a work of painting or architecture. The temporal order of our perceptions is not a part of the composition when we look at sculpture or painting, whereas it is when we look at a dance.

A picture contains one or several dominant themes to which all the rest is subordinated. This hierarchy is valid and comprehensible only when all the relationships it involves are grasped as being coexistent. The observer scans the various areas of the picture in succession because neither the eye nor the mind is capable of taking in everything simultaneously, but it does not matter in what order the exploration occurs. Specific directions indicated by the composition must not be adhered to by the path of the glance in order to be understood. A compositional "arrow" leading from the left to the right is perceived even though the eye may move in the opposite direction or indeed cross the track in an arbitrary zigzag. Barriers erected in the picture by contours or color conflict do not stop the eye. On the contrary, they are noticed and experienced in the course of trespassing. In an experimental study by Buswell the eye movements of observers were recorded while they were looking at pictures. The results showed that there was surprisingly little connection between the order and direction of fixations and the compositional structure of the picture. And even the order of the subjective experiences is largely irrelevant, just as it makes little difference for the final structure of a spider web in what order the threads were woven.

In a dance also there are one or several dominant themes; but their appearance is linked to definite phases of the total development, and different meaning goes with different locations in the perceptual sequence. A theme may be presented at the very beginning, and then demonstrated and explored in its characteristics by a number of changes or variations. Or it may be tested by being subjected to encounters with other themes, and thus it may deploy its nature through the resulting attractions or repulsions, victories or defeats. But the theme, perhaps embodied in the prima ballerina, may also make a late appearance, after a slow build-up that leads through a crescendo to the climax. This produces a completely different structure.

Such a composition evolves step by step and contains two sequences. One of them is inherent in the event represented. It leads from the origin of the "story" to its end. The other may be called the path of disclosure. It is the spectator's approach to and journey through the story, prescribed to him by the work itself. The two sequences do not necessarily coincide. For example, in *Hamlet* the inherent sequence leads from the murder of the king through the wedding of his queen and brother to Hamlet's discovery of the crime, and so to the end. The path of disclosure starts somewhere in the middle of the inherent sequence, moves backward and then forward. It proceeds from the periphery of the problem toward its center, introduces first the watchmen, then Hamlet's friend, then the mysterious ghost. Thus while unfolding the dramatic conflict the play also deals with man's ways of finding out about the mechanisms of life—a secondary plot, of which the spectator is the protagonist. And just as a traveler's route of approach to an unknown city will influence the concept he receives, so the path of disclosure will interpret the subject of the work in a particular way by setting accents that will give precedence to certain of its aspects and withhold others. Shakespeare's indirect approach to the Hamlet story stresses the effects of the crime before presenting the crime itself, and sets the initial accents of night, disturbance of the peace, mystery, and suspense.

It must be recognized, however, that although the play or the dance offers a process of constant change, the presentation, just as that of a picture or statue, adds up to the establishment and interpretation of a constant pattern, independent of the particular sequence in which its manifestations are exhibited. The Hamlet drama reveals an underlying configuration of antagonistic forces, love and hatred, loyalty and treachery, order and crime. The pattern could be represented in a diagram that would contain no reference to the sequence of the story. This pattern is gradually uncovered by the play, explored in its various relationships, tested by the introduction of crucial situations. A man's biography, which carries him from his birth to the grave, must lead to a presentation of the polarity of life and death, which is immutable and permanent. And just as Michelangelo's *Pietà* shows a mother holding her child and at the same time a man leaving his mother behind, so does the story of the Gospel, as every great narrative, contain its end in its beginning and its beginning in its end.

The conclusion seems to be that the difference between the so-called space arts and time arts is merely one of emphasis. In a painting or statue the permanent balance of the total "thing" is built of the actions of forces, which attract and repel each other, push in particular directions, manifest themselves in spatial sequences of shape and color. On the contrary, in a dance or play an over-all action is built of things, which are defined by what they do. Thus one kind of artistic medium defines acting through being; the other defines being through acting. Together they interpret existence in its twofold aspect of permanence and change.

An example will illustrate this point. The forces represented in a painting are defined primarily by space. The direction, shape, size, and location of the shapes that carry them determine where these forces apply, where they go, how strong they are. The expanse of space and its structural features—such as, for example, its center—serve as frame of reference for the characterization of forces. On the contrary, the space of a theater or dance stage is defined by the motor forces that populate it. Expanse becomes real when the dancer runs across it; distance is created by actors withdrawing from each other; and the particular quality of central location is brought to light when embodied forces strive for it, rest at it, rule from it. In short, the interaction of space and force is interpreted with different emphasis.

When Do We See Motion?

Under what conditions do we perceive movement? A caterpillar crawls across the street. Why do we see it in motion and the street at rest rather than seeing the entire landscape, including ourselves, displaced in the opposite direction with the caterpillar alone remaining at the same spot? Surely the phenomenon is not explained simply by learning or knowledge, because we see the sun move across the sky and the moon through the clouds. Dante notes that when a person looks up to one of Bologna's leaning towers from "beneath its leaning" while a cloud moves in the opposite direction, the tower seems to topple over. Sitting in a rocking chair, we find ourselves in motion and the room standing still. But when an experiment makes the whole room turn over, like a wheel, and the observer's chair stand perfectly still, the sensation that the chair is turning is so compelling that the observer must be tied so that he will not fall. This happens even though the observer's sense of balance and muscular feelings indicate the true facts.

The experience of visual motion presupposes that two systems are seen as being displaced in relation to each other. The caterpillar is displaced in relation to the landscape; the leaning tower falls in relation to the clouds. The opposite version would be just as compatible with the retinal image we receive of the scene; or indeed both systems could be seen as moving, each of them assuming a share of the displacement. The psychological rule for what happens in any particular event has been formulated by Duncker. He points out that in the visual field objects are seen in a hierarchic relationship of dependence. The mosquito is attached to the elephant, not the elephant to the mosquito. The dancer is a part of the stage setting, not the stage setting the outer rim of the dancer. In other words, quite apart from motion, the spontaneous organization of the field assigns to certain objects the role of a framework, on which others depend. The field represents a complex hierarchy of such dependences. The room serves as framework for the table, the table for the fruit bowl, the fruit bowl for the apples. Duncker's rule indicates that in displacement the framework tends to remain immobile whereas the dependent object does the moving. When no dependence exists, the two systems may both move symmetrically, approaching each other or withdrawing from each other at identical speed.

Duncker, and later Oppenheimer, established some of the factors that produce dependence. Enclosedness is one of them. The "figure" tends to move, the "ground" to stand still. Variability is another. If one object changes its shape and size and the other remains constant—for example, a line "growing out of" a square—the variable object assumes the motion. The observer sees the line stretching away from the square, rather than the square withdrawing from an immobile line. Size difference is effective in the case of contiguous objects. When two objects lie close to each other, either laterally or in the dimension of depth—the one lying closely in front of the other—the smaller object will assume the motion. Intensity also plays a role. Since the dimmer object is seen as dependent upon the brighter, the dimmer one moves when displacement occurs and the brighter one remains still.

It must not be forgotten that the observer himself acts as a frame of reference. If, for example, one of two bright spots in a dark room is held stationary while the other is moved fast, the observer's impression will approximate the objective conditions because he perceives the displacement in reference to his own location. The observer will also intervene by fixating the one or the other object. The fixated object tends to assume the motion. When the observer stands on a bridge and looks at the moving water, his perception will be "correct"; but when he fixates the bridge, he and the bridge may be seen as moving over the river. Duncker explains the contribution of this factor by pointing out that the object fixated assumes the character of the "figure" whereas the nonfixated part of the field tends to become ground. Since as a rule the "figure" does the moving, fixation makes for motion.

In any particular example several of the factors here enumerated—those referring to the situation in the field itself as well as those depending upon the visual and kinesthetic conditions of the observer—will act with or against each other, so that the resulting perception of motion will be determined by the relative strength of the factors involved.

On the stage the actors are usually seen in motion against the foil of an immobile setting. This happens because the setting is large and enclosing and, in addition, anchored to the even larger environment of the house in which the spectator is seated. It serves as frame of reference for the actors. In consequence the stage presents a concept of life according to which practically all physical and mental activity is invested in man whereas the world of things serves mainly as the base and target of such action. A different concept can be conveyed by the film. The picture taken by a camera that moved along a street does not give the experience we get when we walk in the street ourselves. Then the street surrounds us as a large environment, and our muscular experiences tell us that we are in motion. The street on the screen is a relatively small, delimited part of a larger setting in which the spectator finds himself at rest. Therefore the street is seen as moving. It appears as actively encountering the spectator as well as the characters of the film, and assumes the role of an actor among actors. Life appears as an exchange of forces between man and the world of things, and the things often play the more energetic part. This is so also because the film represents with ease natural motion, such as that of the street traffic or the ocean, which is hardly possible on the stage. In a film like Flaherty's *Man of Aran* the natural motion of the waves is enhanced by the cinematographic motion imposed upon the scene by the moving camera. The film gives the world of things an opportunity to manifest its inherent powers and to inveigh against man. In addition, things on the screen can be made to appear and disappear at will, which is also perceived as a kind of motion and which permits any object, large or small, to enter and leave the scene like an actor.

The predominance of man on the stage is well suited to the drama, which takes place in words and is therefore properly focused on the human figure as the carrier of speech. The combination of speech with the visual language of the screen has destroyed the artistic medium of the silent film without solving the probably insoluble task of how a blend of two different media can produce unified form. The dance, a speechless medium, does not run into this difficulty. On the contrary, the dance film has potentialities that are left untapped by the usual mechanical recordings of stage compositions. Some experimental films, like those by Maya Deren, and the choreography of certain movie musicals have given hints of what can be achieved when the motion of the dancer is integrated with that of objects and of the camera. In such a composition the part of the dancer is no more self-contained or complete in itself than that of an instrument in an orchestra, because it is the image on the screen that performs the dance, availing itself of the moving human body as a part of its raw material.

As long as the dominant framework is without motion, any immobile object will be perceived visually as being "outside of time," just as the framework itself. But when the framework is in motion, the stillness of any dependent object will be interpreted dynamically as its being deprived or incapable of motion or actively resisting displacement. Just as a rock in the middle of a rushing stream will exhibit stubborn opposition to motion, so a person standing still in a surrounding stream of walking or running people will not be outside the dimension of motion, but will appear, in terms of motion, as arrested, petrified, resistant.

The moving framework does not have to comprise the entire field. It suffices for the immobile object to be embedded in a moving subwhole. If a number of people are busy in a room, the motion of the group may be sufficient to give the quality of being majestically at rest to a person who is sitting still in its midst. Lot's wife, turned into a pillar of salt, will hardly interpret her fate effectively to the eye as long as she stands alone in the landscape. She will look no more deprived of motion than the trees and mountains. But when the fugitives rush past her, the paralysis of her body will become apparent as a visual fact.

The mobile framework may exist in time rather than in space. For example, if a still picture is inserted in a film sequence, it will exhibit frozen motion rather than stillness. In the same way a dancer stopping for a moment during a run will look arrested rather than at rest. The musician is familiar with the difference between a dead and a live interval of silence. The pause between two movements of a symphony is not pervaded by movement, because it is excluded from the context. But when the structure of a piece is interrupted by silence, the heart beat of the music seems to have stopped and the immobility of what should be motion creates suspense.

Direction

Whether and where motion is perceived is thus determined by the structure of the context in space and time. The same is true for the more specific properties of motion, such as direction and speed. Under certain conditions the objective direction of motion is reversed in perception. Although physically clouds may move east, we may see the moon speeding west instead. A movie shot taken through the rear window of the gangster's car may show the car of the detective moving backward, although it was actually going forward but more slowly than the car it was chasing.

Oppenheimer projected, on a dark screen in a dark room, two luminous lines in the position shown in Figure 244. Objectively the vertical moved to the right and the horizontal moved upward, so that after a while they assumed the positions indicated by the dotted lines. The observers, however, saw the vertical move downward and the horizontal move to the left (dotted arrows). In other words, the motion was perceived as occurring in the directions of the lines themselves rather than perpendicularly to them. This dependence of dynamics upon shape is relevant to the discussion in Chapter IX.

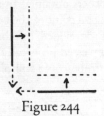

Figure 244

The relation of perceived direction to the context in which the movement occurs was demonstrated also in studies on the rotation of wheels. The hub of a wheel will of course move along a path parallel to that of the whole wheel. Any other point of the wheel will be subjected to two motions: the translatory path and the rotation around the hub. The combination of the two motions will result physically in a wavy path, as indicated in Figure 245.

Figure 245

This is in fact what is seen when the wheel moves in a dark room and nothing of it is made visible except for one luminous point somewhere off center. But if the hub is clearly identifiable, the path of peripheral points observed in the experiment corresponds to what we know from the observation of wheels in daily life. Instead of exhibiting the wavy paths along which all the eccentric points are traveling physically, the motion splits up into horizontal displacement plus rotation around the hub. The wheel is seen spinning around itself and at the same time traveling along its path. Here in the field of motion is a new example of a familiar phenomenon: the subdivision of a pattern into parts that are simpler in structure than the undivided whole.

If this principle of simplicity did not operate, audiences would receive weird experiences from many dance movements. When the dancer turns somersaults, his body is seen as moving across the floor and at the same time as rotating around its center. Any but the simplest movement is a combination of subsystems, which function independently and add up to a whole. When the arms are moved up and down while the body runs forward, the two themes must be—and are—distinguishable. The partial movements, however, do not seem to be strictly independent all the time. Figure 246 shows in a schematic way what happens physically when a bow is combined with a run. It would seem that something of the resulting curve comes through in perception. The structural principles that determine segregation and fusion could be studied fruitfully by comparing film shots of dance movements with others obtained from the same movements executed in the dark while only one point of the body is marked by an attached flashlight, a technique first developed by the French physiologist Jules-Etienne Marey. The path traversed physically by any part of the body can be traced approximately in stroboscopic still photographs.

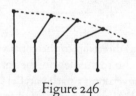

Figure 246

The Revelations of Speed

Motion, as well as other kinds of change, is perceivable only within a limited range of speed. The sun and the moon travel so slowly that they seem to stand still; and the spark of the lightning is so fast that its entire course appears simultaneously as a line. A glance at our watch tells us that the lower limit of perceivable speed is somewhere between that of the minute hand, whose movement remains unnoticed, and the second hand, which is visibly on the march. On Mark Twain's watch, which raced through whole seasons in one day after it had been treated by the watch-repair man, the motion of the hands must have been blurred like that of the blades of an electric fan. We cannot see a child grow up or a man get old; but if we meet an acquaintance after a lapse of time, we can in a split second see him grow tall or shrivel by means of a kind of stroboscopic motion that takes place between a memory trace and the percept of the present moment.

Evidently the speed of change to which our sense organs respond has been keyed during the process of evolution to that of the occurrences whose observation is vital to us. It is biologically essential that we see people and animals move from one place to the other; but we do not need to see the grass grow. The same is true for the observation of size. The lenses of our eyes are keyed to a rate of enlargement that shows many of the important objects small enough to make them appear complete and large enough to reveal essential detail. If we had a pair of telescopes in our head, we should see the stars but neither bread nor water—and microscopes would be equally unsuitable.

We cannot tell whether a turtle, which leads a slow life, sees things move at greater speed than we do. But the traffic of a big city does look faster after we have been away from it for a while. Music and dance also establish adaptation levels for speed; a movement sounds or looks fast when it comes up in a slow context, and vice versa. Some experiments seem to indicate that the rate of the chemical processes in the body influences the perception of time. Thus Piéron asked people to press a Morse key three times a second as nearly as they could estimate this unit of time. When he slightly raised the body temperature of the observers diathermically, they began to press the key faster, thus indicating that the speed of subjective time had increased. Lecomte du Noüy, in citing these and other experiments, speculates that the slowing down of the "chemical clock" during a person's lifetime may account for the well-known fact that as he grows older the years seem to fly faster. It seems questionable, however, whether chemical rather than psychological factors, to which I shall soon refer, are responsible for this phenomenon.

The motion picture has broadened not only our knowledge, but also our experience of life, by making it possible for us to see motion that is otherwise too fast or too slow for our perception. This has become possible because the shooting and the projecting of a film are two independent operations, which can be performed at different speeds. As long as the number of frames taken per unit of time is equal to the number of frames projected, the objects on the screen will move at their natural speed. If the rate of shooting is smaller— for example, if only one frame is exposed every hour—the action on the screen gets faster, and we are enabled to see what otherwise we could only reconstruct intellectually. On the other hand, if the film moves through the camera at high speed, it becomes possible to see a drop of milk bounce back from a surface in the shape of a beautiful white crown or a bullet slowly break up a wooden panel.

The acceleration of natural motion, in particular, has impressed our eyes with a unity of the organic world of which we had at best a theoretical knowledge. The possibility of seeing a plant grow and die within one minute accomplished more than merely making the process surveyable by contraction. The single-frame camera revealed that all organic behavior is distinguished by the expressive and meaningful gestures we formerly considered a privilege of man and animal. For example, the activity of a climbing plant does not appear merely as a displacement in space. We see the vine searching around, fumbling, reaching, and finally taking hold of a suitable support with exactly the kind of motion we considered indicative of anxiety, desire, and happy fulfillment. Sprouts, covered by a glass plate, remove the obstacle by action that does not resemble the mechanical labor of machines. There is a desperate struggle—a visible effort, a proud and victorious escape from oppression to freedom. Organic processes exhibit these "human" traits even at the microscopic level. Sherrington quotes a physiologist's description of a film showing a cell mass making bone. "Team-work by the cell-masses. Chalky spicules of bone-in-the-making shot across the screen, as if laborers were raising scaffold-poles. The scene suggested purposive behavior by individual cells, and still more by colonies of cells arranged as tissues and organs."

Even where the particular appeal of organic movement is lacking, the transformation of long-term changes into visible motion animates the forces of nature and thus impresses the mind with their impact. We know that the sun changes its place in the sky; but when the film, by condensing a day to a minute, shows the play of rapidly moving shadows interpret the relief of architectural shape, we are made to think of light as a happening that assumes its place among the other productive motions of daily life.

A change of velocity not only may make expressive qualities perceivable, but may also modify them qualitatively. It will be remembered that when street scenes were photographed at subnormal speed for the early slapstick comedies, cars did not simply move faster. They were seen dashing around in an aggressive panic—a mood hardly suggested by their normal behavior. Inversely, high-speed shots make the movements of a sportsman or dancer not only slower, but woolly and soft. In addition to the expressive qualities of the moving object, those of the invisible medium are affected. The sloweddown football player seems to be moving through water—that is, through a denser medium, which puts up resistance to motion and cushions the effect of gravitation. Even to the naked eye a school of fast-moving fish makes the water look as thin as air, whereas a lazy goldfish seems to move through oil. This phenomenon is the result of the ambiguity of visual dynamics. The high speed of an object may be perceived as being caused by the great motor power in the object and/or the small resistance of the medium. Slowness is seen as being the result of weakness or lack of effort on the part of the object and/or great resistance of the medium. No experiments seem to have been made on this interesting aspect of perception.

Visual speed also depends upon the size of the objects involved. Large objects seem to move more slowly than small ones. A smaller surrounding field makes for faster motion. Brown had rows of figures move through rectangular frames. When the size of the frame and the figures was doubled, their velocity seemed reduced by one half. In order to appear equal, velocities had to be in equal proportion to the size dimensions. This would make us expect that on a narrow stage dancers will seem to move faster, and that the larger the human figures or other objects on the movie screen, the slower their movement will seem, if they move across the screen at an objectively identical speed.

This dependence of perceived speed upon the size of the framework brings to mind earlier observations on the perception of time. If with increasing age a person finds time flying faster, it is tempting to assume that this happens because a unit of time is experienced in relation to the total span of which it is a part. One year represents one-tenth of a ten-year-old's life, but only one-fortieth of the life of his forty-year-old father. Although this theory sounds convincing, Lecomte du Noüy tended to explain the phenomenon physiologically as a reflection of the slowing down of the chemical processes in the body. As a yardstick for his "chemical clock," he used the time the body takes to heal a skin wound of given size. When he plotted the changing rate of cicatrization during the life of the average individual, and compared it with the length of each year of age in relation to the total preceding life span, he was surprised to find that the two curves were of practically identical shape. This suggests that the question cannot be decided without further investigation.

Stroboscopic Movement

In advertising signboards that display luminous patterns in motion on a panel of light bulbs, letters, ornaments, clowns move although no physical motion occurs on the board. The light bulbs flash on and off, but they do not budge. In order to make a disk-shaped patch move across the panel, the group of bulbs controlling the appearance of the disk changes in a rapid sequence, two phases of which are indicated in Figure 247. This compelling trick raises two psychological questions: Why do we see motion where there is none? Why do we see one disk (in motion) rather than the series of disks formed by light and darkness?

The answers are needed particularly because what happens in the eyes when we see motion is very similar to what happens on the signboard. When the image of a moving automobile is projected upon the retinas, it stimulates different groups of receptors as it crosses the retinal surface. Obviously these stimulations involve no movement, and the stimulus "car" is represented by different nerve fibers at every fraction of time. And yet we see one car move.

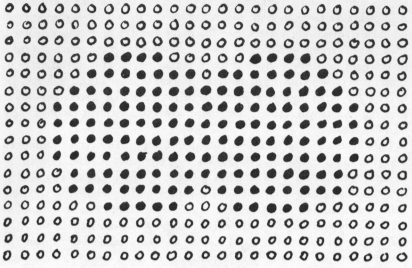

Figure 247

The best-known study of the problem was made by Wertheimer. He investigated the motion perceived when two light spots at suitable distance are flashed on in the dark at a suitable time interval. The phenomenon is recognizable in the signal lights of airplanes and lighthouses. Two spots on the retina are stimulated in succession. When they are far apart in space or the time interval is large, we see first one light appear and disappear and then another light do the same. When they are close together or the time interval is very short, we see them both flash at the same time. But under optimal conditions one light spot moves compellingly from one place to the other.

Since we see motion, motion must be produced somewhere in the brain. Wertheimer concluded that the two stimulations are projected upon a physiological field, presumably located in the cerebral cortex, in which they do not remain isolated. As the two stimulations occur in quick succession and at short distance, a kind of physiological short circuit is brought about, by which the excitation flows from the first spot to the second. The psychological counterpart of this process is the perceived movement. If the principle of what happens to the two stimulations is applied to more complex processes, it offers a theoretical explanation of why we see the car move.

Wertheimer's experiments were suggested by a children's toy invented and first described in 1834 by Horner. A series of pictures representing the phases of movement of some object, for example, a jumping horse, were inserted in a tambour and viewed in succession through slots while the cylinder rotated. This device, called daedaleum by its inventor, and others of the same kind eventually led to the motion-picture technique. Both the simple toy and the modern film projector produce a similar sensation of movement by the rapid succession of pictures in which there is no movement. The fusion of the images is often attributed to the fact that retinal stimulations tend to persist for a moment after their occurrence and thereby to blend with later stimulations in a coherent flow. Film cutters know, however, that under certain conditions a shot only four frames long (about one-sixth of a second) will appear as distinctly separate from the preceding shot. Also, the principle of persistence is incapable of explaining the motion effect produced by distant stimuli in the Wertheimer experiments and under similar conditions in the movies. Factors of structural organization must be considered here.

Why do the stimuli created by the two light spots in the dark blend into a unitary flow of excitation? We notice, first of all, that the phenomenon occurs only when the two spots lie fairly close together, and we remember that similarity of location produces a visual connection among neighbors. Secondly, the two stimuli are alone in an empty field. They play a similar part in the whole. And since similarity was found to connect elements in space, we are led to suspect that it does so also in time.

Consider a flying ball. The positions the ball assumes successively in the visual field are represented in Figure 248 as though they were photographed on the frames of a film. If in this way we eliminate the time dimension, we clearly realize that the object describes a simply shaped path; and we tentatively conclude that the principle of consistent shape, which groups the elements of motionless patterns, may also be instrumental in preserving the identity of the moving object in time.

The other familiar principles of grouping will also play their parts. An object in motion is the more likely to preserve its identity the less it changes its size, shape, brightness, color, or speed. Identity will be threatened if the object changes the direction of its course—for example, if the ball of Figure 248 suddenly turns backward. As usual, in any particular instance these factors will either enhance or counteract each other, and the result will depend upon their relative strength. If a hunted hare makes a sharp double, the change of direction may not prevent us from seeing him still as the same animal. If at the moment of the turn he changes into a turkey, identity may break down and we may see a second animal taking off from where the first disappeared. But if the transformation of shape and color takes place without a change of course, the consistency of path and speed may be strong enough to make us see one and the same animal transforming itself during the chase.

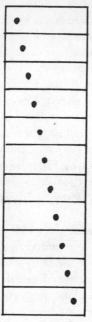

Figure 248

The principles of grouping by similarity were applied to movement by Metzger, who wished to find out what happens when two or more moving objects cross each other's path (Figure 249*a*). At the central meeting point, each object can either sharply change its direction and turn back or continue its path consistently by crossing over to the other side. It was found that the latter version was generally preferred—a result that is in agreement with the principle of grouping by consistent shape. Among other things, the experiments showed that when the objects move in a strictly symmetrical manner (Figure 249*b*) the result is less clear-cut. Then many observers see the objects back up at the point of encounter and remain in their own wing of the field. This indicates that in movement, just as in motionless patterns, symmetry creates a subdivision along its axis, which tends to discourage crossings even where local consistencies of the path favor it.

Wertheimer's experiments had shown that visual objects may appear as identical although their successive locations do not lie close together in space. His basic setup involved only two objects. The question arises as to what

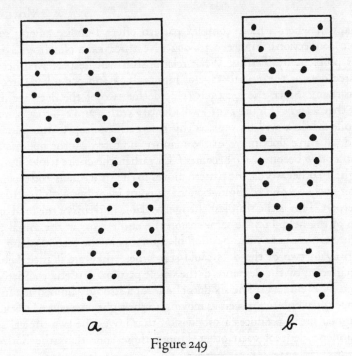

Figure 249

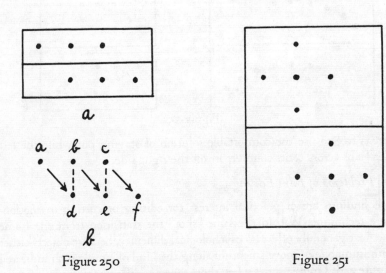

Figure 250

Figure 251

will happen when a more complex pattern offers a choice among several possible connections. Figures 250–252 give three examples from a study of this problem by Ternus. What relationship will be perceived between the three dots at the initial stage of Figure 250*a* and the other three that replace them? Since the locations coincide for two of the dots, we might expect that *b* and *c* (Figure 250*b*) will identify with *d* and *e*—that is, remain immobile while *a* will be replaced by *f* or perhaps leap to the position *f*. Instead, all three dots move in the manner indicated by the oblique lines: *a* becomes *d, b* becomes *e, c* becomes *f*. Or rather, the entire triplet moves to the right. In other words, the pattern moves to the structurally corresponding position in the second configuration. Each point identifies with its structural counterpart. This is the simplest change available in terms of the total organization of the field. For the same reason the entire cross in the initial phase of Figure 251 moves to the position of the cross in the second phase, even though again two of the dots could stay where they are if their behavior was unaffected by the demands of the whole pattern. A useful comparison is afforded by Figure 252. The six dots of *a* form a strongly unified arc. In consequence the whole arc is seen as moving to the right on a curved track. In *b* the angular break produces a subdivision that leaves the two triplets somewhat independent of each other. Under these conditions the horizontal

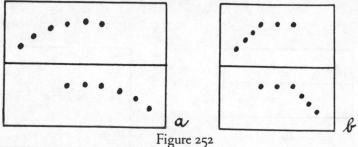

Figure 252

triplet is free to use the comfortable solution of staying put while the left triplet leaps across to its counterpart on the right side.

Some Problems of Film Editing

These findings are of practical interest for editing or cutting in motion-picture technique. Within the same "shot" the transition from one frame to the next generally offers no psychological difficulty, because objects either remain immobile or move smoothly along the kind of simple path indicated in Figure 248. Trouble starts when shots taken at different times in different places follow each other in immediate succession. The spectator knows only what he sees on the screen. Rapid succession suggests unity, and therefore strong means must be used to make the break apparent. Stroboscopic movement is not concerned with the origin of visual patterns. If a policeman in the police station appears on the left side of the screen, and immediately afterward, a little to the right, a woman of about the same size, position, and brightness is shown in her living room, the policeman may be seen jumping to the right and changing into a woman. This can be used for magic tricks, as Georges Méliès did early in the century. Continuity of perceptual factors will bridge over the space-time gap. In one of Maya Deren's experimental films, an actor's leap starts in one setting and is completed in another. The two phases of the leap integrate so perfectly that one unified motion is seen in spite of the change of setting. Usually, however, it is desirable that no such cross-connection between shots should be seen. This implies that objects, characters, or settings meant to be different must be prevented from becoming identical perceptually. The policeman must not change into the woman, and the woman's living room must not be taken to be a part of the police station.

But the opposite problem is just as great. If a scene is composed of shots taken at different camera angles, the same objects, characters, and settings will look different; and it is necessary to make the audience see that the front-face figure at the left in the first shot is identical with the figure shown from the back at the right in the second shot. Similarly, if the first shot presents a corner of a room with a window and a piano, it must be apparent that the other corner with the door and the table in the next shot belongs to the same place. A perceptual connection must be established, which, however, must not be so intimate as to produce stroboscopic jumps.

Here, as in so many other areas, the rules of thumb developed by the practicing artists should be subjected to systematic experimentation by psychologists. The results would benefit both parties. In the meantime, here are a few examples. As far as undesirable stroboscopic movement is concerned, no short circuit is likely to occur as long as objects appear at sufficient distance from each other on the screen. If their location is identical or similar, only a considerable change of appearance will prevent fusion. A mere change of size, as it is obtained when the object is photographed at two different distances from the camera, is unsufficient: the object will be seen magically to shrink or expand. A turn of the head of, say, thirty degrees is likely to produce motion; but a cut from front face to profile involves such a strong change of what I have called the "structural skeleton" that the transition may be safe.

The strongest perceptual factor of the film is directed motion. If a man walks across the screen from the left to the right and immediately afterward from the right to the left, there is no continuity between the two movements and therefore no visible identity between the two human figures. In a similar way, differences of lighting or location can disrupt identity. In strong sunlight the figure of an actor will look very bright when photographed from one side and pitch black when photographed from the other. If other sufficiently effective means of identification are provided, the eye may still make the connection; but the sudden change of mood remains.

The importance of location is illustrated by the following example, which is discussed in an article by Bretz. If a sports match is covered by two television cameras located on opposite sides of the ring, a cut from one camera to the other will naturally invert the picture. The boxer on the left will suddenly be on the right, and vice versa. The obstacle is overcome best by having the cut occur during a pronounced action, which defines the roles of the partners so clearly that correct identification is preserved in spite of the paradoxical location and motion.

Visible Motor Forces

When an object moves, we often see more than simple displacement. The object is perceived as being acted upon by forces; in fact it is the presence of these perceptual forces that gives expression to the motion. Frequently there is a "dead" quality about the motion of motor cars or airplanes. In distinction from the animated activity of horses or birds, they show no sign of being possessed by forces. Magically and incomprehensibly propelled, they exhibit pure, uninspiring locomotion. Obviously this is not true for what can be seen during automobile races, dogfights between fighter planes, or in the aforementioned film comedies; but machines do offer the best examples for dead displacement.

The movements of a dancer, in order to convey expression and thereby be suitable as an artistic medium, must show the action of forces, which they usually do. But since the dance presents human beings in meaningful action, we customarily assume that the activity on the stage is expressive because we have learned to understand what it means. Perhaps the spectator is struck by Orpheus' gesture of wringing his hands only because he has known people to do so when they are in despair and also because the story has told him that Orpheus has lost Eurydice. I have insisted throughout this book, however, that meaning based on mere learning or knowledge is at best secondary for the purposes of the artist. He must rely on the direct and self-explanatory impact of perceptual forces upon the human mind. Therefore it is fortunate that in recent experiments the perceptual effect of motion has been studied in objects that are as free as possible from the connotations of everyday life. In this way we can find out what is achieved by motion as such and under what specific conditions certain expressive phenomena occur. Since thus far these studies have received little attention, I shall discuss them in some detail, rearranging the material and rephrasing the theory somewhat in accordance with my particular objective and procedure. The principal experiments were published by Michotte in 1946.

I have pointed out that unified motion is perceived when the successive locations of an object in space add up to a simply shaped, consistent path. The unifying power of a simple motion is such that the moving object is seen as identical throughout its path even when its shape changes abruptly. In one of Michotte's experiments—which puts my example of the hare and the turkey to test—a small, black square (A) appears on the left side of a white field and moves horizontally toward the center. At a given moment it disappears and is replaced by a red square of the same size (B), which appears next to it and immediately moves on in the same direction and at the same speed. The observers see one object, which in the course of a unitary movement changes its color.

A different effect results from the following demonstration. The black square A, again at the left, starts moving horizontally and stops directly above or beneath the red square B, which has been present but immobile (Figure 253). At the moment of A's arrival, B begins to move in the same

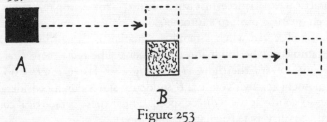

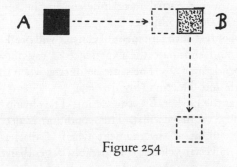

Figure 253

direction. In this experiment, observers see two objects performing two movements, which are all but independent of each other. The same is true for the setup of Figure 254, in which B moves at right angles to A.

Between the limits of undivided, unitary movement on the one hand

Figure 254

and fairly or completely independent movements on the other, a number of revealing phenomena can be observed. Michotte's basic experiment is the following. The red square (B) is in the center of the field; the black one (A) is at some distance from it to the left. At a given moment A begins to move horizontally in the direction of B. At the moment when the two touch, A stops and B starts moving. The observers see A give B a push that makes it move. In other words, the occurrence involves cause and effect.

Of course no physical causality is involved, because the two squares are drawn or projected on a screen. Why, then, do the observers see a causal process? According to Hume's well-known opinion, the percept itself contains nothing but a neutral succession of events. The mind, having become accustomed to the fact that one kind of happening is followed by another, assumes the connection to be necessary and expects it to take place every time. The quality of cause and effect is thus added secondarily to the percept by an association formed during a lifetime.

In opposition to this view, Michotte demonstrates that causality is as much an aspect of the percept itself as the shape, color, and movement of the objects. Whether and to what extent causality is seen depends exclusively upon the perceptual conditions. Strong causality results under conditions where practical experience must call it absurd—for example, when a wooden ball is seen giving a push to a luminous disk projected on a screen. Causality may also be observed when a familiar situation is turned into its opposite, as, for example, in the following experiment. The red square B is moving fairly rapidly toward the right. A, moving even faster, catches up with B. At the moment of their contact, B suddenly slows down considerably and continues its course at the reduced speed. Under these paradoxical conditions perceived causality is particularly compelling.

The general condition may be stated as follows. Causality is perceived when the objects are sufficiently distinguished from each other to appear as not identical and when at the same time the sequence of their activities is sufficiently unified to appear as one unitary process. When these prerequisites are fulfilled, the perceptual force inherent in the primary object is transmitted to the secondary object.

A slight interval of rest at the moment of contact will break the continuity of the movement and eliminate the experience of causality. B's action is then seen as independent of A's. The same holds true when there is no inner consistency of path and direction (Figure 254).

Why is A seen as the pusher, B as the victim? The obvious answer is that this happens because A moves first. This condition is necessary but not sufficient. If, for example, at the moment when A reaches its immobile partner, B starts to move at a velocity considerably larger than that previously seen in *A, B*'s motor energy no longer seems acquired from *A. B* starts to move under its own power. There is still causality, but it is reduced to *A*'s "giving the starting signal" to *B*. Michotte's observers describe this release effect in various ways. "*A*'s arrival is the occasion for *B*'s departure." "*A* throws an electric switch, which makes *B* go." "*B* is frightened by *A*'s arrival and escapes." This last description is an example of the humorous effect often produced by the release but not by pushing. Michotte explains it by the disproportion between the small antecedent and the big consequence.

On the other hand, pushing is most effective when *A*'s motion is faster than *B*'s, because here the hierarchy between the two is not only established by *A*'s time priority of action but reinforced by *A*'s superiority of speed. *B* is seen as acquiring some of *A*'s energy. In mere release, *B*'s energy does not seem a gift of *A*, although *A*'s arrival is still seen as the cause of *B*'s departure. It is thus apparent that the perceptual unity of a movement that is carried by two or more objects in succession requires, not only consistent path and direction, but also a constant level or—preferably—a falling gradient of energy. If either of the two factors is absent, the effect of causality is reduced.

Obviously motor energy as such is not visible, nor is it contained physically in the squares on the screen. In fact, even when we observe a man of flesh and blood walking in the street, the energy we perceive is in no way the physical power that moves the body. Nothing but visual displacements are given to the eyes. What I am discussing is the psychological counterpart of the physiological forces stirred up in the nervous system of the observer by the stimulus of visual motion. It is remarkable indeed how subtly and precisely these perceived forces depend upon the stimulus conditions.

For example, when an object enters the field at a constant velocity, energy is naturally involved; but there is no telling whether the object moves under its own steam or is pushed or pulled. We get the fairly neutral, inexpressive sensation of mere displacement, often present when an airplane is seen moving across the sky. In Michotte's basic experiment, *A* is at rest for a moment before it begins to move toward *B*. With no other source of energy in sight, *A* is thus seen as "taking off," that is, as generating its own motor energy. Hence the expression of inherent vigor conveyed by *A*. We could imagine that *A* might also be seen as being attracted magnetically by *B*. But this does not happen. Michotte reports that under no condition did he succeed in producing the effect of attraction, the reason evidently being that he found no way of characterizing an object visually as being the seat of the kind of energy that would attract others.

The essential point is that in these experiments the visual object turns out to be "implicitly defined." It conveys no properties but the ones revealed perceptually by its presence and behavior. A square at rest will not seem a center of attraction just because the observer imagines it to be such. At more complex levels, the evidence of attractiveness can be brought about in various ways. In a movie a shiny apple or a pretty girl may be supplied by the observer with the forces that are seen to attract a hungry admirer; or the body of the attracted actor himself may show that he is pulled passively. But even under such conditions it holds true that the effect will be the more compelling perceptually and therefore artistically, the more immediately the forces at work are made accessible to the eyes.

Just as the power to influence other objects must be explicitly apparent, so will *B* qualify for the role of the passive victim only if there is direct evidence that it does not possess enough energy of its own. Michotte modified the basic experiment in the following way. *B* is absent. *A* moves toward the right, and stops as usual. At this moment, *B* appears next to *A* and immediately moves to the right. In this case, some observers see *A* pushing *B,* but a larger number perceive *B*'s action as autonomous, the reason being probably that *B* has not been seen immobile before *A* arrived and therefore has not been clearly defined as "dead."

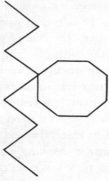

Figure 255

A further experiment deserves to be cited in this connection. Before *A* starts to move, *B* sets itself in motion, travels to the right, turns backward to where it came from, and repeats this zigzag course several times. *A* takes off and meets *B* at the moment when it has returned to its point of departure for a last trip. Unless the observers concentrate their attention on the meeting point, they see no pushing under these conditions, although the last phase of the performance duplicates the basic experiment. By its zigzag course *B* has defined itself as moving under its own power, and its last trip to the right appears simply as a part of its autonomous movement, even though *A* has by now arrived. The experiment closely parallels one of

Wertheimer's demonstrations for immobile patterns (Figure 255). At the meeting point the zigzag line continues its own path although there is a straight-line connection with one of the sides of the octagon. Both experiments show that the inner consistency of two parts will not lead to connection if the structure of the whole pattern separates them from each other.

A Scale of Complexity

An object is perceived as generating its own motor power when after a period of immobility it suddenly takes off. This effect is greatly enhanced when the change from immobility to motion does not occur for the whole object simultaneously but when a part of it starts the motion and imparts it to the rest. Then both cause and effect are located within one and the same object. Michotte used a horizontal bar of the proportions 2:1, located at the left of the field. The bar starts getting longer at its right end until it has reached about four times its original length. As the right end stops, a contraction begins at the left end until the bar has become as short as it was originally. Now the left end stops, the whole performance starts all over, and is repeated three or four times, which carries the bar to the right side of the field. Figure 256 shows the main stages for two full periods.

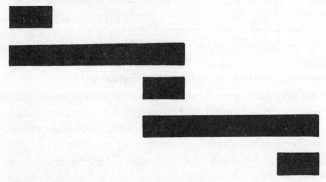

Figure 256

The effect is very strong. The observers exclaim: "It is a caterpillar! It moves by itself!" A notable feature is the internal elasticity exhibited by the bar. The entire body participates in the change imposed upon it by the displacement of its ends. There is no rigid distinction between the immobile and the moving part. The body begins to stretch at one end, and the extension gradually involves a larger and larger part of the body. The same happens in the contraction. This inner flexibility produces a strikingly organic quality.

A very different effect is obtained by the following modification (Figure 257). The experiment starts as before with the 2:1 rectangle at the left side of the field; but, instead of getting longer, the rectangle now splits up into two squares, the left one remaining immobile, the right one moving forward. Otherwise the performance is that of the caterpillar (Figure 256). Now *A* is seen as running after *B* and pushing it forward. The two squares are rigid, and the whole process looks mechanical rather than organic.

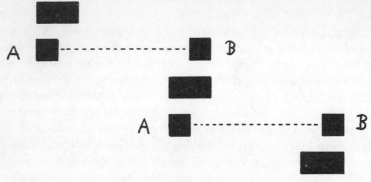

Figure 257

These experiments bring up the question: Are there precise perceptual criteria for the distinction between organic and inorganic behavior? Offhand we might assume that such a distinction will depend simply upon whether an observed motion reminds us more of machines or more of animals. Such an explanation, however, would neglect the most relevant aspect of the phenomenon.

It is well known that the distinction between inorganic and organic things is a fairly late one. At early stages of development primitives as well as children, guided by what they see, do not in principle separate dead things from living ones. Thus stones are believed by some primitives to be either male or female, to have offspring, and to grow. They live forever, whereas animals and humans die. Perception suggests no split in nature; rather does it indicate various degrees of liveliness. Spring water looks more alive than a flower. But what is observed here is not just differences in the amount and speed of motion. There is also a scale that leads from simpler to more complex behavior. And here it must be realized that the distinction between things that have consciousness, feelings, desires, intentions, and others that do not is equally foreign to a world view based on immediate perception. There is a difference in degree between the rain that falls without much consideration of what it is hitting and a crocodile going after his prey. But this is not a difference between having or not having a mind or soul. Rather does it concern the extent to which behavior seems directed by external goals as well as the complexity of the observable reactions. A

Westerner of the twentieth century is supposed to distinguish sharply between a man walking along a hotel corridor in search of his room number and a wooden cart, steered by a pair of photoelectric cells, that will set itself in motion and run after any bright light. But even the Westerner is strongly impressed by the "human" qualities of the phototropic robot. And there are good reasons for the comparison. The behavior of both the hotel guest and the wooden cart is distinguished by a visible striving toward specific aims, which is quite different from what we observe when the pendulum of a clock moves to and fro or when a bored watchman in a museum strolls through the rooms of which he is in charge. It might well be maintained that the difference between high-level and low-level performance is more essential than the fact that the hotel guest and the watchman are supposed to have consciousness whereas the robot and the pendulum are not.

In his interviews with children, Piaget studied the criteria for what is considered alive and endowed with consciousness. At the lowest age level anything that "has an activity" is considered alive and conscious, regardless of whether it moves or not. At the second stage, movement makes the difference. A bicycle has consciousness, a table has not. At the third level, the child bases its distinction on whether the object generates its own movement or is moved from the outside. Older children consider only animals alive and in possession of consciousness, although they may count plants among the living creatures.

It will be seen that the modern scientist's way of separating the inanimate from the animate, and the mindless from the mindful, does not hold for spontaneous perception. It does not hold for the artist either. To a film director a thunderstorm can be more alive than the passengers of a streetcar. A dance is not a means of conveying to us the feelings or intentions of the person represented by the dancer. When we see agitation or calm, escape or pursuit, we watch the behavior of forces, whose perception does not require an awareness of a physical outside and a mental inside.

What counts is the level of complexity in the observed behavior. If we attempt informally to sketch some of the pertinent criteria, we find the following. In agreement with the opinions of children, I cite first the difference between what moves and what does not move. Second, flexible movement, which involves internal change, is at a higher level of complexity than the mere displacement of rigid objects or parts of objects. Third, an object that mobilizes its own power and determines its own course is higher than one that is moved and steered—that is, passively pushed, pulled, repelled, attracted—by an external agent. Fourth, among the "active" objects there is the distinction between those that move merely by an internal impulse and others whose behavior is influenced by the existence of external centers of reference. In this latter group there is behavior of a lower level, which requires the direct contact of the outer agent—for example, object B's "taking off" when touched by A. At a higher level, there is response to the object of reference across a distance in space—for example, A is seen as moving "toward" B, or B escapes while A is approaching.

The level of the fourth group does not presuppose that the objects are "having awareness." Nothing is implied but that the behavior pattern of the observed forces is more complex when they involve an interplay between the object and its environment. Such interplay may occur when the forces are purely physical, as in the phototropic robot; whereas the primitive "blindness" of the lower level may be found in a sophisticated dreamer, who pursues his path with no regard for what is going on around him.

Complexity of the object's path will also indicate a complex pattern of the steering forces. Compare, for example, the difference between A moving toward B in a straight line and at constant speed with the following possibilities. A slows down while approaching, and suddenly "leaps at" B with a sharp increase of speed. Or A slows down, stops, proceeds again, stops again, and suddenly turns around and withdraws very quickly. Or A starts out in the "wrong" direction, moves slowly through the zigzag path indicated in Figure 258, and after the last turn joins B very quickly. Presumably these demonstrations would give the impression of sneaking up, hesitating and escaping, searching. Their dynamics is more complex than that of the straight movement at constant speed, because we observe the effect of an interplay of force and counterforce, of contradictory forces taking over at different times, of changes of the course because of what is found or not found at a given place, and so on.

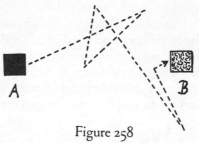

Figure 258

These expressive qualities appear not only in the behavior of visible objects, but also in the indirectly perceived movements of the film camera. As long as these movements are relatively simple—for example, when the camera travels forward or backward in a straight line and at constant speed, or when it rotates on the tripod for a horizontal or vertical panorama shot—they appear as fairly neutral displacements. The spectator's attention is concentrated on the new aspects uncovered by the camera movement in the photographed setting. But the path of the camera can describe curves of a higher order. Its motions can become quite irregular, particularly when it is controlled by hand. Its speed can vary. It can search and hesitate, explore, turn its attention suddenly to some event or object, leap at its prey. Such complex motions are not neutral. They portray an invisible self, which assumes the active role of a character in the plot. The strivings and reactions of this character are conveyed by a pattern of forces, which becomes manifest in the motor behavior of the camera.

At an even more complex level, we may observe "feedback" effects of what happened before upon what happens later. For example, while A approaches, B suddenly runs toward A and pushes it back. A approaches again; but while B starts for a new attack, A withdraws "in time." A short film in which a large triangle, a small triangle, and a circle act out a story was prepared by Heider and Simmel for experimental purposes. It was found that the observers spontaneously endowed the geometric figures, on the basis of their motions, with "human" properties. For example, the larger triangle was described by 97 per cent of the observers as: "Aggressive, warlike, belligerent, pugnacious, quarrelsome, troublesome, mean, angry, bad-tempered, temperamental, irritable, quick to take offense, bully, villain, taking advantage of his size, picking on smaller people, dominating, power-loving, possessive." The surprisingly strong expression of geometrical figures in movement has been demonstrated in the more elaborate "abstract" films of Oskar Fischinger, Norman MacLaren, Walt Disney, and others.

The more complex the pattern of forces that manifests itself in motor behavior, the more "human" the performance looks. But we cannot indicate a particular level of complexity at which behavior begins to look human, animate, conscious; nor are we dealing here with a mere comparison between what appears on the screen and what various things and creatures are observed to do in daily life. The decisive facts would seem to be that human behavior is relatively complex, that animate behavior is often more complex than inanimate behavior, and that the same holds true for creatures that we assume to have consciousness as distinguished from those that seem to have no senses, emotions, intellect, strivings. Human behavior is, however, often strikingly mechanical. In fact Bergson has maintained in his book on laughter that what strikes us as comical is the discovery of mechanical aspects in the behavior of people. On the other hand, inanimate objects often seem uncannily alive.

Therefore, from the point of view of perception and of art, it is appropriate not to insist on the categories set up by biologists, physiologists, and psychologists, but to inquire what level of complexity is exhibited by the observed behavior. Almost always various levels of complexity will be found in the same object. Among the organs of the human body the hand has the most refined motor behavior to be encountered anywhere in nature, whereas the knee shows little beyond what the ball-and-socket joint of a machine can accomplish.

These considerations hold also for immobile shape. Some artists—for example, the cubists—have given the human figure the simplicity of inorganic shape; whereas van Gogh has represented trees and even hills and clouds by means of flexible curves, which humanize these objects. In the work of Henry Moore we find the whole range of complexity from rigid cubes to subtly inflected curves of high order. Associations with things living and dead will frequently be aroused by shape and movement. But it is not the association that endows them with expression and meaning. On the contrary, the level of behavior and form exhibited by the things of nature determines the place assigned to them by the eye in the scale that leads from the simplest pattern of existence to the most elaborate.

The Body as an Instrument

As a person, the dancer has a body of flesh and blood, whose physical weight is controlled by physical forces. He has sensory experiences of what happens inside and outside of his body, and also feelings, wishes, goals. As an artistic instrument, however, the dancer consists—at least for his audience—of nothing but what can be seen of him. His properties and actions, just as those of Michotte's squares, are implicitly defined by how he looks and what he does. One hundred and sixty pounds of weight on the scales will not exist if to the eye he has the winged lightness of a dragonfly. His yearnings are limited to what appears in posture and gesture. He has no more and no less of a soul than a painted figure in a picture.

This does not mean that the human figure is the same as an abstract pattern. Figure 259*a* shows an attempt of the painter Kandinsky to translate a photograph of the dancer Palucca, looking roughly like Figure 259*b*, into a line pattern. It will be seen that the design retains—and perhaps even intensifies—certain properties of the dancing body, its symmetry, its squat proportion, the irradiation of limbs from a massive base. But it lacks characteristics that spring from our knowledge of the human body. The picture of the dancer derives strong dynamic properties from the fact that we perceive the pose as a deviation from a normal or key position. The legs are not just a flat circular curve; they are stretched apart. The arms are not just directed upward; they are raised. The head is more than one of three dots; it is the seat of the sense organs—that is, the center of incoming and outgoing forces.

Thus some of the known properties and functions of the body are part of its visible character. This poses a peculiar problem for the dancer. The center of the nervous system, which receives all information and directs all action, is not located in the visible center of the body, but in the head, a relatively small and detached appendage. Only in a limited way can activity be shown as issuing from this appendage—for example, in facial expression or when the head turns toward an object of interest or nods or shakes. But even these motions are difficult to coördinate with the rest of the body. In daily life the head alone performs much action while the body rests as an essentially unconcerned party. The same is true for the hands. The dancer can frankly exclude the body, as in Hindu dances; these dances can be performed even when the person is seated, and consist of stories told by the hands while the head and face supply an accompaniment of emotional reactions. But if the whole body is to be involved, action must issue from its visible and motor centers in the torso rather than from the center of the nervous system. If man were constructed like a starfish there would be no trouble. But the peculiar discrepancy of the human build moves the appropriate center of the dancer's action away from the visible locus of the mind.

Figure 259

The French dance teacher Delsarte maintained that "the human body, as an instrument of expression, was divided into three zones: the head and neck being the mental zone; the torso, the spiritual-emotional zone; the abdomen and hips, the physical zone. The arms and legs are our contact with the outer world—but the arms, being attached to the torso, take on a predominantly spiritual-emotional quality; the legs, being attached to the heavy lower trunk, take on a predominantly physical quality. Each part of the body subdivides again into the same three zones; in the arm, for instance, the heavy upper arm, physical; the forearm, spiritual-emotional; the hand, mental. In the leg: thigh, physical; foreleg, spiritual-emotional; foot, mental." This interpretation, which has its roots in Greek tradition, is essentially in keeping with what I have said about the different levels of complexity found in the various parts of the human body, and relates to the distribution of the sense organs and the localization of other physiological functions.

Isadora Duncan reasoned as a dancer when she asserted that the solar plexus was the bodily habitation of the soul because the visual and motor center of the dance movement is the torso. But her statement hides the fact that when movement issues from the torso, human activity is represented as directed by the vegetative functions, particularly sex, rather than by the higher human capacities of the mind. In other words, the torso-centered dance shows man primarily as a child of nature, not as a carrier of the spirit. Many a young dancer's difficulties involve a conscious or unconscious resistance to shifting from the safe control of reason to an "immodest" acknowledgment of instinct, which has its parallel in some trends of modern psychology.

In the dance, however, as in all art the subject matter is symbolic—that is, the presentation of the human figure aims at a representation of life and nature in general. On this universal plane there is more justification for considering the unique faculties of the human mind as a mere island of high achievement in a world of unreasoning, unconscious forces.

It would be tempting to follow up the parallel with sculpture, where the compositional theme is also frequently developed from the center of the body and sometimes limited to a headless and limbless, that is, despiritualized torso.

Just as in any other work of art, all action must be subordinated to a dominant theme of movement. In daily life the body accomplishes motor coördination with little difficulty once the initial stages of training are overcome. When a child learns to walk, each step is innervated deliberately and separately. The same lack of integration can be observed whenever a new motor skill is being acquired. For the purposes of dancing and acting, all motor behavior must be learned afresh until it becomes again spontaneous at a higher level of form and control. When we feel self-conscious, the smooth submission to the dominant theme of motion is disturbed by the sudden conscious control of secondary centers of action. In an essay on the puppet theater the poet Kleist recommended to the dancer the example of the marionette, which in his opinion has the negative advantage of never being affected. "For affectation, as you know, appears when the soul (vis motrix) finds itself at a point other than that of the center of gravity of the movement. Since the puppeteer, when he holds this wire, has no other point in his power but this one, all other limbs are what they should be, dead; they are only pendula and just follow the law of gravitation; an excellent quality, which we seek in vain with most of our dancers. . . . Look at young F. when, as Paris, he stands among the three goddesses and hands the apple to Venus: his soul—it is awful to look at—is seated in his elbow. Such mistakes . . . are unavoidable since we have eaten of the tree of knowledge. But Paradise is bolted, and the cherub is behind us; we must make the voyage around the world and see whether, perhaps, it is open again somewhere at the back." To be sure, Kleist simplified the condition of grace. No model of perfection is produced at the lowest level of·integration when dead limbs drag behind the motion of a central point. Even the puppeteer is faced with the delicate task of organizing the various centers of motion in accordance with their functions in the whole.

The Kinesthetic Body Image

In dancing—and the same holds true for acting—the artist, his tool, and his work are fused into one physical thing: the human body. One curious consequence is that the dance is created essentially in a different medium than the one in which it appears to the audience. The spectator receives a strictly visual work of art. The dancer uses a mirror occasionally; he also has at times a more or less vague visual image of his own performance, and of course as a member of a group or as a choreographer he sees the work of other dancers. But as far as his own body is concerned, he creates mainly in the medium of the kinesthetic sensations in his muscles, tendons, and joints. This fact should be noted, if only because some aestheticians have maintained that only the higher senses of vision and hearing yield artistic media.

I have insisted that all visual shape is dynamic. This is equally true for kinesthetic shape. Michotte has observed that "movement seems to be essential to the phenomenal existence of the body, and posture is probably experienced only as the terminal phase of motion." Merleau-Ponty points out that "my body appears to me as posture"; and that, in contrast to visually observed objects, it does not have a spatiality of position but one of situation. "When I stand in front of my desk and lean upon it with both hands, the accent is all on my hands, while my entire body trails behind them like the tail of a comet. Not that I am unaware of the location of my shoulders or hips, but it is only implied in that of my hands, and my entire posture is, as it were, readable through their leaning on the desk."

The dancer builds his work from the feelings of tension and relaxation, the sense of balance, which distinguishes the proud stability of the vertical from the risky adventures of thrusting and falling. The dynamic nature of

kinesthetic experiences must be kept in mind in speculating about the surprising correspondence between what the dancer creates on the basis of his
muscular sensations and the image of his body seen by the audience. The
dynamic quality is the common element, which unites the two different
media. When the dancer lifts his arm, he primarily experiences the tension
of raising. A similar tension of raising is visually conveyed to the spectator
through the image of the dancer's arm.

Dancers and actors have to learn, in order to coördinate the two media,
mainly how much to give. Their initial uncertainty in this matter may be
partly the result of the fact that, as Michotte has pointed out, our dynamic
body image has poorly defined limits. It is a "kinesthetic amoeba"; it has no
contour. Michotte explains that this is true because the body is the one and
only content of the kinesthetic field. There is nothing beyond and around
it, no "ground" from which it could detach itself as the figure. Thus we can
judge the size and strength of our motions in relation to each other, but we
have little concept of their impact in the surrounding visual field. The
dancer must learn how large or fast a gesture should be in order to achieve
the desired effect.

Of course the proper dimensions depend also upon the function of the
movement pattern in the whole performance and upon the size of the image
received by the spectator. The movement of the dancer can be more extensive than that of the actor, with whom it is subservient to speech. For the
same reason gestures had to be toned down when the sound film added
dialogue to the picture. Stage acting requires larger movement than screen
acting, and the slight raising of an eyebrow in a close-up will equal an extensive gesture of surprise in a long shot. To meet these requirements the dancer
and the actor have to develop appropriate kinesthetic size and speed scales.

Mechanical and Recorded Motion

For a long time the artistic use of visual shape in motion remained limited
to the performance of live dancers and actors. This meant that invention and
composition in this field were unable to go beyond the kind of motion
pattern derivable from the mechanics of the human skeleton. The physical
weight of the body had always to be included as a compositional factor, and
there was no getting away from the human figure as the subject matter.
Also the use of a physical body allowed no more than an approximation of
the desirable precision of shape and motion. Finally, all performance contains
an element of improvisation, since impulses and imperfections of the moment cannot be corrected. Thus the performing arts must by necessity
remain halfway between the raw material of nature and the precision of
controlled form.

On the other hand, the creation of artificial movement remained a primitive medium as long as it had to depend on mechanical means. Clockworks could produce only quaint toys; and when certain modern sculptors started to experiment with motion, they had only the choice between controlling it and limiting it to simple rotations—which hardly agreed with the elaborate shape of their figures—or leaving the joints of their mobiles free to form the kind of playful, accidental pattern that we observe with pleasure but without admiration in kaleidoscopes. Similar limitations hampered the attempts to produce symphonies of moving lights on the screen by means of mirrors, lenses, and projectors.

Only the motion picture rendered visual movement independent of mechanics. In combination with photography this new technique made it possible to record and manipulate, not only human motion, but just as well that of other natural things, large or small. By the movement of the camera it put immobile objects in action and limited the rule of gravitation. In particular, the animation technique added the dimension of motion to pictorial shape. This most promising new medium has so far been used artistically only by a few pioneers. What we have been able to see makes us feel that motion will greatly strengthen the immediate expressive appeal of "abstract" art, without which arrangements of form remain a mere entertainment of the eye.

IX   TENSION

When we say that a person sees movement, we generally mean that he sees
something changing its place. Such displacement may be observed in physical objects either directly, as in a flying bird, or indirectly, for example, when
the moon seems to rise above the horizon. Motion also may be seen where
physically there is none. The pictures on the movie screen are an example.
So are the so-called autokinetic sensations: in a dark room a small bright
light seems to perform an erratic dance, owing perhaps to muscular strains
on the eyes. Whatever the origin of the percept, locomotion is seen in all
these cases.

Movement without Motion

The term "movement" is also used in quite a different sense. T. S. Eliot says
of a Chinese jar that it "moves perpetually in its stillness." There is movement in the marble folds of a Greek statue or in the spiral scrolls of a baroque
façade. Artists attribute great importance to this quality. If a painted figure
lacks it, it is, according to Leonardo da Vinci, "doubly dead, since it is dead
because it is a figment and dead again when it shows neither movement of
the mind nor of the body." Evidently no locomotion is perceived here. If
Tintoretto's angels looked as though they were actually being propelled
through pictorial space, we should think we were witnessing a frightening
miracle.

The phenomenon is clearly different from what happens when we watch
a dancer or a movie. There is neither physical motion nor the illusion of it.
In a painting or statue visual shapes are seen as striving in certain directions.
They convey a happening rather than a being. They contain, as Kandinsky
has put it, "directed tensions." What are the nature and origin of this perceptual quality?

The traditional explanation follows familiar lines. The phenomenon is said not to spring from the observation itself, but to be added to it secondarily because of what has been experienced at other occasions. We have learned to associate motion with the visual images of a running man or a waterfall. When we see an image commonly connected with motion, we supply the element of displacement where it is absent in the perceptual experience itself. This theory can be found, for example, in the writings about the Rorschach test as an explanation of people's "movement responses" to the ink blots.

Snapshot photography proves every day, however, that whereas some action pictures show a football player or dancer in vivid motion, others have the human figure awkwardly arrested in mid-air as though struck by sudden paralysis. In a good work of painting or sculpture, bodies swing freely. In a bad one, they may be stiff and rigid. These differences occur although the good and the bad photographs, paintings, or statues have equal chances of being associated by the observer with past experiences. In bad ones, we understand that motion is represented; but not only do we not see it, we find it painfully absent.

This objection can be met by another more refined version of the same theory, which might maintain that the association is not based on the objects as such (running man, waterfall), but on the shapes, directions, brightness values, by which objects are represented. From everyday experience certain perceptual properties are known to be connected with motion and with objects that move. For example, movement through water leaves a wedge-shaped trace. Fish, boats, arrows, birds, airplanes, motorcars are outlined, wholly or in part, by converging straight lines or curves. Similarly, oblique position of objects suggests potential or actual motion, since it deviates from the positions of rest, that is, from hanging perpendicularly or lying on the ground horizontally. Again, blur or scales of shading are observed in fast-moving wheels, cars, flags, arms, legs. Therefore, according to this version of the traditional theory, it can be assumed that any visual image that presents objects by means of such perceptual qualities as wedge shape, oblique direction, shaded or blurred surface will give the impression of movement; whereas the same objects will look stiff in pictures that do not fulfill the perceptual conditions.

Essentially, this assertion is borne out by the facts. The theory also has the advantage of suggesting an explanation of the strong dynamic effect often produced by patterns not directly related to objects of daily life experience, for example, in architecture or "abstract" art. A wedge-shaped form shows the effect regardless of whether or not it reminds the observer of an arrow, a boat, or anything at all.

Both versions of the theory, however, neglect the difference between the perception of locomotion and that of directed tension. Since they explain the dynamic quality of immobile patterns as an aftereffect of perceived locomotion, they would make us expect one of two things: either that works of the visual arts should produce the illusion of locomotion; or the fact that they do not, although they contain subject matter and perceptual features commonly accompanied by motion, should make pictures and statues look paralyzed, as if they had been suddenly stopped in their course, like still shots inserted in a motion picture.

The least we would assume to happen would be that if, say, a pictorial composition showed a tendency to actual locomotion, this tendency would greatly enhance the dynamic effect. Instead, the opposite is true. I have pointed out that in imperfectly balanced compositions, shapes do not stabilize each other's locations, but look as though they wanted to move to more suitable places. This tendency, far from making the work appear more dynamic, produces the painful effect of paralysis. Shapes look frozen, arrested in arbitrary positions. The dimension of time, which does not belong in the immobile arts, has been introduced and creates a false interpretation. In El Greco's *St. Jerome* (Figure 260) the slight movement of the beard to the right counterbalances the location of the hands and the book at the left. If the section below the dotted line is covered, balance is destroyed. The beard now looks as though it was being blown sideways by an electric fan and wanted to return to a vertical state of rest. Does this tendency make it appear more dynamic? On the contrary, whereas the beard flows freely in the complete picture, it is awkwardly kept from motion in the incomplete composition. Paradoxical as it may sound, the quality that painters and sculptors call the "movement" of immobile form does not appear unless any indication that the object might actually change or move is rigorously checked.

Directed Tension

If this dynamic effect were nothing but a secondary attribute applied to the percept by the observer on the basis of what his past experience makes him expect, it would be indirect, weak, and therefore of little value for the artist. But it will be evident by now that we are not dealing here with the projection of one kind of perceptual experience (locomotion) upon another. Rather, we are confronted with a perceptual phenomenon in its own right, directly inherent in what we see. What, then, is its psychological origin and condition? An answer suggests itself as soon as we remember that all perception is dynamic. The experience of vision is not adequately described as the presence of objects with certain static properties definable by distance, angle, or wave length. Perception reflects an invasion of the organism by external forces, which upset the balance of the nervous system. We must not think

Figure 260

of stimulation as stable patterns peacefully printed upon a passive medium. More nearly, we might imagine a hole being torn into a resistant tissue. A battle must be assumed to result from the impact of the invading forces trying to maintain themselves against the tendency of the physiological field forces to eliminate the intruder or at least to reduce it to the simplest possible pattern. The relative strength of the antagonistic forces determines the resulting percept.

At no time does stimulation congeal to a static arrangement. As long as light affects the brain centers of vision, the pushing and pulling keep going on, and the relative stability of the result is nothing but the balance of opposing forces. Is there any reason to assume that only the outcome of the struggle is reflected in visual experience? Why should not the play of the physiological forces itself also find its counterpart in perception? I suggest that it is these forces which we perceive as "directed tension" or "movement" in immobile patterns. In other words, we are dealing with the psychological counterpart of the physiological processes that result in the organization of perceptual stimuli. These dynamic aspects belong to any visual experience as intimately and directly as the static qualities of shape, size, color. To the sensitive eye, the simplest picture—a dark spot on a light ground—presents the spectacle of an object expanding from its center, pushing outward, and being checked by the counterforces of the environment. The fact that all visual being is visual action brings about expression and thus makes it possible to use percepts as an artistic medium.

A few words should be said here about the theory that the dynamics of visual objects is due to kinesthetic sensations in the body of the observer. In the reasoning of Rorschach and his followers, visual perception in itself contains nothing but static patterns. When the subject matter suggests it, some kind of movement, not further defined as to its nature, is added to the percept by association. In order to endow the movement with its dynamic impact, the observer must call on remembrances of how his own body felt when it was in situations similar to that represented in the picture. The picture of a man with a raised fist evokes the muscular tension of fist raising in the observer's own body.

I have previously attempted to show that the widespread tendency to explain the accomplishments of space perception as donations from a nonvisual source is due to the mistaken assumption that touch has more direct contact with the perceived object than vision. It is equally fallacious to assume that experiences of tension will arise more directly from kinesthetic percepts than from visual ones. The physical forces that move muscles, joints, and tendons are not transmitted by the sensory nerves to the brain. Only information about their effects—that is, about the extensions and contractions they produce in the body—is so transmitted. If these messages are accompanied by experiences of tension, this surely is not due to a direct grasp of muscular energies, but to perceptual forces aroused within the cortical brain centers by the stimulation. If it is admitted that such experiences of tension are inherent in kinesthetic perception, there is no reason why they should not accompany visual perception in the same way. In other words, recourse to kinesthesis is of no help in explaining the dynamic properties of visual perception, since this requires assumptions about the nature of kinesthetic stimulation that can be made with equal justification, or lack of it, for visual stimulation itself.

This remark is not meant to deny the fact that visual perception can be accompanied by kinesthetic sensations. But these will be expected to occur only when and because visual tension is experienced in the first place. Rather than being indispensable for the perception of tension, they are a secondary reinforcement, a kind of sympathetic resonance, which arises sometimes, but not necessarily always, in the neighboring medium of the muscle sense.

Information about the nature of directed tension in visual patterns can be obtained indirectly from two kinds of studies dealing with certain aspects of perceived locomotion. First, there are reports on the so-called "gamma motion," which is observed when an object suddenly appears or disappears. A traffic light that flashes on at night seems to expand from its center toward the outside in all directions. Similarly, its disappearance is seen as a centripetal shrinking toward the inside. Experiments have shown that this motion varies with the shape and orientation of the object. It occurs essentially along the axes of what I have called the structural skeleton of the pattern or, to use Newman's language, along the lines of force. It issues from a vaguely circular central spot and, in a disk-shaped object, irradiates in all directions (Figure 261a). A square or rectangle unfolds in the directions of its sides (b), but there is also motion in the directions of the corners (c). A star appears through the outward shooting of its corners (d). When an equilateral triangle stands on one of its sides, the base remains quiet whereas the other two sides strike energetically outward and upward as though they were hinged on the apex (e). The same figure will come about by a violent upward thrust of the apex from the base if the exposure time is very short (f). When the square or triangle stands on edge, the corners push outward more or less symmetrically (g, h). There is, however, a tendency of the motion to be strongest in the horizontal directions, and in the vertical there is more upward than downward push. This is demonstrated in the square (b). The lateral motion is most pronounced, the upward one weaker, the downward one almost absent.

The gamma motion permits us to observe the perceptual forces at work

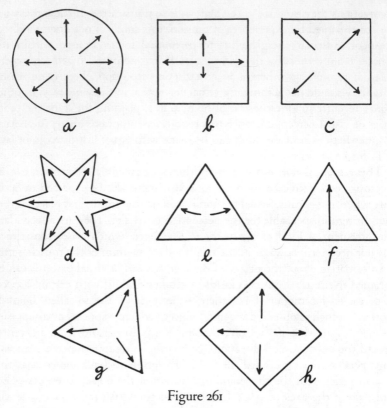

Figure 261

in the creation of patterns. And perhaps it is not too daring to assume that it also furnishes a kind of anatomy of the forces or tensions characterizing the dynamics of patterns when they are observed at rest under normal conditions. At the present time the procedure has been applied only to a very few, elementary patterns. It would be in the interest of the psychologist as well as of the artist if these experiments were continued with more complex shapes and configurations.

Another kind of indirect evidence comes from the studies on locomotion by Oppenheimer and Brown, mentioned in the foregoing chapter. Straight lines or rectangles were seen to move faster through the field when they were oriented with the direction of the movement than when at right angles to it. Also visual objects preferred to move with the direction of their main axis, second choice being the direction perpendicular to that of the main axis. These findings suggest that perceived locomotion is enhanced when it conforms to the directed tensions within the object. Brown also observed that disks seemed to move much faster in the upward than in the horizontal direction. This corresponds to what is shown by the gamma motion of the square. If upward motion takes a greater effort than lateral motion, it can be expected to look faster at objectively identical speed. (It will be remembered that a similar phenomenon occurs with regard to size. A square with objectively equal sides looks "too high.")

What Creates Movement?

No attempt experimentally to explore the nature and conditions of directed tension in immobile patterns seems to have been made. We must rely on the eyes of the individual observer. Valuable material is available, for example, in Wölfflin's studies on the baroque style, one of whose main characteristics is "movement." In the following I shall refer also to examples already discussed in various contexts.

In the first place, movement depends upon proportion. For example, as the Renaissance develops into the baroque, the architectural preference shifts from circular forms to oval ones, from the square to the rectangle, thus creating "tension in the proportions." This can be observed particularly in the ground plans of rooms, courtyards, churches. In the circle the dynamic forces irradiate symmetrically in all directions and thereby compensate each other. The circle rests in its place. It is the first shape mastered by the child, who in his drawings cannot yet conceive of a distinguished direction. Similarly, in a square the vertical and the horizontal axes counterbalance each other, and so do the diagonals. In the oval and the rectangle there is directed tension along the greater axis. Rather than invade the environment in all directions, such a shape pushes toward a specific aim. In particular, every line exhibits movement along its own course. This is the most elementary dynamic feature of all drawing.

Strictly speaking, the proportion of an oblong or line defines only the orientation but not the direction of the movement. A horizontal rectangle may move to the left or the right. The action may also proceed symmetrically from the center in both directions, as in the gamma motion of the rectangle or in the façades of symmetrically designed buildings. This ambiguity can be eliminated by the context. If an oblong is rooted in a heavy base, the tension will be directed toward the free end. Thus arms and legs and the branches of trees are seen to move outward from the trunk. In the vertical the preference for upward over downward motion, suggested by the gamma phenomenon, helps to define direction. Columns tend to strive upward rather than downward.

The movement in a rectangle or homogeneous line is not strong, probably because the shape is symmetrical and balanced. No such symmetry exists along the main axis of a wedge or triangle. Here the glance shifts back and forth between the broad and the narrow end. Dynamically the wedge shape represents a crescendo or decrescendo of breadth—a first illustration of the general rule that all perceptual gradients make for movement.

A characteristic remark on the dynamic quality of the wedge shape is contained in a treatise by Lomazzo, painter and writer of the sixteenth century. Speaking about the proportions of the human figure in paintings, he said: "For the greatest grace and life that a picture can have is that it express motion, which the painters call the spirit of a picture. Now there is no form so fit to express this motion as that of the flame of fire, which according to Aristotle and the other philosophers is an element most active of all others because the form of the flame is most apt for motion. It has a cone or sharp point with which it seems to divide the air so that it may ascend to its proper sphere." Lomazzo concludes that a human figure having this shape will be most beautiful.

There is less ambiguity of direction in the wedge than in the square. Movement is preferably oriented toward the point. It produces the arrow effect. Presumably this is so because the broad end fulfills the function of a heavy base, from which movement issues toward the slim point. In steeples, pyramids, or obelisks the effect is reinforced by the mass of the building or the ground on which they rest and by the preference for upward movement in the vertical.

In Chapter V, I pointed out that three-dimensionality arises from tensions inherent in the two-dimensional pattern. In terms of the present discussion, this means that in surface patterns that tend to be seen three-dimensionally there is always "movement" in the direction toward simpler shape. This tension is only partly resolved in the three-dimensional version; for example, groups of convergent lines do not become completely parallel, but retain some of their wedge shape. The pointing, decrescendo effect of the wedge greatly contributes to the dynamic quality of three-dimensional space. Central perspective produces a system of arrows, which move from their basis in the foreground toward the vanishing point on the horizon. Thus depth is perceived not merely as a static agglomeration of distances but as a dimension of directed action, which leads from the observer to infinity. But ambiguity of direction is evident here too. At their near, broad sides the perspective wedges are endless. They are merely overlapped, but not closed off by the frame of the picture or the delimitations of the observer's visual field. On the other hand, their narrow ends are often firmly anchored to some object at a finite distance. For example, converging side walls, ceiling, and floor of a room find their base in the back wall. Consequently under certain conditions there is in perspective space also a crescendo movement from the distant base toward the "free ends" in the open area around the observer.

A variety of the wedge shape is the stepwise connection between spatial levels, which replaces an abrupt and relatively static right-angular break with an oblique profile and a gradual diminution of breadth. Wölfflin exemplifies this device by the so-called pilaster bundles, favored by baroque architects. The wall level is made to advance gradually to the pilaster level by a mediating scale of steps, "which often recalls the chromatic scales of music." A decrescendo of breadth makes the pilaster grow dynamically out of the wall. Exterior staircases fulfill the similar function of making the vertical block of the building emerge gradually from the horizontal ground or—if the pattern is read downward—of making the structure dissolve toward the ground. Rather than resting statically on the ground, the building is interpreted to the eyes dynamically as an event of rising or descending.

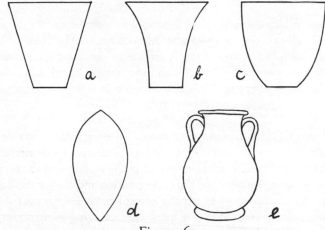

Figure 262

Convergent straight lines retain as a static element the fact that the gradient of decreasing breadth has a constant rate. A comparison of *a* with *b* and *c* of Figure 262 shows that the movement of the profiles becomes more compelling when a crescendo or decrescendo of rate is added to mere wedge shape. In *b* divergence is enhanced by a bold pushing outward; in *c* it is softened by a slowing down of speed. In both, the dynamics is livelier, and the more complex formula of shape makes for a more "organic" effect (cf. Chapter VIII). The movement is even freer when, in leaves or vases (*d, e*), turns of orientation occur. If you cover the drawings with a piece of paper and then slowly uncover them vertically, you will best experience the wealth of expansions and contractions, which occur at varying speeds.

The baroque style uses the swelling of curved shape to increase the inner tension of its compositions. If the straight-edged gables over windows are replaced by arches, the geometry of the triangle gives way to a more active process of rising and falling. Similarly, barrel vaults sometimes seem to convey "a growing of space in the upward direction." Figures 263*a* and *b*,

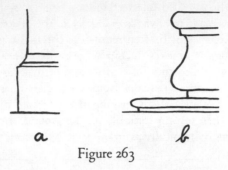

a   *b*

Figure 263

taken from Wölfflin, compare the profile of a typical foot from a building of the early Renaissance with one by Michelangelo. The festoons of fruit and leaves, so popular with baroque architects, combine the curve of the crescent with a swelling of breadth, and the oblique spiral volutes serve to present the stepwise enlargement of the façade as a growing expansion.

The Dynamics of Obliqueness

Oblique orientation is probably the most elementary and effective means of obtaining directed tension. Obliquity is perceived spontaneously as a deviation from the basic spatial framework of the vertical and the horizontal. This involves a tension between the norm position and that of the deviating object, the latter appearing as striving toward rest, being attracted by the framework, pulling away from the framework, or being pushed away by it. With the mastery of oblique orientation the child as well as the primitive artist acquire the main device for distinguishing action from rest, for example, a walking figure from a standing figure. Auguste Rodin states that in order to indicate movement in his busts, he often gave them "a certain slant, a certain obliquity, a certain expressive direction, which would emphasize the meaning of the physiognomy."

Obliquity is indispensable for almost any distinction between two-dimensional and three-dimensional representation. Wölfflin describes how, during the transition from Renaissance to baroque painting, oblique views become more and more dominant. At first only single figures and objects are given in diagonal position. "Finally, the axis of the entire picture, architectonic space and group composition, is directed obliquely toward the observer." The result may be studied, for example, in Tintoretto's work (cf. Figure 217).

In many paintings and drawings, the texture provides a dynamic element through obliquely oriented brush strokes or lines of shading.

The effect of obliquity is sometimes reinforced by the spectator's knowledge of the object's norm position, from which the perceived position deviates. A Y-shaped pattern shows more tension when it represents a man with raised arms than when it represents a tree; for whereas the branches are seen in a "normal" position, the arms are known to be momentarily raised. (Compare here my remarks on Kandinsky's drawing after the photograph of a dancer.) Then the perceived position is in a relation of tension, not only to the framework directly inherent in the picture, but also to the memory trace of the object's normal attitude (arms hanging at rest).

We must not assume, however, that obliquity involves movement because it is understood as a momentary phase of actual locomotion. The primary condition for the effect is the amount of deviation from more stable orientations. The windmills in Dutch landscapes stand still if their arms are painted in a vertical-horizontal position (Figure 264a). The arms move little when they are a pair of symmetrically oriented diagonals (b), and most strongly in an asymmetrical, unbalanced position (c), although all three kinds of orientation are known to be phases of possible actual motion or rest.

Figure 264

Every action picture is perceived as representing the maximum movement of the action. In Muybridge's serial photographs—for example, the sequence showing a blacksmith at work—the full impact of the blow appears only in those pictures in which the hammer is lifted high. In-between phases are not seen as transition stages of the smashing blow, but as a more or less quiet lifting of the hammer, the intensity depending upon the angle represented. In snapshots of a man walking, the step will look small or large depending upon the given angle between the legs.

An amusing illustration of the independence of pictorial movement is given by the fact that, according to Reinach, "of the four attitudes in which European art had represented the galloping horse during the various periods of its history only one was confirmed by photographic snapshots, and this one, used by the Attic artists of the fifth century B.C., had been almost completely abandoned by Roman art and remained unknown to medieval and modern art up to the discovery of the Parthenon frieze." The three others turned out to be entirely "wrong." The conventional attitude of the galloping horse with outstretched legs, as seen in Géricault's *Derby at Epsom* (Figure 265) was used in Mycenaean, Persian, and Chinese art, and reappeared in Europe in the British color prints of the late eighteenth century, possibly under Chinese influence. When photography disavowed this ancient pattern, painters maintained rightly that the snapshots were wrong and the artists right; for only the maximum spread of the legs translates the intensity of the physical motion into pictorial dynamics, even though no running horse can ever assume that position except during a leap.

Figure 265

For the same reason, Carl Justi and others have objected to the theory of the "pregnant moment" in the visual arts expounded by Lessing in his *Laocoön*. Lessing maintained that action should be represented in sculpture or painting, not at its climax, but at a point a few moments before the maximum, because only in that way would the imagination of the spectator be given free play to conceive a dynamic increase beyond the given phase. Justi knew that Lessing's notion of imagination was alien to the nature of art. The artist "will not leave free play to phantasy but fasten it to the spell of his creation." The spectator "must not add this and that in his mind but grasp the thought of the artist, if he is capable of it. The highest belief to which he can aspire is not the belief of seeing *more* but the recognition of what the artist has seen."

It should be noted that, strictly speaking, no painting or statue can actually represent the motion of limbs but only the tension inherent in the deviation from the normal attitude. The disk thrower does not throw, the sling of Bernini's David does not propel the rock, the swords of Dürer's angels do not strike, and Millet's sower does not spread the seeds. In an essay on illustrations and interpretations, Wölfflin has scored the mistake of accepting works of Renaissance art as representations of a specific moment of the plot. He shows that they give the essence of the story as a whole, often combining elements that belong to different episodes. Donatello's David "still" holds the rock in his hand, although Goliath's head lies "already" at the feet of the victor. And when the same sculptor's Judith raises her sword, she is not about to decapitate Holofernes but performs a gesture of fight and victory independent of momentary motion.

The great artists of the past knew intuitively that motion is not a subject matter of the immobile arts. They translated it into gestures loaded with tension, which have the timeless permanence appropriate to their media. It is significant that a painting by Rembrandt, which shows Moses holding the tablets in his raised hands, was reproduced in a recent catalogue under the title: "Moses Breaking the Tablets of the Law" with the remark: "Scholars have recently suggested that the subject represents Moses showing the tablets." Works actually intended to show the fleeting moment endow transitory gestures with embarrassing duration or fail to render any activity at all. An extreme example is the representation of the winking eye in commercial posters. We see one eye open and one closed, but no movement.

Tension in Deformation

Obliquity has been shown to produce directed tension because it is perceived as a deviation from a norm position. In the examples discussed thus far, the deviation concerned location. It may also concern shape. Distortion of shape, it will be remembered, is one of the incentives for three-dimensional perception. A rhomb may be transformed into the simpler figure of a square or rectangle by being seen as tilted in the depth dimension. This eliminates the tension created by the distortion. It is true, however, that this straightening of shape is hardly ever complete. Thus the perspective convergence of parallels is perceived to some extent, and creates a compression, which gradually increases toward the vanishing point. Foreshortening also is perceived dynamically as a contraction, and brings about a resistant counterforce similar to that of a charged spring.

The baroque style offers many examples of tension produced by distorted shape. Wölfflin points out that when the square yields to the rectangle, the favorite proportion of the rectangle is rarely that of the golden section, which was popular during the Renaissance because of its harmonious and more stable character. The baroque prefers the slimmer or squatter proportions, which contain more tension because they appear as compressed or drawn-out versions of more simply proportioned oblongs. Further, "the gay arch acquires depressed, elliptic shape." The coiled columns give the impression of a violent twist applied to a more simply shaped stem. In particular, the characteristic swing of the facade gives tension to the entire building. "The façade is somewhat curved inward at the ends while its center exhibits a vivid forward movement, directed toward the observer." This forward and backward movement is so strong because it seems obtained by a lateral compression of the building. In resisting this compression, the facade dramatizes for the eye the symmetrical outward pushes from the center indicated in the gamma motion of the rectangle.

Not only the shape of objects is dynamic, but also that of the intervals between them. The empty space that separates objects or parts of objects from each other in sculpture, painting, and architecture is being compressed by the objects, and compresses them in turn. According to rules that are entirely unexplored, this dynamics depends not only upon the size, shape, and proportion of the intervals themselves, but also upon those of the neighboring objects. Given a set of windows of a particular dimension and shape, the wall spaces between them will look too large, oppressive, or too small, squeezed, or just right. The same phenomenon can be studied in the mats of framed pictures, the white margins of the printed page, or under much more complex conditions in the relations between figure and ground in pictorial compositions. In baroque architecture, says Wölfflin, "the quickening of the pulse is clearly indicated in the changed proportions of the arches and the intervals between pilasters. The intervals keep getting narrower, the arches slimmer, the speed of succession increases."

Pottery illustrates particularly well how inner tension, and thereby expression, is brought about through shapes that are perceived as deformations of simpler ones. The design of vases, bottles, or jugs, for example, derives psychologically from the elementary concepts of the spherical belly, the cylindrical neck and foot, the triangular spout (Figure 266). But these forms are rarely used in their geometrically pure version. Often the various organs do not appear as sharply separate shapes, but are fused into a more unified whole. Consequently, the sphere is perceived as being stretched upward or downward, the cylinders are pulled outward, and so on. These pulls and pushes, expansions and contractions, all produce directed tensions, which give life to the object.

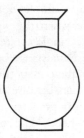

Figure 266

In the representational arts the distortion effect of certain shapes is again enhanced by the notions of normal shape the spectator has formed through experience in his memory. El Greco's and Lehmbruck's figures or the oval faces in Modigliani's portraits owe their tense slimness not only to the perceptual properties of the patterns as such, but also to their deviations from the familiar proportions of the human body. In addition, the extent to which a pattern looks normal depends also upon taste—that is, upon the psychical needs of the individual or period. The grotesquely elongated women in fashion designs look normal to us, not simply because we are used to them, but because their slim bodies conform to an image of the desirable woman deeply rooted in modern man. There are, however, limits beyond which the frame of reference will not stretch. It is probable that for many a beholder the flagpole-shaped figures of the sculptor Giacometti or the obese nudes of Lachaise are not fully relatable to the human body; these figures appear as creatures of their own kind, whose visual dynamics are perceived only in part with reference to the human norm and otherwise in accordance with their own inherent shape and proportion, as happens when we look at a giraffe or a pig.

The incompleteness of a well-structured pattern produces a tension toward closure. Thus in Moslem architecture the horseshoe arch, which presents circular shape beyond the halfway mark, clearly contains forces in the direction of the completed circle (Figure 267). Incompleteness is frequently brought about by overlapping. As discussed earlier, the overlapped pattern tends to get free from the intruder by detaching itself from it in depth.

Figure 267

Nevertheless the superposition remains visible and makes the interlocking units strive to pull apart. In the baroque style this device is used to reinforce the movement toward freedom by the pressure of imprisonment. In the library of San Lorenzo in Florence, Michelangelo buries the back of the columns in the wall; and in some of his unfinished statues, notably in the so-called *Slaves,* the body remains partly embedded in the block of marble and thus exhibits an impressive struggle for completeness, that is, for liberty. Often units are made to overlap each other in fuguelike scales, and painted or sculptured figures and ornaments reach beyond the limits assigned to them by the architectural skeleton of the building. Such devices are sought or avoided by individual artists and cultural periods, depending upon whether they welcome or reject the tension created in this way. Recently the cubists have obtained highly dynamic compositions by building up volumes from irregularly crowded units, which constantly interfere with each other's shape.

A Stroboscopic Effect

Strong movement results also from what may be termed the immobile equivalent of stroboscopic motion. It will be remembered that stroboscopic motion occurs between visual objects that are essentially alike in their appearance and function in the whole field, but differ in some perceptual feature—for example, location, size, or shape. Under suitable conditions such constellations produce a dynamic effect also in simultaneity, the most obvious example being stroboscopic photographs, which show the same object at a number of locations in the same picture or series of pictures. The sequence of the locations forms a simply shaped, consistent path, and the internal changes of the object—for example, the change of posture in a leaping athlete—also occur gradually. The similarity of the images and the consistency of the changes produce a perceptual whole distinguished by movement, which is strongest when the pictures overlap. The effect has been used by artists, notably by the futurists, who tried to render motion through the multiplication of figures or parts of figures. Duchamp's *Nude Descending a Staircase* and Balla's many-legged dog are well-known examples. In a less obvious way other artists have used the same device throughout the ages. Brueghel's blind men have been cited earlier. Auguste Rodin, in his conversations with Paul Gsell, maintains that "movement is the transition from one attitude to another," and that therefore the artist, in order to express movement, often represents in the different parts of a figure successive phases of the action.

In many pictures different figures are perceived spontaneously also as the same figure in different positions. Thus the weeping angels in the sky of Giotto's *Lamentation* represent gestures of despair in such a way that the group as a whole appears as a highly dynamic composite picture of one and the same activity (Figure 271). Riegl has pointed out that Michelangelo's figures of Night and Day, at the monument for Giuliano de' Medici in Florence, together create an effect of rotation. The eye groups them together because of their symmetrical positions in the whole and because of their almost identical outlines. Yet the two figures are inversions of each other. Night is seen from the front and seems to approach, whereas Day shows its back and seems to recede. Hence the rotation of the group.

A useful study of these "stroboscopic" phenomena could be based on the practice of some modern painters, particularly Picasso, to duplicate parts of figures or objects. Figure 268a shows a double profile head. The two heads are placed obliquely. They are clearly distinguished from each other; but at the same time they prevent each other from being complete, and together also form a unified perceptual whole. The intimate connection of the incompatible as well as the similarity and fuguelike parallelism of the two overlapping units produce tension in the oblique direction established by the corresponding elements, particularly the two eyes. This forward and upward thrust enhances the vigorous activity of the profile. It will also be noticed that the transition from the lower to the higher head involves an increase in articulation and directed action. The lower head has no profile line, and the pupil of its eye rests in a central position. A pulpy front develops into a sharply defined profile and a dreamingly inactive eye into the intensely directed forward glance of the upper head. We experience a crescendo of increasing keenness, entirely in keeping with the subject of the painting.

Figure 268

The opposite procedure leads to a rather terrifying result in Figure 268*b*. In the painting from which this detail is taken, Picasso makes an articulate profile, equipped with an explicit eye, change into a flat mask, in which a glanceless circle represents the eye. Here intense life is seen as degenerating into a dead hull.

In Figure 268*c* the device is limited to a pair of eyes, which stand for the two eyes of the human face but at the same time are a duplication of one profile eye. Again this serves to strengthen the forward movement of the head—the expression of an active, exploring mind. (Figure 268*c* is the head of a woman painter at work.)

Picasso's figures demonstrate also that the dynamic effect of such displacements does not depend primarily upon what the observer knows about the "correct" spatial position of the elements involved, but rather upon the structure of the perceptual pattern. The combination of profile and front face, as it can be seen, for example, in the *Girl before a Mirror* (Figure 268*d*), makes for a fairly static substitution effect rather than movement as we switch from one version to the other. This happens although the observer knows that in physical space either he himself or the perceived object would have to make a turn of ninety degrees in order to bring about the change. The two versions, however, are so smoothly integrated and the pattern as a whole rests so stably on an essentially vertical-horizontal skeleton that little tension results. Similarly, when two eyes in a profile face are placed horizontally rather than obliquely, there is hardly any movement, The same is true for vertically oriented eyes or mouths (Figure 268*e*). Past experience would require a switch from the familiar horizontal, but the perceptual stability of the vertical excludes movement.

Physical Forces Made Visible

Often the strong visual movement observed in natural objects derives from the fact that their shapes are the traces of physical forces, which have created them through motion, expansion, contraction, or the processes of growth. The highly dynamic curve of an ocean wave is the result of the upward thrust of the water bent by the counterpull of gravitation. The traces of waves on the wet sand of a beach owe their sweeping contours to the motion of the water; and in the expansive convexities of clouds and the rising and breaking outlines of mountains, we directly perceive the nature of the mechanical forces that originated them. The winding, twisting, swelling shapes of tree trunks, branches, leaves, and flowers retain and repeat the motions of growth. Burchartz says: "Snails in building their shells offer an example of rhythmical construction. The shells are made from excretions of liquid chalk paste, which is shaped by rhythmical motions of the body and then

crystalizes. Snails' shells are fixated expressive movements of the first order."
Thus nature is alive to our eyes partly because its shapes are fossils of the
events that gave rise to them. The past history is not merely inferred intellectually from clues, but directly experienced as forces and tensions present
and active in visible shape.

With similar directness we sense the motions of the hand in the traces
of the pen on paper in writing. Here the standardized shapes of letters are
re-created by motor activity, and the graphologist is accustomed to weighing
the contribution of motion against the effect of the intention to copy the
model pattern. When the motor factor is strong, it is found to tilt the letters
obliquely in the direction of the ·movement—that is, mostly toward the
right—to cut corners, slur angles, omit detail. The line shows an unbroken
over-all flow, which often reduces the intended patterns to illegibility. In
this way the graphologist indirectly gauges the strength of temperament
and vital impulses in their relation to the controlling will, which tends to
guide activity in accordance with the prescribed task. Handwriting is a live
diagram of psychophysical forces.

In the works of the visual arts we are also faced with the traces of motor
acts intent on realizing visual images, and we can evaluate the relative
strength of the two factors in any particular example. Drawings that Picasso
executed by moving a flashlight in a dark room were recorded photographically. The swinging curves clearly showed dominance of the motor factor
over visual organization, and thus differed from what is seen in Picasso's
drawings on paper. Quick sketches are similarly distinguished from careful
elaboration, and the style of any individual artist or period reveals a characteristic state of mind by the extent to which the motor factor is given free
play. When during and after the Renaissance there developed a tendency
to consider and appreciate the work of art as a product of individual creation,
the plainly visible brush stroke became a legitimate element of artistic form,
and the imprints of the sculptor's fingers were preserved, somewhat paradoxically, even in the bronze casts of clay figures. Drawings, formerly mere
preparatory stages of the workshop process, were now collected as works of
art in their own right. The dynamics of the act of creation had been added
to whatever movement was contained in the created shapes themselves.

Graphologically significant differences can be discovered between the
uninhibited, spontaneous strokes of a Velázquez or Frans Hals, the violently
twisted ones of van Gogh, the carefully but lightly applied layers of touches
in the paintings of the impressionists or Cézanne. There is something painfully mechanical about the uniform stipples of the pointillists, and the
careful leveling of any personal trace in the texture and line of Mondrian's
work is related to the absence of curves and obliquities in his patterns and

the withdrawal from the subject matter of life and nature in his themes.

Artists know that the dynamic traits of the physical motor act leave their traces in the work and show up as movement qualities of corresponding character. Not only do they practice relaxed wrist and arm motion, which will translate itself into fluent, life-giving line, but many will even attempt to put their body in a kinesthetic state appropriate to the nature of the subject to be represented. Bowie discusses the principle of "living movement" (*Sei Do*) in Japanese painting: "A distinguishing feature in Japanese painting is the strength of the brush stroke, technically called *fude no chikara* or *fude no ikioi*. When representing an object suggesting strength, such, for instance, as rocky cliff, the beak or talons of a bird, the tiger's claws, or the limbs and branches of a tree, the moment the brush is applied the sentiment of strength must be invoked and felt throughout the artist's system and imparted through his arm and hand to the brush, and so transmitted into the object painted." The dead quality of many printed reproductions and plaster casts is due partly to the fact that the strokes, touches, lines, and edges have not been produced, as is true in the originals, by forces active along the trails of movement but by the perpendicular pressure of the printing press or the shapeless liquid of the plaster.

Thus the physical motor forces give an animating "bite" to shape that records their strength and course. It goes without saying, however, that a visual pattern can exhibit strong tension even though the forces that created it have little relation to those it conveys to the eye. The deforming upward pull of the vase belly does not have to be produced by a corresponding physical pull. No physical power has protracted the bodies of El Greco's figures, and the swelling muscles of Michelangelo's Moses have not come about by expansion from the inside but by the chiseling away of the marble from the outside. Here visual forces are put to work by the eye for the eye.

Dynamic Composition

The dynamics of a composition will be successful only when the movement of each detail fits logically in the movement of the whole. The work of art is organized around a dominant dynamic theme, from which movement irradiates throughout the entire area. From the main arteries the movement flows into the capillaries of the smallest detail. The theme struck up at the higher level must be carried through consistently at the lower level, and elements at the same level must go together. It is not difficult to draw one line of good inherent movement; it is much more difficult to add to it a second line in such a way that the dynamic patterns of both produce one common movement. The eye perceives the finished pattern as a whole together with the interrelations of its parts, whereas the process of making a picture or statue requires each part to be made separately. Thus attention is tempted to concentrate on the part at hand in isolation from its context.

More clearly than in any other period of history, the shortcomings of the piecemeal approach have shown up in the minor artists of the nineteenth century who concentrated on carefully copying models from nature. The lack of integration carries over even to their free inventions. Examples such as Hans Thoma's picture reproduced in Figure 269 make us marvel how movement can be so completely absent even in subjects eminently suited to convey it. If we examine the figure of the angel more closely, we observe first of all a number of rigid breaks in the hips, the elbows, and the knees. Angular breaks as such do not interfere with movement, as can be easily seen in Gothic art. In the etchings of Martin Schongauer angularity dominates the entire picture, the relations of the figures to each other, the posture of each figure, and every detail of fold or finger. In Thoma's drawing there is no such unified conception of form. The breaks in the joints stop the movement because they conflict with the soft flow of the outlines. Furthermore, the front line of the chest or the contour of the shoulder and the upper left arm show a halfhearted wavering rather than a consistently swinging shape because they are constructed piece by piece. Their elements stop each other rather than being inserted in an over-all movement. If we consider the shape of the volumes, we find that most of them show complex, irregular relationships among the contours. Once this high level of complexity is set, the simplicity of the horn-shaped lower arms produces inorganic stiffness. In the left leg the two corresponding contours do not add up to volumes of understandable form or movement, and the sudden simple parallelism between the cap and the pit of the knee stops the intended rhythm of the entire leg. Interferences of mechanically realistic and therefore visually incomprehensible shape with movement can be found also in the lines of the trees, mountains, and clouds.

Examples of this kind make it clear why artists consider movement, or directed tension, so fundamental. If movement is absent, the work is dead; and none of the other virtues it may possess will make it speak to the beholder. Movement of shape presupposes that the artist conceives of every object or part of object as a happening rather than a static piece of matter, and that he thinks of the relationships between objects not as geometric configurations but as mutual interaction. Occasionally this dynamic nature of vision is expressed even in the way artists talk about their work; thus when Matisse, discussing a series of self-portraits, points to "the way in which the nose is rooted in the face—the ear screwed into the skull—the lower jaw hung— the way in which the glasses are placed on the nose and ears—the tension of the gaze and its uniform density in all the drawings. . . ."

The foregoing demonstrates that movement is not limited to objects meant to convey physical action. In a painted landscape no difference in principle exists between the movement perceived in the sinuous contour of a coastline and the shape of the waves. The swinging contour of a beret in a Rembrandt portrait can be just as dynamic as the skirt of a dancer drawn by Toulouse-Lautrec, even though the beret is known to be motionless whereas the skirt is known to be moving. In fact the meaning of a work may be conveyed through a complete reversal of the dynamics suggested by physical action. In Piero della Francesca's *Resurrection* (Figure 270) the figure of the rising Christ is given a minimum of pictorial movement. He is located in

Figure 270

the center of the picture, and his position is strictly frontal—that is, symmetrical. The posture of his body, the flag he holds in his hand, the tomb from which he emerges—all conform to a vertical-horizontal framework. The resurrection is not interpreted materially as a transition from death to life. Christ is given a permanent existence, which contains the aspects of both death and life, represented in the bare trees to the left and those full of leaf to the right. These trees also do not indicate any transition. They are vertical, like the figure of Christ, and flank it symmetrically like a pair of wings. Perceptually as well as symbolically they appear as attributes of Christ. The motif of rising is indicated only as a secondary theme in the folds of the robe, whose convergence forms a wedge pointing to the right— the direction of life. Forceful pictorial movement is reserved to the four Roman soldiers, who are physically at rest. Many perceptual devices are used

Figure 269

to obtain the dynamic effect. The main axes of the bodies run obliquely. The heads and arms offer varying phases of posture, almost adding up to the picture of a man tossing in uneasy sleep. The figures strongly interfere with each other by overlapping; together they form a triangle, whose left side bulges outward, is burst like a bubble by the tread of Christ's foot, and culminates obliquely in the head of the man with the spear. Evidently Piero's picture sets the unrest of temporal material life in opposition to the monumental serenity of Christ, who, as the top of the pyramid, rules between life and death.

The movement pattern of a picture and its relation to the content will be examined now with more detail in a particular example. In one of Giotto's frescoes in Padua, the subject of the *Lamentation* (Figure 271) is interpreted by the painter as a story of death and resurrection, which in formal terms calls for an interplay between the horizontal and the vertical. The horizontal of death is indicated but left behind by the body of Christ, which has been lifted and thus endowed with the dynamic quality of oblique position. The arms, in turn, are made to deviate obliquely from the body—a further element of animation. This motif of revival is taken up and developed into one of the two dominant themes of movement by the diagonal ridge of the hill, which, just broad enough for a man to walk upward, leads through the entire picture, from the horizontal of death to the verticals of the two upright men, the vertical edge of the picture frame, and the tree. The tree takes over where the diagonal of the hill is about to end, and turns the oblique climbing into straight rising. The concentrated vertical of the tree trunk is gently dispersed in all directions by the branches. As the movement rises, it dematerializes, spreads throughout space, becomes universal, and gradually disappears from sight.

But, owing to the ambiguity of direction in all movement, the diagonal of the hill also points downward, indicating the great fall that has occurred. This descending arrow is directed significantly from the right to the left. The eye follows it only reluctantly, because it is made to run against the direction of the glance. A man who was upright like the two standing men has been felled. There is "stroboscopic movement" between the two standing male figures and the dead body on the ground. The ninety-degree turn of the fall is just being completed by the dead body. The falling movement of death occurs from the right to the left, and is superseded by the rising movement toward resurrection from the left to the right.

The angels are spread irregularly about the sky like a swarm of birds stirred up in panic. The motion of despair that they enact is not given in gradual stages, but in its extreme phases; thus, in shifting from the central angel to his neighbors and back, we see the body convulsively thrown up and down.

Figure 271

Similarly, in the group of the humans to the left the standing woman with
the clasped hands is placed next to one with outstretched arms—again a
movement leap from extreme to extreme. With equal abruptness the outburst
is hushed by the two motionless and faceless women squatting on the
ground. But out of this low, in which distress has paralyzed action and left
the mind blank, feeling rises again; and the face, distorted by grief, reappears
in the seated woman to the right. Yet the posture is still passive. It serves
as a base for the forward thrust of the next woman. The arms, no longer
reposing in the lap, now reach out to hold the hands of Christ. And finally,
in another violent contrast of movement, the arms are spread apart desperately in the figure of St. John rising above and behind the crouching woman.

Consider the second dominant theme of movement—the expressive curve
formed by the row of the mourners. It starts on the left with the praying
woman, moves backward to her neighbor; then, by a tensely stretched
interval, it arrives at its extreme and turning point in the hooded woman
crouching in the corner. The curve is "taken aback" and brought to a standstill by the fall of Christ. Broken by the figure of the dead man, but resumed
in the second hooded woman, it now swings upward in a release of emotion
to the standing figure with the outstretched arms. It reminds me of the
curve of the melodic line in the recitative that tells of Peter's weeping in
Bach's *Passion According to St. Matthew* (Figure 272).

Figure 272

But next to the climax of emotion stands the concluding vertical. We see
the two men watching in quiet contemplation. Beyond the temporal tragedy
they indicate the positive aspect of the sacrifice, the stability of the doctrine
to be carried on, and—in their visible relation to the tree of resurrection
above their heads—the immortality of the spirit.

Tension and Simplicity

The work of different artists and periods of art varies in the amount of tension they give to their compositions. We need only compare the paintings
of Carracci or Tiepolo with the solemn figures of Byzantine mosaics or the
vehement protrusions and contractions in the profiles of Daumier's faces
with the stillness of Greek profiles. An attempt could be made to assign
every particular style its place on a scale that would lead from a minimum
to a maximum of visual tension.

How, it may be asked, is this concern with movement to be reconciled with my assertion that all perception tends toward greatest simplicity? To make a pattern simpler means to reduce its internal tension. The vertical and horizontal directions are simpler than the oblique ones. Elementary geometrical shapes are simpler than distorted ones. But artists often seek the oblique and the distorted. There is, then, in the arts a widespread tendency to nonsimple form.

In order to deal with this apparent contradiction we must remember, first of all, that if the tendency to simplicity persisted all the way, there would be no seeing whatsoever. The nonhomogeneity caused by any stimulus introduces tension and makes the visual field less simple. Now it is true that, to the extent to which the organism participates in the universal striving of the physical world for the elimination of tension, the stimulus will be reduced to the simplest obtainable pattern. But I have also pointed out that the most characteristic feature of the organism is its revolt against what the physicist calls the increase of entropy. By constantly drawing energy from its environment, the organism charges itself with fuel for action. The processes of growth and the striving for vital aims are most typically organic. At the same time there is always the tendency to keep the given pattern of forces as simple as the situation permits. This duality was revealed even at the level of perception when we found that there is not only a tendency to simplicity and balance (leveling) but also one to an increase of tension by stressing disequilibrium and deviation from simpler pattern (sharpening). At the higher psychical level we find that man prefers life to death, activity to inactivity, and that laziness, far from being a natural impulse, is generally a manifestation of weakness, fear, protest, or some other disturbance. But in pursuing his aims, man will also strive for tension-reducing fulfillment and satisfaction. He will try to balance his needs against the requirements of the environment and to organize the various drives within himself in such a way that they form the most harmonious pattern.

This twofold dynamics is reflected in every work of art. A work of art is no more described sufficiently by its inherent harmony, balance, and order than an organism by its tendency to simplicity and minimum tension. The reason why art is often discussed in this one-sided manner may be partly a surviving preference of classicist aesthetics for simplicity and stillness, partly the fact that simplicity of shape can be analyzed purely as a matter of formal relations without any reference to content and meaning, whereas the dynamic theme makes little sense without such a reference. Thus a formalistic analysis talks about balance or unity but avoids the question without which the existence of the work remains incomprehensible: What is being balanced and unified?

If we wish to understand a work of art, either by intuitive contemplation or by explicit analysis, we must inevitably start with the pattern of forces that sets its theme and states the reason for its existence. But, as was shown above in the discussion of Giotto's painting, the dynamic theme is meaningful only when it is referred to the content of the work, that is, to the statement the artist wishes to make. This holds true regardless of whether or not the work represents objects of nature. The dynamic theme of a building or a "mobile" depends upon a statement about a content just as much as a picture full of people, animals, and trees.

X   EXPRESSION

Every work of art must express something. This means, first of all, that the content of the work must go beyond the presentation of the individual objects of which it consists. But such a definition is too large for our purpose. It broadens the notion of "expression" to include any kind of communication. True, we commonly say, for example, that a man "expresses his opinion." Yet artistic expression seems to be something more specific. It requires that the communication of the data produce an "experience," the active presence of the forces that make up the perceived pattern. How is such an experience achieved?

Inside Linked to Outside

In a limited sense of the term, expression refers to features of a person's external appearance and behavior that permit us to find out what the person is feeling, thinking, striving for. Such information may be gathered from a man's face and gestures, the way he talks, dresses, keeps his room, handles a pen or a brush, as well as from the opinions he holds, the interpretation he gives to events. This is less and also more than what I mean here by expression: less, because expression must be considered even when no reference is made to a mind manifesting itself in appearance; more, because much importance cannot be attributed to what is merely inferred intellectually and indirectly from external clues. Nevertheless this more familiar meaning of the term must be discussed briefly here.

We look at a friend's face, and two things may happen: we understand what his mind is up to; and we find in ourselves a duplicate of his experiences. The traditional explanation of this accomplishment may be gathered from a playful review of Lavater's *Physiognomic Fragments for the Advance-*

ment of the Knowledge and Love of Our Fellow Man written by the poet
Matthias Claudius around 1775. "Physiognomics is a science of faces. Faces
are *concreta* for they are related *generaliter* to natural reality and *specialiter*
are firmly attached to people. Therefore the question arises whether the
famous trick of the 'abstractio' and the 'methodus analytica' should not be
applied here, in the sense of watching out whether the letter *i,* whenever it
appears, is furnished with a dot and whether the dot is never found on top of
another letter; in which case we should be sure that the dot and the letter
are twin brothers so that when we run into Castor we can expect Pollux not
to be far away. For an example we posit that there be one hundred gentlemen, all of whom are very quick on their feet, and they had given sample
and proof of this, and all of these hundred gentlemen had a wart on their
noses. I am not saying that gentlemen with a wart on their noses are cowards
but am merely assuming it for the sake of the example. . . . Now *ponamus*
there comes to my house a fellow who calls me a wretched scribbler and spits
me into the face. Suppose I am reluctant to get into a fist fight and also cannot tell what the outcome would be, and I am standing there and considering
the issue. At that moment I discover a wart on his nose, and now I cannot
refrain myself any longer, I go after him courageously and, without any
doubt, get away unbeaten. This procedure would represent, as it were, the
royal road in this field. The progress might be slow but just as safe as that on
other royal roads."

In a more serious vein, the theory was stated early in the eighteenth
century by the philosopher Berkeley. In his essay on vision he speaks about
the way in which the observer sees shame or anger in the looks of a man.
"Those passions are themselves invisible: they are nevertheless let in by the
eye along with colors and alterations of countenance, which are the immediate object of vision, and which signify them for no other reason than
barely because they have been observed to accompany them: without which
experience, we should no more have taken blushing for a sign of shame
than gladness." Charles Darwin, in his book on the expression of emotions,
devoted a few pages to the same problem. He believed that external manifestations and their psychical counterparts are connected by the observer
either on the basis of an inborn instinct or of learning. "Moreover, when a
child cries or laughs, he knows in a general manner what he is doing and
what he feels; so that a very small exertion of reason would tell him what
crying or laughing meant in others. But the question is, do our children
acquire their knowledge of expression solely by experience through the
power of association and reason? As most of the movements of expression
must have been gradually acquired, afterwards becoming instinctive, there
seems to be some degree of *a priori* probability that their recognition would
likewise have become instinctive."

Recently a new version of the traditional theory has developed from a curious tendency on the part of many social scientists to assume that when people agree on some fact it is probably based on an unfounded convention. According to this view, judgments of expression rely on "stereotypes," which individuals adopt ready-made from their social group. For example, we have been told that aquiline noses indicate courage and that protruding lips betray sensuality. The promoters of the theory generally imply that such judgments are wrong, as though information not drawn from the individual's firsthand experience could never be trusted. The real danger does not lie in the social origin of the information, but rather in the fact that people have a tendency to acquire simply structured concepts on the basis of insufficient evidence, which may have been gathered firsthand or secondhand, and to preserve these concepts unchanged in the face of contrary experience. Whereas this may make for many one-sided or entirely wrong evaluations of individuals and groups of people, the existence of stereotypes does not explain the origin of physiognomic judgments. If these judgments stem from tradition, what is the tradition's source? Are they right or wrong? Even though often misapplied, traditional interpretations of physique and behavior may still be based on sound observation. In fact, perhaps they are so hardy because they are so true.

Within the framework of associationist thinking, a step forward was made by Lipps, who pointed out that the perception of expression involves the activity of forces. His theory of "empathy" was designed to explain why we find expression even in inanimate objects, such as the columns of a temple. The reasoning was as follows. When I look at the columns, I know from past experience the kind of mechanical pressure and counterpressure that occurs in them. Equally from past experience, I know how I should feel myself if I were in the place of the columns and if those physical forces acted upon and within my own body. I project my own kinesthetic feelings into the columns. Furthermore, the pressures and pulls called up from the stores of memory by the sight tend to provoke responses also in other areas of the mind. "When I project my strivings and forces into nature I do so also as to the way my strivings and forces make me feel, that is, I project my pride, my courage, my stubbornness, my lightness, my playful assuredness, my tranquil complacence. Only thus my empathy with regard to nature becomes truly aesthetic empathy."

The characteristic feature of traditional theorizing in all its varieties is the belief that the expression of an object is not inherent in the visual pattern itself. What we see provides only clues for whatever knowledge and feelings we may mobilize from memory and project upon the object. The visual pattern has as little to do with the expression we confer upon it as words have to do with the content they transmit. The letters "pain" mean "suffer-

ing" in English and "bread" in French. Nothing in them suggests the one
rather than the other meaning. They transmit a message only because of
what we have learned about them.

Expression Embedded in Structure

William James was not so sure that body and mind have nothing intrinsic-
ally in common. "I cannot help remarking that the disparity between
motions and feelings, on which these authors lay so much stress, is somewhat less absolute than at first sight it seems. Not only temporal succession,
but such attributes as intensity, volume, simplicity or complication, smooth
or impeded change, rest or agitation, are habitually predicated of both
physical facts and mental facts." Evidently James reasoned that although
body and mind are different media—the one being material, the other
not—they might still resemble each other in certain structural properties.

This point was greatly stressed by gestalt psychologists. Particularly
Wertheimer asserted that the perception of expression is much too immediate and compelling to be explainable merely as a product of learning.
When we watch a dancer, the sadness or happiness of the mood seems to be
directly inherent in the movements themselves. Wertheimer concluded that
this was true because formal factors of the dance reproduced identical factors
of the mood. The meaning of this theory may be illustrated by reference to
an experiment by Binney in which members of a college dance group were
asked individually to give improvisations of such subjects as sadness,
strength, or night. The performances of the dancers showed much agreement. For example, in the representation of sadness the movement was slow
and confined to a narrow range. It was mostly curved in shape and showed
little tension. The direction was indefinite, changing, wavering, and the
body seemed to yield passively to the force of gravitation rather than being
propelled by its own initiative. It will be admitted that the psychical mood
of sadness has a similar pattern. In a depressed person the mental processes
are slow and rarely go beyond matters closely related to immediate experiences and interests of the moment. In all his thinking and striving are softness and a lack of energy. There is little determination, and activity is often
controlled by outside forces.

Naturally there is a traditional way of representing sadness in a dance,
and the performances of the students may have been influenced by it. What
counts, however, is that the movements, whether spontaneously invented
or copied from other dancers, exhibited a formal structure so strikingly
similar to that of the intended mood. And since such visual qualities as
speed, shape, or direction are immediately accessible to the eye, it seems
legitimate to assume that they are the carriers of an expression directly comprehensible to the eye.

If we examine the facts more closely, we find that expression is conveyed not so much by the "geometric-technical" properties of the percept as such, but by the forces they can be assumed to arouse in the nervous system of the observer. Regardless of whether the object moves (dancer, actor) or is immobile (painting, sculpture), it is the kind of directed tension or "movement"—its strength, place, and distribution—transmitted by the visible patterns that is perceived as expression.

Many already cited examples have illustrated the expressive meaning of visual forces. In Giotto's *Lamentation* the upsurge of the diagonal expressed the dynamic motif of the Resurrection, and the retreat and rise of the curve formed by the row of the mourners expressed awe and despair. It may be worth while to add here two examples of abstract form in order to demonstrate that expression is contained in the pattern itself without necessary reference to objects of nature.

In comparing two curves—one a part of a circle, the other a part of a parabola—it will be found that the circular curve looks more rigid, the parabolic one more gentle. What is the cause of this difference? Instead of looking around for objects of nature with which the two objects might be associated, examine the structure of the curves themselves. Geometrically, the constant curvature of the circle is the result of only one structural condition: it is the locus of all points that are equally distant from one center. A parabola satisfies two such conditions and therefore is of variable curvature. It is the locus of all points that have equal distance from one point and one straight line. The parabola may be called a compromise between two structural demands. Either structural condition yields to the other. In other words, the rigid hardness of the circular line and the gentle flexibility of the parabola can be derived from the inherent make-up of the two curves.

Now for a somewhat similar example from architecture. In the outlines of the dome that Michelangelo designed for St. Peter's in Rome, we admire the synthesis of massive heaviness and free rising. This expressive effect is obtained in the following way. The two contours that make up the section of the outer cupola (Figure 273) are parts of circles, and thus possess the firmness of circular curves. But they are not parts of the same circle. They do not form a hemisphere. The right contour is described around the center *a*, the left around *b*. In a Gothic arch the crossing of the curves would be visible at the apex. The cupola hides it by the gallery and the lantern on top of it. In consequence both contours appear as part of one and the same curve, which, however, does not have the rigidity of a hemisphere. It represents a compromise between two different curvatures, and thus appears flexible while at the same time preserving circular hardness in its elements. The total contour of the dome appears as a deviation from a hemisphere, which has been stretched upward. Hence the effect of vertical striving. It will also be seen that line *A* contains the horizontal diameters of the circles for both contours of the section. Therefore at the intersection with *A* the contours would reach verticality. This would give the cupola a stable, rather static orientation. Now this verticality is hidden by the drum between *B* and *A*. The cupola rests on *B* rather than on *A*. This means that the contours meet the base at an oblique rather than a right angle. Instead of moving straight upward, the cupola tilts inward, which produces an oblique sagging—that is, the effect of heaviness. The delicate balancing of all these dynamic factors produces the complex and at the same time unified expression of the whole. "The symbolic image of weight," says Wölfflin, "is maintained, yet dominated by the expression of spiritual liberation." Michelangelo's dome thus embodies "the paradox of the Baroque spirit in general."

The Priority of Expression

The impact of the forces transmitted by a visual pattern is an intrinsic part of the percept, just as shape or color. In fact, expression can be described as the primary content of vision. We have been trained to think of perception as the recording of shapes, distances, hues, motions. The awareness of these measurable characteristics is really a fairly late accomplishment of the human mind. Even in the Western man of the twentieth century it presupposes special conditions. It is the attitude of the scientist and the engineer or of the salesman who estimates the size of a customer's waist, the shade of a lipstick, the weight of a suitcase. But if I sit in front of a fireplace and watch the flames, I do not normally register certain shades of red, various degrees of brightness, geometrically defined shapes moving at such and such a speed. I see the graceful play of aggressive tongues, flexible striving, lively color. The face of a person is more readily perceived and remembered as being alert, tense, concentrated rather than as being triangularly shaped, having slanted eyebrows, straight lips, and so on. This priority of expression, although somewhat modified in adults by a scientifically oriented education, is striking in children and primitives, as has been shown by Werner and Köhler. The profile of a mountain is soft or threateningly harsh; a blanket thrown over a chair is twisted, sad, tired.

The priority of physiognomic properties should not come as a surprise. Our senses are not self-contained recording devices operating for their own sake. They have been developed by the organism as an aid in properly reacting to the environment. The organism is primarily interested in the forces that are active around it—their place, strength, direction. Hostility and friendliness are attributes of forces. And the perceived impact of forces makes for what we call expression.

If expression is the primary content of vision in daily life, the same should

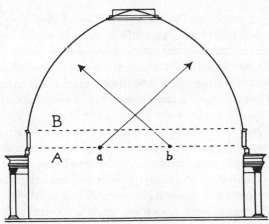

Figure 273

be all the more true for the way the artist looks at the world. The expressive qualities are his means of communication. They capture his attention, through them he understands and interprets his experiences, and they determine the form patterns he creates. Therefore the training of art students should be expected to consist basically in sharpening their sense of these qualities and in teaching them to look to expression as the guiding criterium for every stroke of the pencil, brush, or chisel. In fact many good art teachers do precisely this. But there are also plenty of times when the spontaneous sensitivity of the student to expression not only is not developed further, but is even disturbed and suppressed. There is, for example, an old-fashioned but not extinct way of teaching students to draw from the model by asking them to establish the exact length and direction of contour lines, the relative position of points, the shape of masses. In other words, students are to concentrate on the geometric-technical qualities of what they see. In its modern version this method consists in urging the young artist to think of the model or of a freely invented design as a configuration of masses, planes, directions. Again interest is focussed on geometric-technical qualities.

Such teaching follows principles of description often employed in mathematics or physical science rather than those of spontaneous vision. There are, however, other teachers who will proceed differently. With a model sitting on the floor in a hunched-up position, they will not begin by making the students notice that the whole figure can be inscribed in a triangle. Instead they will ask about the expression of the figure; they may be told, for example, that the person on the floor looks tense, tied together, full of potential energy. They will suggest, then, that the student try to render this quality. In doing so the student will watch proportions and directions, but not as geometric properties in themselves. These formal properties will be perceived as being functionally dependent upon the primarily observed expression, and the correctness and incorrectness of each stroke will be judged on the basis of whether or not it captures the dynamic "mood" of the subject. Equally, in a lesson of design, it will be made clear that to the artist, just as to any unspoiled human being, a circle is not a line of constant curvature, whose points are all equally distant from a center, but first of all a compact, hard, restful thing. Once the student has understood that roundness is not identical with circularity, he may try for a design whose structural logic will be controlled by the primary concept of something to be expressed. For whereas the artificial concentration on formal qualities will leave the student at a loss as to which pattern to select among innumerable and equally acceptable ones, an expressive theme will serve as a natural guide to forms that fit the purpose.

It will be evident that what is advocated here is not the so-called "self-expression." The method of self-expression plays down, or even annihilates, the function of the theme to be represented. It recommends a passive, "projective" pouring-out of what is felt inside. On the contrary, the method discussed here requires active, disciplined concentration of all organizing powers upon the expression that is localized in the object of representation.

It might be argued that an artist must practice the purely formal technique before he may hope to render expression successfully. But that is exactly the notion that reverses the natural order of the artistic process. In fact all good practicing is highly expressive. This first occurred to me many years ago when I watched the dancer Gret Palucca perform one of her most popular pieces, which she called "Technical Improvisations." This number was nothing but the systematic exercise that the dancer practiced every day in her studio in order to loosen up the joints of her body. She would start out by doing turns of her head, then move her neck, then shrug her shoulders, until she ended up wriggling her toes. This purely technical practice was a success with the audience because it was thoroughly expressive. Forcefully precise and rhythmical movements presented, quite naturally, the entire catalogue of human pantomime. They passed through all the moods from lazy happiness to impertinent satire.

In order to achieve technically precise movements, a capable dance teacher may not ask students to perform "geometrically" defined positions, but to strive for the muscular experience of uplift, or attack, or yielding, that will be created by correctly executed movements. (Comparable methods are nowadays applied therapeutically in physical rehabilitation work. For example, the patient is not asked to concentrate on the meaningless, purely formal exercise of flexing and stretching his arm, but on a game or piece of work that involves suitable motions of the limbs as a means to a sensible end.)

The Physiognomics of Nature

The perception of expression does not therefore necessarily—and not even primarily—serve to discover the state of mind of another person by way of externally observable manifestations. Köhler has pointed out that people normally deal with and react to expressive physical behavior in itself rather than being conscious of the psychical experiences reflected by such behavior. We perceive the slow, listless, "droopy" movements of one person as contrasted to the brisk, straight, vigorous movements of another, but do not necessarily go beyond the meaning of such appearance by thinking explicitly of the psychical weariness or alertness behind it. Weariness and alertness are already contained in the physical behavior itself; they are not distinguished in any essential way from the weariness of slowly floating tar or the energetic ringing of the telephone bell. It is true, of course, that during a business conversation one person may be greatly concerned with trying to read the other's thoughts and feelings through what can be seen in his face and gestures. "What is he up to? How is he taking it?" But in such circumstances we clearly go beyond what is apparent in the perception of expression itself, and secondarily apply what we have seen to the mental processes that may be hidden "behind" the outer image.

Particularly the content of the work of art does not consist in states of mind that the dancer may pretend to be experiencing in himself or that our imagination may bestow on a painted Mary Magdalen or Sebastian. The substance of the work consists in what appears in the visible pattern itself. Evidently, then, expression is not limited to living organisms that we assume to possess consciousness. A steep rock, a willow tree, the colors of a sunset, the cracks in a wall, a tumbling leaf, a flowing fountain, and in fact a mere line or color or the dance of an abstract shape on the movie screen have as much expression as the human body, and serve the artist equally well. In some ways they serve him even better, for the human body is a particularly complex pattern, not easily reduced to the simplicity of shape and motion that transmits compelling expression. Also it is overloaded with nonvisual associations. The human figure is not the easiest, but the most difficult, vehicle of artistic expression.

The fact that nonhuman objects have genuine physiognomic properties has been concealed by the popular assumption that they are merely dressed up with human expression by an illusory "pathetic fallacy," by empathy, anthropomorphism, primitive animism. But if expression is an inherent characteristic of perceptual patterns, its manifestations in the human figure are but a special case of a more general phenomenon. The comparison of an object's expression with a human state of mind is a secondary process. A weeping willow does not look sad because it looks like a sad person. It is more adequate to say that since the shape, direction, and flexibility of willow branches convey the expression of passive hanging, a comparison with the structurally similar state of mind and body that we call sadness imposes itself secondarily. The columns of a temple do not strive upward and carry the weight of the roof so dramatically because we put ourselves in their place, but because their location, proportion, and shape are carefully chosen in such a way that their image contains the desired expression. Only because and when this is so, are we enabled to "sympathize" with the columns, if we so desire. An inappropriately designed temple resists all empathy.

To define visual expression as a reflection of human feelings would seem to be misleading on two counts: first, because it makes us ignore the fact that expression has its origin in the perceived pattern and in the reaction of the brain field of vision to this pattern; second, because such a description unduly limits the range of what is being expressed. We found as the basis of expression a configuration of forces. Such a configuration interests us because it is significant not only for the object in whose image it appears, but for the physical and mental world in general. Motifs like rising and falling, dominance and submission, weakness and strength, harmony and discord, struggle and conformance, underlie all existence. We find them within our own mind and in our relations to other people, in the human community and in the events of nature. Perception of expression fulfills its spiritual mission only if we experience in it more than the resonance of our own feelings. It permits us to realize that the forces stirring in ourselves are only individual examples of the same forces acting throughout the universe. We are thus enabled to sense our place in the whole and the inner unity of that whole.

Some objects and events resemble each other with regard to the underlying patterns of forces; others do not. Therefore, on the basis of their expressive appearance, our eye spontaneously creates a kind of Linnean classification of all things existing. This perceptual classification cuts across the order suggested by other kinds of categories. Particularly in our modern Western civilization we are accustomed to distinguishing between animate and inanimate things, human and nonhuman creatures, the mental and the physical. But in terms of expressive qualities, the character of a given person may resemble that of a particular tree more closely than that of another person. The state of affairs in a human society may be similar to the tension in the skies just before the outbreak of a thunderstorm. Further, our kind of scientific and economic thinking makes us define things by measurements rather than by the dynamics of their appearance. Our criteria for what is useful or useless, friendly or hostile, have tended to sever the connections with outer expression, which they possess in the minds of children or primitives. If a house or a chair suits our practical purposes, we may not stop to find out whether its appearance expresses our style of living. In business relations we define a man by his census data, his income, age, position, nationality, or race—that is, by categories that ignore the inner nature of the man as it is manifest in his outer expression.

Primitive languages give us an idea of the kind of world that derives from a classification based on perception. Instead of restricting itself to the verb "to walk," which rather abstractly refers to locomotion, the language of the African Ewe takes care to specify in every kind of walking the particular expressive qualities of the movement. There are expressions for "the gait of a little man whose limbs shake very much, to walk with a dragging step like a feeble person, the gait of a long-legged man who throws his legs forward, of a corpulent man who walks heavily, to walk in a dazed fashion without looking ahead, an energetic and firm step," and many others. These distinctions are not made out of sheer aesthetic sensitivity, but because the expressive properties of the gait are believed to reveal important practical information on what kind of man is walking and what is his intent at the moment.

Although primitive languages often surprise us by their wealth of subdivisions for which we see no need, they also reveal generalizations that to us may seem unimportant or absurd. For example, the language of the Klamath Indians has prefixes for words referring to objects of similar shape or movement. Such a prefix may describe "the outside of a round or spheroidal, cylindrical, discoid or bulbed object, or a ring; also voluminous; or again, an act accomplished with an object which bears such a form; or a circular or semi-circular or waving movement of the body, arms, hands, or other parts. Therefore this prefix is to be found connected with clouds, celestial bodies, rounded slopes on the earth's surface, fruits rounded or bulbed in shape, stones and dwellings (these last being usually circular in form.) It is employed too, for a crowd of animals, for enclosures, social gatherings (since an assembly usually adopts the form of a circle), and so forth."

Such a classification groups things together that to our way of thinking belong in very different categories and have little or nothing in common. At the same time, these features of primitive language remind us that the poetical habit of uniting practically disparate objects by metaphor is not a sophisticated invention of artists, but derives from and relies on the universal and spontaneous way of approaching the world of experience.

Georges Braque advises the artist to seek the common in the dissimilar. "Thus the poet can say: The swallow knifes the sky, and thereby makes a knife out of a swallow." It is the function of the metaphor to make the reader penetrate the concrete shell of the world of things by combinations of objects that have little in common but the underlying pattern. Such a device, however, would not work unless the reader of poetry was still alive, in his own daily experience, to the symbolic or metaphoric connotation of all appearance and activity. For example, hitting or breaking things normally evokes, if ever so slightly, the overtone of attack and destruction. There is a tinge of conquest and achievement to all rising—even the climbing of a staircase. If the shades are pulled in the morning and the room is flooded with light, more is experienced than a simple change of illumination. One aspect of the wisdom that belongs to a genuine culture is the constant awareness of the symbolic meaning expressed in concrete happening, the sensing of the universal in the particular. This gives significance and dignity to all daily pursuits, and prepares the ground on which the arts can grow. In its pathological extreme this spontaneous symbolism manifests itself in what is known to the psychiatrist as the "organ speech" of psychosomatic and other neurotic symptoms. There are people who cannot swallow because there is something in their lives they "cannot swallow" or whom an unconscious sense of guilt compels to spend hours every day on washing and cleaning.

Symbols in Art

In the more popular sense of the term, we do not call a work of art symbolic unless the individual facts it represents can be understood only by reference to an underlying idea. A Dutch genre painting that shows a group of peasants around the inn table may be called devoid of symbolism. But when Titian paints a picture in which two women, one fully dressed and one almost naked, are placed symmetrically on a well, or when in one of Dürer's engravings a winged woman with a goblet in her hand stands on a sphere that moves through the clouds, we are convinced that the mysterious scene has been invented to convey an idea. Such symbolism may be standardized to the kind of picture language that is found, for example, in the allegories of religious art. A lily stands for the virginity of Mary, lambs are disciples, or two deer drinking from a pond show the recreation of the faithful.

But symbolic meaning is expressed only indirectly by what our reasoning or learning tells us about the subject matter. In the great works of art the deepest significance is transmitted to the eye with powerful directness by the perceptual characteristics of the compositional·pattern. The "story" of Michelangelo's *Creation of Adam,* on the ceiling of the Sistine Chapel in Rome (Figure 274), is understood by every reader of the book of Genesis. But even the story is modified in a way that makes it more comprehensible and impressive to the eye. God, instead of breathing a living soul into the body of clay—a motif not easily translatable into an expressive pattern— reaches out toward the arm of Adam as though an animating spark, leaping from fingertip to fingertip, was transmitted from the creator to the creature. The bridge of the arm visually connects two separate worlds: the self-contained, complete roundness of the mantle that encloses God and is given forward motion by the diagonal of his body; and the incomplete, flat slice of the earth, whose passivity is expressed by the backward slant of its contour. There is passivity also in the concave curve over which the body of Adam is molded. It is lying on the ground and enabled partly to rise by the attractive power of the approaching creator. The desire and potential capacity to get up and walk are indicated as a subordinate theme in the left leg, which also serves as a support of Adam's arm, unable to maintain itself freely like the energy-charged arm of God.

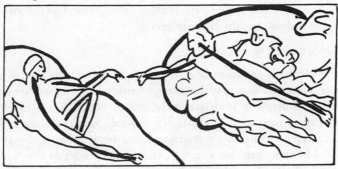

Figure 274

The analysis shows that the structural skeleton of the pictorial composition reveals the dynamic pattern of the story. There is an active power making contact with a passive object, which is being animated by the energy it receives. The essence of the story appears in what strikes the eye of the observer first: the dominant perceptual pattern of the work. And since this pattern is not simply recorded by the nervous system, but presumably arouses a corresponding configuration of forces, the observer's reaction is more than a mere taking cognizance of an outer object. The forces that characterize the meaning of the story become active in the observer, and produce the kind of stirring participation that distinguishes artistic experience from the detached acceptance of information.

But there is more. The structural pattern does not only elucidate the meaning of the individual story presented in the work. The dynamic theme revealed by this pattern is not limited to the Biblical episode at hand, but is valid for any number of situations that may occur in the psychical and the physical world. Not only is the perceptual pattern a means of understanding the story of the creation of man, but the story becomes a means of illustrating a kind of event that is universal and therefore abstract and therefore in need of being clad with flesh and blood so that the eye may see it.

The perceptual pattern of a work of art is neither arbitrary nor a purely formal play of shapes and colors. It is indispensable as a precise interpreter of the idea the work is meant to express. Similarly, the subject matter is neither arbitrary nor unimportant. It is exactly correlated with the formal pattern to supply a concrete application of an abstract theme. The kind of connoisseur who looks only for the pattern does as little justice to the work as the kind of layman who looks only for the subject matter. When Whistler called the portrait of his mother *Arrangement in Grey and Black,* he treated his picture as one-sidedly as someone who sees nothing in it but a dignified lady sitting on a chair. Neither the formal pattern nor the subject matter is the final content of the work of art. Both are devices of artistic form. They serve to give body to the invisible universal.

The Psychoanalytic Way

It will be evident why we must hesitate to accept the interpretation of artistic symbols presented by some psychoanalytic writers. In their analyses we find, first of all, a tendency to understand the artistic object as a representation of other objects, such as the womb, the genitals, or the artist's father or mother. Extreme examples are contained in a book, *Man as Symbol,* by Groddeck. He maintains, for example, that the attitudes of the figures in Rembrandt's *Anatomy,* read from the back of the picture toward the front, and the Roman *Laocoön,* read from the right to the left of the group, are representations of the male genital in the stages of excitation and slackening. The most common objection to this kind of interpretation points to its one-sidedness, that is, to the presupposition that sex is the most basic and important human experience, to which everything else is spontaneously referred. Psychologists have remarked that this assumption is unproved. At best the theory holds true for certain psychoneurotic individuals or even cultural periods in which "an over-emphasized sexuality is piled up behind a dam" of severe moral restrictions and in which other aims of life have been deprived of their weight by an empty existence under unfavorable social conditions. As Jung has remarked in this connection, "It is well known that when we have a bad toothache, we can think of nothing else."

But another objection seems even more pertinent. The psychoanalytic theory describes the visible facts of the work of art as a representation of other, equally concrete and individual facts. If after penetrating the work of a master we are left with nothing but references to organs and functions of the human body or to some close relative, we wonder what makes art such a universal and supposedly important creation of the human mind. Its message seems pitifully obvious. A little thought shows that sex is no more final and no less symbolical than other human experiences. It is true that in the arts as well as in common usage "neutral" situations are often employed to point to a veiled sexual meaning, as, for example, when Rabelais warns husbands to be wary of the monks because "the very shadow of an abbey's steeple is fertile." But equally often we find the less refined device of describing "neutral" situations by colorful sexual images. Thus Cézanne was fond of distinguishing between substantial and insubstantial art by the epithets *"bien couillard"* and *"pas couillard."* For our purposes it is especially significant that sex stands often for a highly abstract power. According to Jung, "As was customary throughout antiquity, primitive people today make a free use of phallic symbols, yet it never occurs to them to confuse the phallus, as a ritualistic symbol, with the penis. They always take the phallus to mean the creative *mana,* the power of healing and fertility, 'that which is unusually potent,' to use Lehmann's expression."

Similarly, some psychoanalysts have come recently to interpret narrative plots in a less restricted manner. For example, Fromm says of the Bible story of Jonah: "We find a sequence of symbols which follow one another: going into the ship, going into the ship's belly, falling asleep, being in the ocean, and being in the fish's belly. All these symbols stand for the same inner experience: for a condition of being protected and isolated, of safe withdrawal from communication with other human beings."

Symbolic interpretations that make one concrete object stand for another equally concrete one are almost always arbitrary and unprovable. There is no telling whether a particular association was or is on the conscious or unconscious mind of the artist or beholder unless we obtain direct information, which may require a depth analysis. The work of art itself does not offer the information, except in the case of symbols standardized by convention or in those few individual instances in which the overt content of the work appears strange and unjustified unless it is considered as a representation of different objects of similar appearance. Since the underlying theme of any work of art is so universal that it can fit an infinite number of concrete situations, an observer has no trouble in associating it with any one of them that happens to be on his mind. But whereas the associations produced by some one in reaction to his own dream are valid because the dream is a spontaneous product of his own making, associations to a work of art are often purely personal responses, which lead away from the meaning of the work rather than elucidating it. This is true even for the artist himself. The first concept of a work may be as spontaneously private as that of a dream. But in the course of the creative process the work goes through elaborations that require that the artist distinguish, with severe discipline, between what suits the nature of his subject and what is accidental impulse.

The psychoanalytic approach is somewhat too limited also when it defines, as Fromm has recently, the symbolic language as one "in which the world outside is a symbol of the world inside, a symbol for our souls and our minds." Undoubtedly artists often represent relatively abstract psychical situations through concrete outer themes; and Freud, for example, has attempted interesting analyses of Shakespeare, the Oedipus legend, or Leonardo's painting *Virgin and Child with St. Anne*. We cannot, however, describe art as a mere projection of human personalities without restricting its scope unduly.

Finally, progress has been made beyond Freud's original conviction that symbols serve to camouflage an objectionable content. In an early paper, *The Poet and Fantasy,* Freud asserts that the artist makes his "daydreams" acceptable essentially by two devices: he "tones down the character of the egotistic daydream by modifications and concealments and seduces us by purely formal, that is, aesthetic pleasure offered to us in the presentation of his fantasies." In other words, artistic form serves to hide the true content of the work and to sugar-coat the repulsive ingredients of the pill by external "beauty." In opposition to Freud's view of dream symbols, Jung has maintained that symbols reveal rather than veil the message. "When Freud speaks of the 'dream-façade,' he is really speaking not of the dream itself but of its obscurity, and in so doing is projecting upon the dream his own lack of understanding. We say that the dream has a false front only because we fail to see into it."

This reinterpretation opens our eyes to the similarity between the language of the dream and that of the work of art. During sleep the human mind seems to descend to the more elementary level at which life situations are described not by abstract concepts but by significant images. We cannot but admire the creative imagination awakened by sleep in all of us. It is this dormant power of picture language on which the artist also draws for his inventions.

All Art Is Symbolic

If art could do nothing better than reproduce the things of nature, either directly or by analogy, or to delight the senses, there would be little justification for the honorable place reserved to it in every known society. Art's reputation must be due to the fact that it helps man to understand the world and himself, and presents to his eyes what he has understood and believes to be true. Now everything in this world is a unique individual; no two things can be equal. But anything can be understood only because it is made up of ingredients not reserved to itself but common to many or all other things. In science, greatest knowledge is achieved when all existing phe-

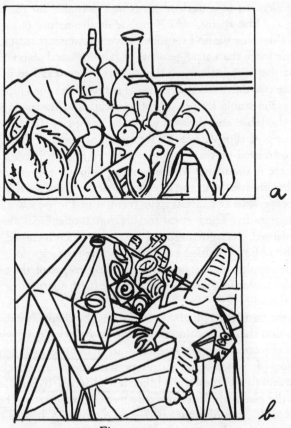

Figure 275

nomena are reduced to a common law. This is true for art also. The mature work of art succeeds in subjecting everything to a dominant law of structure. In doing so, it does not distort the variety of existing things into uniformity. On the contrary, it clarifies their differences by making them all comparable. Braque has said: "By putting a lemon next to an orange they cease to be a lemon and an orange and become fruit. The mathematicians follow this law. So do we." He fails to remember that the virtue of such correlation is two-fold. It shows the way in which things are similar and, by doing so, defines their individuality. By establishing a common "style" for all objects, the artist creates a whole, in which the place and function of every one of them are lucidly defined. Goethe said: "The beautiful is a manifestation of secret laws of nature, which would have remained hidden to us forever without its appearance."

Every element of a work of art is indispensable for the one purpose of pointing out the theme, which embodies the nature of existence for the artist. In this sense we find symbolism even in works that, at first sight, seem to be little more than arrangements of fairly neutral objects. We need only glance at the bare outlines of the two still lifes sketched in Figure 275 to experience two different conceptions of reality. Cézanne's picture (a) is dominated by the stable framework of verticals and horizontals in the background, the table, and the axes of bottles and glass. This skeleton is strong enough to give support even to the sweeping folds of the fabric. A simple order is conveyed by the upright symmetry of each bottle and that of the glass. There is abundance in the swelling volumes and emphasis on roundness and softness even in the inorganic matter. Compare this image of prosperous peace with the catastrophic turmoil in Picasso's work (b). Here we find little stability. The vertical and horizontal orientations are avoided. The room is slanted, the right angles of the table, which is turned over, are either hidden by oblique position or distorted. The four legs do not run parallel, the bottle topples, the desperately sprawling corpse of the bird is about to fall off the table. The contours tend to be hard, sharp, lifeless, even in the body of the animal.

Since the basic perceptual pattern carries the theme, we must not be surprised to find that art continues to fulfill its function even when it ceases to represent objects of nature. "Abstract" art does in its own way what art has always done. It is not better than representational art, which also does not hide but reveals the meaningful skeleton of forces. It is no less good, for it contains the essentials. It is not "pure form," because even the simplest line expresses visible meaning and is therefore symbolic. It does not offer intellectual abstractions, because there is nothing more concrete than color, shape, and motion. It does not limit itself to the inner life of man, or to the unconscious, because for art the distinctions between the outer and the inner world and the conscious and the unconscious mind are artificial. The human mind receives, shapes, and interprets its image of the outer world with all its conscious and unconscious powers, and the realm of the unconscious could never enter our experience without the reflection of perceivable things. There is no way of presenting the one without the other. But the nature of the outer and the inner world can be reduced to a play of forces, and this "musical" approach is attempted by the misnamed abstract artists.

We do not know what the art of the future will look like. But we know that "abstraction" is not art's final climax. No style will ever be that. It is one valid way of looking at the world, one view of the holy mountain, which offers a different image from every place but can be seen as the same everywhere.

Back to the Start

Expression is the crowning aspiration of all perceptual categories. It is the statement to which they all contribute by arousing visual tension. We noted some of the tension-creating properties of shape and color, location, space, and light and, in fact, began our enquiry by observing that all perceived patterns are dynamic. This most elementary attribute turns out to be most significant artistically as well; for if pictures and sculpture did not convey dynamic tension they could not portray life. In our more limited, perceptual sense, expression is based on tension alone. It refers to the universality of the patterns of forces experienced in the particular images we receive: to expansion and contraction, conflict and concordance, rising and falling, approach and withdrawal. When these dynamisms are understood as symbols of the powers that shape human destiny, then expression assumes a deeper meaning. To it our interpretations of some specific works of art inevitably alluded; but its systematic scrutiny is not in the realm of a study devoted to what the eyes can see.

NOTES

Notes to Chapter I

BALANCE

(pages 1–31)

P. 3. The "magnetic" effects described here have been tested preliminarily by one of my students, Toni Cushing. They deserve to be subjected to quantitative experimentation on a broader basis.

P. 3. The repulsion of the disk from the edge of the square brings to mind certain findings by Köhler and Wallach (166) in their experiments with the visual aftereffect. A line figure was fixated by observers for a few minutes, after which a new figure was introduced for inspection in order to test the influence of the previously fixated pattern. It was found that visual objects recede from areas previously occupied by other visual objects. The effect was found to be weak when the objects were closer together, to approach a climax at a certain distance, and to

weaken again as distance increased further. A physiological explanation is offered by the authors.

P. 5. Wertheimer (303), p. 79.

P. 5. Duncker (67), p. 164.

P. 6. Compare Kepes (152), p. 29: "The actual visual elements are only the focal points of this field; they are the concentrated energy."

P. 7. Wertheimer (301).

P. 7. Köhler and Held (165).

P. 8. See, for example, the use of the mirror in Jean Cocteau's film *The Blood of the Poet*.

P. 10. Ross (257), p. 23.

P. 11. *St. Michael Weighing Souls*, Austria (Salzburg ?), painted around 1470. Reproduced by permission of the Allen Memorial Museum, Oberlin College.

P. 12. Based on Arnheim (19), p. 267.

P. 12. Compare Ross (257), p. 25: "In any unsymmetrical relation of positions (directions, distances, intervals), in which

445

the balance-center is not clearly and sufficiently indicated, there is a suggestion of movement. The eye, not being held by any balance, readily follows this suggestion."

P. 13. Figures 6–9 are adapted from figures 21, 24, 1, and 9 of Graves (110) by permission of the Psychological Corporation, New York.

P. 13. In Graham Sutherland's painting for the church of St. Matthew in Northampton, England, the body of the crucified Christ is given in complete frontal symmetry, except for the head, which hangs sideways. To judge from a photograph, the head looks unrelated to the body because the symmetry of the whole is so strong that the one local deviation from it is simply cast off as an interference.

P. 14. Pelt (235), p. 144.

P. 14. For the lever principle and other factors of balance see Langfeld (173), chapters 9 and 10 and the earlier literature cited there.

P. 14. Puffer (243) on the vista effect.

P. 15. Mock and Richards (212), p. 43. By permission of Penguin Books, Ltd.

P. 15. On emphasis by isolation on the stage see Dean (59), p. 146.

P. 17. Toulouse-Lautrec's *At the Circus: The Tandem* (1899) is in the Knoedler Collection, New York.

P. 18. Erle Loran, in his analysis of Cézanne's compositions (189) uses double-headed arrows to indicate the double direction created by shape. See diagram ii on p. 41 of his book.

P. 19. For perceptual aftereffects found in experiments by J. J. Gibson and others see Köhler and Wallach (166), p. 269.

P. 19. A systematic study of compositional patterns has been made by Rudrauf (260). He distingushes between *compositions diffuses,* in which units are evenly and homogeneously distributed without center of radiation or accent (Bosch, Brueghel, Persian miniatures), and *com-*

positions scandées, which have spatial rhythm and a hierarchy of accents. He divides the latter into (1) axial compositions, organized around the pivot of a principal figure or group; (2) centered compositions, radiating from a point of gravitation; and (3) polarized compositions, made up of two opposing figures or groups, between which there is a dynamic relation.

P. 20. Langfeld (173), p. 223.

P. 20. Quoted from Greenough (112) by permission of the University of California Press, Berkeley.

P. 20. Compare p. 12 on balance and locomotion.

P. 22. One of my students, Charlotte Hannaford, used three paintings by Rudolf Bauer and one each by Mondrian and Kandinsky. The result obtained from twenty observers for the four possible orientations (*A* being the one intended by the artist) was as follows:

	A	B	C	D
Bauer I	15	3	1	1
Bauer II	4	3	3	10
Bauer III	10	5	3	2
Mondrian	11	1	4	4
Kandinsky	10	2	8	0
	50	14	19	17

The over-all result showed exactly 50 per cent correct judgments. The result was negative for Bauer II (notice, however, the high agreement on one "wrong" judgment), weak for Kandinsky, and clearly positive for the other three. Mere probability would have made for only 25 per cent correct judgments. The comments obtained from observers in such experiments are enlightening and deserve more study.

P. 22. Wölfflin published two papers on the right-left problem (319).

P. 22. Gaffron's first observations are contained in a book on Rembrandt's etchings (90). An article of hers in English cites the earlier literature (91).

P. 23. Dean (59), p. 132.

P. 23. Cobb (52), p. 28.

P. 24. Gaffron (91), p. 329. Owing to the crossing of nerve connections, the right visual field belongs to the left brain center.

P. 25. Freud (80), p. 1.

P. 25. Whyte (307).

P. 25. The definition of motivation is quoted from Freeman (79), p. 239. Compare also Krech and Crutchfield (168), chapter ii and Weber (298).

P. 25. Regarding the organism and the law of entropy see Köhler (161), pp. 314 ff.

P. 27. Leonardo da Vinci (178), vol. ii, p. 284.

P. 27. Cézanne's portrait is reproduced by permission of the Chicago Art Institute.

P. 30. Ross (257), p. 26.

P. 31. For the analysis of a similar portrait by Cézanne see Loran (189), plate 17.

Notes to Chapter II

SHAPE

(pages 32–81)

P. 32. For a report on the brain-injured man see Gelb and Goldstein (95), p. 324.

P. 33. Plato, *Timaeus*, paragraph 45.

P. 33. T. S. Eliot (70), p. 4.

P. 33. Köhler (159), p. 320.

P. 34. Lorenz (190), pp. 162–163. Compare also Gombrich's article in the same book (107) and Tinbergen (286).

P. 34. Jung (142), p. 147.

P. 34. See Gellermann (96) and more recently Hebb (122), pp. 12 ff., who stresses the fact that the grasping of perceptual features seems to develop gradually.

P. 34. Lashley quoted by Adrian (2), p. 85.

P. 34. Based on Arnheim (13). By per-

mission of the American Psychological Association.

P. 36. Compare Gibson's article on form (99).

P. 39. For the experiment on the effect of verbal instruction see Carmichael (47).

P. 40. Gottschaldt (109). Figure 22 is not one of Gottschaldt's patterns. I found it sketched in pencil on the margin of Gottschaldt's paper by the late Max Wertheimer in his personal copy of the *Psychologische Forschung*.

P. 40. Genetically, the grasping of shape may not be immediate. Compare Hebb (122), pp. 12 ff.

P. 40. Gombrich (107), p. 216. See also Bruner and Krech (42), pp. 15–31.

P. 42. Figure 24 is reproduced from an engraving contained in Leon Battista Alberti, *Della Pittura e della Statua*, Milan, Società Tipografica De' Classici Italiani, 1804, p. 123.

P. 43. Gelb and Goldstein (95), p. 317.

P. 44. Figure 28 is after Berliner (29), p. 24.

P. 44. Simplicity and order are not the same thing, but certain observations on the nature of one of them hold good also for the other. Spinoza's remark on the subjectivity of order (*Ethics*, part i) is cited in a paper by Hartmann and Sickles on the theory of order (117). These authors, who seem to think of order mainly, or perhaps exclusively, as a characteristic of grouping—that is, as a relationship between discrete objects—assert that "order is the term applied to any subjective quality or sensation which is produced by, and dependent upon, the number of straight lines which can be drawn through three or more actual or supplied points or centers of the sensory field; it varies directly with the degree to which these lines tend to become parallel with each other and with the vertico-horizontal coordinate system natural to the organism." This definition, which can also be applied to simplicity, is valuable as a first attempt to solve the problem in exact terms. It points correctly to the importance of the spatial frame of reference and of parallel orientation. But it describes the effect of parallelism in terms of a summation of elements and is inadequate also by considering only two specific factors. For example, circles, which contain no parallels, have a high degree of order. In a second paper Sickles (274) realizes that a circular arrangement of objects would possess order, but maintains that no such arrangement is ever perceived, because "the eyes never see curves save when these are objectively present—all subjective intervals being straight lines." This consideration is based on insufficient observation, and also refutes Hartmann and Sickles' own definition, according to which order is supposed to exist only as a subjective quality or sensation (and as a property of "underlying electrodynamic laws," which govern processes in the nervous system).

P. 45. Peter Blake, in a review of the book *The Road Is Yours,* by R. M. Cleveland and S. T. Williamson, published in the *New York Times,* 1951.

P. 45. Quotes are translated, by permission of the author, from an unpublished essay, "Ueber die Einfachheit," by Kurt Badt, written in the 1920's (22).

P. 46. Cohen and Nagel (53), pp. 212 and 384.

P. 46. Newton (224), Book III, Rule I, p. 398.

P. 47. Ben Nicholson's relief is illustrated in *Circle* (203), plate 6.

P. 50. Psychologists are accustomed to distinguishing between the proximal and the distant stimulus. Compare Koffka (158), p. 79. If a person looks at a table, the material object in the room is the distant stimulus whereas the retinal image of the table is the proximal stimulus. The distant and the corresponding prox-

imal stimuli often differ in simplicity, but the structure of the distant stimulus can be neglected here for the moment. It will come up later when I discuss the representation of three-dimensional bodies.

P. 51. *Victory Boogie-Woogie,* a painting by Piet Mondrian (214), p. 55. *Rebellion Tamed by Wise Government* is the title of a picture by Rubens, painted around 1631.

P. 52. Personal communication by S. Kracauer.

P. 52. The Valéry quote is translated from "L'Homme et la Coquille" (289), p. 12.

P. 53. Köhler (163), p. 132, quotes Ernst Mach's assertion that in orderly distributions the pattern of forces is as regular as the distribution of the material.

P. 53. L. L. Whyte (307).

P. 53. The reference to Leopardi is taken from Tsanoff (287), p. 217.

P. 54. Leonardo da Vinci (178), volume ii, p. 238.

P. 54. A detailed survey of the experiments on the reactions to subdued stimuli can be found in Woodworth (322), chapter iv, "Memory for Form." Consult also Koffka (158), pp. 493–505. Considerable controversy has been aroused by the experiments based on the effect of memory. The pioneer study by Wulf (324) was done under the guidance of Koffka. Among the more recent publications, the study by Goldmeier (104) is particularly relevant. Hebb and Foord (123) obtained negative results from a memory experiment with two figures: an incomplete circle and an arrowhead. The material on the reactions to Figure 36, which is adapted from Wohlfahrt (314), derives from demonstrations in my classes. Figure 38a is based on Wulf, Figure 38d on Allport (4), Figures 39a and 40 on Hanawalt (116), and Figure 39c on Hempstead (128).

P. 57. Wulf described both leveling and sharpening as manifestations of the "law of prägnanz." This was in keeping with the terminology of Wertheimer, who had introduced the term to designate a tendency to clear-cut structure, the German word "prägnant" meaning just that. It will be seen from my presentation that the law of prägnanz covers cases which show the gestalt tendency to simplest form as well as others that do not. This is one of the reasons why the term "prägnanz" is not used here. In addition, the word has produced confusion by its similarity with the English word "pregnant," which means something else.

P. 59. On simplicity of shape in physics see Köhler (163), p. 131, and Koffka (158), p. 132.

P. 59. It has been shown that the principles of visual organization hold also for animals. The reactions of jay birds to patterns like Figure 41*d* have been studied by Hertz (129).

P. 60. Figure 44 is after Arnheim (18), p. 202.

P. 62. Wertheimer's example of the bridge on p. 336 of the German original (302). The drawing is mine.

P. 62. Stein (279), p. 11. On camouflage in nature see Cott (56).

P. 63. Compare Köhler (163), pp. 156–160. Wertheimer explains the correspondence of perceptual and physical organization as an evolutionary adaptation of the nervous system to the environment; p. 336 of the German original (302), omitted in the summary by Ellis (303).

P. 63. Edouard Manet's *Guitarist* is reproduced by permission of the Metropolitan Museum of Art, New York City.

P. 65. Waddington's article on biological form (295), p. 44. The paper also contains critical remarks on modern sculpture from the point of view of the anatomist.

P. 65. Figure 49 on p. 323 of Wertheimer's original paper (302).

P. 66. In a "gestalt" the structure of the whole is determined by the structure of the parts, and vice versa. For a list of definitions of "gestalt" see Katz (151), p. 91. For an introduction to the theory see Wertheimer (304), Köhler (163), and Koffka (158).

P. 67. On rules of grouping see Wertheimer (303). My presentation differs from Wertheimer's, principally because all the rules are described here as special examples of one of them—the rule of similarity. This also necessitates changes in terminology.

P. 67. Figures 51–55 are adapted from Arnheim (18), p. 200.

P. 67. "Similarity of direction" was called the "factor of common fate" by Wertheimer.

P. 70. In Ramakrishna's account of the parable (245), p. 191, one of the blind men said that the elephant was like a pillar—he had touched only its leg. Another said it was like a winnowing fan—he had touched only its ear. The meaning given to the story is that "a man who has seen only one aspect of God limits God to that alone." I am indebted to Mr. Joseph Campbell for this reference.

P. 70. The piecemeal character of the rules of grouping is often overlooked. Wertheimer himself was well aware of it. After having introduced his rules he called them "a poor abstraction," thus giving his paper a dramatic turning point. He described the law of similarity as "a special case of the law of good gestalt," and asserted that visual patterns should not be treated in terms of "distances and relations between pieces."

P. 70. Weird composite pictures were painted by Giuseppe Arcimboldi in the sixteenth century. The Vienna Gemäldegalerie possesses symbolic portraits of his, in which human figures are made up of such things as fruit.

P. 71. Figure 59 is adapted from Wertheimer, who called this factor "good continuation." Meyer Schapiro has suggested to me that Wertheimer's principle of "good continuation" ("consistent shape") could be described as a special case of "similarity."

P. 72. Walter Piston (240), p. 20. Some of the other principles found in visual organization could also be beneficially applied to music.

P. 73. Picasso's gouache *Seated Woman* (1918) is reproduced here by permission of the Museum of Modern Art, New York.

P. 74. Gombrich (106), p. 259.

P. 74. For Rudrauf's concept of "diffuse composition" see the note to p. 19 on p. 446.

P. 74. Seurat's *La Grande Jatte* is in the Art Institute, Chicago.

P. 74. Constantin Brancusi's *Lovers* is in the Philadelphia Museum of Art.

P. 74. Cézanne's *Uncle Dominic,* formerly in the Frick Collection, is now in a private collection in New York.

P. 76. Figure 66 is taken from Arnheim (18), p. 202.

P. 77. Five versions of El Greco's *Expulsion from the Temple* are known. I am referring to the one in the Frick Collection, New York.

P. 78. Brueghel's *Parable of the Blind Men* is in the Museo Nazionale, Naples.

P. 78. Delacroix (61), I. *Etudes Esthétiques,* p. 69.

P. 80. Figure 73 is derived from a procedure suggested by Wertheimer on p. 318 of the original paper (302).

Notes to Chapter III

FORM

(pages 82–154)

P. 82. Gellermann (96).

P. 83. Once a normal orientation has been established, the world will look upside down when it is inverted by means of lenses or in a picture. See Stratton

(281). Berkeley, in his *New Theory of Vision,* paragraphs 88–102, discusses the inversion of the retinal image in an interesting way.

P. 84. A simplified description of one of Witkin's experiments is given here. For further detail see Witkin (312).

P. 84. Picasso's still life *The Red Tablecloth,* painted in 1924, is reproduced as plate 187 by Barr (26).

P. 85. Figure 77 is taken from Kopfermann (167), p. 353.

P. 86. The influence of orientation on the shape of the square was pointed out first in 1896 by Mach (199), p. 106.

P. 86. The observation on obliquely oriented right angles is taken from Kopfermann (167), p. 352.

P. 86. On the copying of figures in intelligence tests see Terman and Merrill (282), pp. 92, 98, 219, 230.

P. 87. Köhler (162), p. 29, in the course of a detailed discussion of the problem. For other statements on spatial orientation see Koffka (158), pp. 212–219, and Kopfermann (167), pp. 349–353.

P. 87. Gibson and Robinson (100) on the influence of past experience on orientation.

P. 87. On children's responses to orientation see Stern (280) and Rice (253).

P. 88. Koffka (156), p. 314, quoting from Pechuël-Loesche, *Volkskunde von Loango,* 1907, pp. 76–77.

P. 88. Stratton's report on his experiment (281).

P. 88. Lewin's paper on changes of spatial orientation (182).

P. 90. Distortion of an object because of the angle of observation does occur, even apart from the obvious perspective changes of relative size due to differences of distance. Wölfflin, in a paper on the reproduction and interpretation of works of art (317), pp. 66–76, complains about the distorting effect of photographs that show pieces of sculpture from inappropriate points of view. In a photograph such distortion occurs more easily than in direct perception because it presents an isolated aspect under conditions of greatly reduced three-dimensionality. When the shape of a statue is rather complex, an obliquely taken picture may produce a "pseudo-front," that is, the impression that the observer is facing the front view of the statue—hence the distortion.

P. 90. Projective geometry deals with a similar problem by determining the structural "invariants," which remain untouched by distortion through projection. See Courant and Robbins (57), pp. 165 ff.

P. 90. Francis Galton (93), p. 68.

P. 91. The back view of a seated nurse in Seurat's *Grande Jatte* in Chicago comes close to my example of the Mexican.

P. 92. Chesterton in "The Eye of Apollo," one of his Father Brown stories.

P. 93. Kerschensteiner (154), pp. 229–230.

P. 95. Schaefer (265), pp. 202, 207, 253, 254.

P. 97. Schaefer (265), pp. 74–75.

P. 97. If we think of the sections of the foreshortened bodies, we realize that this rule of completion is an application of the rule of consistent shape to the third dimension (see Figure 276).

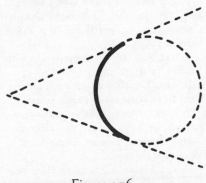

Figure 276

P. 98. Figure 89 is drawn after a detail from an Attic amphora of the early sixth century, in the possession of the Metropolitan Museum of Art, New York City (illustrated in *Greek Painting* [111], p. 8). The fact that such monstrosities occur in a period in which the sense of the visually significant was so strict otherwise that even mild foreshortenings—for example, of faces—were avoided shows the compelling power of structurally simple patterns. The symmetry of the front view is so inviting that its inadequacy is overlooked. It also affords a simple solution of the problem how to represent a set of four horses (see also p. 85). Rathe (247), p. 37, mentions similar cases in Far Eastern art as examples of the "Durchschlagskraft" of such projections.

P. 99. Delacroix, *Journal* (63), vol. iii, p. 13, entry of January 13, 1857.

P. 100. Andrea Mantegna's foreshortened Christ is in the Brera, Milan.

P. 100. Figure 92b is sketched from a detail of a drawing by Matisse, reproduced as number 225 in the catalogue of the Matisse exhibition of the Philadelphia Museum of Art, 1948.

P. 101. Figure 91 is enlarged from Fernand Léger's film *Ballet Mécanique* (1924). I am indebted for the photograph to Guido Aristarco, editor of *Cinema Nuovo*.

P. 102. The Barlach quotation is translated from one of his letters, written in June, 1889 (25), p. 17.

P. 102. Low-cut dresses that end in a horizontal line slice the shoulders from the rest of the body whereas the oblique V-shaped cut sufficiently deviates from the axes of the body and thus does not interfere with its unity.

P. 103. Apologies are due Rockwell Kent, a detail of whose woodcut *The Lovers* gave me the idea for Figure 94.

P. 103. Britsch (39), pp. 82 ff., has drawn attention to the remnants of the "Egyptian" method in Leonardo and Michelangelo.

P. 103. My presentation of the relationship between perspective projection and visual conception has profited greatly from conversations with Henry Schaefer-Simmern.

P. 104. The vague term "Western" is meant here to indicate the style of representation epitomized by Renaissance art.

P. 106. Figure 98 is taken from an Egyptian relief at Abydos (about 1300 B.C.) representing King Sethos I and the goddess Isis.

P. 106. Rubens' *Shepherd Embracing a Young Woman* (1636–1638) is in the Munich Pinakothek.

P. 106. For further examples of how superposition is used to convey meaning in films see Arnheim (10), pp. 47 ff.

P. 106. Alschuler and Hattwick (5), vol. ii, p. 129.

P. 107. Wölfflin (321), p. 63.

P. 109. The picture of St. Ursula from a calendar manuscript in Stuttgart is reproduced by Gombrich (106), p. 129.

P. 109. The parallel noted in the development of music and the visual arts refers mainly to the sequence of comparable steps, not to coincidence in time. It may be mentioned, however, that although in Western culture visual overlapping precedes musical harmony by thousands of years, the arrangement of pictures in horizontal rows gives way to an integrated organization of the third dimension only in the Renaissance.

P. 110. The group in Figure 102 is a detail of a scroll, reproduced here by permission of the Boston Museum of Fine Arts. Painted by an emperor of the Sung Dynasty, Hui Tsung (1082–1135), the scroll is a copy of a work of the Tang period.

P. 113. Concerning the ambiguity of dynamic effects see also p. 403.

P. 113. Rathe (247) has observed the dynamic effect of foreshortening but does not specify its perceptual basis. In Mantegna's Christ the head is blocked toward the back by a cushion, whereas

the feet act as "free ends," which give an outlet to expansion toward the front. We may observe also how the inclined foot to the left promotes this effect more clearly than the more vertical foot to the right. These are examples of the perceptual factors that may control the phenomenon.

P. 113. The influence of the observer's personal attitude upon the interpretation of dynamic effects has been studied by Rorschach and his followers. Compare Schachtel (264), pp. 78–81.

P. 114. Kühn's book on the art of the primitives (171).

P. 115. Freud's reference to the artist is found at the end of the 23rd of his *Introductory Lectures* (84), pp. 327–328. Consult also his paper on the relation of the poet to the daydream (85) as well as the essay on civilization (81).

P. 116. On the lifelikeness of images see Panofsky (231) and Blanshard (32).

P. 116. Boccaccio's *Decamerone*, fifth novel of the sixth evening.

P. 117. Jacques Lipchitz in a lecture at Sarah Lawrence College.

P. 118. Lévy-Bruhl (180), pp. 47 ff., gives this and other examples of the reality character of images.

P. 119. Meyer Schapiro (268), p. 11.

P. 119. Picasso's *School Girl,* painted in 1919, is in the Collection Douglas Cooper, London. Reproduced on p. 136 of Skira (275).

P. 119. Cézanne in conversation with Vollard (293), p. 180.

P. 120. The Klee quotation is retranslated from Kahnweiler (145), p. 25.

P. 121. Klee's *Brother and Sister,* painted in 1930, is in the Collection Roland Penrose, London. Reproduced in Skira (275), p. 165.

P. 123. Figure 108 is taken from Boas (33), pp. 224–225.

P. 124. Morin-Jean (217), pp. 86, 87, 138, 139, 152.

P. 125. Figure 109a is taken from a

drawing by a five-and-a-half-year-old child, 109b from *Still Life with an Enamel Saucepan,* painted by Picasso in 1945 (Musée d'Art Moderne, Paris).

P. 125. See, for example, Laporte's article on Picasso (174).

P. 126. Picasso's head of a bull is sketched from *Mise à Mort* (1934).

P. 126. Parts of the following discussion are adapted from Arnheim (13). A pertinent analysis can be found in Worringer's book on abstraction and empathy (323). See also Blanshard (32).

P. 127. Worringer (323), p. 68, quoting von den Steinen without specifying the reference.

P. 128. I am not concerned here with the special problem of realism in paleolithic and bushman art. Although the animal pictures of the Altamira type have the earmarks of a late, mature style, the question remains whether highly realistic pictures are ever produced at a primitive level of development by a kind of spontaneous "photographic" recording of momentary visual impressions, that is, whether under special conditions the visual conception of the object may be overruled by the impact of a specific percept.

P. 129. On primitive thinking consult Lévy-Bruhl (180) and Radin (244).

P. 129. For a characteristically modern reëvaluation of Byzantine art see Malraux (202), vol. 2, "The Creative Act."

P. 130. A survey of the literature on the "artistic behavior in the abnormal" has been published by Anastasi and Foley (7). For a recent presentation see Reitman (252). Nijinsky's drawings are reproduced in his diary (225). A good characterization of the schizoid temperament is given in the tenth chapter of Kretschmer's book on physique and character (170).

P. 134. Coomaraswamy (54), pp. 85–99, has pointed out that traditionally an ornament or decoration is an integral part of the work of art and not "millinery," as it is considered today. Etymologically the Latin "ornare" means primarily to "fit out, furnish, provide with necessaries," and even in the sixteenth century we read of the "tackling or ornaments of a ship." Similarly, asserts Coomaraswamy, "décor" is related to "decorous" or "decent," meaning "suitable to a character or time, place, and occasion" and to "decorum," that is, "what is befitting."

P. 137. Hogarth (133), chapters iii and vii.

P. 137. For the observation that symmetry is frequent in the staging of comedies I am indebted to my student Toni Cushing.

P. 137. Bergson in his book on laughter (28).

P. 143. Michelangelo painted the frescoes on the ceiling of the Sistine Chapel in the Vatican in the years 1508–1512.

P. 144. See Rudrauf (260).

P. 144. Ingres' *La Source* is in the Louvre.

P. 144. Muther (221), vol. iii, p. 163.

P. 150. Leonardo da Vinci's *Notebooks* (178), vol. i, p. 105.

P. 152. The subway map is reproduced by permission of London Transport.

P. 153. *Notebooks* (178), vol. i, p. 107.

Notes to Chapter IV

GROWTH

(pages 155–212)

P. 155. "If for ages two great principles, that of the imitation and that of the transformation of reality, have vied for the right truly to express the essence of artistic activity, a settlement of the dispute would seem to be possible only by replacing these two principles with a third, namely that of the production of reality. For art is nothing but one of the primary means by which man acquires reality." Konrad Fiedler (75), p. 151.

P. 155. For the story of Zeuxis' composite statue and the maidens of Croton see Blanshard (32), p. 17, and Panofsky (231), p. 99.

P. 156. The main ideas presented in the first section of this chapter were developed earlier in a paper of mine on perceptual abstraction and art (13).

P. 157. Compare Herbert Read's remarks on the "conceptual fallacy" (249), p. 134. Read discusses many of the most important among the innumerable books and papers that have been written on the subject of the present chapter. Luquet (196) asserts that the child's drawings go through three main stages: incapacity for synthesis, intellectual realism, and visual realism. See also Goodenough (108).

P. 158. On the fusion of perception and thought in primitive mentality and on "concrete abstraction" see Werner (300), chapter ix, "Conception."

P. 160. There are of course exceptions from perceptual constancy. The sun, the moon, or persons in the street, watched from a window on the sixtieth floor, do not look their size. For the theory of the phenomenon see Chapter V.

P. 161. The basketry pattern of Figure 119 is drawn after Boas (33), p. 90. Strictly speaking, not even straight lines are possible in basketry. Straightness is represented by a sequence of oblique units.

P. 162. Picasso's pencil drawing (1937) is reproduced here by permission of the owner, Roland Penrose, London.

P. 163. The line of poetry is quoted from W. B. Yeats, "Shepherd and Goatherd" (326), p. 140.

P. 163. The Matisse anecdote is reported by Gertrude Stein (279), p. 17.

P. 164. The question whether or not the drawings and paintings of children should be called "art" may be safely left to the philosophers.

P. 164. The literature on comparisons between children's art and primitive art is summarized by Anastasi and Foley (7), ii, pp. 48–65. In particular see Levinstein (179), Eng (72), Britsch (39), and Löwenfeld (191).

P. 165. Only little of Gustaf Britsch's teaching is available in his own words. The book, *Theorie der Kunst* (39), which was published in 1926 under his name, with his student Egon Kornmann indicated as editor, was actually written by Kornmann after Britsch's death. He relied on oral communication and on Britsch's notes and papers, some of which are quoted verbatim in the last part of the book. The main ideas are summarized in English in the introduction to (267) by Britsch's student Schaefer-Simmern, who applied and developed them. Frequent conversations with Schaefer-Simmern have been of the greatest value for me in writing the present chapter.

P. 166. The sculptor Hildebrand, in his book on the problem of form, maintains that "sculpture undoubtedly evolved from drawing" (130), p. 125. For the remnants of drawing in early sculpture see p. 209 of the present book.

P. 166. Köhler on "painting" by apes (159), p. 96.

P. 167. The example of the horses was sometimes used by Wertheimer in his lectures.

P. 167. Cott (56) on animal camouflage.

P. 167. Charlotte Rice (253), p. 133.

P. 167. We often read that children endlessly repeat "stereotyped schemas" they have worked out. The adult tends to pay more attention to the basic patterns that keep reappearing in the drawings than to the variations obtained with these patterns. It is true that children will cling to a formal discovery and experiment with its capacities until its virtues are exhausted and something new is needed. This, however, is good practice, fortunately not limited to children.

P. 167. On the nature of line see Hayter (121) and Badt (23), pp. 46 ff.

P. 168. The pioneer investigation on the properties of contour lines was made by Rubin (258).

P. 168. Gelb's and Granit's experiments on the color threshold in figure-ground situations are discussed by Koffka (158), p. 187.

P. 168. Köhler and Wallach on the aftereffect of contour figures on size in (166). For a less technical, earlier report by Köhler see (162), pp. 82–100.

P. 169. For an example of a disconnected drawing by a weak-sighted child see Löwenfeld (193), p. 155, figure 3. Occasionally such drawings occur also in normal children, but they are not frequent enough to represent a typical phase ("incapacity for synthesis"), as Luquet has maintained (196). Luquet arrived at his conclusion by including in this category the so-called "tadpole" drawings. He relied here on the common erroneous view that in these drawings arms are attached to the head or the legs. Compare also Piaget (239), p. 65.

P. 172. Koffka (156), p. 357, on the speech of children. For a similar observation on the Chinese language see Fenollosa (73).

P. 172. Experiments in which children were asked to copy geometrical figures have shown that between the ages of three and four they often employ two concentric circles to represent a triangle inscribed in a circle or two obliquely overlapping, oblong hexagons. Piaget (239), p. 75, and Bender (27), chapters 2 and 4.

P. 173. Figure 125*k* is drawn after Werner (300), p. 122; *a* and *g* are originals; the other examples are copied from originals.

P. 174. Goodenough (108).

P. 175. Kerschensteiner (154), p. 17.

His statement is substantially—but not entirely—correct, since the very first two samples he reproduces show a linear trunk, misinterpreted by him as "one leg, to which feet are attached." However, even in these samples, heads, fingers, and feet are given as outline figures, which keep the whole pattern, as it were, visually afloat.

P. 175. Delacroix's *Journals* in the year 1843 (60), p. 8. Not contained in (63) or the American translation (62).

P. 177. Wölfflin (317), p. 79.

P. 184. For an early drawing of a person sitting on a chair see Eng (72), p. 69.

P. 184. Five-year-old children who have become aware of the perspective effect but are not yet able to tackle the deformation of shape will sometimes draw a tilted disk as a smaller but perfectly round circle rather than as an ellipse. Piaget (239), p. 214.

P. 186. The tapestry, designed around the year 1380, depicts chapter xi of Revelations. See plate 29 in Lejard (177). In realistic painting or photography objective size differences are often compensated by perspective. Thus a large figure in the foreground may hold its own against an entire city which lies at a distance. This is a sophisticated way of satisfying the need for visual equality among corresponding members of a pictorial statement.

P. 187. Piaget (239).

P. 187. Löwenfeld (193), pp. 25–31, and (191), fig. 26, p. 167.

P. 188. For the experiments with geometric figures see the references given in the note to page 172.

P. 188. See pp. 41, 47, 49, 77, 127 in Löwenfeld (193), who is inclined to explain the long arms as an expression of the muscular feeling of stretching experienced in such situations. There seems to be no need for resorting to a specific kinesthetic factor when a universal visual factor provides a full explanation.

P. 189. A characteristic in-between position is assumed by Luquet in (197), where he realizes that the omission of the trunk may be only apparent, but attributes it to lack of importance for the child.

P. 190. Figure 141 is traced from Kerschensteiner (154), table 82.

P. 191. Abbott (1).

P. 192. Figure 142 is a schematic composite, not an actual drawing by a child.

P. 192. Clark (50).

P. 195. I am indebted to Hildegarde Herold Sexton for her permission to publish the picture of the *Bear Village* (Plate 2), which she drew at the age of six.

P. 195. Piaget (239), chapter vi.

P. 195. For a monograph on children's drawings of houses see Kerr (153).

P. 195. Occasionally we see drawings of cubes in which a top face is added; for example, Werner (300), p. 124, or Katz (149). I wonder whether this is a spontaneous solution; it may come about when children are pressed to copy a model cube with all its details.

P. 196. Piaget (239), p. 219.

P. 196. Figure 146 is adapted from a Persian manuscript of 1525, now in the possession of the Metropolitan Museum, New York, illustrated in (237), plate 13. The figures and all detail are eliminated in the tracing.

P. 196. "Different positions are marked by changing the direction of the figure, but the figure is not changed in itself." Piaget (239), p. 206.

P. 196. Löwenfeld (191, 193; particularly 192, pp. 103–105) has asserted that the difference between the drawing of undistorted, right-angular shape and perspectively oblique shape is the result of a difference of attitude between a "haptical" and a "visual type" of person. Starting from the traditional assumption that the visual percept duplicates the retinal projection, he believes that the right-angular procedure is nonvisual. He is unaware of the fact that he is dealing with an entirely visual, but genetically earlier, type of representation, which is based on the perceptual "constancy of size" and is not limited to one type of people but occurs universally. For the further assumption that perception by touch ascertains the shape of objects directly "as it is" compare p. 259 of the present book.

P. 197. Figure 148*a* is taken from a Spanish altarpiece, dated 1396, at the Chicago Art Institute.

P. 197. On "inverted perspective" see, for example, Wulff (325), p. 38.

P. 198. *The Window,* a gouache by Picasso (1919), is in the Collection Alice Paalen, Mexico.

P. 199. The term "painterly" ("malerisch") was introduced by Wölfflin (320). Venturi on contour (291), p. 278.

P. 200. On Schönberg as a teacher see Wellesz (299), pp. 49 ff. For the application of the genetic approach to art education consult particularly Schaefer-Simmern (267).

P. 200. Symposia on the interrelationship of perception and personality have been edited by Bruner and Krech (42) and by Blake and Ramsay (30).

P. 200. Herbert Read (249), plate 18*b*.

P. 201. See Wilhelm (311), pp. 96 ff. Jung, in his comment on Wilhelm's translation of the Chinese text, reproduces ten paintings by Western patients in order to demonstrate their similarity with symbolic pictures of the East. Read (249), pp. 183–195, relates Jung's findings to the drawings of children and contributes a theory based on the gestalt psychology of perception.

P. 204. Figure 151 shows a Mycenaean terra-cotta figure of an ox, made between 1400 and 1100 B.C. It is reproduced here by permission of the Metropolitan Museum of Art, New York.

P. 206. A curious solution of the head-face problem may be seen in the small

Sumerian bronzes that show divinities with four faces symmetrically arranged around the head. Examples are in the Oriental Institute, Chicago. Illustrated in *Master Bronzes* (205), plates 1 and 2.

P. 206. On the flatness of early faces in the work of beginners see, for example, Schaefer-Simmern (267), pp. 98–99.

P. 207. Compare plates 83, 86, 404–409, in Bossert's book on ancient Crete (35).

P. 209. Lange's law of frontality (172).

P. 209. The fusion of units in sculpture may be compared with the analogous development in drawings (pp. 181 ff.).

P. 209. Hildebrand (130), pp. 80–82.

P. 210. The saying by Michelangelo is quoted by Gallatin (92) without indication of source.

P. 210. Schäfer (266), p. 23.

P. 210. Löwy (194).

P. 211. Figure 157 is drawn after plate viii of Perrot and Chipiez (236), vol. ii, p. 130.

P. 212. For the quote from Lomazzo see Holt (134), p. 260.

P. 212. Compare, here again, Schaefer-Simmern (267).

Notes to Chapter V

SPACE

(Pages 213–291)

P. 214. Klee's painting is reproduced by permission of the Curt Valentin Gallery, New York. It is dated 1940.

P. 216. The soap-film experiments are described by Courant and Robbins (57), pp. 386 ff. It would be mistaken to assume that in physics simplest possible shape and shortest connection always go together. For example, the solution of Plateau's problem for the edges of a cube does not lead to a cube. Similarly, the shortest connections between three or four points do not necessarily form triangles or quadrilaterals. See Figure 277,

taken from Courant and Robbins, pp. 355 and 361.

P. 217. Figure 162 is after Hempstead (128).

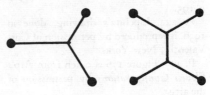

Figure 277

P. 217. For the copying of geometric figures see Piaget (239), pp. 72 ff. The experiment with the honeycomb design was made by Rupp (261).

P. 218. Picasso's *La Vie*, painted in 1903, is in the Cleveland Museum. The example best known to psychologists is the goblet whose outlines can be seen as two profile faces. Introduced by Rubin (258), it has found its place in most textbooks.

P. 220. A thorough analysis of the figure-ground phenomenon can be found in chapter 5 of Koffka (158).

P. 221. Matisse's *Reclining Nude* is reproduced from Duthuit (68) by courtesy of Wittenborn, Schulz, Inc., New York.

P. 222. Koffka (158), pp. 275 ff., on the anisotropy of space. Compare also the discussion of top and bottom in pictorial composition, p. 20 of the present book.

P. 222. The evidence on the spatial distance and density of color is discussed by Argelander (8), pp. 106–109. See also the figure-ground experiment of Goldhamer (103), who tentatively suggests that the brighter surface is likely to be the ground. If the brighter color is the visually more powerful one, it might be expected to seize the ground whenever a brighter and a darker pattern interrupt each other mutually. Being confronted with the choice between the uninterrupted ground and the interrupted figure, the brighter color may use its power to assume the simpler shape. But this is mere conjecture.

P. 223. On the effect of symmetry see Bahnsen (24), discussed by Koffka (158), p. 195.

P. 224. Lipchitz's drawing, done in 1936, is reproduced by permission of Curt Valentin, New York.

P. 227. Figure 176 is taken from Arp's *Eleven Configurations* by permission of the artist.

P. 228. It goes without saying that art historians have recorded a wealth of observations on the depth relief of works of art. A systematic monograph could organize and complete this material.

P. 229. I am referring here to van Gogh's portrait of Mme Ginoux (1888) in the Lewisohn Collection, not to the one in the Bakwin Collection, which was painted in 1890 after a drawing by Gauguin.

P. 230. Figure 179 is reproduced from an Attic red-figured cup by Douris (about 470 B.C.) with the permission of the Metropolitan Museum of Art, New York.

P. 231. Figure 180 is from Rupp (261), p. 277.

P. 231. On the Rorschach test see Arnheim and Klein (20) and Rapaport and Schaefer (246), ii, p. 39.

P. 231. The framing of modern paintings is discussed by Kahnweiler (144), p. 86.

P. 233. The section on concavity in sculpture is based on Arnheim (14) by permission of the *Journal of Aesthetics and Art Criticism*. A useful series of photographs illustrating five stages of sculpture (1, blocklike; 2, modeled or scooped out; 3, perforated; 4, suspended; 5, mobile) can be found in Moholy-Nagy (213).

P. 234. The plane surfaces of the cube, neither convex nor concave, delimit a volume whose compactness makes for figure character.

P. 234. Gibson (98), p. 183, notes the underestimation of interspaces and the overestimation of solids.

P. 235. For a psychoanalytic interpretation of the same subject see Wight (310).

P. 235. Henry Moore's *Family Group* exists in a small version (1946) as well as a life-sized one (1949). Bronze casts of both are in the Museum of Modern Art, New York.

P. 236. Maillol's *Resting Nude* (1912) and Moore's *Reclining Figure* (1945) are reproduced by courtesy of the Curt Valentin Gallery, New York.

P. 238. Hogarth (133), p. 106.

P. 238. Moholy-Nagy (213).

P. 238. St. Ivo's chapel in the courtyard of the Sapienza in Rome was built by Borromini around 1650. The photograph by Ernest Nash is reproduced here with his permission.

P. 239. There is some indication that under certain conditions specific rules determine whether one of two complete and overlapping line figures appears in front of or behind the other. The phenomenon seems to be somewhat ambiguous and fluctuating and to depend upon a number of different factors. Experiments carried through by one of my students, Barbara Lindemann, suggested the following possibilities. Squares seemed to lie more readily in front than circles, particularly when the squares were in normal, vertical - horizontal orientation. Larger figures were seen in front more often than smaller ones. Figures in central position seemed to lie in front more readily than those in peripheral position. It is also possible that lower position favors the front. These results cannot be considered as safely established. They only indicate what directions the investigation of this unexplored phenomenon might take.

P. 239. The passage from Helmholz (125), pp. 283–284, is quoted by Ratoosh

(248), whose mathematical formulation asserts that "continuity of the first derivative of the object's contour at the points of intersection is the sole determiner of relative distance."

P. 240. Gibson (98), p. 142.

P. 241. The film director Josef von Sternberg told me once that to him space was most visible when crowded with objects. For the eyes of others an empty expanse may do the same service.

P. 241. Mary Cassatt's painting (1893) is in the Chester Dale Collection, New York.

P. 242. Klee's gouache, dated 1939 and owned by Douglas Cooper, is illustrated in (55), plate 26.

P. 243. Kopfermann (167), pp. 344–349.

P. 243. The remark on stage design may seem to amount to the naïve statement that depth is seen more clearly when there is any than when there is none. But neither the psychologist nor the stage designer can take it for granted that every physical fact has its equivalent in the observing mind.

P. 244. The fact that a distortion is a deviation from what "ought to be" does not make it undesirable. The artist uses it to describe digressions from a norm. These may be welcome or deplorable ethically.

P. 246. In Figure 191 the square is transformed into the rhomb by an upward rotation around the left edge and a leftward rotation around the bottom edge. The same transformation can be obtained also by different rotations. Different three-dimensional concepts correspond to the different directions in which the distortions are seen to occur. For the mathematical theory of transformation see Courant and Robbins (57), chapter 4.

P. 247. Groups of fibers that issue from the retinal receptors are combined by so-called synapses. But this fact does not alter the situation under discussion.

P. 247. The shape of the retinal surface does have an influence on the shape of the projective pattern. A flat projection screen, such as the photographic plate in a camera, will produce a different picture than a curved one. These differences, however, are relevant only in the peripheral areas of the screen; and since acute vision is limited to the centers of the retinas, the resulting distortions of shape seem to be of no practical consequence.

P. 248. Köhler and Emery (164), p. 176.

P. 249. Koffka (157), p. 166.

P. 253. On the architectural illusions see Panofsky (230). On Borromini consult also Hempel (127).

P. 254. Vitruvius (292), book 3, chapter 3.

P. 254. Plato's *Sophist,* paragraph 236.

P. 254. Vasari (290), "On Sculpture," chapter 1, paragraph 36.

P. 254. For the Ames demonstrations see Lawrence (175) and Blake and Ramsay (30), pp. 99–103.

P. 255. See, for example, Thouless' studies on the constancy of shape (284).

P. 256. The study on Indian and British students was made by Thouless (285), who—strangely enough—assumed that inherent racial traits accounted for the difference in both perception and art. He forgot that central perspective is a recent acquisition of Western culture.

P. 256. Gibson (98), pp. 175–177, reports on an experiment that strikingly demonstrates the destructive effect of a simple frontal pattern upon depth perception.

P. 257. The main source on the visual experiences of the blind after operation is Senden (271). Some of the findings are reported and discussed by Hebb (122), chapter 2. Compare also the critical remarks by Wertheimer (305).

P. 258. For perspective drawing by means of tracings on vertical glass plates see p. 279.

P. 258. Gibson (98), p. 111, has argued against the theory of "muscular cues." Any textbook of psychology furnishes a fuller description of these factors. Consult particularly Woodworth (322), chapter 26.

P. 258. Merleau-Ponty (209), pp. 294–309.

P. 260. In Hastorf's experiment (119), the observer looked with one eye through a hole in the screen at the luminous disk, which appeared in a totally dark room.

P. 260. Figure 202 illustrates the principles used by the Hochbergs (132), rather than being an exact reproduction of their drawings. The authors also tested the mirror images of the drawings to make sure that the difference between left and right was not responsible for the outcome. In another set of drawings the figures were placed at equal height. The outcome was not significantly different. Apart from any influence of the figures, the screen itself can be expected somewhat to favor the version in which it is seen standing on the ground, rather than the opposite version in which at least one of the panels is seen as suspended in mid-air.

P. 261. Compare here Pratt's critique of the empiricist theory (241).

P. 265. Experiments of this type have been made by Gibson (97), pp. 170–171, and Adelbert Ames, Jr., at the Hanover Institute, Hanover, New Hampshire.

P. 265. Wertheimer's experiments are unpublished. He occasionally repeated them during his lectures.

P. 265. Compare Gilinsky (101), p. 464, and Gibson (98), pp. 183–186.

P. 266. On Euclidean and non-Euclidean space consult Courant and Robbins (57), pp. 214 ff.

P. 267. To call visual space pyramidal is probably a simplification. Experiments and mathematical calculations based upon them have suggested that straight lines in visual space correspond to curves

in physical space, and vice versa (cf. Luneburg, 195). This is not necessarily a statement on what we are actually aware of. However, there are some indications that such curvatures are noticed. In the field of art, Ames (6), p. 29, has maintained that straight lines are represented as curves in Leonardo's *Last Supper,* as well as in works by Rembrandt, de Hoogh, Puvis de Chavannes, Millet, Turner, and others. Compare also the so-called "refinements" of Greek temples.

P. 267. Even in a flat plane a bundle of beams issuing from a center causes distortions similar to those observed in three-dimensional pyramidal space. It is hard to believe that the two verticals in Figure 278 are of equal size. The one closer to the "vanishing point" appears much larger. Similar distortions of squares, circles, and straight lines, caused by an asymmetrical spatial environment, are well known as "optical illusions." See, for example, Berliner (29), p. 35.

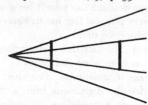

Figure 278

P. 267. Gibson (98), p. 181.

P. 268. Gibson (98).

P. 269. Gibson, who was the first to point out the importance of textural gradients, writes as though they were effective because they made the image more realistic. He considers line drawings "ghostly abstractions." But perceptually there is no difference in principle between drawings, photographs, and the direct perception of physical reality. The degree of the depth effect depends upon the number of the gradients present and the visual strength of their appearance. A simple geometrical drawing will often be inferior to a photograph by lacking some of the gradients, and yet produce the stronger depth effect because of the precise structure of what it does contain.

P. 270. In his work for the Army Air Forces (97) Gibson showed that the point of the environment toward which an airplane or car is directed becomes the center of a centrifugal expansion imparted to the entire surroundings. The world seems to fly apart. In looking backward, we find that the point from which the vehicle is moving away marks the center of a constriction or centripetal movement.

P. 270. Wallach and O'Connell (297).

P. 273. The fact that the mechanism of vision produces the image of a cube from a pattern that is no projection of a cube poses a physiological problem. Apparently there is more flexibility in the third dimension than in the two frontal ones. The brain field does not seem to exert upon the projective pattern the rigid constraints we should assume to exist if our abacus model were to be taken literally. It will be remembered, however, that receding lines drawn parallel tend to be seen as diverging toward distance (cf. p. 250).

P. 273. What I am calling "frontal perspective" is commonly known as "parallel perspective," a term that is often taken to mean the isometric method.

P. 276. The historical development leading to the discovery of central perspective is analyzed by Panofsky (232) and Bunim (44).

P. 277. Figure 214 is traced from a representation of St. Matthew in the museum of the Aachen cathedral. Illustrated in Hauttmann (120), p. 342. For a Roman example see the murals from a villa in Boscoreale, now in the Metropolitan Museum, New York.

P. 278. The quotation from Cennini's *Il Libro dell' Arte o Trattato della Pittura* is given by Bunim (44), p. 138.

P. 279. The first treatise on central perspective, *Della Pittura Libri Tre,* was written by Leon Battista Alberti in 1435.

P. 279. Ivins (138), p. 9.

P. 283. Tintoretto's *Last Supper,* painted around 1560, is in the church of S. Giorgio Maggiore in Venice.

P. 284. On Cézanne's use of perspective see Novotny (226).

P. 285. Henry Moore's water color *Tube Shelter Perspective* (1941) is reproduced here by permission of the Trustees of the Tate Gallery, London.

P. 286. On perspective in film photography see Spottiswoode (278), pp. 40–43, and Arnheim (10), pp. 69–76.

P. 287. Spengler (276), pp. 175 ff.

P. 287. On the philosophy of "process" see Whyte (307 and 308).

P. 288. De Chirico's *Lassitude of the Infinite,* painted in 1912, is in the Collection Pierre Matisse, New York. Figure 220, *Melancholy and Mystery of a Street,* painted two years later, is reproduced here with the permission of the owners, Mr. and Mrs. Stanley R. Resor; photo by courtesy of the Museum of Modern Art, New York.

P. 291. Hungerland (137), pp. 99 and 102, in an essay on inconsistency, has demonstrated the effect by combining a Rembrandt figure with a Matisse-like background and by pasting the cut-out portrait of an eighteenth-century family on an "abstraction."

P. 291. Marianne Moore's "Poetry" is contained in her *Collected Poems* (215), p. 40.

Notes to Chapter VI

LIGHT

(pages 292–322)

P. 293. Piaget (238), chapters 8 and 9.
P. 293. Driver (65), p. 6.
P. 293. Job xxxviii: 19–20.

P. 294. Piaget (238), chapter 9.

P. 294. On the relativity of brightness see Wallach (296) and MacLeod (200).

P. 295. The Alberti quote is taken from Holt (134), p. 112.

P. 295. Compare Helson's discussion of the adaptation level (126).

P. 298. Figure 221 is taken from a publicity folder by permission of Cinema 16, New York. In theory, it is just as possible to see the white beam at the bottom, overlaid by transparent black numbers. In practice, this version seems much more difficult to produce. The conditions that determine which unit will assume spontaneous transparency deserve further experimental investigation. The basic studies on transparency have been made by Fuchs (89).

P. 299. Delacroix (63), January 13, 1857, notes that the "true tone" of the object is always found next to the luminous point because that area is hit by the full light.

P. 300. Quotation from MacLeod (200), pp. 11–12, who later investigated the effect of the "penumbra" systematically (201).

P. 300. On the three-dimensional effect of brightness gradients see Turhan (288) and Gibson (98), pp. 94 ff.

P. 301. Gehrke and Lau (94).

P. 303. On the discontinuity of gradients see Gibson (98), pp. 92–94.

P. 303. The quote from Piles' *Principles of Painting* is taken from Holt (134), pp. 412–413.

P. 304. The passage on "obliterative shading" in animals is taken from Cott (56), p. 124.

P. 304. For the quote from Piles see Holt (134), p. 413.

P. 305. Rembrandt's *Night Watch*, painted in 1642, is in the Rijksmuseum in Amsterdam. A detailed analysis of the use of light in this picture is given by Fromentin (87), chapters 21 and 22.

P. 306. On the primitive view of shadows consult Lévy-Bruhl (180), pp. 54–56, and (181), pp. 136 ff.

P. 307. Jung (141), p. 173.

P. 308. Figure 228 is taken from an advertisement for *Eleven Came Back,* a novel by Mabel Seeley, Doubleday, 1943.

P. 309. Brunswik (43), p. 387, writes of perceptual distortions as though they were essentially a nuisance. "The task of the perceiving organism is, then, to keep its reactions free from variations of projective stimulus-size." Instead, these variations are vitally important for the organism. They are clearly and carefully perceived, even though within certain limits we are aware of them only as translated into spatial values.

P. 310. Bunim (44), p. 27, notes that Apollodorus, a painter of the fifth century B.C., was famous for his effects of light and shade. The evidence is of course indirect, since no works of the early Greek painters have survived.

P. 311. Britsch (39), pp. 34–35, and Schaefer-Simmern (267), pp. 22–25.

P. 311. A striking example is provided by the dark cloud behind the face in Piero di Cosimo's portrait of Simonetta in Chantilly.

P. 311. Carpenter (48). Figure 231 is a detail from Titian's *Noli Me Tangere* in the National Gallery, London.

P. 313. Goethe's conversations with Eckermann, April 18, 1827. The description of the picture matches best, although not completely, with Rubens' *Return from the Labor in the Fields,* painted around 1640, in the Palazzo Pitti in Florence. Perhaps the engraving was made after this landscape.

P. 313. Wölfflin (320).

P. 313. See the article on "Light and Darkness" in Hastings (118), volume 8.

P. 314. Rembrandt's *Holy Family,* painted around 1644, is in the Lennox Collection in Scotland. *The Descent from the Cross* (1634) is in the Hermitage, Leningrad.

P. 315. *The Wedding of Samson* (1638) belongs to the Dresden Gallery. *The Toilet of Bathsheba* (1643) is in the Metropolitan Museum of Art, New York.

P. 315. Katz (150), pp. 7 ff. on the appearance of colors. The relation between luminosity and surface quality is discussed by Wallach (296).

P. 316. Interpretations of Dürer's *Melencolia* are given by Panofsky and Saxl (233) and by Wölfflin (318), pp. 96–105.

P. 316. On the use of illumination in the movies see Arnheim (10), pp. 76–83.

P. 316. For the Rembrandt paintings see the notes to pp. 314 and 315. Two representations of the Potiphar story, both painted in 1655, belong to the Berlin and Leningrad museums.

P. 318. Wölfflin (320), chapter 1.

P. 318. *The Third Man* is a British film, directed by Carol Reed in 1949.

P. 320. Georges Braque's *Painter and Model* (1939) is in the collection of Walter P. Chrysler, Jr.

P. 322. Compare the Freudian antagonism of the ego and the id or the dialectic process in Marxism.

Notes to Chapter VII

COLOR

(pages 323–359)

P. 324. Werner (300), pp. 234–237.

P. 324. Rorschach (256).

P. 324. Schachtel (263).

P. 324. Kretschmer (169), chapter 13 ("Experimentelle Typenpsychologie"), pp. 190–191, refers to experiments according to which cyclothymes are more sensitive to color, schizothymes to shape. The former group comprises people whose temperament is represented in its pathological extreme by manic-depressive patients. They are warmhearted, emo-

tional, sociable. The schizothymes are epitomized by the schizophrenics. They are cold, speculative, withdrawn. The chapter, which was added to Kretschmer's book in the seventh edition, is not contained in the English translation. However, the translation does contain Kretschmer's reference to the way the two types express themselves in the visual arts (170), pp. 239–241. Kretschmer's report on the behavior of cyclothymes partly contradicts the findings of Rorschach, who asserts that a cheerful mood produces rich color responses whereas depression does the opposite. This suggests that in order to describe the behavior of cyclothymes correctly it may be necessary to distinguish reactions during depressive phases from those during manic phases.

P. 325. The English word "shape" is related etymologically to the German word "schaffen" ("to create").

P. 325. Matisse (207), p. 15.

P. 326. Poussin quoted from Holt (134), p. 369.

P. 326. Kant, *Critique of Judgment*, part 1, section 1, book 1, paragraph 14.

P. 326. Charles Blanc (31), p. 23.

P. 327. Féré (74), pp. 43–47, as quoted by Schachtel (263), p. 403.

P. 327. Goldstein (105). Volume 1942 of "Occupational Therapy and Rehabilitation" contains several other articles on color therapy.

P. 327. Kandinsky (148), pp. 61–62.

P. 327. Pressey (242).

P. 328. Allesch (3), pp. 234–235.

P. 328. Can it be shown that unmixed colors are used in styles of art distinguished by low tension as far as over-all mood and shape patterns are concerned? For example, is there not a parallel between Mondrian's preference for the relatively static shapes of bars, squares, and rectangles and his use of pure reds, yellows, and blues? Each of these unmixed colors possesses little tension in itself, and in addition their company produces little tension, because they are essentially unrelatable to each other. On the other hand, the baroque style seems to prefer color mixtures that are not only strongly dynamic in themselves, but also interact by an expressive play of attractions and repulsions.

P. 330. On structural qualities shared by different sensory media compare Hornbostel (135).

P. 331. Katz (150), p. 69, reports on an experiment about the apparent distance of red and blue. See also Argelander (8), pp. 106–109.

P. 331. Allesch (3), pp. 53–56.

P. 331. Kandinsky (148), pp. 60–62.

P. 331. Goethe (102), section 1 ("Physiological Colors"), pp. 45–46.

P. 331. On the expressiveness of colors see the psychological material quoted by Chandler (49), chapter 6. Goethe's classical treatment of the subject is contained in the sixth section of his *Theory of Color* (102). Kandinsky on the "language of form and color" (148), pp. 63–72. For the views of the "color and design engineer" Howard Ketcham see *The New Yorker,* March 8, 1952, pp. 39–53.

P. 332. On the controversy about the nature of green consult Boring (34), p. 131.

P. 334. Chandler (49), pp. 70 ff., opens his discussion of color preferences with the characteristic phrase: "The first efforts in the experimental aesthetics of color were naturally directed to the problem of the pleasantness and unpleasantness of color." Such an approach is "natural" only when a hedonistic theory of art is taken for granted. Allesch (3), pp. 9–21, found no agreement on color preferences. Observers frequently contradicted their own as well as other observers' judgments. Findings of this kind do not prove that color preferences obey no law; they merely indicate the complexity of the determining factors.

P. 335. Rorschach (256), p. 35.

P. 335. The history of color diagrams is described by Boring (34), pp. 145–154. Characteristic attempts at color classification are the systems described by Ostwald in his introduction to the theory of color (229) and by Munsell in his work on color notation (219).

P. 335. Ostwald (229), pp. 137, 146–148.

P. 335. Munsell (219), pp. 44, 88 ff.

P. 337. The influence of subject matter on color is discussed by Kandinsky (148), pp. 82–85.

P. 338. Schönberg (269), p. 8. Retranslated from the German original.

P. 339. Chandler (49), pp. 69–70, maintains that an average of 214 gradations of gray can be discriminated. Freeman (79), p. 380, speaks of 700 such gradations.

P. 340. The anecdote about Père Tanguy is reported by Vollard (294), p. 47.

P. 341. Goethe (102) ("Erstes Stück"), p. 305.

P. 342. Experiments on the wave lengths corresponding to colors are cited by Woodworth (322), p. 543, Allesch (3), pp. 23 ff., Boring (34), p. 129, Hiler (131), p. 209. According to Morgan (216), p. 32, recent experiments by Granit, in which the retinas of various animals were stimulated by small electrodes, have shown that some nerve cells have peak responses at a wave length of 580 millimicrons, others at 450, and others at 530 and 600. It is tempting to relate these physiological findings to the perception of the colors yellow, blue, green, and red.

P. 343. In the table of mixtures green is treated as a mixture, since between green and yellow and between green and blue there do not seem to exist stably balanced mixtures of the kind found between blue and red and between red and yellow. For this reason green itself is considered one of the three stable mixtures.

P. 345. I am indebted to Meyer Schapiro for the suggestion to illustrate my discussion of color pairs with triangular diagrams.

P. 347. On the theory of complementary colors see Parsons (234), pp. 38 ff., Woodworth (322), pp. 552–553, Boring (34), pp. 141–145.

P. 348. Hiler (131), p. 211.

P. 349. If the reader will color the circular arcs of Figures 241 and 242 with crayons as indicated, he may find the analysis in the text a little less confusing.

P. 352. *Moby Dick,* chapter 42.

P. 352. Rabelais, *Gargantua,* book 1, chapter 10.

P. 352. Badt (22), pp. 47–48.

P. 353. McCandless (198), p. 56, talking about stage lighting says: "By using warm and cool colors on opposite sides and varying the intensity between the two, it is possible to retain a considerable amount of the plastic quality." Carpenter (48), p. 180, maintains that there is no such thing as modeling without gradation of brightness, "and Cézanne rarely tries to model form just with changes of hue." He concludes that modeling with change of color alone does not work. Compare, however, Delacroix in his *Journals* (July 10, 1847). Speaking of the head of Magdalen in the *Christ in the Tomb* (Boston Museum), he says that "it was sufficient to color the whole shaded area with warm, reflected tones, and although the bright and shaded areas are almost of the same brightness value, the cold tones of the one and the warm ones of the other are sufficient to set the accents in the whole."

P. 354. Ruskin (262), p. 138.

P. 354. Allesch (3), p. 46.

P. 354. In psychological language a phenomenon is called "reliable" when it produces similar reactions in different observers or in the same observer at different times.

P. 354. Allesch (3), p. 38.

P. 354. Liebmann (184), pp. 308 ff.

P. 355. Matisse's *Le Luxe II,* painted in 1907 or 1908, is in the Copenhagen Statens Museum for Kunst. A sketchier version, *Le Luxe I,* is at the Musée National d'Art Moderne in Paris. It should be understood that, given the considerable inaccuracies of color reproductions at the present time, the reader may find discrepancies between the descriptions given here and his own impressions of a work. In the present case, a color print may reproduce the foreground and the hill to the right a rusty brown rather than orange; the left hill may appear violet rather than purple.

P. 356. El Greco's *The Virgin with St. Inés and St. Tecla,* painted between 1597 and 1599, is reproduced here by courtesy of the National Gallery of Art (Widener Collection), Washington, D. C.

Notes to Chapter VIII

MOVEMENT

(pages 360–395)

P. 360. Wertheimer (301), p. 63.

P. 362. The discussion of time given here is influenced by Merleau-Ponty's treatment of the subject (209), pp. 469 ff.

P. 363. On the spatialization of time in memory see Koffka (158), p. 446. For the psychological concept of the past as an aspect of the present see Lewin (183). Compare also Freud's assertion that the dream translates temporal relations into spatial ones (83), p. 41.

P. 363. Persons who maintain that motion and time are inherent in painting and sculpture just as much as they are in the dance or the movies, because the eyes and the legs of the spectator move, may find their thinking clarified by Gregory's remark (113), pp. 25–26, that time is involved in applied geometry "in the first degree only, i.e., in the purely qualitative sense that to observe, to test, to measure, to advance, to retreat, to rotate a line about a point, a plane about a line, etc., all take time, and change of some kind is involved. The important thing is, however, that the amount of time taken is of no consequence, [whereas] with rotating and revolving bodies, swinging pendulums, wave motion generally, and changing currents in electric circuits, the rate of motion is an additional quantity to be determined." That is, in the latter cases, motion is an integral part of the phenomenon itself.

P. 364. Buswell (46).

P. 364. For examples of "exposition" in film and literature see Arnheim (10), pp. 146–151.

P. 365. Michelangelo's early *Pietà* (1498–1500) is in St. Peter's, Rome. Firestone (76) has asserted that the motif of the sleeping Christ child was intended and understood during the Renaissance as a prefiguration of the death of Christ.

P. 365. Lessing, in the sixteenth section of his *Laocoon,* points out that sculpture and painting represent action through objects whereas literature, a "time art," describes objects through action.

P. 366. *Divine Comedy,* "Inferno," canto 31, verses 136–138.

P. 366. Duncker (67), p. 170.

P. 366. Oppenheimer (228).

P. 366. Duncker, pp. 247–248 of the German original (66), not contained in the English summary (67).

P. 367. The documentary film *Man of Aran* was produced by Robert Flaherty in 1933–1934.

P. 368. When different media are combined successfully—such as words and music in the song, or visual movement and music in the dance—they are not blended into one form unit, but present parallel patterns, each complete in itself. Compare Arnheim (11), an essay on the combinations of artistic media.

P. 368. In the experiment of Oppen-

heimer (228), p. 36, just as in others performed by her and by Duncker, the speed of the visual pattern was kept so low that the observer could see motion only in the relation of the objects to each other, whereas the objects seemed to stand still when viewed separately. This was done to prevent the location of the observer from acting as a frame of reference.

P. 369. On the rotation of wheels see Rubin (259) and Duncker (67), pp. 168–169.

P. 371. Piéron cited by Lecomte du Noüy (176), chapter 9, pp. 145–177.

P. 371. Spottiswoode (278), pp. 120–122, on synthesizing space and time.

P. 372. In T. H. White's *The Sword in the Stone* the young son of King Arthur is introduced by his tutor, the owl Archimedes, to the goddess Athene, who, divinely independent of human time perception, shows him the moving life of the trees and the geological ages. (306), pp. 244–251.

P. 372. Dru Drury quoted by Sherrington (273), p. 120. On accelerated motion see also Arnheim (10), pp. 118–119.

P. 373. Brown (40 and 41), discussed by Koffka (158), pp. 288 ff.

P. 373. Lecomte du Noüy (176), pp. 165–168.

P. 374. Wertheimer (301). On the perception of stroboscopic motion consult Boring (34), pp. 588–602.

P. 374. Wertheimer's physiological theory (301), §21.

P. 375. Horner (136). On the technical history of the motion picture see Liesegang (185). An illustration of the daedaleum is given by Boring (34), p. 591, who also describes the stroboscopic devices of Plateau and Stampfer.

P. 377. Figure 249 adapted from Metzger (210), p. 12. To produce the effect of movement, the reader may cut a narrow horizontal slot in a piece of white cardboard and make the drawing slide vertically underneath it.

P. 377. Figures 250–252 are adapted from Ternus (283), pp. 150 and 159.

P. 379. Maya Deren's film *Pas de Deux* (*Choreographies for Camera*) is of the year 1945.

P. 379. On the technique of editing see, for example, May's detailed treatment of "montaggio continuo" (208), pp. 78–133, as well as Reisz (251) and Bretz (38).

P. 381. Michotte (211).

P. 382. Michotte distinguishes the pushing effect (*effet lancement*) from the release effect (*effet déclenchement*).

P. 385. Wertheimer (302), p. 323, of the German original. Not contained in the English summary by Ellis (303).

P. 386. Lévy-Bruhl (181), introduction, pp. 15 ff., and Piaget (238), part 2. Also Köhler (160).

P. 387. For a description of the phototropic robots see Wiener (309), pp. 191–195.

P. 387. Piaget (238), pp. 173, 194–195.

P. 389. Physicists speak of a feedback when a mechanism changes its behavior in accordance with the effect its action produced earlier. See Wiener (309) and the special issue of the *Scientific American*, September, 1952, on "Automatic Control."

P. 389. For the reader who wishes to look up Michotte's experiments in his book here are the references in the order in which they are cited on pages 381–386 of the present book. Black changing into red: exp. 5, p. 42 *B* below *A*; exp. 33, p. 96. *B* at right angle: exp. 34, p. 96. Basic experiment of pushing: exp. 1, p. 17. Wooden ball pushing disk: exp. 28, p. 79. *B*'s motion slowed down by *A*: p. 66. Effect of time interval: p. 19. *B* moving faster than *A*: exp. 40, p. 103. *B* moving more slowly: p. 116. Attraction unobtainable: p. 210. *B* without initial immobility: exp. 61, p. 159. Zigzag course of *B*: exp. 21, p. 69. Caterpillar exps. 65 and 66, pp. 176–177. Two squares: exp. 70, p. 187. The experiments illustrating

complexity of pattern are hypothetical.

P. 389. Heider and Simmel (124).

P. 389. Bergson (28).

P. 390. Compare Focillon's essay on the human hand (78).

P. 390. In the individual and historical development of art we find that as form becomes more complex it begins to look more organic, more "human" (cf. Chapter IV).

P. 390. Based on Arnheim (12).

P. 391. Figure 259 is adapted from Kandinsky (147).

P. 391. See A. K. Coomaraswamy's article on the dance in India in the *Encyclopædia Britannica*.

P. 391. The description of Delsarte's system is quoted from Shawn (272), p. 14.

P. 392. Kleist (155). Translation revised.

P. 393. Michotte (211), p. 196.

P. 393. Merleau-Ponty (209), p. 116.

Notes to Chapter IX

TENSION

(pages 396–424)

P. 396. This chapter is based in part on Arnheim (19).

P. 396. Eliot (70), p. 7.

P. 396. Leonardo, quoted by Justi (143), vol. 3, p. 480.

P. 396. Kandinsky (147).

P. 397. On the so-called "M-responses" in the Rorschach test see Rorschach (256), pp. 22, 25–29, and more recently Schachtel (264). Compare also the discussion of "empathy" in chapter x, p. 427 of the present book.

P. 399. El Greco's *St. Jerome* is reproduced here by courtesy of the Frick Collection, New York.

P. 400. The kinesthetic theory is presented by Langfeld (173), chapters 5 and 6. For a critique of the corresponding approach to space perception see p. 259 of the present book.

P. 401. Lindemann (186) and Newman (223) have investigated gamma motion.

P. 402. Oppenheimer (228), p. 45; Brown (40), pp. 100–101, and (41), p. 222.

P. 403. "Heaviness (Massigkeit) and movement are the principles of the baroque style. Its aim is not the perfect architectonic body . . . but rather a happening, the expression of a particular movement in that body," Wölfflin (315), p. 59. See also Fleming (77).

P. 403. Compare the history of the plan for St. Peter's in Rome, first intended as a centrically symmetrical Greek cross and later redesigned as an oblong basilica. On the preference of Renaissance architects for centralized plans and their philosophical interpretation see Wittkower (313), part 1.

P. 404. The Lamazzo quote is adapted from the translation given by Holt (134), p. 261.

P. 406. Figures 263a and b after Wölfflin (315), p. 47; a is from the Cancelleria, b from the Palazzo Farnese, both in Rome.

P. 406. Rodin (255), p. 66.

P. 407. Muybridge (222).

P. 407. Reinach (250). Rodin (255), p. 77, justifies the outstretched legs of the galloping horse in a way differing from ours. Ogden (227), pp. 213–215, reproduces the Gericault painting (Louvre, Paris, 1824) and compares it with a more "correct" but grotesquely motionless drawing of a running horse.

P. 408. Justi (143), p. 479. Lessing's *Laocoon*, section 3.

P. 408. Wölfflin (317), pp. 72–76.

P. 409. *Masterpieces from the Berlin Museums* (206), p. 27. Rembrandt's picture is of the year 1659.

P. 412. Rodin (255), chapter 4. It would seem, however, that in the examples from sculpture cited by Rodin, move-

ment is obtained not so much because the figure represents different phases of a time sequence as because there is a gradual change of visual dynamics—for example, in the *Age of Iron*—from the relaxed posture of the legs to the high charge of tension in the chest, the neck, and the arms.

P. 412. Riegl (254), p. 33.

P. 413. Figures 268a–e are tracings from works by Picasso reproduced as numbers 249, 209, 268, 246, 216 by Barr (26).

P. 414. Burchartz (45), p. 156.

P. 416. Bowie (36), pp. 35, 77–79, quoted by Langfeld (173), p. 129.

P. 417. Matisse (207), p. 33.

P. 418. Piero della Francesca's *Resurrection* was painted around 1450 in the town hall of Borgo San Sepolcro.

P. 419. Hans Thoma's picture is taken from *Quickborn*, vol. 1, October 15, 1898.

P. 420. It is worth while to compare Giotto's work with similar representations, which may be equally well "composed" but in which the pattern does not seem to interpret to the eye the underlying meaning of the scene symbolically. In this sense, Raphael's *Entombment* in the Villa Borghese in Rome is hardly a religious picture although it presents the Biblical episode dramatically enough.

P. 422. Bach, *St. Matthew Passion*, number 46, recitative.

P. 423. Compare the discussion of leveling and sharpening in chapter ii, p. 57.

Notes to Chapter X

EXPRESSION

(pages 425–443)

P. 425. Parts of this chapter are based on Arnheim (16 and 17).

P. 426. Quotation translated from Claudius (51), vol. 1, pp. 177–178.

P. 426. Berkeley, *An Essay Towards a New Theory of Vision,* paragraph 65.

P. 426. Darwin (58), pp. 356–359.

P. 427. The quotation is translated from Lipps (188), p. 359. Compare also his (187) and Langfeld's presentation of empathy (173), pp. 113 ff. Lipps' rather complex theoretical position is discussed in Arnheim (16), pp. 159–160. For the purpose of the present chapter we are less concerned with the exact attitude of any particular theorist than with possible clear-cut approaches to the phenomenon of expression.

P. 428. James (139), chapter 6, p. 147. He is referring to a somewhat different subject—the relations between the nervous system and psychical experience—but his reasoning applies to the problem of expression as well.

P. 428. On the gestalt psychology of expression see Wertheimer (304), pp. 94–96, Köhler (163), pp. 216–247, Koffka (158), pp. 654–661, Arnheim (16), and Asch (21), chapters 5–7.

P. 428. Jane Binney, a student of mine, made the experiment at Sarah Lawrence College a few years ago. It is discussed in more detail in (16), pp. 169–170.

P. 429. Werner (300), pp. 67–82, distinguishes "geometric-technical" from "physiognomic" properties.

P. 429. In terms of projective geometry the parabola as a conic section is intermediate between the horizontal section of the cone—namely, the circle—and the vertical section—namely, the straight-edged triangle.

P. 430. The quotation is from Wölfflin (315), p. 306.

P. 430. Werner (300), pp. 67–82, and Köhler (160).

P. 430. Köhler (163), pp. 260–264.

P. 431. Figure 273 is derived from Wölfflin (315), p. 297. I have corrected a mechanical error in Wölfflin's drawing, by which the centers of the circles are placed slightly too high.

P. 433. A baby, who quickly distinguishes between a gentle and a harsh motion, finds it difficult to learn the meaning of facial expression. According to Spitz (277), children between the third and sixth month of age will still react to a terrifying grin with an amused smile. The spasmodic muscle distortions and outbursts of sound we call laughter are in themselves so far from suggesting mirth that they permanently remain a cause of panic for the chimpanzee, who otherwise, according to Köhler (159), p. 307, "at once correctly interprets the slightest change of human expression, whether menacing or friendly."

P. 435. Lévy-Bruhl (180), pp. 153, 165, 166.

P. 435. Braque (37).

P. 436. On the function of the metaphor compare Arnheim (15), pp. 153–159.

P. 436. Schizophrenics seem to revert to a primitive kind of logic. E. von Domarus, in his study on the relations between normal and schizophrenic thinking, formulates the following principle: "Whereas the normal person accepts identity only upon the basis of identical subjects, the paleologician accepts identity based upon identical predicates." See Arieti (9).

P. 436. Titian's *The Sacred and Profane Love* (1510–1512) is in the Borghese Gallery in Rome. Dürer's etching *Nemesis* belongs to the period 1500–1503.

P. 438. Groddeck (114), pp. 11 and 78. Selections from the book are translated in (115).

P. 438. Jung (142), p. 139.

P. 439. Rabelais, *Gargantua,* book 1, chapter 45.

P. 439. On Cézanne's informal terminology see Vollard (293), p. 30.

P. 439. Jung (142), p. 26. On *mana* see Lévy-Bruhl (180).

P. 439. Fromm (88), p. 22.

P. 440. Fromm (88), p. 12.

P. 440. Freud on Oedipus in the 21st of his *Introductory Lectures* (84); the discussion of his interpretation by Fromm (88), pp. 196–231, and Mullahy (218). Among Freud's many comments on Shakespeare see, for example (86). His analysis of Leonardo's painting is given in (82).

P. 440. Freud (84) and (85), pp. 327–328.

P. 440. Jung (142), p. 15.

P. 441. Braque (37).

P. 442. Cézanne's still life is in the National Gallery in Washington. Picasso's *Still Life with Dead Fowl* (1942) is reproduced by Janis (140), plate 57.

BIBLIOGRAPHY

1. Abbott, Edwin A. Flatland. A romance of many dimensions by A Square. New York, 1952.
2. Adrian, E. D. The physical background of perception. Oxford, 1947.
3. Allesch, G. J. von. Die ästhetische Erscheinungsweise der Farben. Psychologische Forschung, 1925, vol. 6, pp. 1–91, 215–281.
4. Allport, Gordon W. Change and decay in the visual memory image. British Journal of Psychology, 1930, vol. 21, pp. 133–148.
5. Alschuler, Rose H., and La Berta Weiss Hattwick. Painting and personality. Chicago, 1947.
6. Ames, Adalbert, Jr., C. A. Proctor, and Blanche Ames. Vision and the technique of art. Proceedings of the American Academy of Arts and Sciences, 1923, vol. 58, # 1.
7. Anastasi, Anne, and John P. Foley, Jr. A survey of the literature on artistic behavior in the abnormal. I. Journal of General Psychology, 1941, vol. 25, pp. 111–142; II. Annals of the New York Academy of Sciences, 1941, vol. 42, pp. 1–112; III. Psychological Monographs, 1940, vol. 52, # 6; IV. Journal of General Psychology, 1941, vol. 25, pp. 187–237.
8. Argelander, Annelies. Das Farbenhören und der synaesthetische Faktor der Wahrnehmung. Jena, 1927.
9. Arieti, Silvano. Special logic of schizophrenic and other autistic thought. Psychiatry, 1948, vol. 11, pp. 325–338.
10. Arnheim, Rudolf. Film. London, 1933.
11. Arnheim, Rudolf. Nuovo Laocoonte. Bianco e Nero, 1938, # 8, pp. 3–32.
12. Arnheim, Rudolf. Psychology of the dance. Dance Magazine, August, 1946, pp. 20 and 38.
13. Arnheim, Rudolf. Perceptual abstraction and art. Psychological Review, 1947, vol. 54, pp. 66–82.

14. Arnheim, Rudolf. The holes of Henry Moore. On the function of space in sculpture. Journal of Aesthetics and Art Criticism, 1948, vol. 7, pp. 29–38.
15. Arnheim, Rudolf. Psychological notes on the poetical process. In Arnheim et al., Poets at Work. New York, 1948.
16. Arnheim, Rudolf. The gestalt theory of expression. Psychological Review, 1949, vol. 56, pp. 156–171.
17. Arnheim, Rudolf. The priority of expression. Journal of Aesthetics and Art Criticism, 1949, vol. 8, pp. 106–109.
18. Arnheim, Rudolf. Gestalt psychology and artistic form. In Whyte (308), pp. 196–208.
19. Arnheim, Rudolf. Perceptual and aesthetic aspects of the movement response. Journal of Personality, 1951, vol. 19, pp. 265–281.
20. Arnheim, Rudolf, and Abraham Klein. Perceptual analysis of a Rorschach card. Journal of Personality, 1953, vol. 22, pp. 60–70.
21. Asch, Solomon E. Social psychology. New York, 1952.
22. Badt, Kurt. Ueber die Einfachheit. Unpublished manuscript.
23. Badt, Kurt. Eugène Delacroix' drawings. Oxford, 1946.
24. Bahnsen, Poul. Eine Untersuchung über Symmetrie und Asymmetrie bei visuellen Wahrnehmungen. Zeitschrift für Psychologie, 1928, vol. 108, pp. 129–154.
25. Barlach, Ernst. Aus seinen Briefen. Munich, 1949.
26. Barr, Alfred H. (ed.). Picasso—forty years of his art. New York, 1939.
27. Bender, Lauretta. A visual motor gestalt test and its clinical use. New York, 1938.
28. Bergson, Henri. Laughter. New York, 1911.
29. Berliner, Anna. Lectures on visual psychology. Chicago, 1948.

30. Blake, Robert R., and Glenn V. Ramsay (eds.). Perception, an approach to personality. New York, 1951.

31. Blanc, Charles. Grammaire des arts du dessin. Paris, 1870.

32. Blanshard, Frances Bradshaw. Retreat from likeness in the theory of painting. New York, 1945.

33. Boas, Franz. Primitive art. Cambridge (Mass.), 1927.

34. Boring, Edwin G. Sensation and perception in the history of experimental psychology. New York, 1942.

35. Bossert, Helmuth Theodor. The art of ancient Crete. London, 1937.

36. Bowie, Henry P. On the laws of Japanese painting. San Francisco, 1911.

37. Braque, Georges. Notebook 1917–1947. New York, n. d.

38. Bretz, Rudy. Television cutting technique. Journal of the Society of Motion Picture Engineers, 1950, vol. 54, pp. 247–267.

39. Britsch, Gustaf. Theorie der bildenden Kunst. Munich, 1926.

40. Brown, J. F. Ueber gesehene Geschwindigkeiten. Psychologische Forschung, 1928, vol. 10, pp. 84–101.

41. Brown, J. F. The visual perception of velocity. Psychologische Forschung, 1931, vol. 14, pp. 199–232.

42. Bruner, Jerome S., and David Krech (eds.). Perception and personality. Durham (N.C.), 1950.

43. Brunswik, Egon. The psychology of objective relations. In Marx (204), pp. 386–391.

44. Bunim, Miriam Schild. Space in medieval painting and the forerunners of perspective. New York, 1940.

45. Burchartz, Max Albrecht. Gleichnis der Harmonie. Munich, 1949.

46. Buswell, G. Th. How people look at pictures. Chicago, 1935.

47. Carmichael, Leonard, H. P. Hogan, and A. A. Walter. An experimental study of the effect of language on the reproduction of visually perceived form. Journal of Experimental Psychology, 1932, vol. 15, pp. 73–86.

48. Carpenter, James M. Cézanne and tradition. Art Bulletin, 1951, vol. 33, pp. 174–186.

49. Chandler, Albert R. Beauty and human nature. New York, 1934.

50. Clark, Arthur B. The child's attitude towards perspective problems. Studies in Education, 1897, vol. 1.

51. Claudius, Matthias. Sämtliche Werke des Wandsbecker Boten. Dresden, 1938.

52. Cobb, Stanley. Borderlands of psychiatry. Cambridge (Mass.), 1944.

53. Cohen, Morris R., and Ernest Nagel. An introduction to logic and scientific method. New York, 1934.

54. Coomaraswamy, Ananda K. Figures of speech or figures of thought. London, 1946.

55. Cooper, Douglas. Paul Klee. Harmondsworth, 1949.

56. Cott, Hugh B. Animal form in relation to appearance. In Whyte (308), pp. 121–156.

57. Courant, Richard, and Herbert Robbins. What is mathematics? New York, 1951.

58. Darwin, Charles. The expression of the emotions in man and animals. New York, 1896.

59. Dean, Alexander. Fundamentals of play directing. New York, 1946.

60. Delacroix, Eugène. Mein Tagebuch. Berlin, 1918.

61. Delacroix, Eugène. Oeuvres littéraires. Paris, 1923.

62. Delacroix, Eugène. The journal of Eugène Delacroix. New York, 1937.

63. Delacroix, Eugène, Journal de. Paris, 1950.

64. Dennis, Wayne (ed.). Readings in general psychology. New York, 1950.

65. Driver, S. R. The book of Genesis. London, 1926.

66. Duncker, Karl. Ueber induzierte Bewegung. Psychologische Forschung, 1929, vol. 12, pp. 180–259.

67. Duncker, Karl. Induced motion. In Ellis (71), pp. 161–172.

68. Duthuit, Georges. The fauvist painters. New York, 1950.

69. Ehrenfels, Christian von. Ueber "Gestaltqualitäten." Vierteljahrsschrift für wissenschaftliche Philosophie, 1890, vol. 14, pp. 249–292.

70. Eliot, T. S. Four Quartets. New York, 1943.

71. Ellis, Willis D. (ed.). A source book of gestalt psychology. New York, 1939.

72. Eng, Helga. The psychology of children's drawings. New York, 1931.

73. Fenollosa, Ernest Francisco. The Chinese written characters as a medium for poetry. London, 1936.

74. Féré, Charles. Sensation et mouvement. Paris, 1900.

75. Fiedler, Konrad. Vom Wesen der Kunst. Munich, 1942.

76. Firestone, G. The sleeping Christ child in Italian Renaissance representations of the Madonna. Marsyas, 1942, vol. 2, pp. 43–62.

77. Fleming, William. The element of motion in Baroque art and music. Journal of Aesthetics and Art Criticism, 1946, vol. 5, pp. 121–128.

78. Focillon, Henri. Vie des formes. Paris, 1939.

79. Freeman, Ellis. Principles of general psychology. New York, 1939.

80. Freud, Sigmund. Beyond the pleasure principle. London, 1922.

81. Freud, Sigmund. Civilization and its discontent. New York, 1930.

82. Freud, Sigmund. Leonardo da Vinci. New York, 1932.

83. Freud, Sigmund. New introductory lectures, New York, 1933.

84. Freud, Sigmund. A general introduction to psychoanalysis. Garden City, 1943.

85. Freud, Sigmund. The relation of the poet to daydreaming. In Collected Papers, vol. 4. London, 1949.

86. Freud, Sigmund. The theme of the three caskets. In Collected Papers, vol. 4. London, 1949.

87. Fromentin, Eugène. The masters of past time. New York, 1948.

88. Fromm, Erich. The forgotten language. New York, 1951.

89. Fuchs, Wilhelm. On transparency. The influence of form on the assimilation of colors. In Ellis (71), pp. 89–103.

90. Gaffron, Mercedes. Die Radierungen Rembrandts. Mainz, 1950.

91. Gaffron, Mercedes. Right and left in pictures. Art Quarterly, 1950, vol. 13, pp. 312–331.

92. Gallatin, A. E. (ed.). Of art. New York, 1945.

93. Galton, Francis. Inquiries into human faculty and its development. New York, 1908.

94. Gehrcke, E., and E. Lau. Ueber Erscheinungen beim Sehen kontinuierlicher Helligkeitsverteilungen. Zeitschrift für Sinnesphysiologie, 1922, vol. 53, pp. 174–178.

95. Gelb, Adhémar, and Kurt Goldstein. Analysis of a case of figural blindness. In Ellis (71), pp. 315–325.

96. Gellermann, Louis W. Form discrimination in chimpanzees and two-year-old children. Pedagogical Seminary and Journal of Genetic Psychology, 1933, vol. 42, pp. 2–27.

97. Gibson, James J. Motion picture testing and research. Report # 7. U.S. Army Air Forces Aviation Psychology Program. Washington, 1947.

98. Gibson, James J. The perception of the visual world. Boston, 1950.

99. Gibson, James J. What is a form? Psychological Review, 1951, vol. 58, pp. 403–412.

100. Gibson, James J., and Doris Robinson. Orientation in visual perception, Psychological Monographs, 1935, vol. 46, # 6, pp. 39–47.

101. Gilinsky, Alberta S. Perceived size and distance in visual space. Psychological Review, 1951, vol. 58, pp. 460–482.

102. Goethe, Johann Wolfgang von. Zur Farbenlehre. Leipzig, n.d.

103. Goldhamer, H. The influence of area, position, and brightness in visual perception of a reversible configuration. American Journal of Psychology, 1934, vol. 46, pp. 189–206.

104. Goldmeier, Erich. Progressive changes in memory traces. American Journal of Psychology, 1941, vol. 54, pp. 490–503.

105. Goldstein, Kurt. Some experimental observations concerning the influence of colors on the function of the organism. Occupational Therapy and Rehabilitation, 1942, vol. 21, pp. 147–151.

106. Gombrich, E. H. The story of art. New York, 1950.

107. Gombrich, E. H. Meditations on a hobby horse, or the roots of artistic form. In Whyte (308), pp. 209–222.

108. Goodenough, Florence L. Measurement of intelligence by drawings. Yonkers, 1926.

109. Gottschaldt, Kurt. Gestalt factors and repetition. In Ellis (71), pp. 109–122.

110. Graves, Maitland. Design judgment test. Psychological Corporation. New York, 1946.

111. Greek painting. The Metropolitan Museum of Art. New York, 1944.

112. Greenough, Horatio. Form and function. Berkeley and Los Angeles, 1947.

113. Gregory, C. C. L. Shape and distance considered by an astronomer. In Whyte (308), pp. 23–42.

114. Groddeck, Georg Walther. Der Mensch als Symbol. Vienna, 1933.

115. Groddeck, Georg Walther. The world of man. London, 1934.

116. Hanawalt, Nelson Gilbert. Memory traces for figures in recall and recognition. Archives of Psychology, 1937, # 216.

117. Hartmann, George W., and William R. Sickles. The theory of order. Psychological Review, 1942, vol. 49, pp. 403–421.

118. Hastings, James (ed.). Encyclopedia of religion and ethics. New York, 1916.

119. Hastorf, A. H. The influence of suggestion on the relationship between stimulus size and perceived distance. Journal of Psychology, 1950, vol. 29, pp. 195–217.

120. Hauttmann, Max. Die Kunst des frühen Mittelalters. In Propyläen-Kunstgeschichte, vol. 6. Berlin, 1929.

121. Hayter, Stanley William. The convention of line. Magazine of Art, 1945, vol. 38, pp. 92–95.

122. Hebb, D. O. The organization of behavior. New York, 1949.

123. Hebb, D. O., and Esme N. Foord. Errors of visual recognition and the nature of the trace. Journal of Experimental Psychology, 1945, vol. 35, pp. 335–348.

124. Heider, Fritz, and Marianne Simmel. An experimental study of apparent behavior. American Journal of Psychology, 1944, vol. 57, pp. 243–259.

125. Helmholtz, Hermann von. Treatise on physiological optics. New York, 1925.

126. Helson, Harry. Adaptation-level as frame of reference for prediction of psychological data. American Journal of Psychology, 1947, vol. 60, pp. 1–29.

127. Hempel, Eberhard. Francesco Borromini. Vienna, 1924.

128. Hempstead, L. The perception of visual form. American Journal of Psychology, 1900, vol. 12, pp. 185–192.

129. Hertz, Mathilde. Figural perception in the jay bird. In Ellis (71), pp. 238–252.

130. Hildebrand, Adolf. The problem of form. New York, 1907.

131. Hiler, Hilaire. Some associative aspects of color. Journal of Aesthetics and Art Criticism, 1946, vol. 4, pp. 203–217.

132. Hochberg, Carol Barnes, and Julian E. Hochberg. Familiar size and the perception of depth. Journal of Psychology, 1952, vol. 34, pp. 107–114.

133. Hogarth, William. The analysis of beauty. Pittsfield, 1909.

134. Holt, Elizabeth Gilmore (ed.). Literary sources of art history. Princeton, 1947.

135. Hornbostel, Erich M. von. The unity of the senses. In Ellis (71), pp. 210–216.

136. Horner, W. G. On the properties of the Daedaleum, a new instrument of optical illusion. London and Edinburgh Philosophical Magazine and Journal of Science, 1834, vol. 4, pp. 36–41.

137. Hungerland, Helmut. Consistency as a criterion in art criticism. Journal of Aesthetics and Art Criticism, 1948, vol. 7, pp. 93–112.

138. Ivins, William M., Jr. On the rationalization of sight. Metropolitan Museum of Art Papers, # 8. New York, 1938.

139. James, William. The principles of psychology. New York, 1890.

140. Janis, Harriet and Sidney. Picasso—the recent years, 1939–1946. Garden City, 1946.

141. Jung, Carl Gustav. The integration of the personality. New York, 1939.

142. Jung, Carl Gustav. Modern man in search of a soul. London, 1947.

143. Justi, Carl. Winckelmann und seine Zeitgenossen. Leipzig, 1923.

144. Kahnweiler, Daniel-Henry. Juan Gris, his life and work. New York, 1947.

145. Kahnweiler, Daniel-Henry. Klee. Paris, 1950.

146. Kainz, Friedrich. Gestaltgesetzlichkeit und Ornamententwicklung. Zeitschrift für angewandte Psychologie, 1927, vol. 28, pp. 267–327.

147. Kandinsky, Wassily. Punkt und Linie zur Fläche. Munich, 1926.

148. Kandinsky, Wassily. On the spiritual in art. New York, 1946.

149. Katz, David. Ein Beitrag zur Kenntnis der Kinderzeichnungen. Zeitschrift für Psychologie, 1906, vol. 41, pp. 241–256.

150. Katz, David. The world of color. London, 1935.

151. Katz, David. Gestalt psychology. New York, 1950.

152. Kepes, Gyorgy. Language of vision. Chicago, 1944.

153. Kerr, Madeline. Children's drawings of houses. British Journal of Medical Psychology, 1936, vol. 16, pp. 206 ff.

154. Kerschensteiner, Georg. Die Entwickelung der zeichnerischen Begabung. Munich, 1905.

155. Kleist, Heinrich von. Essay on the puppet theatre. Partisan Review, January–February, 1947, pp. 67–72.

156. Koffka, Kurt. The growth of the mind. New York, 1924.

157. Koffka, Kurt. Some problems of space perception. In Murchison (220), pp. 161–187.

158. Koffka, Kurt. Principles of gestalt psychology. N Y 1935.

159. Köhler, Wolfgang. The mentality of apes. New York, 1931.

160. Köhler, Wolfgang. Psychological remarks on some questions of anthropology. American Journal of Psychology, 1937, vol. 50, pp. 271–288.

161. Köhler, Wolfgang. The place of value in a world of facts. New York, 1938.
162. Köhler, Wolfgang. Dynamics in psychology. New York, 1940.
163. Köhler, Wolfgang. Gestalt psychology. New York, 1947.
164. Köhler, Wolfgang, and David A. Emery. Figural after-effects in the third dimension of visual space. American Journal of Psychology, 1947, vol. 60, pp. 159–201.
165. Köhler, Wolfgang, and Richard Held. The cortical correlate of pattern vision. Science, 1949, vol. 110, pp. 414–419.
166. Köhler, Wolfgang, and Hans Wallach. Figural after-effects. An investigation of visual processes. Proceedings of the American Philosophical Society, 1944, vol. 88, # 4, pp. 269–357.
167. Kopfermann, Hertha. Psychologische Untersuchungen über die Wirkung zweidimensionaler Darstellungen körperlicher Gebilde. Psychologische Forschung, 1930, vol. 13, pp. 292–364.
168. Krech, David, and Richard Crutchfield. Theory and problems of social psychology. New York, 1948..
169. Kretschmer, Ernst. Körperbau und Charakter. Berlin, 1936.
170. Kretschmer, Ernst. Physique and character. New York, 1936.
171. Kühn, Herbert. Die Kunst der Primitiven. Munich, 1923.
172. Lange, Julius. Die Darstellung des Menschen in der älteren griechischen Kunst. Strassbourg, 1899.
173. Langfeld, Herbert Sidney. The aesthetic attitude. New York, 1920.
174. Laporte, Paul M. The space-time concept in the work of Picasso. Magazine of Art, January, 1948, pp. 26–32.
175. Lawrence, Merle. Studies in human behavior. Princeton, 1949.
176. Lecomte du Noüy, Pierre. Biological time. New York, 1937.
177. Lejard, André. Les tapisseries de l' apocalypse de la cathédrale d'Angers. Paris, 1942.
178. Leonardo da Vinci, The notebooks of. New York, n.d.
179. Levinstein, Siegfried. Kinderzeichnungen bis zum vierzehnten Lebensjahr. Leipzig, 1905.
180. Lévy-Bruhl, Lucien. How natives think. London, 1926.
181. Lévy-Bruhl, Lucien. The "soul" of the primitive. London, 1928.
182. Lewin, Kurt. Ueber die Umkehrung der Raumlage auf dem Kopf stehender Worte und Figuren in der Wahrnehmung. Psychologische Forschung, 1923, vol. 3, pp. 210–261.
183. Lewin, Kurt. Defining the "field at a given time." In Lewin, Field theory in social science, pp. 43–59. New York, 1951.
184. Liebmann, Susanne. Ueber das Verhalten farbiger Formen bei Helligkeitsgleichheit von Figur und Grund. Psychologische Forschung, 1927, vol. 9, pp. 300–353.
185. Liesegang, F. Paul. Zahlen und Quellen zur Geschichte der Projektionskunst und Kinematographie. Berlin, 1926.
186. Lindemann, Erich. Gamma movement. In Ellis (71), pp. 173–181.
187. Lipps, Theodor. Aesthetische Einfühlung. Zeitschrift für Psychologie und Physiologie der Sinnesorgane, 1900, vol. 22, pp. 415–450.
188. Lipps, Theodor. Aesthetik. In Lipps et al., Systematische Philosophie. Berlin, 1907.
189. Loran, Erle. Cézanne's composition. Berkeley and Los Angeles, 1943.
190. Lorenz, K. Z. The role of gestalt perception in animal and human behavior. In Whyte (308), pp. 157–178.
191. Löwenfeld, Viktor. The nature of creative activity. New York, 1939.

192. Löwenfeld, Viktor. Tests for visual and haptical aptitudes. American Journal of Psychology, 1945, vol. 58, pp. 100–111.
193. Löwenfeld, Viktor. Creative and mental growth. New York, 1947.
194. Löwy, Emanuel. Die Naturwiedergabe in der älteren griechischen Kunst. Rome, 1900.
195. Luneburg, Rudolf K. Mathematical analysis of binocular vision. Princeton, 1947.
196. Luquet, Georges Henri. Les dessins d'un enfant. Paris, 1913.
197. Luquet, Georges Henri. Les bonhommes têtards dans le dessin enfantin. Journal de Psychologie, 1920, vol. 27, pp. 684 ff.
198. McCandless, Stanley. A method of lighting the stage. New York, 1939.
199. Mach, Ernst. The analysis of sensations. Chicago and London, 1914.
200. MacLeod, Robert Brodie. An experimental investigation of brightness constancy. Archives of Psychology, 1932, # 135.
201. MacLeod, Robert Brodie. The effects of artificial penumbrae on the brightness of included areas. Miscellanea Psychologica, Albert Michotte. Louvain, 1947.
202. Malraux, André. The psychology of art. Vol. 1: Museum without walls; vol. 2: The creative act; vol. 3: The twilight of the absolute. New York, 1949–1950.
203. Martin, J. L., Ben Nicholson, and N. Gabo (eds.). Circle. International survey of constructive art. London, 1937.
204. Marx, Melvin H. (ed.). Psychological theory. New York, 1951.
205. Master bronzes. Albright Art Gallery. Buffalo, 1937.
206. Masterpieces from the Berlin museums. The Cleveland Museum of Art. Cleveland, 1948.
207. Matisse, Henri. Catalogue of the Philadelphia Museum of Art. Philadelphia, 1948.
208. May, Renato. Il linguaggio del film. Milan, 1947.
209. Merleau-Ponty, M. Phénoménologie de la perception. Paris, 1945.
210. Metzger, Wolfgang. Beobachtungen über phänomenale Identität. Psychologische Forschung, 1934, vol. 19, pp. 1–60.
211. Michotte, A. La perception de la causalité. Louvain, 1946.
212. Mock, Elizabeth, and J. M. Richards. An introduction to modern architecture. New York, 1947.
213. Moholy-Nagy, L. The new vision. New York, 1947.
214. Mondrian, Piet. Plastic art and pure plastic art. New York, 1945.
215. Moore, Marianne. Collected poems. New York, 1952.
216. Morgan, Clifford T. Some structural factors in perception. In Blake and Ramsay (30), pp. 25–55.
217. Morin-Jean. Le dessin des animaux en Grèce d'après les vases paints. Paris, 1911.
218. Mullahy, Patrick. Oedipus, myth and complex. New York, 1948.
219. Munsell, A. H. A color notation. Boston, 1919.
220. Murchison, Carl (ed.). Psychologies of 1930. Worcester, 1930.
221. Muther, Richard. Geschichte der Malerei. Berlin, 1912.
222. Muybridge, Eadweard. The human figure in motion. London, 1901.
223. Newman, Edwin B. Versuche über das Gamma-Phänomen. Psychologische Forschung, 1934, vol. 19, pp. 102–121.
224. Newton, Sir Isaac. Mathematical principles. Berkeley, 1934.
225. Nijinsky, Romola (ed.). The diary of Vaslav Nijinsky. New York, 1936.
226. Novotny, Fritz. Cézanne und das Ende der wissenschaftlichen Perspektive. Wien, 1938.

227. Ogden, Robert Morris. The psychology of art. New York, 1938.
228. Oppenheimer, Erika. Optische Versuche über Ruhe und Bewegung. Psychologische Forschung, 1935, vol. 20, pp. 1–46.
229. Ostwald, Wilhelm. Einführung in die Farbenlehre. Leipzig, 1919.
230. Panofsky, Erich. Die Scala Regia im Vatikan und die Kunstanschauungen Berninis. Jahrbuch der königlich preussischen Kunstsammlungen, 1919, vol. 40.
231. Panofsky, Erich. "Idea." Studien der Bibliothek Warburg. Leipzig and Berlin, 1924.
232. Panofsky, Erich. Die Perspektive als "symbolische Form." Vorträge der Bibliothek Warburg, 1924–1925, pp. 258–330. Leipzig and Berlin, 1927.
233. Panofsky, Erwin, and Fritz Saxl. Melencolia I. Studien der Bibliothek Warburg. Leipzig, 1923.
234. Parsons, John Herbert. An introduction to the study of color vision. Cambridge, 1924.
235. Pelt, John Vredenburgh van. The essentials of composition as applied to art. New York, 1913.
236. Perrot, Georges, and Charles Chipiez. A history of art in Chaldaea and Assyria. London, 1884.
237. Persian miniatures. A picture book. The Metropolitan Museum of Art. New York, 1944.
238. Piaget, Jean. The child's conception of the world. New York, 1929.
239. Piaget, Jean, and Bärbel Inhelder. La représentation de l'espace chez l'enfant. Paris, 1948.
240. Piston, Walter. Harmony. New York, 1941.
241. Pratt, Carroll C. The role of past experience in visual perception. Journal of Psychology, 1950, vol. 30, pp. 85–107.
242. Pressey, Sidney L. The influence of color upon mental and motor efficiency. American Journal of Psychology, 1921, vol. 32, pp. 326–356.
243. Puffer, Ethel D. Studies in symmetry. Psychological Monographs, 1903, vol. 4, pp. 467–539.
244. Radin, Max. Music and medicine among primitive peoples. In Schullian and Schoen (270), pp. 3–24.
245. Ramakrishna, Sri, The Gospel of Sri Ramakrishna. New York, 1942.
246. Rapaport, David, and Roy Schaefer. Manual of diagnostic psychological testing. Publications of the Josiah Macy, Jr., Foundation. New York, 1946.
247. Rathe, Kurt. Die Ausdrucksfunktion extrem verkürzter Figuren. London, 1938.
248. Ratoosh, P. On interposition as a cue for the perception of distance. Proceedings of the National Academy of Sciences, 1949, vol. 35, # 5, pp. 257–259.
249. Read, Herbert. Education through art. New York, 1945.
250. Reinach, Salomon. La représentation du galop dans l'art ancien et moderne. Revue Archéologique, 1900–1901, vol. 36, pp. 217–251, 441–450; vol. 37, pp. 244–259; vol. 38, pp. 27–45, 224–244; vol. 39, pp. 1–11.
251. Reisz, Karel. The technique of film editing. London and New York, 1953.
252. Reitman, Francis. Psychotic art. New York, 1951.
253. Rice, Charlotte. The orientation of plane figures as a factor in their perception by children. Child Development, 1930, vol. 1, pp. 111–143.
254. Riegl, Alois. Barockkunst in Rom. Vienna, 1923.
255. Rodin, Auguste. Art. Boston, 1912.
256. Rorschach, Hermann. Psychodiagnostics. New York, 1942.
257. Ross, Denman W. A theory of pure design. New York, 1933.
258. Rubin, E. Visuell wahrgenommene Figuren. Copenhagen, 1921.
259. Rubin, E. Visuell wahrgenommene wirkliche Bewegungen. Zeitschrift für Psychologie, 1927, vol. 103, pp. 384–392.
260. Rudrauf, Lucien. L'annonciation. Etude d'un thème plastique et de ses variations en peinture et en sculpture. Paris, 1943. Summarized in Journal of Aesthetics and Art Criticism, 1949, vol. 7, pp. 325–354.
261. Rupp. Hans. Ueber optische Analyse. Psychologische Forschung, 1923, vol. 4, pp. 262–300.
262. Ruskin, John. The elements of drawing in three letters to beginners. New York, 1889.
263. Schachtel, Ernest G. On color and affect. Psychiatry, 1943, vol. 6, pp. 393–409.
264. Schachtel, Ernest G. Projection and its relation to character attitudes and creativity in the kinesthetic responses. Psychiatry, 1950, vol. 13, pp. 69–100.
265. Schäfer, Heinrich. Von ägyptischer Kunst, besonders der Zeichenkunst. Leipzig, 1922.
266. Schäfer, Heinrich. Grundlagen der ägyptischen Rundbildnerei und ihre Verwandtschaft mit denen der Flachbildnerei. Leipzig, 1923.
267. Schaefer-Simmern, Henry. The unfolding of artistic activity. Berkeley and Los Angeles, 1948.
268. Schapiro, Meyer. On a painting of Van Gogh. View, Fall 1946, pp. 9–14.
269. Schönberg, Arnold. Theory of harmony. New York, 1948.
270. Schullian, Dorothy M., and Max Schoen. Music and medicine. New York, 1948.
271. Senden, M. von. Raum- und Gestaltauffassung bei operierten Blindgeborenen vor und nach der Operation. Leipzig, 1932.
272. Shawn, Ted. Fundamentals of a dance education. Girard, 1937.
273. Sherrington, Charles, Man on his nature. New York, 1941.
274. Sickles, William R. Psycho-geometry of order. Psychological Review, 1944, vol. 51, pp. 189–199.
275. Skira, Albert (ed.). History of modern painting from Picasso to Surrealism. Geneva, 1950.
276. Spengler, Oswald. The decline of the West. New York, 1932.
277. Spitz, René A. The smiling response. Genetic Psychology Monographs, 1946, vol. 34, pp. 57–125.
278. Spottiswoode, Raymond. Film and its techniques. Berkeley and Los Angeles, 1951.
279. Stein, Gertrude. Picasso. London, 1939.
280. Stern, William. Ueber verlagerte Raumformen. Zeitschrift für angewandte Psychologie, 1909, vol. 2, pp. 498–526.
281. Stratton, George M. Vision without inversion of the retinal image. Psychological Review, 1896, vol. 3, pp. 611–612, and 1897, vol. 4, pp. 342–351, 466–471. Reprinted in: Dennis (64), pp. 24–40.
282. Terman, Lewis M., and Maud A. Merrill. Measuring intelligence. Boston, 1937.
283. Ternus, Josef. The problem of phenomenal identity. In Ellis (71), pp. 149–160.
284. Thouless, Robert H. Phenomenal regression to the real object. British Journal of Psychology, 1931, vol. 21, pp. 339–359.
285. Thouless, Robert H. A racial difference in perception. Journal of Social Psychology, 1933, vol. 4, pp. 330–339.
286. Tinbergen, N. The study of instinct. Oxford, 1951.
287. Tsanoff, Radoslav A. The nature of evil. New York, 1931.
288. Turhan, Müntaz. Ueber räumliche Wirkungen von Helligkeitsgefällen. Psychologische Forschung, 1937, vol. 21, pp. 1–49.

289. Valéry, Paul. Variété V. Paris, 1945.

290. Vasari, Giorgio. Vasari on technique. London, 1907.

291. Venturi, Lionello. Il gusto dei primitivi. Bologna, 1926.

292. Vitruvius Pollio. The ten books on architecture. Cambridge (Mass.), 1914.

293. Vollard, Ambroise. Paul Cézanne. Paris, 1924.

294. Vollard, Ambroise. Paul Cézanne. New York, 1937.

295. Waddington, C. H. The character of biological form. In Whyte (308), pp. 43–52.

296. Wallach, Hans. Brightness constancy and the nature of achromatic colors. Journal of Experimental Psychology, 1948, vol. 38, pp. 310–324.

297. Wallach, Hans, and D. N. O'Connell. The kinetic depth effect. Journal of Experimental Psychology, 1953, vol. 45, pp. 205–217.

298. Weber, Christian O. Homeostasis and servo-mechanisms for what? Psychological Review, 1949, vol. 56, pp. 234–239.

299. Wellesz, Egon. Arnold Schönberg. Leipzig, 1921.

300. Werner, Heinz. Comparative psychology of mental development. Chicago, 1948.

301. Wertheimer, Max. Experimentelle Studien über das Sehen von Bewegung. Zeitschrift für Psychologie, 1912, vol. 61, pp. 161–265. Also in Wertheimer, Drei Abhandlungen zur Gestalttheorie. Erlangen, 1925.

302. Wertheimer, Max. Untersuchungen zur Lehre von der Gestalt, II. Psychologische Forschung, 1923, vol. 4, pp. 301–350.

303. Wertheimer, Max. Laws of organization in perceptual forms. In Ellis (71), pp. 71–88.

304. Wertheimer, Max. Gestalt theory. Social Research, 1944, vol. 11, pp. 78–99.

305. Wertheimer, Michael. Hebb and Senden on the role of learning in perception. American Journal of Psychology, 1951, vol. 64, pp. 133–137.

306. White, T. H. The sword in the stone. New York, 1939.

307. Whyte, Lancelot Law. The unitary principle in physics and biology. New York, 1949.

308. Whyte, Lancelot Law (ed.). Aspects of form. London, 1951.

309. Wiener, Norbert. The human use of human beings. Boston, 1950.

310. Wight, Frederick S. Henry Moore: the reclining figure. Journal of Aesthetics and Art Criticism, 1947, vol. 6, pp. 95–105.

311. Wilhelm, Richard (translator). The secret of the golden flower. A Chinese book of life. With a European commentary by C. G. Jung. New York, 1938.

312. Witkin, H. A. The nature and importance of individual differences in perception. In Bruner and Krech (42), pp. 145–170.

313. Wittkower, Rudolf. Architectural principles in the age of humanism. Studies of the Warburg Institute, vol. 19. London, 1949.

314. Wohlfahrt, E. Der Auffassungsvorgang an kleinen Gestalten. Neue Psychologische Studien, 1928–1932, vol. 4, pp. 347–414.

315. Wölfflin, Heinrich. Renaissance und Barock. Munich, 1888.

316. Wölfflin, Heinrich. Gedanken zur Kunstgeschichte. Basle, 1941.

317. Wölfflin, Heinrich. Ueber Abbildungen und Deutungen. In Wölfflin (316), pp. 66–82.

318. Wölfflin, Heinrich. Zur Interpretation von Dürers "Melancholie." In Wölfflin (316), pp. 96–105.

319. Wölfflin, Heinrich. Ueber das Rechts und Links im Bilde. Das Problem der Umkehrung in Raffaels Teppichkartons. In Wölfflin (316), pp. 82–96.

320. Wölfflin, Heinrich. Principles of art history. New York, 1950.

321. Wölfflin, Heinrich. Classic art. London, 1952.

322. Woodworth, Robert S. Experimental psychology. New York, 1939.

323. Worringer, Wilhelm. Abstraktion und Einfühlung. Munich, 1911.

324. Wulf, Friedrich. Tendencies in figural variation. In Ellis (71), pp. 136–160.

325. Wulff, Oscar. Die umgekehrte Perspektive und die Niedersicht. In Kunstwissenschaftliche Beiträge August Schmarsow gewidmet. Leipzig, 1907.

326. Yeats, W. B., The collected poems of W. B. Yeats. New York, 1951.

INDEX

477